IBSEN

AND

HITLER

THE PLAYWRIGHT, THE PLAGIARIST, AND THE PLOT FOR THE THIRD REICH

STEVEN F. SAGE

CARROLL & GRAF PUBLISHERS
NEW YORK

IBSEN AND HITLER:

The Playwright, the Plagiarist, and the Plot for the Third Reich

Published by
Carroll & Graf Publishers
An Imprint of Avalon Publishing Group, Inc.
245 West 17th Street • 11th floor
New York, NY 10011-5300

AVALON
publishing group incorporated

Copyright © 2006 by Steven F. Sage

Library of Congress Cataloging-in-Publication Data is available.

ISBN-10: 0-78671-713-0
ISBN-13: 978-0-78671-713-2

9 8 7 6 5 4 3 2 1

Designed by India Amos, Neuwirth & Associates, Inc.
Printed in the United States of America

CONTENTS

AUTHOR'S NOTE

IN PAINTING, THE term *pentimento* refers to a faint trace of an early sketch that the artist altered when adding layers of pigment. Decades, even centuries may elapse before such traces become evident. A ghostly hand, ear, or other feature might then appear displaced from its spot in the final version. Pentimenti occur when slow chemical changes degrade the refractive index of the surface paint layer to allow some transparency. Once discerned, pentimenti offer a glimpse into how a work evolved. Literary critics sometimes borrow the word pentimento to indicate a vestige of a writer's first draft. However, the term has not been much used by historians.

It is now apt, though, for discussing Adolf Hitler. Here the subject is not the young vagabond watercolorist but the politician and dictator. The Hitler pentimenti presented in these pages comprise a long obscured master blueprint for the Nazi Third Reich and the Holocaust. Historians never suspected this hidden underlying source. It is neither a political tract nor an archived state document. The source consists instead of dramas written for the stage by the Norwegian playwright, Henrik Ibsen (1828–1906). On empirical grounds, it appears that Hitler secretly contrived major events to follow selected Ibsen scripts. He did so over the course of his life and career.

I virtually stumbled over this finding after being drawn by chance to investigate a Third Reich topic. As a historian, I was astonished to encounter recurrent echoes from Ibsen's plays in what Hitler said, and particulars of their plots in what he did. For awhile I remained skeptical, although more confirming evidence came to light the deeper I looked. Even so, I stayed aware that I had interloped on other scholars' turf from a separate field of History. The circumstances counseled caution. Yet the methodology of my own discipline stressed the patient, minute comparison of texts. Employing that approach, I continued to uncover still more of Ibsen in Hitler. It seemed reasonable; many contemporary observers had detected a thespian at the core of the man. My discovery that key Hitler moves followed theatrical scripts thus conformed to his established nature. The new element was only the identification of Ibsen as the author of the scripts Hitler borrowed and warped.

The implications of the find seemed tremendous. It would be audacious, in the least, to seek a hearing for any new evidence on the subject, especially evidence such as this. The Dutch novelist Harry Mulisch summed up the problem in his story *Siegfried*, published in 2001: "By now a hundred thousand studies have been devoted to [Hitler], if not more . . . more than about anyone else but it hasn't gotten us anywhere . . . He has remained the enigma that he was to everyone from the very beginning—or no, he has simply become more incomprehensible. All those so-called explanations have simply made him more invisible." Thus the opacity of Hitler is an article of faith, a dogma born of failure and a lack of new leads.

But certain Ibsen plays matched Hitler's plots too well, defying the dogma of an ever-elusive "Führer." Enough Ibsen pentimenti underlay the Hitler canvas to substantiate the point. Moreover, a line of dots led from the plagiarist back to the playwright, via a small German cult that called Ibsen a "prophet" and hailed Hitler as destiny's agent. The full evidence is presented here. When all the dots are joined the emergent picture compels an audacious claim: Yes, in this 100,001st study, new facts at last unlock the enigma to define the method of

Hitler's madness. Betrayed by his own words, the Nazi tyrant becomes comprehensible and visible beneath the surface pigment.

Altogether, I documented the presence of three Ibsen plays, each systematically adapted by the Führer over the course of decades. He paraphrased their lines and restaged highlights of their plots. He adhered to the scripted sequence of those events he mimicked. The three scripts ran concurrently and proved mutually supportive, like the three legs of a stool. A reason existed for each play in Hitler's repertoire. And the plays provided a rationale that linked several disparate, murky episodes of the dictator's personal life to the life of the monstrous state he led. Hitler assigned himself three starring roles from the three Ibsen plays. He cast unwitting associates in supporting roles. This was no parlor game, however. When the script called for a death the real life character would perish. Nearly six million Jews fell victim, although the first to die on cue was Hitler's own niece.

Several Ibsen pentimenti had long hid in plain sight, in *Mein Kampf* and other recorded utterances of the despot. The bona fides of these texts are not in doubt. Had their barely veiled subtext been glimpsed decades ago, the mystique of an unfathomable Hitler could not have taken hold. Harry Mulisch resolved, "It's time that was changed. Perhaps fiction is the net he can be caught in." An inspired verdict. The Führer had all along enmeshed himself, and his Third Reich, in dramatic fiction.

The evidence for Ibsen's plays in Hitler's plots is arranged here in a logical progression. Consequently, the chapters are best read in order to make the dots connect.

STEVEN F. SAGE

WASHINGTON, D.C., JANUARY 2006

PROLOGUE

Theater of War

The ideals of our time, while falling apart, are tending toward what in my play *Emperor and Galilean* I called by the term "the third Reich."
—HENRIK IBSEN IN A SPEECH,
SEPTEMBER 24, 1887

DURING THE AUTUMN of 1941, the master of Europe usually dined in a concrete command bunker. There he would prattle to guests while a stenographer took down what he said. His conversation ranged from the grandiose to the giddy. On the Eastern Front, the largest military campaign of all time had been under way since June. By mid-October, the situation had turned critical for both sides. If Hitler's armies could seize the Kremlin and bring on a Soviet collapse, the war would be effectively won. If not, then Germany would face a resurgent Russia, a rearmed Britain, and a looming USA. All the world watched in awe and expectation. And all the world recalled Napoleon, who had stood at the same juncture a hundred and twenty-nine years before.

All the world except Hitler himself. He looked back to a remoter age. This is the stenographer's transcription of how the Führer assessed things on October 19, 1941:

Christianity was proto-Bolshevism, the mobilization by the Jew
of the slave masses with the aim of undermining the structure
of the state; therefore the decent Roman elements kept aloof
from the new doctrine.

Yet Rome wants to reproach Bolshevism for having destroyed
the Christian churches. As if Christianity hadn't done the same
with pagan temples!

What is this all about? Something seems anomalous here. Wehrmacht troops had run short of ammunition, fuel, food, and winter gear. They were starting to bog down. The invaders would soon be racked by hunger and numbed by frost in Russia's vast white hell. Meanwhile, back at his cozy bunker, the leader carped over early Christians ripping down ancient pagan shrines. To deem him distracted seems to understate the case.

Yet the Führer's words reveal an inner logic, linking this strife from the hoary Roman past to his faltering lunge toward Moscow. He was eager to immerse himself deeper in antiquity, urgent pleas from the war zone notwithstanding. Two days later, on October 21, Hitler urged a volume on his dinner guests:

I really hadn't known how clearly a man like Julian had judged
the Christians and Christianity. One must read this.

And what was this all about? The hero he upheld was Julian the Apostate, a Roman emperor who reigned from 361 to 363 C.E. Julian had tried, in vain, to stifle Christian churches and restore the pagan past. Hitler continued:

Christianity was destructive Bolshevism. Nevertheless, the
Galilean, who later was called the Christ, meant something quite
different. He was a popular leader (*ein Volksführer*) who took a
stand against Jewry.

So Christ ("the Galilean") was not really the foe, but Judeo-Christianity was.

Most remarks are prompted by some stimulus. What then prompted Hitler's distant concerns at this hinge of fate in World War II? It is a question worth pursuing, because Julian proved no mere passing interest. Three months later, on January 27, 1942, the head of the Reich mused again at lunch:

> What Christianity wrote against Julian is the same drivel as the stuff the Jews pour forth about us, while the writings of Julian are the pure truth.

The unchallenged head of a modern industrial state, embroiled in a war to the death, was likening his own quest to that of a ruler from the classical twilight. He proceeded to augment what he already knew by poring through Julian's theological tracts. Inexplicably but consistently, the Nazi conqueror aligned his own cause with the last pagan sovereign of ancient Rome.

By the time Hitler spoke those latter words, the German armies had retreated. Moscow had held fast. America had entered the war, adding the might of its factories, farms, and fleets to the fight. The Führer faced certain doom. But a mystery remains. Why the failed apostate? How far did Hitler's emulation of him really go? What had prompted Hitler's self-stated identity with Julian from among the many histories, novels, and plays about that bygone tragic figure? And if a prompt source can be found, how could it revise what is known about the widest conflict and the most-analyzed tyrant ever?

So, why Julian? Identifying the Führer's prompt source is a thread worth pursuing. It could lead to another, hidden World War II: the prototype concept that raged in the mind of the man who literally called the shots. What was this mental fount of the real war really all about?

There is, as it happens, a source that seems to fit. The Norwegian playwright Henrik Ibsen (1828–1906) wrote a drama about Julian the Apostate, *Emperor and Galilean*. He drafted parts of it at a place called Berchtesgaden, the same Bavarian resort with breathtaking alpine views that would later lure the Führer. The script was completed in 1873. Here and there its phrasing matches Hitler's later words, even including a dirge over ruined pagan shrines. And in *Emperor and Galilean,* Julian seeks to found a "third Reich." It is prophesied, as he dies on stage, that the emperor will be reborn in a new guise, someday, to accomplish that goal.

But purloined metaphors are just the start.

Far beyond borrowed phrases, over a score of episodes from the Ibsen script correlate with moves Hitler later made. Hitler's analogs to the plot of the play occurred in the same order as those in the script, instance after instance. The sequence of matching events played out over nearly two decades. It began with ritual actions and progressed to deeds of gravest effect. All told, certain selections from *Emperor and Galilean* match up, like a transparent map overlay, with the record of what the Führer said and did. Here, better late than never, is the Führer's Ur-text.

Why Ibsen? The bard of Norway and Father of Modern Drama was already a bit retro when Hitler was spouting forth during that fateful winter of 1941–42. In his heyday, though, Ibsen had been Europe's premier gadfly writing for the stage. "Scandalous," "provocative," and "ironic" issued from the critics' adjectival grab bag in assessments of his work. Ibsen detested hypocrisy in any form. George Bernard Shaw called him one "who declares that it is right to do something hitherto regarded as infamous." He pioneered a genre of unfettered social comment in dramatic form. Whether loved or loathed, the gruff Ibsen was, to all, an iconoclast.

And, to some, a "prophet." A loose German literary cult read the playwright's scripts like the sayings of a modern Nostradamus. Ibsen disciples split over what their master really meant. Some veered toward feminism, socialism, anarchism, reform; others toward a mystical racist creed. One such latter cultist, Dietrich Eckart, tutored the Führer. Another, in print, pointed to Hitler as the anointed one to usher in what the seer foretold: a "third Reich." Hitler, it appears, took the cue. Yet his minions never caught on to the source. Albert Speer, the Reich architect and also armaments minister, was as close a friend to the leader as any underling could be. After his postwar imprisonment, the released war criminal Speer reminisced on his own youthful theatrical fare:

> Upon seeing Ibsen's *The Wild Duck*, I decided that we could not find the characteristics of the leaders of society as other than ridiculous. These people were "farcical," I wrote.

Sound judgment, although a bit belated, and the right playwright. Wrong script, though. If only Speer had shunned politics or seen more Ibsen plays—for example, *The Master Builder,* or the epic *Emperor and Galilean,* which mattered most to his boss. That much can be gleaned by matching these scripts, in minute detail, to what Hitler said and did. Even so, the drama about Julian was not the first to echo in the speech of the man who started World War II. Still another Ibsen play preceded it in guiding Hitler's plans.

1

AN ENEMY OF THE PEOPLE

ASLAKSEN THE PRINTER: This gathering of
citizens unanimously declares the medical
officer of the Baths, Dr. Thomas Stockmann, an
enemy of the people.

—HENRIK IBSEN,
AN ENEMY OF THE PEOPLE, ACT IV

Munich People's Court. Judgment against Mr. Hitler.
At 11 A.M. on April 1, 1924 it is undertaken that the
following be sentenced to fortress detention:
Adolf Hitler, 5 years confinement.

—JUDICIAL VERDICT IN
THE BEER HALL PUTSCH TRIAL

DRAMA LURED HITLER. He never denied it. He boasted of seeing the same play seventeen times, the same opera forty times. From boyhood on, his reading mostly consisted of popular novels and stage scripts. Schooling for the future "Führer" ended shy of a diploma, at age sixteen. His real classroom was a darkened theater in Linz, upper Austria.

If the child be the father of the man, such a man may be suspected of blurring the real world with the world of the stage. His aides took it for granted. They dubbed his essence thespian, his talents histrionic. Percy Ernst Schramm kept stenographic notes at the wartime command bunker. He concluded that the Führer was "never entirely free" from the theater's grip. The longtime adjutant Julius Schaub said after the war that Hitler had been "extremely partial to the theater." Albert Speer confirmed: "Theater always played a leading role in his life."

Colonel-General Alfred Jodl, Chief of the General Staff, recalled a telling instance. It seems that at table one lighthearted day, Hitler lapsed into an impromptu impersonation. Something stirred him to mimic the accent and manners of a typical upper-Bavarian peasant. The one-man skit came off without flaw. Jodl remarked that had the then-master of Europe not gone into politics, he might have become the greatest actor ever on the German stage.

MAYBE HE WAS. Friend and foe agreed: Hitler acted, quite literally, on impulse. Actors ad-lib on occasion, and this actor did many an off-the-cuff routine. A long performance, though, requires a script.

WHO WROTE HITLER'S SCRIPT?

From time to time, journalists and historians have speculated that some literal script guided Adolf Hitler's actions. Wagner operas topped the list of suspect works. After all, Nazidom all but beatified the composer. A formal Führer state soirée almost invariably included a night at the opera, meaning Wagner. It was thus within reason to suspect some carryover to policy. And Wagner was, after all, a noted anti-Semite.

So, was he the Führer's muse? Wyndham Lewis, a British critic who viewed Hitler up close, wrote in 1939 with war on the horizon:

> It is as if we heard that the fate of the world hung upon a novel of Hugo's, to learn that it might be decided by the score of *Parsifal!*

Wagner definitely composed the tunes that played on, and on, and on, in Hitler's head. The Nazi phantom of the opera knew long

Wagner selections by heart. Yet somehow their lyrics fail to turn up in *Mein Kampf,* or in speeches, or in the transcripts of Hitler's dinnertime chats. Nary a Hitler line has ever been traced to *Parsifal,* the *Ring* cycle, *Lohengrin,* or to any other Wagner work.

Was there some other, secret bard? A passage from *Mein Kampf* offers a curious clue. Convict Hitler wrote Volume I in 1924. Part memoir, part manifesto, the manuscript emerged with its author after confinement in the Landsberg fortress prison. The Führer of the Nazi party served nine months in jail for fomenting the abortive Beer Hall Putsch. He turned the time into a writing sabbatical and caught up on his reading. And, so it seems, he saw himself mirrored in a play.

A play by Henrik Ibsen. Author Hitler never uttered Ibsen's name on the record. But the words of an Ibsen character veer suspiciously close to his own. Like Hitler, Dr. Thomas Stockmann was officially "an enemy of the people," so labeled by a citizens' assembly in a small spa town.

In *An Enemy of the People* (1882), Stockmann is responsible for certifying water quality at the town's public baths. He raises an epidemic alarm when he finds the waters rife with germs fed by some pollutant. Stockmann proceeds with scientific care and eventually traces the bacilli to noxious wastes dumped by a tannery located some distance upstream. Guided by a sense of duty, the doctor urges closing the baths until the germs are eradicated. With the town's tourist trade at stake, no one pays heed, so Stockmann is put off by the local press. Frustrated, he calls a municipal meeting to air the facts. There he stands alone. The town consensus is to deny that there is any risk to public health. Vested interests confront one conscientious scientist speaking the truth. At a stormy session in Act IV, Stockmann is forsaken even by his own brother, the sly, unprincipled mayor. The townsfolk try to hoot the physician down.

Dr. Stockmann's impassioned tirade (left column in the paired selections below) is a lone voice of reason against the mob. Something suspiciously like that voice resounds again in *Mein Kampf,* chapter 3 (right column). Bold italics emphasize the likeness to the Ibsen play.

DR. STOCKMANN VS. THE MOB

FURIOUS VOICES: So we're not the people, aren't we? So it's only the **aristocrats** who have the right to rule? . . .

DR. STOCKMANN: Let me be the **freethinker**, then. From my knowledge of **natural science** I shall now reveal to you all that the *People's Tribune* is deceiving you most shamefully when it tells you that you, the common millions, the masses, the **mob**, are the true heart and core of the people! That's just **a newspaper lie!** The masses are nothing but raw material which may, some day, be refined into individuals! . . . You've only got to look at that smug, "respectable" **mayor** of yours! He's about as low as any man that ever walked on two feet.

HOVSTAD: So it's the aristocrats who are the liberals in this country? That really is a new discovery!

DR. STOCKMANN: Yes, that's part of my discovery too. And the reason is that liberality is almost the same as morality. And I say it's quite indefensible of the *Tribune* day after day to mention the false gospel that the masses, the mob, the solid majority have a monopoly on liberality and morality, and

HITLER'S VIEWS ON MAJORITY RULE

By rejecting the authority of the individual and replacing it by the numbers of some momentary **mob,** the parliamentary principle of majority rule sins against the basic **aristocratic principle of Nature,** though it must be said that this view is not necessarily embodied in the present-day decadence of our upper ten thousand.

The devastation caused by this institution of modern parliamentary rule is hard for the reader of Jewish **newspapers** to imagine, unless he has **learned to think and examine independently.** It is, first and foremost, the cause of the incredible inundation of all political life with the most inferior, and I mean the most inferior, characters of our time. Just as the true leader will withdraw from all political activity which does not consist primarily in creative achievement and work, but in bargaining and haggling for the favor of the majority, in the same measure this activity will suit the small mind and consequently attract it.

The more dwarfish one of these present-day **leather merchants** is in spirit and ability, the more clearly his own insight makes him aware of the lamentable figure he actually

DR. STOCKMANN VS. THE MOB	HITLER'S VIEWS ON MAJORITY RULE
that vice and corruption and every kind of spiritual filth are a kind of pus that oozes out of culture, just as all that beastly stuff in the baths oozes down from the *tanneries* at Moelledal!	cuts—that much more will he sing the praises of a system that does not demand of him the power and genius of a giant, but is satisfied with the craftiness of a *village mayor*, preferring in fact this kind of wisdom to that of a Pericles.

While not quite a one-to-one congruence, in a roughly matching sequence Hitler echoes Stockmann's points:

⊕ Aristocracy is a natural principle, decreeing some persons intrinsically superior to others.
⊕ Majority rule defies that principle of nature.
⊕ Mob rule is promoted by the press, which Hitler dismissed as controlled by Jews.
⊕ It takes a freethinker to discover truth.
⊕ The polluting tannery in the Ibsen play correlates with Hitler's odd allusion to a leather dealer.
⊕ Both Stockmann and Hitler take a swipe at the mayor.

The shared theme here is an old one: the genius versus a tyrannical majority. The (self-proclaimed) Genius here might have pleaded with an original voice. Or he could have quoted from Plato on the trial of Socrates, or from John Stuart Mill's *On Liberty,* or from James Madison in the *Federalist Papers.* Yet his dramatic bent took him instead to *An Enemy of the People.* He appropriated not only the broad gist but enough particulars of Stockmann's speech to show that he identified with the brave spa doctor. Together, the presence of the village mayor and the "leather dealers" (*Lederhändler*) function like a painter's pentimenti in revealing a substratum. They all but confirm that Hitler cribbed from Ibsen. "Leather dealers" merits a closer look, as does the odd reference to Pericles.

WHEREFORE LEATHER DEALERS? AND PERICLES?

An enduring cultural distaste toward leather curing existed primarily because of the filth and foul odor emitted by tanneries. But taken purely on its own, no stretch of meaning in the *Mein Kampf* sequence can accommodate dragging in leather merchants. The allusion is so incongruous here that one unauthorized English translation substituted a more general "petty tradesman" for Hitler's *Lederhändler.* It was no accident, though, that the author had specified a tradesman in leather. His hidden reason explains the baffling reference to Pericles. Hitler connects the two incongruities later on.

Lederhändler did double duty. While recalling the polluting tannery in Ibsen's play, Hitler looked much farther back as well to another leather dealer. This was Cleon, an ancient Athenian craftsman turned politician and rival of Pericles during the fifth century B.C.E. Five years after writing *Mein Kampf,* Volume I, Hitler wrote of Cleon—and thus offered a link to Pericles—in an article. It is dated October 12, 1929, a contribution to the *Illustrierte Beobachter* ("Illustrated Observer"). There he made the same points as in *Mein Kampf,* but with varied examples. This time he cited the defiant heroes as Caesar, Frederick the Great, Napoleon, and Bismarck. They are counterposed in the 1929 article with the leather merchant Cleon "and his widespread ilk" (*ebenso wie den Lederhändler Kleon und seine weitverzweigte Sippschaft*).

So the hinge word *Lederhändler* connects with Cleon. Since the latter was hardly a household name, the mention of him among more familiar modern figures was no accident. Cleon as symbol for the vulgar politician in Hitler's mind accounts for his reference to Cleon's noble antagonist, Pericles. They are polar opposites. A "dwarfish" conniver who drags politics down to the level of his putrid trade has dared to challenge the visionary ruler and patron of architecture. The typically Hitlerian mishmash fuses an allusion from classical antiquity with the Ibsen material. Noble Dr. Stockmann conflates with Pericles by still another line of metaphoric logic. In the context of an alarm over deadly germs, Hitler had to know that Pericles succumbed to a plague along with thousands of other Athenians besieged during a long war. It was a very well known episode. Despite such a cruel end for the man, though, his Parthenon stood for all time.

Dr. Stockmann fought noxious germs and blockheads; Pericles commissioned great buildings like the Parthenon. Both Stockmann and Pericles are linked, in vivid metaphor, to the person of Hitler, in Hitler's own writing. About three pages of *Mein Kampf*'s chapter 3 amount to an adapted, abridged gloss of *An Enemy of the People*, Act IV—with Pericles tacked on.

HITLER HAD READ Ibsen in German translation. At least two German versions were easily obtainable in the early 1920s. Their wordings are too close to pin down which of the two Hitler consulted, but both include the reference to tanneries corresponding to his giveaway use of *Lederhändler.*

WHY IBSEN?

The full quotation from *An Enemy of the People*, Act IV runs to some three pages of text in most editions, whereas the *Mein Kampf* passage takes up only half a page or so. Their likeness was therefore best shown by somewhat truncating the Ibsen quotation, as indicated with ellipses in the paired passages. But much of Dr. Stockmann's speech excised above is also simpatico to what Hitler thought. Here Ibsen's physician lectures to the hostile mob about superior and inferior breeds:

> DR. STOCKMANN: The masses are only the raw material which some day may be refined into individuals. (*murmuring, laughter, general disturbance*) It's the same thing in all other forms of life. Fine animals are created by breeding and selection. Take an ordinary common hen, for instance—she's not much good for eating, and her eggs are not much better than a crow's eggs—or a raven's; she can't be compared with a really fine strain of poultry. But now take a Japanese or Spanish hen—a pheasant or a turkey—and you'll soon see the difference! Or in the case of dogs—so closely related

to mankind; think first of a common ordinary cur—one of those filthy, ragged, plebian mongrels that haunt the gutters and dirty up the sidewalks; and compare that mongrel with a pedigreed poodle, bred for generations from the finest stock, used to good food and accustomed to well-modulated voices and the sound of music. Don't you suppose the poodle's brain shows a marked superiority? Of course it does! A trainer can take a poodle pup like that and teach it the most fantastic tricks—things a common mongrel could never dream of learning! [*noise, laughter*]

A MAN (*shouting*): Are you comparing us with dogs?

ANOTHER: We're not animals, Doctor!

DR. STOCKMANN: Of course you are! We're all animals, my friend! What else are we? But there aren't many well-bred animals among us. There's a tremendous difference between poodle-men and mongrel-men.

This is racism, by twenty-first-century standards. Now, Ibsen was a man of the nineteenth century; he must not be burdened with the onus for Nazi racial madness. But such statements were clearly compatible with the German Third Reich's eugenic doctrine and practice. In Ibsen's day, these ideas were on the cutting edge of what people then called progressive science. Ibsen's ideas were "so startling that they struck the smug, complacent society of the time with the force of a tidal wave, and revolutionized not only plays and players but the pattern of thought of men and women everywhere." That was how one translator put it. The plays gave a voice to impassioned reason and modernity. They supplied lesser writers with metaphors.

By the time Hitler echoed *An Enemy of the People* in *Mein Kampf,* he had already taken material from it via an intermediate source. The Swedish novelist Per Hallström (1866–1960) earlier drew on the drama in a 1915 pamphlet, *Folkfeinden,* with four essays backing German war aims.

Hallström found in the Ibsen play an analogy for Germany's unpopularity among the democratic European neutral states. He too depicted majority opinion as flouting the natural aristocratic principle that vests rule in the hands of a talented few. As archetype he used Frederick the Great of Prussia during the Seven Years' War. Since 1870, Germany had shown again how a nation could strengthen and modernize under the firm guidance of aristocrats and qualified specialists, leaving but token parliamentary power to the elected Reichstag. Hallström took Ibsen's small-minded mob to portray parliamentary majorities. As he put it, "Yes, this aristocrat and enemy of the people [i.e., Germany, meant ironically] has discovered the holy source [i.e., parliaments] of the democratic microbe and has taken cold and conclusive sanitary measures." It was thus Hallström who likened majority rule to microbial contamination.

The chauvinist Munich publisher Hugo Bruckmann brought out a German translation of Hallström's pamphlet in 1916 under the title *Der Volksfeind*. Bruckmann was a patron of the Nazi playwright Dietrich Eckart and a backer of the nascent Nazi party. And so it is not surprising that phrases from the Hallström essay found their way into Hitler speeches, given the close nurturing relationship of Eckart to Hitler from 1920 to 1922. A standard, undated example delivered numerous times before *Mein Kampf* turns up in an authorized Nazi collection.

This text appears to be prompt notes, consisting of a few simple sentences. "German parliamentarianism is the downfall and the end of the German nation." "Our democracy today cannot breed leadership or responsibility. It hides behind anonymous majorities." "The Jewish democracy of majority consent is now and for all time but a means toward the extermination of actual Aryan leadership." And "If a Frederick [the Great] were to appear today, he'd probably wind up sentenced to be shot." A complete text version bears the date May 4, 1923. Here Frederick serves as the lexical fingerprint, corroborating Hitler's resort to Hallström. The fourth essay in Hallström's booklet was a paean to Frederick as the paragon of stern leadership in adversity.

More notes, in Hitler's handwriting, are dated July 20, 1921, incidentally a week before his formal recognition as the Nazi party Führer. A nine-page scribbled speech outline winds up with "Minorities, not majorities, make world history" and "No majority will save Germany," then "No dictatorship of Jewry, only a dictatorship of genius" and the dramatic finale, "We are creating a new age." That could correspond to Stockmann's announcement to the town meeting of having discovered a new truth.

For about three years prior to *Mein Kampf,* Hitler had spouted a rhetorical trope derived first, it seems, from Hallström's pamphlet, then directly from Ibsen. Once he was immured at Landsberg, the Ibsen play fit his situation even better. Dr. Stockmann, denounced as an enemy of the people, had mulled leaving for America but finally resolved to stay in town and fight. Hitler during his trial likewise faced the chance of forced deportation to his native Austria, should the Bavarian authorities move to do so. It remained a possibility through much of 1924.

Repatriation would have ruined the Führer's future in his adopted land. Politically, he knew he was better off in a jail on German soil. It made him that much more of a German.

Other features in *Mein Kampf,* chapter 3 substantiate its borrowing of narrative structure from *An Enemy of the People,* Act IV. The Ibsen and Hitler segments quoted above were each preceded by reminiscences of the narrators' formative years. Stockmann talked about his medical internship in a remote northern district. Hitler digressed to his youth in Vienna before turning to matters closer at hand. There was also a curiously titled article in the Nazi party's daily organ *Völkischer Beobachter* for June 6, 1923. Bearing the headline "Fighting an Enemy of the People," it touts a medicinal remedy against tuberculosis. The byline is that of a "Dr. A. Friedman." A note accompanying the piece states that the story was placed by some individual "outside the authority of the editorial board." Did anyone apart from the top-ranked Nazi leader wield enough clout to override the party paper's regular editors? Apparently this "Dr. A. Friedman" had the phrase "enemy of the people" on his mind, and in a medical context at that.

He retained it in mind. By working the Ibsen script into *Mein Kampf* a year later, Hitler privately assumed the persona of Dr. Thomas Stockmann along with the scientific reason and social responsibility possessed by physicians. *An Enemy of the People* was, after all, about battling insidious microbes. Stockmann had sounded the klaxon. Hitler believed he must, too.

JEWS = GERMS

Jews had long been maligned as ogres, dogs, or swine. But these insults did not prescribe a truly definitive, final solution. The souls of ogres may be redeemed. Dogs or even a rare pig may attain pet status. Not so with germs. Germs are irredeemable. A germ cannot be baptized as some higher order of being. A baptized Jew is merely a moistened germ, while still a Jew. All germs pose a danger, and germs were always bad according to common belief in Hitler's day. Jews spread disease—or, more ominously, they were themselves a disease.

Practical consequences ensue. The notion "Jews = germs" evoked the dread of the fourteenth-century bubonic plague and its subsequent visitations. Jews incurred blame as perpetual social outsiders, scripturally accursed. To scripture was added the panache of modern science going back to one of its early martyrs, Giordano Bruno (1548–1600).

A victim of the Inquisition, Bruno had burned at the stake for espousing a version of Copernican cosmology. That made him a martyr for science and a precursor of Ibsen's Dr. Stockmann. Along the way, Bruno condemned the Jews for posing such a "pestilential, leprous, and hazardous genus that they deserve to be exterminated before birth." That was how Hitler encountered Bruno in a 1920 pamphlet by his mentor Dietrich Eckart, *That's the Jew* (*Das ist der Jude*). During the early 1920s, Hitler met with Eckart at least weekly, oftentimes almost daily. It would be unrealistic to suppose that he did not know of Eckart's pamphlet, which itself rested on a pedigreed tradition. In 1887, the philologist and anti-Semitic ideologue Paul de Lagarde had also brandished a rhetorical test tube and warned of the microbes within. Hitler's own underlined copy of Lagarde's book is extant, among the other volumes of the Führer's personal collection now in the Library of Congress.

Jews and bacilli, or viruses, germs, agents of tuberculosis, syphilis, and plague are juxtaposed in the Hitler corpus with a frequency approaching that of "wine-dark sea" in Homer. His own rhetorical equation of Jews with bacilli went back at least to a letter he sent in July 1920 calling Jews the perennial "racial tuberculosis of the nations." A month later, Hitler uttered the same words in a speech at Salzburg. Ever consistent, he again used the formula on May Day 1923. Germ references feature in *Mein Kampf,* Volume I, chapter 11: "He [the Jew] is like a noxious bacillus"; Jewry then became the "world plague" in a statement made to a pro-Nazi journalist during his Landsberg jail time.

His lexicon drew upon the global post-Armistice influenza epidemic that had only just run its course, having taken a human toll exceeding that of all the battles of World War I. A horror of germs and viruses pervaded the popular mind more than ever before. Hitler used the germ image on the podium and in casual talk, again and again. From this, but one conclusion can be drawn: he meant it.

In similar contexts, Heinrich Himmler would loosely use the term "lice," biologically a higher form of vermin than bacilli or viruses. Lice are visible to the naked eye; ordinary people can control lice; and, although a nuisance, lice do not kill. Germs do. Battling invisible microbes requires the scientific expertise of a qualified professional, and a long-term commitment. Seventeen years passed from the writing of *Mein Kampf* to the start of the Nazi genocide against the Jews. Yet Dr. Hitler kept at it.

Proud of his research, on the evening of July 10, 1941 he remarked at headquarters:

> I feel like Robert Koch in politics. He discovered the bacilli and pointed many things in a new direction. I discovered the Jews and the bacillus and their fermenting agent of social decomposition.

In a conference with a Croatian military representative a week later, Hitler stated:

> When even one state, for any reason whatsoever, tolerated one single Jewish family in its midst, this would constitute a source of bacilli touching off new infection. Once there are no more Jews in Europe, there will be nothing to interfere with the unification of the European nations.

Nothing if not consistent, on February 22, 1942 Hitler expounded at the dinner table, again comparing himself to Robert Koch with Louis Pasteur thrown in for good measure:

> The discovery of the Jewish virus is one of the greatest revolutions that have taken place in the world. The battle in which we are engaged today is of the same sort as the battle waged, during the last century, by Pasteur and Koch. How many diseases have their origin in the Jewish virus!

The culture samples were back from the lab. To guard public hygiene, the self-appointed Surgeon General of Europe ordered a prescription:

> We shall regain our health only by eliminating the Jews.

THE GERM OF THE FINAL SOLUTION

It is not news that Hitler usurped the microbial metaphor. What is new is the uncovering of Ibsen's *An Enemy of the People* behind his antiseptic campaign, the Final Solution (*Endlösung*) to world Jewry.

Dr. Stockmann had explicitly demanded not only the extermination of harmful bacilli, but also those human communities deemed unworthy of life. Again, Stockmann's speeches correlate with Hitler's. The link involves another set of words: liars, lies, and lying. *Mein Kampf,* Volume I, chapter 11 got down to cases. Jews are defined there as a group that, being without their own state, must prevaricate in order to survive.

> The Jew's life as a parasite in the body of other nations and states explains a characteristic which once caused Schopenhauer, as has already been mentioned, to call him the "great master in lying."
> Existence impels the Jew to lie, and to lie perpetually, just as it compels the inhabitants of the northern countries to wear warm clothing. His life within other peoples can only endure for

any length of time if he succeeds in arousing the opinion that he is not a people but a "religious community," though of a special sort. And this is the first great lie.

So far, Hitler merely reflected tradition. The Schopenhauer remark on Jews turns up in material by Dietrich Eckart. Also staple was Martin Luther's notorious tract *On the Jews and Their Lies,* which Eckart also quoted. Yet for all his third-hand cribbing, something marked Hitler as special. He would settle with those he called liars, not individually but as a community of congenital liars. For them the final solution drew afresh from Ibsen. Dr. Stockmann had pointed the way in his forthright scientific manner. It is communities of liars that are unworthy of existence. A society built on lies should be exterminated.

The left column below comes again from *An Enemy of the People,* Act IV. The right column comes from the Führer's post-prandial chat at midday on February 8, 1942. Present at table were Albert Speer and Heinrich Himmler:

It hardly matters if a lying society (*Gesellschaft*) is run into the ground! I say it should be razed to the earth! Like noxious pests they must be exterminated (*ausgerottet*), all of them, who live by lies! In the end they infest the whole land and bring it to ruin. And if it comes to that then I say from full, inner conviction (*Überzeugung*): "Let the whole land go to ground! Let the whole people be exterminated!"	I'm convinced (*überzeugt*) in ten years things will look different. Because we haven't yet reached the fundamental solution. If one thinks it's really essential to build a human society (*Gesellschaft*) on a basis of untruth, then such a society is unworthy to exist. If one takes truth as the necessary firmament, then the conscience is tasked to intervene on behalf of truth and to exterminate untruth (*die Unwahrheit auszurotten*).

To compare:

* The same German keywords appear in both passages.
* Both speakers take for their topic a society based on lies, which is unworthy of existence.

⊕ Both are convinced of the justice of a radical solution.

⊕ And to both speakers, extermination offers the only sure answer.

But lots of frustrated people could throw such a tantrum. Identifying *An Enemy of the People* as Hitler's source text might be debatable here, were it not for the clear pentimenti from the same play in *Mein Kampf*, written in 1924. With an astonishing continuity in 1942, Hitler picked up again from Act IV, about a page away from where he had left off some eighteen years earlier. It is evident that by the date of these latter words, Hitler had once again mentally donned the good doctor's white lab smock.

In these two sets of paired quotations, we have some pages of a lost playbill from the matinee in Hitler's head. Entering late, we grope along the aisle; our eyes are unaccustomed to the dark. But in the dim-lit loge of his cerebrum, we catch phrases of a recital in progress. They are chilling. Could it be? Did this theater maven and self-described microbe hunter link his monstrous program to Ibsen's crusading physician every single time he called the Jews "germs"? By adducing Pasteur and Koch in 1941–42, he all but confirmed it. The two historical germ fighters were surrogates for Stockmann. A head of state may cite the work of famous scientists, but must find it less prudent to admit he has taken his act from a doctor concocted for the stage. *An Enemy of the People* remained a clinical secret.

The Führer adopted theatrical roles, or so it seems, in a mad game that took scripted metaphors at their literal word. It argues on behalf of his basic conviction. And that is a point perennially at issue among Hitler scholars. Was he a posing charlatan? or a lunatic propelled by some inner sense of mission? Hitler-as-Stockmann fits the latter. Sincerity comes through not only in his unwavering resolve but also in the wary cloaking of his textual source. Instead of openly crediting Ibsen, Hitler co-opted the imagery of the Ibsen character into his own argument. The 1924 dictation that became *Mein Kampf*, chapter 3 bears enough marks of *An Enemy of the People* to reasonably infer that a copy of the play was present in Hitler's cell, pages open to Act

IV. By 1942, though, the fleeting reference may more likely reflect a recent rereading of the text, internalized and regurgitated without conscious thought. The phenomenon is sometimes called "crypt-amnesia," derivation without deliberate plagiaristic intent. Hitler's conscious choice lay in the material he chose to read, review, and absorb as a part of himself. What emerged was an action program, directed against the Jewish "germs," worthy of Dr. Stockmann.

Hitler acted, believed, and acted on his beliefs. A certain weary cynicism might grow in any politician giving the same speech again and again: Each time he must convey verve, as if it were the first time. The best stage actors manage to project belief in their roles by immersing themselves into their part, sometimes for years. If that was Hitler's method, it accounts for his oratorical appeal. He projected mission. He also had enough sense to realize that the mission would be jeopardized should the public realize how much was taken from theatrical scripts. This, then, was Hitler's quandary as a method actor, living a role on a long performance run.

TAKING STOCK

Taken alone, *An Enemy of the People* is not that elusive Grail long sought by scholars, the very wellspring of Hitler's hatred for the Jews. But it bears upon his genocidal acts. Hitler swore himself to be destiny's instrument, having said so often enough. The literary selections he internalized thus assume a status like holy writ. They show what animated Hitler and define who he thought he was, or wanted to be.

A "Führer" who aped Dr. Thomas Stockmann is, at the very least, a bit different from the Hitler conjectured by scholarly biographers and Freudian psychohistorians. To be sure, Ibsen comprised only one ingredient among many in Hitler's mental mix. But Ibsen, like yeast, made an active ingredient. A small, measured amount is essential. More still may be in the mix.

In sum so far, these propositions are given as demonstrable:

- Enough well-placed people at different times remarked on Hitler's theatrical bent for this trait to be taken as highly significant, if indeed not crucial.
- A portion of *Mein Kampf,* Volume I, chapter 3 was reworked from Henrik Ibsen's *An Enemy of the People,* Act IV, as shown by a sequence of metaphors too close to dismiss as mere chance replication.
- Further ruling out chance replication are references in Hitler's speaking notes from 1921, and an odd story headline in the Nazi newspaper *Völkischer Beobachter* in mid-1923 showing the presence of this play in the mind of the party leader.
- A political pamphlet by Per Hallström evidently reinforced the value of *An Enemy of the People* to Hitler.
- Hitler's off-the-cuff paraphrases, as opposed to verbatim quotations, show that material from *An Enemy of the People* had become deeply embedded in his own thinking.
- Hitler tacked an allusion from classical antiquity onto the Ibsen material from *An Enemy of the People,* showing a tendency to mix themes and historical periods.
- The *Mein Kampf* paraphrase of *An Enemy of the People* and its resumption in Hitler's chitchat eighteen years later underscores this play's long and abiding grip on him.
- The speech from *An Enemy of the People,* Act IV bears significance beyond its merely literary echo in the text of *Mein Kampf,* since the eradication of germs urged by Dr. Stockmann offered an action plan for a tyrant equating the germs with the Jews.

So the stakes are high indeed. The hold of this play on Hitler went beyond mere parroted words, an adopted character, and an adapted theme. And to be sure, the dictator knew that Ibsen wrote other plays as well.

2

"ADOLF READ IBSEN'S DRAMAS IN VIENNA"

BROVIK: I've begun to have doubts about the
boy. In all these years you've never uttered
so much as a single word of encouragement
about him. But it must be there. I can't believe
he hasn't got the ability.
MASTER BUILDER SOLNESS: He doesn't
know anything. Not really. Except how to draw.
—IBSEN, *THE MASTER BUILDER*, ACT I

"Adolf read Ibsen's dramas in Vienna . . ."
—AUGUST KUBIZEK,
HITLER'S ROOMMATE IN VIENNA, 1908

HAULED BEFORE THE Munich court that would sentence him in 1924, the Nazi party Führer was required to state an occupation. His reply readily rang out: "master builder"—*Baumeister*, in German.

Baumeister implied a qualified and licensed practitioner. Adolf Hitler never attended classes at any architecture school. He had never held a contract to design or erect a building, a bridge, a monument, or really anything. He had neither been employed by an architect or contractor, nor ever labored on any construction site.

The response he supplied to a pro forma courtroom query was thus a fantasy.

Yet, inwardly at least, not quite an outright lie. The German word for a profession is *Beruf,* carrying the sense of a "calling." In court Hitler thus distanced the evident fact of his being a politician from his ideal inner essence. He had always proclaimed himself an aspiring architect, from his Austrian schoolboy days through his time as a struggling artist and then his army service. Former acquaintances and comrades in the trenches concurred on that point. The dream career traced back to sketches he made, at age fourteen, for structures he someday hoped to build. His only friend in Linz, August Kubizek, recalled architecture as Adolf's "mania."

> Usually he carried around in his head a dozen different build-
> ing projects, and sometimes I could not help feeling that all
> the buildings of the town were lined up in his brain like a giant
> panorama.

He did show a flair for draftsmanship. But Adolf gave indifferent effort to essentials like mathematics and physics, the disciplines of the builder's trade. His grades were poor, his attitude worse: "obstinate, high-handed, dogmatic, and irascible," one teacher judged, adding: "He found it very difficult to fit into a school situation." It appears that another Muse lured this pupil, one more compelling than girls, sports, hobbies, or study toward his avowed metier.

The Muse was Drama. Hitler made the Linz Landschaftlichen Theater his haunt, going there alone, sitting in the dark, watching plays. He acknowledged that they went to his head. When Adolf deigned to attend middle school classes, he would, to use a British term then in fashion, Ibsenize.

"IBSENIZING"

"Ibsenizing" referred to biting social commentary written for the stage. If Hitler mimicked Ibsen's style per se this early, circumstances may explain why. The Landschaftlichen featured an Ibsen cycle in 1903. That year was just when the teenaged Adolf idled there, according to a knowledgeable hometown source, the theater's director. Hugo Rabitsch wrote an account published years later. It reveals much, despite an adulatory intent. Rabitsch credited theater as the decisive ingredient in molding the future Führer. Rabitsch's book, *Aus Adolf Hitlers Jugendzeit* ("From the Youth of Adolf Hitler"), proceeds to list the Landschaftlichen repertoire for 1903–05. The latter-day equivalent might be to append pages of "TV Guide" to the formative-years chapter in a biography of some academic zero of a baby-boomer turned chief of state.

Pupil Adolf's "Ibsenizing," if it may be so called, found a human target. Rabitsch and Hitler himself agree on who it was. Father Franz Sales Schwarz (d. 1912) served as religion instructor at the Catholic middle school. Rabitsch remembered the priest as a "sick old man." His irascible student did naught to improve the cleric's health. Some provocations were political. When Schwarz upheld the Habsburg dynasty of the polyglot Austro-Hungarian empire, Hitler played the pan-German chauvinist. He would flaunt red, black, and yellow pencils in his hand, wordlessly declaring loyalty to the tricolor flag of Germany. Other taunts were religious. When Schwarz taught the holy faith, Hitler played the rebel apostate with endless nuisance questions on theological points. They pair waged a memorable vendetta; remembered best, that is, by the boy who would be Führer.

On the night of January 8–9, 1942, the most powerful man in Europe looked back. He still seethed over this simple parochial school teacher:

> I was the eternal questioner. Grades showed my peerless mastery over the material. In religion I was laudable and preeminent, but in conduct unsatisfactory. I had a penchant for risky themes from the Bible. "Herr Professor, what's meant by that?" An evasive answer. I'd ask again and again until finally Professor Schwarz would lose patience: "Sit down, already!"

One day Schwarz asked whether this self-appointed gadfly recited daily prayers. Adolf rose to his glory. "No, Herr Professor, I don't pray at all since I don't think God takes any interest in the prayers of a middle-school pupil." It got personal. The Führer rambled on, that night in 1942:

> Schwarz would pull out a large blue handkerchief he kept in the lining of his cassock. It would crackle when he unfolded it. One day he left it in class. While he was talking to some other teachers, I handed the rag back to him, at arm's length, and said "Herr Professor, you've forgotten your handkerchief." What a ruckus in the class!

Father Schwarz threatened eternal perdition. Hitler laughed that off, denying faith in an afterlife. Short of delivering on Hell, Schwarz issued demerits for bad behavior. The grown Führer looked back on those days:

> He never knew what to think of me, and that bothered him. I had read a lot of free thinkers' works, and he knew it. When I irked him with my half-baked scientific knowledge, I almost drove him out of his wits.

It got worse. An acquaintance later retold pupil Hitler's story of how he wrote, mimeographed, and circulated a sheet satirizing the Catholic dogma of the immaculate conception. This was outright blasphemy. Schwarz threatened thirty-six hours' detention for the class until the culprit came forward. Hitler admitted the prank and did the time in twelve installments of three hours each. Then he upped the ante.

Adolf the Apostate needed moral support. So he joined—of all groups in Linz—an association of separated persons agitating for revised marriage laws. However bizarre for a never-married youth, this was the closest Hitler could find to an anti-Church league in Catholic upper Austria, where civil divorce was banned. The teenager added this social issue to the seditious pan-Germanism he already touted in class, to goad Schwarz.

What matters is the protest format: drama.

At the divorce-law league, he heard impassioned orators plead for legal reform. Then he went home and began composing a play on the theme. "Writing" is not a strictly accurate word for what he did. Instead, he would pace up and down, dictating acts and scenes to his half-sister Angela. At last the scribe tired. No finished play ever emerged; but with this script attempt, the boy refreshed his stock of rhetoric for prodding the parochial pedagogue.

In that, he succeeded. He won his classroom battles, only to lose the scholastic war. Hitler was a year shy of graduation when the school denied him enrollment for 1904–05. A term at a less-prestigious academy in Steyr proved abortive too. So Father Schwarz got the last laugh. Acting up in class, bad boy Adolf had committed educational suicide. Rabitsch had attended the Linz middle school six years behind Hitler. He knew the milieu and the leading characters, including Schwarz. Confirmed by Hitler's own subsequent words, it is evident that their confrontation led the priest to engineer the expulsion of what Rabitsch called "the little rejected student Baumeister."

RABITSCH TOLD THE miseries of Hitler's years in Linz. AWOL from school, he sat in the theater's cheap section. He went solo. Theater was not a social event for young Adolf: it comprised the basis of his learning. He was neither jock, nor nerd, nor ladies' man, nor hale-fellow-well-met. A sympathetic writer cast him instead as an insatiable drama fan. Hitler substantiated the Rabitsch portrait. In May 1906, he stayed with his godparents for some three weeks in Vienna. From there, he sent ecstatic postcards back to his only boyhood friend, August Kubizek, recounting the operas he attended. Kubizek recalled that Hitler saw Wagner's *Lohengrin* fully ten times. The Linz schedule confirms that it was performed "often."

Kubizek remembered, too, how Wagner's *Rienzi* moved Hitler when the boys went to this show, in Linz. *Rienzi* is about a fourteenth-century tribune of Rome who tries to free the city from noble oligarchs. He fights and fails. At the end, Rienzi dies gloriously amidst the burning Roman Capitol. A normally talkative Adolf was struck dumb by the performance. Enchanted beneath the night sky after the show, the teenager at last regained his tongue. "In that hour it began," was how a grownup Hitler revered the moment.

It.

By "it," one may safely infer that Hitler meant his career. "It" thus began with a show, which happened to be a show written by Wagner. The self-admitted impact of a Wagner musical just then may hint at how "it"—the life's mission of Adolf Hitler—might in due course have assimilated other themes from other plays by other writers—although, for the time being in 1906–07, Wagner dominated the "it."

According to Kubizek, the appeal of Wagner even induced young Hitler to try his own hand at composing opera. He set out to complete a piece left undone by Wagner, about a medieval character called Wieland the Smith. Adolf banged out melodies on the Hitlers' family piano for the musically trained Kubizek to record in notation. Hitler also outlined the opera plot and scenes. Again, he could dictate but not actually bring himself to scrawl. And again, as with the play he had dictated to Angela, the ambitious project was left incomplete.

The stage pulled one way, painting another, and architecture still another. In September 1907, Hitler sought acceptance at the Vienna Academy of Art but failed to make the cut. Turning him down, the rector said his talents seemed better geared for architecture than for painting. Those consoling words steered the applicant to the Vienna Academy of Architecture, only to be stymied by unmet prerequisites. Hitler had no secondary-school diploma. His run-in with Father Schwarz was exacting its toll.

Shortly, however, he gained an independent income. The settlement following his mother's death in December that year allotted him some family funds and a government welfare allotment for orphans. Here was a windfall, ready cash for show tickets.

AS OF EARLY 1908, Hitler was a jobless daydreaming dropout with a theatrical bent. The Hitlers' landlady in Linz had some connection in Vienna to a noted stage designer, Alfred Roller, who designed sets at the Hofoper and taught at the Academy of Arts and Crafts. Adolf was provided with a letter of introduction. An appointment with Roller was his putative reason for leaving Linz. But as with school, the Linz building plans, and the drama writing attempts, this job hunt also fizzled.

The nineteen-year-old Hitler arrived in Vienna from Linz in February 1908, still smarting from his rejection by the art and architectural academies the previous autumn. He had been told he could sketch buildings, not badly, but that was all he could do. The next logical step would have been to prepare his best drawings as a portfolio, print up a business card, and shop himself around for work with some architect, somewhere. Vienna offered a timely chance for such a job search. The Eighth International Architects' Congress would meet there from May 18 to 23. Held in a different city biennially, these meetings assembled the leading names from Europe and the Americas. As of early 1908, Adolf had ample time and funds to prepare a credentials package and prospect for employment. Work, however, was not on his agenda. In Vienna he rented a room at No. 29 Stumpfergasse. He sent word inviting August Kubizek to share lodgings while the latter studied at the Vienna conservatory. Kubizek arrived later in February. Hitler put on airs, concealing his own failures to matriculate. Yet instead of pursuing a practical fallback plan or a job, he tried one more forlorn approach to the architecture school.

This was delusional. If Adolf had been somehow unaware in 1907 that the Academy required a high-school diploma, he surely knew it in 1908. His talk of attending, minus credentials or connections, betrays a disengagement from facts. It showed again in his blithe ignorance of the upcoming architects' congress. In all his correspondence, his writings, in his transcribed monologue ramblings about his youth, and in Kubizek's memoir of their friendship, there is not a hint that Hitler even knew of the May convention. Distracted and out of the loop, he bungled a chance. Building was his steady conversational refrain. But his activities led elsewhere, as Kubizek confirms. The boys roomed together until early July. During that time, Adolf went to theaters—not to paint sets, heft props, and learn stage design, but to sit in the audience. He squandered time, effort, and cash, using shows as an anodyne in Vienna as he had in Linz. The capital city offered many more shows to see.

ENTER JULIAN THE APOSTATE

The present issue concerns the historical consequences of this young man's theatrical craze. It goes beyond whether Hitler merely liked shows. He relished them, but that too may understate the point. To voluntarily attend the same opera ten times is to pursue rapture. Having long since ceased attending Catholic services, he later stated flatly: "For me, Wagner is something godly and his music is my religion. I go to his concerts as others go to church." The fixation on Wagner, at least, was out in the open. He would make less public fuss about other favorites.

Kubizek named two more dramas he and Hitler viewed: "We saw Frank Wedekind's *Frülings Erwachen* ('Spring Awakening') and Adolf Wilbrandt's *Der Meister von Palmyra* ('The Master of Palmyra')." Kubizek's memory checks out against the newspaper listings. The Deutsche Volkstheater in Vienna staged the Wedekind play during May and June 1908. Risqué for its time, it dealt with puberty, the coming of age in Mitteleuropa. But Adolf bothered little with girls. More important was the historical extravaganza *Der Meister von Palmyra*, on the themes of architecture, statecraft, war, faith, and paganism, all of which would loom large in Hitler's later words and deeds. The Hofburg Theater gave two performances in late February 1908, just when Kubizek arrived to room with Hitler.

Adolf Wilbrandt (1837–1911) completed *Der Meister von Palmyra* in 1889, setting the drama in the Hellenized eastern lands of the late Roman Empire. It was meant to glorify paganism's last gasp. The title character Apelles is the master of Palmyra, at once its proficient architect and wise governor. His great buildings in an opulent Hellenistic style adorn Palmyra, a Roman client state bordering Persia. Apelles was inspired by the historical Palmyrene ruler Odenathus, although Wilbrandt changed the name and embellished. Blessed by longevity, Apelles ages but slowly over the fourth century while those around him are born, mature, and perish.

In each act, Apelles has a principal interlocutor. Wilbrandt stipulated that one actress—female—play all these roles to convey the idea of reincarnation. The same spirit, or *Geist*, is supposed to successively inhabit the Christian martyr Zoë; a Roman courtesan Phoebe, who then marries Apelles as Persida; their grandson Nymphas; and finally Zenobia, Palmyra's queen after Apelles. In Act II, it is said that "The vital spirit leaps from form to form," gender notwithstanding. A Fräulein Hohenfeld acted the multiple part in the performance attended by Hitler and Kubizek.

The notions of rebirth and of gender-switching bear significance because Hitler would go on to extol a supposedly reincarnated character, Julian the Apostate, from an Ibsen historical play. He would also paraphrase the lines spoken by a female character from still another Ibsen script.

A theme of paganism versus Christianity suffuses *Der Meister von Palmyra*. Apelles suffers at the hands of Christian fanatics. He supports the Roman emperor Julian the Apostate, who has renounced Christianity. A character asks: "What are they quarreling about?" The answer comes from Nymphas, the male pagan figure played by an actress:

> About the man who is now turning the world upside down, about the great emperor Julian. Some curse him—I heard it in the open market place—because he has fallen off from the faith of his uncle, the Christian Constantine, they call him the renegade, the Apostate; the others proclaim to the people how wise and good he is, and prophesy a rebirth of the old times. If he overcomes the Persians whom he is now fighting, he will come as conqueror to Palmyra and here too cast down the spite of the Christians before him. And the fallen grandeur of the old Roman Empire will arise again.

A Christian character is unmoved: "You think so? It lies dead, will never rise again . . . those times are past." Yet Apelles takes a longer view:

> Let us leave time alone. To live timeless, as we do, is happiness for man . . . above us the ever steadfast citadel of peace, the dome wrought by the world's Master Builder, of unfathomable

blue—till those silver mysteries, the flames of night, break
through it.

Apelles opts for paganism. He declares:

Our goal is to be free, not to surrender. Down with the enemies
of the ancient gods!

But Apelles rules only a small oasis state. All really depends on
the emperor Julian. Then Julian's sudden demise postpones his grand
historical reckoning with Christianity. An offstage voice intones
somberly through several scenes:

Julian the Apostate is no more!
The emperor is slain!

At length Apelles expires too, amidst Palmyra's ruined architectural grandeur. It could hardly fail to awe a certain self-declared
young apostate seated in the audience. Hitler had to know, though,
that Apelles never actually lived.

THE "THIRD REICH" IN *EMPEROR AND GALILEAN*

Yet Julian did. Wilbrandt built his drama upon the same historical
themes as Henrik Ibsen took up in his two-part epic *Kaiser und
Galiläer* ("Emperor and Galilean"). This play became available in
German translation in 1888, just when Wilbrandt was writing *Der
Meister von Palmyra*. A connection between these two plays is apparent. For instance, both promoted reincarnation and a cyclical view
of history, as well as incorporating Rome's last pagan emperor. Ibsen
had portrayed Julian as a flawed prophet who himself must bow to
fate. In *Emperor and Galilean,* he foretold a revived pagan future,
which he called a "third Reich."

Julian's apostasy from the Church emerges early in the Ibsen play. By Part One, Act III, Julian consults a seer known as Maximus the Mystic.

> MAXIMUS: There are three empires [*Reich*, in the German].
> JULIAN: Three?
> MAXIMUS: First, the Reich founded on the tree of knowledge; then the Reich founded on the tree of the cross.
> JULIAN: And the third?
> MAXIMUS: The third is the Reich of the great mystery, the Reich which shall be founded on the tree of knowledge and the tree of the cross together, because it hates and loves them both, and because it has its living springs under Adam's grove and Golgotha.
> JULIAN: And that empire will come?
> MAXIMUS: It is at hand. I have calculated and calculated again.

In the second part of the Ibsen drama, Emperor Julian announces his goal to reconstruct the great Jewish temple at Jerusalem, defying a hex on the project. Rebuilding the Temple would incur the "curse of Golgotha" and incite the wrath of Christ. Julian scoffs—and pays the price.

Ibsen's historical prophecy resounds in Part Two, Act III. Maximus the Mystic appears again. It is the dramatic highlight.

> MAXIMUS: *That* is the third Reich, Julian.
> JULIAN: Yes, Maximus, that is the third Reich.
> MAXIMUS: In *that* empire, truth shall bear out all the inspiring words of those who came before.

From Maximus, Julian hears of an anointed spirit who shall return in successive incarnations through history. On each appearance, he will strive to establish the state of absolute truth, called the third Reich (*das dritte Reich*) in the play's German text. Julian takes this as repudiating Christ the Galilean. Maximus hints at the fact that making this third Reich also entails confronting Old-Testament monotheism.

JULIAN: Who will break the power of the Galilean?

MAXIMUS: Wherein lies the power of the Galilean?

JULIAN: I have asked myself but found no answer.

MAXIMUS: It is written somewhere: "Thou shalt have no other gods but me."

And a few lines further on:

JULIAN: The third Reich? The Messiah? Not that of the Jews, but the Messiah of the empire of the spirit and the empire of the world—?

MAXIMUS: The god-Kaiser.

JULIAN: The Kaiser-god.

MAXIMUS: Logos in Pan—Pan in Logos.

Two familiar biblical allusions are conjoined here. They are the First Commandment revealed to Moses, from Exodus 20:3, demanding exclusive service to the one deity, and an allusion to the opening lines of the New Testament Gospel of St. John, "I am the Word (*Logos*)." Church sermons and religious services do not customarily juxtapose these excerpts. The pairing is peculiar. As such, the pair may be taken to comprise an identifying marker.

The same paired allusions crop up in a discourse of the adult Hitler, at a most crucial juncture. Along with other baggage from the Ibsen play, the oddly coupled bits of Bible phrasing provide evidence, twenty-three years later, that Adolf Hitler had indeed read this Ibsen drama.

In *Emperor and Galilean*, Part Two, Maximus hints to Julian his true identity and his mission. But an epiphany still eludes the apostate emperor.

JULIAN: Worst of all is the crucified Jew.

MAXIMUS: Then have done with this division of authority! . . . You must come in your own name, Julian! Did Jesus of Nazareth come as another man's envoy? Didn't he say he was the one who sent him? Truly, in you lies the fulfillment of time, and you see it not. Do not all signs and omens point with an unerring finger to you?

Maximus keeps hinting. The prophesied one shows up periodically to make a new try. Part Two, Act IV goes on.

MAXIMUS: There is one who always reappears at certain intervals in the life of the human species. He is like a rider in a corral, taming a wild steed. Each time, the steed tosses him off. A little while later, the rider is sitting in the saddle again, always more assured and more skilled, but down he had to come in his various forms up to this very day. Down he had to come as the divinely begotten man in the Garden of Eden; down he had to come as the founder of the world-empire; down he must come as the ruler of God's kingdom. Who knows how often he has walked among us, unrecognized by any man? Are you sure, Julian, that you were not in him whom you now persecute?

Julian cannot grasp the paradoxical duality of this prophesied redeemer. The expected one will be an avatar of Jesus, returned to disavow the distorted Christianity preached by the Church. In Ibsen's heady play, Maximus suspects Julian to be the second coming of Christ, the Galilean. Julian fails to comprehend this possibility, so his program falters. He tries to fight church dogma by mocking Christ. He even allies with the Jews, dooming his great project. Julian hopes to demonstrate a power superior to that of Christ while militarily expanding the empire. He favors pagan soldiers over Christians. He turns his sights eastward, concludes a peace pact with the Persian king, then shortly unilaterally annuls it and invades. Yet many of Julian's troops stubbornly go on worshipping Christ. They reject their emperor's program and pretensions. Julian is mortally wounded by one such Christian in the ranks. He dies near the front, the fulfillment of his task postponed to some future incarnation. At the end of Ibsen's play, Maximus pronounces a final prophecy: "The third Reich will come!"

THE HIGHEST FORM OF FLATTERY

Two years after Ibsen's death, 1908 would have been the time to take note of *Emperor and Galilean*. It had a rare one-month run at Berlin's Schiller Theater during February and March, prompting reviews. George Bernard Shaw also helped matters along. An homage to Ibsen that he had written in 1891 appeared in a German edition in 1908, doting favorably on the Julian play. An appreciation also appeared in a volume of essays by the German critic Paul Schulze-Berghof. He praised *Emperor and Galilean* as no less than Ibsen's acme and a statement of the heroic Nordic *Geist*. The fact that Julian ruled over Rome was of little account—the play is seen as a lesson for Germans in Schulze-Berghof's discourse, "The Ethical Spirit of the Times in Ibsen's Works." A literary cult was emerging. Another book published in 1908 carried the intriguing title *Ibsen als Prophet*. So, did Hitler know this play as early as 1908?

Forty-five years later, August Kubizek recorded how one day during that spring of 1908, he came upon his roommate busily scrawling words in a notebook. Adolf was yet again attempting a drama. Hitler excitedly outlined the concept. His setting was "a holy mountain in Bavaria," where pagans resisted Christian intrusions. Shamans sacrifice a black bull (*schwarzen Stier*), recalling Julian the Apostate's revival of similar pagan rituals in Part Two of *Emperor and Galilean*. According to Kubizek, the scene in Hitler's script consecrated an oath to slay the Christian missionaries. Adolf might as well have stuck pins in a Father Schwarz voodoo doll. The antagonism plainly replays that religion class back at the Linz Realschule. On one side are Christian clerics, the bad guys. Resisting them are unambiguously German mountain men, the good guys. The Bavarian locale harks back to what Hitler declared in Father Schwarz's class: He would rather be a pagan and a German than a Christian subject of the polyglot Habsburg domain. Yet once again the playwriting attempt came to nil. At least as of 1908.

There had to have been some stimulus enticing Hitler to write a script on this theme, just as the divorce league's meetings had earlier sparked him to attempt a play and Wagner operas had moved him to try composing librettos. Heroic pagans abound in literature. For instance, the Icelandic *Njal's Saga,* then available in German, offered Thorwald as a pagan martyr. Yet there is reason too to consider *Emperor and Galilean* by that latter-day Norseman, Ibsen. In 1908, an Ibsen cult was in the offing with a spate of current books. Hitler had recently attended a performance of Wilbrandt's *Der Meister von Palmyra* with its mentions of Julian. And later Hitler remarks would show traces—pentimenti—that he had read Ibsen's Julian play.

When, though?

Along with mentioning how he and Hitler had seen *Der Meister von Palmyra*, August Kubizek recalled:

> Adolf read Ibsen's dramas in Vienna but without receiving any particular impression. None I can remember, anyway.

There are two problems. One concerns a hostile critique, by a rival author, of the Kubizek account in general. The other concerns Kubizek's statement that Ibsen made no notable impression on his roommate. Had Kubizek reported a Hitler bowled over by Ibsen, then Ibsen's messianic "third Reich" in *Emperor and Galilean* would likely have been noted before by biographers of the Nazi dictator.

For its overall worth, the Kubizek memoir has quite fairly been subjected to scrutiny. It is the principal eyewitness account of the young Hitler on which biographers have freely drawn. At issue is nothing less than what made the monster tick—that is, the formative years of the most destructive figure in twentieth-century Europe. Hitler's youthful diet of literary and dramatic fare is thus of paramount historical interest.

An Austrian archivist, Franz Jetzinger, slandered Kubizek's contribution in his own book, *Hitlers Jugend,* published three years after that of Kubizek. Jetzinger said he had interviewed Kubizek before Kubizek's book came out. He found Kubizek hazy on who was who in the Hitlers' Linz household. There are discrepancies on dates too. Civil residential archives showed that Kubizek and Hitler roomed together in Vienna for just over four months, from late February up to early July 1908. Yet Kubizek had claimed sixteen months, beginning in 1907 and ending in July 1908. Sixteen months cheek by jowl with

Hitler would yield a Kubizek four times more important to History. And there Kubizek undoubtedly fibbed.

With Kubizek's credibility thus tarnished, Jetzinger looked askance at Hitler's readings as listed by Kubizek for the four months they were indeed roommates. The authors named were Dante, Schopenhauer, Stifter, Rosegger, Ganghofer, and Nietzsche, along with Ibsen. Jetzinger made the point that in earlier accounts, dated 1938 and 1949, Kubizek had not mentioned any reading by Hitler at all. Then under Jetzinger's browbeating, Kubizek had supposedly pared down Hitler's reading list. It pleased Jetzinger to dismiss the nineteen-year-old Hitler as vacuous and unread and the highbrow reading syllabus, in whole or part, as probably nothing more than an invention of Kubizek's publisher. But Kubizek had been critical in places. He stated that Hitler at that age lacked the depth to appreciate Dante and that he had learned nothing from reading Ganghofer, but he did remember Hitler having relished the light dramas of Otto Ernst, which neatly fits a passion for the stage.

Next comes the problem of what impression Ibsen did or did not make on Hitler. Kubizek was privileged to observe which books lay about their room, but only Hitler knew what he actually read and retained. Given Adolf's know-it-all airs, Kubizek had learned to back off during their time together. And Kubizek did qualify his pronouncement on the impression Ibsen had made. That is, he was certain Hitler had read Ibsen, but conceded that his own memory might be fallible regarding the plays' impact on his roommate.

On Kubizek's credibility, it must also be said that he and Jetzinger pursued conflicting agendas. In post–World War II Europe, both were out to sell books: their own. Kubizek aimed to puff himself up as the tyrant's boyhood sidekick. He naïvely added a year to their Vienna time as if no one would check. Jetzinger did check, snared Kubizek in a falsehood, but held back fair credit when Kubizek's word did jibe, such as on matters of theater. The ticket stubs are gone, but the performance runs as reported in newspapers substantiate Kubizek at least on that score. Whatever Jetzinger's misgivings toward Kubizek, there is no cause to doubt that Hitler loved theater, or that he attended certain specified theater performances. Or that Hitler read

Ibsen's plays as reported. Reading theater scripts fully conformed to the tastes of a nineteen-year-old who on occasion felt moved to try writing them himself.

The Kubizek detail that Hitler read Ibsen, as opposed to seeing the plays on stage, is also worth noting. There were four Ibsen productions in Vienna during the months that Hitler and Kubizek shared a room. In March and April 1908, *John Gabriel Borkmann* was given at the Hofburg Theater, while *Rosmersholm* and *Hedda Gabler* played at the Theater-an-der-Wien. In late June, *Gespenster* ("Ghosts") played at the Hofburg. Going to a show can inspire reading in the playwright's works; yet Kubizek does *not* mention his roommate seeing these performances. That by itself need not rule out Hitler's attendance, but it does suggest that Kubizek had no agenda urging him to concoct stories about Hitler and Ibsen.

In some places the Kubizek account (published in 1953) is tinged by Hitler's own *Mein Kampf*, written in 1924 and including some reminiscences of Vienna. But Ibsen is not mentioned by name in *Mein Kampf*. Ibsen has never hitherto been an issue among historians with regard to Hitler. Thus to sum up, Kubizek's recollection about Hitler reading Ibsen in 1908 must be taken as simply that, a factoid offered without artifice. Ibsen was then current. Ibsen wrote dramas; Adolf Hitler was a theater fan. Jetzinger's caveats on the Kubizek memoir offer balance. But in the final analysis it was August Kubizek, not Franz Jetzinger, who shared a room with Adolf Hitler for four months in the spring of 1908.

Accepting the statement that Hitler "read Ibsen's plays" need not imply that he read every one of them. It is hard to imagine Hitler persisting through each play, one after another, either with equal ardor or equal ennui. They vary in appeal for persons at successive stages of life. Several of them explore themes remote from the concerns of a nineteen-year-old single youth. Some deal with love, but this bachelor did not date girls. If he read a fair number of Ibsen's works, they were bound to impress him unevenly as discerned by his roommate. Yet no one persists in reading the works of an author without forming some inward impression. Something kept Hitler going to read "Ibsen's dramas," in the plural.

For Hitler the would-be master builder, one play sure to attract notice (besides *Emperor and Galilean*) was *Baumeister Solness*. That was the German title of the play now well known in English as *The Master Builder*. Cheap paperback editions were readily available in German; one more appeared in 1907. The Residenz Theater in Munich incidentally presented *The Master Builder* in 1908. Hitler is not known to have traveled there at this time, but the Munich performance stimulated reviews and something of a revival. There were almost two hundred performances of *Baumeister Solness* between 1906 and 1912, four times as many as there had been from 1899 to 1906. As a would-be architect and a drama fan, Hitler could scarcely have read Ibsen's dramas and remained unaware that one had been written about a self-made contractor who rises to the top of his profession with the help of some unseen benefactor.

HOWEVER, FOR 1908 it need not be assumed that Hitler took on a persona from among the drama's characters. Not yet. His own outward circumstances then most closely resembled those of Ragnar, master builder Solness's assistant and the only young man in the play. Ragnar showed drafting talent, as did Hitler. With that the likeness ends, however. Ragnar had a fiancée and held a job. He suffered slights by the master builder, as did Hitler at the hands of the Academy of Architecture admissions board. But Ragnar pursued his calling undaunted. He bided his time and strove as a good apprentice must, preparing for the day when he would turn his own designs into great structures.

Unlike Ragnar, Adolf could not be bothered to work at all, much less jump at a master builder's beck and call. Adolf's architecture literally remained on the drawing boards. Apart from his sketch pads, he had substituted theater for a life. He often read plays when not watching them. In 1908, he read Ibsen's dramas. These made no impression that Kubizek discerned, but then reading is essentially a private pursuit. Like any reader save for the most prattling bore, Hitler kept some impressions to himself. If he read *The Master Builder*, he stayed quiet about it; the contrast to Ragnar could only put him to shame. And when Hitler did get enthused enough to try writing a play, he adopted a theme common to another one by Ibsen, *Emperor and Galilean.*

Kubizek told no more. The roommates went their separate ways in July 1908, keeping in touch for a while only via an occasional postcard. But as of 1910, another informant states that Adolf was still reading Ibsen. By then he had moved into cheaper accommodations at a men's hostel. A fellow lodger there, Josef Greiner, conversed enough with Hitler to recall some of the latter's books decades later. Listed among the modern authors were Scheffel, Stifter, Hammerling, Hebbel, Rosegger, Hauptmann, Sudermann, Zola—and Ibsen. That 1910 list makes for a partial overlap (Rosegger, Stifter, Ibsen) with Kubizek's list referring to two years earlier. Greiner revealed this information in a memoir published in 1947, before the Kubizek account appeared. Greiner gains credibility by his inclusion of Hitler's tale out of school, wherein the young Austrian pan-Germanist brandished colored pencils to symbolize the German tricolor flag. The Hitler retelling of this anecdote in January 1942 did not see print until the "Table Talk" transcripts appeared, four years after the Greiner book was out. It is thus reasonable to take Greiner at his word on this much. He knew Hitler in 1910, and recalled a story that Hitler subsequently kept reciting to people in his vicinity. Greiner also knew Hitler well enough to remember some of the items the latter read—including Ibsen, who crops up on an author list from two years earlier. Unfortunately Greiner, like Kubizek, did not state which of the Ibsen plays Hitler favored.

IN SPRING 1913, dodging Austria's military callup, the 24-year-old artist sought haven in Munich. This had been Ibsen's favorite German city, and now it became Hitler's as well. Exalting all things German, he enlisted in the Bavarian ranks once war broke out. Most of the period from late 1914 to autumn 1918 he spent in combat zones on the Western Front as a regimental message runner. One month before the war's end, he faced a British attack that used searing gas south of Ypres. It briefly affected his eyes. Hitler went rearward to an army hospital, where he regained full vision about a week later. A few days after the Armistice, he rejoined his outfit at its Munich home base. He was fit for duty and stayed on as a soldier for another year. Wartime comrades recalled nothing about any Hitler interest in Ibsen, although theatrical taste was not a top concern for most soldiers huddled in the trenches.

But then in Munich during the autumn of 1919, the just-demobilized corporal joined a newly formed political group, the German Workers' Party. Among its leading lights was a playwright, Dietrich Eckart, who had made a name by adapting an Ibsen play to the German stage.

3

PEER GYNT, A.K.A.
DIETRICH ECKART

Can't people just read what I write? I only write about
people. I don't write symbolically. Just about people's
inner life as I know it, psychology.

—HENRIK IBSEN (IN A LETTER FROM 1892)

From the drama of Ibsen again and again issues
operetta *cum* masquerade.

—DIETRICH ECKART

DIETRICH ECKART LIVED from 1868 to 1923. For the following multiple-choice quiz on this playwright, promoter, poet, and pamphleteer, sharpen a no. 2 lead pencil and prepare to shade the appropriate box. Dietrich Eckart was:

[A] by far the most significant guru to Adolf Hitler, who concluded *Mein Kampf* with a paean to Eckart's memory;

[B] an influential German literary figure during the last decade of his own life and posthumously a Nazi icon through the twelve years of the Third Reich;

[C] a writer of anti-Semitic screeds who proposed that eliminating the Jews would deprive Christianity of its basis and prepare the world for a pagan revival;

[D] a theater man who adapted Ibsen's play *Peer Gynt* to the German stage;
[E] Peer Gynt.

The answer, of course, is All of the Above. Heinous, deluded, drugged, besotted though he was, Dietrich Eckart did have a way with words and an impact on events.

PEER GYNT INCARNATE

A close Nazi associate depicted Eckart with "a shaved head, a high, lined forehead, dark-rimmed glasses shielding blue eyes, the nose slightly curved, somewhat too short and fleshy, a full mouth, a broad, rather brutal chin." This character wrote the first Nazi anthem, fostered the party newspaper, coached the party leader, promoted the use of the title "Führer," and coined the party's first slogans. As a tabloid journalist, Eckart set new lows in the time-tested genre of Jew-baiting.

Before Nazism, though, Eckart had made a cause of Ibsen.

Peer Gynt had already been translated into German verse, by Louis Passarge in 1881 and then by the poet Christian Morgenstern (1871–1914), who had worked with Ibsen himself in Norway. Morgenstern had studied Norwegian and rendered four other Ibsen plays into German from the original. His authorized *Peer Gynt* saw print in 1901 under the imprimatur of Ibsen's executor in Germany. This was Georg Morris Cohen Brandes, a Dane—of Jewish family origins—author, Shakespeare scholar, and longtime confidant who oversaw the playwright's interests after Ibsen suffered a disabling stroke in 1900.

Still, a decade later, Eckart appointed himself to rework *Peer Gynt* as an "adaptation for the German stage," challenging what Morgenstern had done. His rather different version was ready in 1912, in time to compete in an ongoing *Peer Gynt* revival throughout the German-speaking world. Productions proliferated, Eckart's among them.

Ibsen once cautioned: "Anyone who wishes to understand me fully must know Norway." Eckart knew little of Scandinavia, though he had a feel for the German box office, aiming to universalize Peer Gynt by downplaying his Norwegianness. To a friendly critic, Eckart's hero was "not a Norwegian adventurer but a symbol of earthbound man attempting to shed his fetters." The surreal script invited such liberties. Peer Gynt leaves his backwoods village and faithful girlfriend to roam the world. He is trying to discover who he is. He cons his way through Egypt, the Near East, America, and an insane asylum. Along the way he converses in turn with the Sphinx, a sultan, a mountain king, trolls, a gaunt man, and a button maker. Each seems symbolic, although of what is unclear. But after all his travels, Peer Gynt is still lost. He peels an onion layer by layer to search for its core. None can be found. At last, he returns home, his identity as elusive as the onion's core.

Eckart need not be imagined rifling through dictionaries, conjugating verbs, or troubling over what Ibsen meant. He liberally consulted the various published translations. Then like Peer Gynt himself, he proceeded to make a virtue of piracy. His wordier rhymed version somehow won acclaim. If Eckart bothered little with Norwegian essence, he made up for it with a feel for German taste, helped too by the accompanying music of Edvard Grieg, which sold tickets no matter what. Eckart hyped his upstart *Peer Gynt* on grounds of mystical empathy with an unassailable position: He declared himself, Dietrich Eckart, the embodiment of the title character. That is, he did not merely grasp *Peer Gynt* the play: He *was* Peer Gynt made animate, and so stated in a July 1911 letter just as he began work on the drama:

> It is my own life, the main point of which I see reflected in *Peer Gynt* sometimes with frightening clarity.

There followed several months in an asylum at Schwarzeck. Certified crazy but by no means stupid, Eckart secured release by marrying one of the nurses. He had his text ready during the course of 1912. The death of Morgenstern in March 1914 removed a key competitor, easing Eckart's effort to market the new script. In that year, one of six producers tried the Eckart rendition. A battle of rival

Peer Gynt productions was on. When his version failed to immediately monopolize the field, Eckart resorted to attacking the deceased Morgenstern in pamphlets.

Meanwhile, the war in the trenches got bloodier. Germany needed scapegoats and, by and by, the Jews fit the bill.

Heightened anti-Semitism arrived at a convenient moment for Eckart. His rivals were either Jews or people who could be labeled as such. Besides Georg Brandes, there was the incongruous identity of the late Morgenstern, whose surname occurred mainly among Jews. The odd combination of "Christian" and "Morgenstern" suggested a person of ethnic Jewish origins whose family had converted. For Eckart, though, a baptismal font could never wash away Jewishness. He would make that point repeatedly in published tracts to come. By assailing Morgenstern, he could adopt the pose of saving Ibsen from the Jews.

Too old for the Somme or Verdun, Eckart fought on the *Peer Gynt* front. The year 1916 brought a breakthrough in his struggle, if not the Kaiser's. *Peer Gynt* productions played in nine German cities. Of these, five followed the Eckart text. Of seven *Peer Gynt* productions in 1917, six used the Eckart text, as did five of seven in 1918. Ten of twelve productions in 1919 and another nine of twelve productions in 1920 were also Eckart's. The popularity of his script went on expanding over the next few years. Eckart became a celebrity, riding in automobiles when they were still mainly the province of the well-to-do, dining well, and drinking more. The Great *Peer Gynt* War was won decisively by Eckart, a.k.a. Peer Gynt, in the flesh as his own legend would have it.

Hypnosis may conceivably have had some part in prompting the Peer Gynt pose. Back in 1892, Eckart's very first article as a critic had been "Hypnosis and the Novel." If he too dabbled in the trance state, he risked the psychological damage it can wreak. Generations of experience have since shown hypnosis capable of blurring the line between a subject's memory of real-world experience and impressions gleaned from hearsay, reading, or the stage. Trances can induce quasi-recollections of past lives and beliefs in alternate selves, mental artifacts real enough to the post-hypnotic subject. The "Bridey

Murphy" case of the 1950s is a classic instance. For Eckart there were also the delusionary powers of morphine and drink.

PAUL SCHULZE-BERGHOF

However inane or insane, Eckart won support for his take on the Ibsen script. In 1918, a fellow German playwright and critic, Paul Schulze-Berghof, came forth with a book relating *Peer Gynt* to the Great War. In ninety-four pages titled *Thoughts on Ibsen's Peer Gynt* (*Zeitgedanken zu Ibsens Peer Gynt*), Schulze-Berghof estimated the worth of the playwright and his output:

> The writer of *Peer Gynt* was already a prophet of his time, but only a Jeremiah, not a savior, not a liberator and redeemer of mankind.

That is, Ibsen—and by extension Eckart—were heralds in a new pantheon. The actual "liberator and redeemer of mankind" (*Befreier und Erlöser der Menschheit*) had not yet arrived as of 1918. But he was expected imminently.

Schulze-Berghof admired the Eckart work as an advance over prior German versions of *Peer Gynt*, which had been predicated on mere fidelity to the text. He applauded Eckart for intuiting what Ibsen had *really* meant, and judged the Eckart *Peer Gynt* as "a mirror for contemporary mankind, the contemporary character." To Schulze-Berghof, Ibsen's works expounded political truths. Germany was engaged in war against the Anglo-Saxons. Schulze-Berghof trumpeted the German people as summoned by a higher power to be "world rulers" and "creative god-men." He attributed this notion to Nietzsche's *Zarathustra*, the "god-man of the third Reich." A new German ethic, wrote Schulze-Berghof, would be based on a synthesis of the long Nietzsche poem and selected inspiring works by Ibsen.

It is not clear whether Schulze-Berghof knew of Eckart's claim to another self, as "Peer Gynt." Peer Gynt was for Schulze-Berghof a warning of what Germans should avoid being like. Germans, as "god-men" (a Nietzsche concept), were by nature spiritual. Peer Gynt signified crass materialism, the real foe of Germany. When Peer Gynt said he would be happy as the king of England, Schulze-Berghof took the words as an attack on England as the premier commercial nation. This mechanistic equivalency was elaborated by Schulze-Berghof in his exegesis of Act IV. Again discerning irony in the Ibsen–Eckart script, he saw Peer Gynt as symbolizing a Mammon-worshipping American president. Peer Gynt's sorry fate at the end stood to warn Germans against materialism. President Wilson's magnanimous Fourteen Points had been offered as a peace formula. Many war-weary Germans welcomed Wilson's ideals, but Schulze-Berghof was not among them. Meanwhile, on the Western Front, the combined industrial might of the English-speaking powers had crushed the Kaiser's army.

Schulze-Berghof's discourse on *Peer Gynt* may have differed in detail from what Eckart had in mind, but the critic favored Eckart's work over preceding versions. A *Peer Gynt* construed as national-istic allegory was a play many more would pay to see, with ensuing financial benefit for Eckart. It may be presumed that Eckart knew of Schulze-Berghof's book. Many writers live and die by what critics say, and here was as fine an appraisal, from another playwright, as could ever be wished. Schulze-Berghof maintained that Ibsen, through the legacy of his works, would reshape the postwar world. But first came the birth of Nazism and the encounter of Eckart and Hitler.

"PEER GYNT" CREATES A FÜHRER

The Great War exerted a politicizing effect on many writers. Eckart, like Schulze-Berghof, saw a future in both allegorical drama and political journalism. Eckart came to savor the role of polemicist in the wake of his *Peer Gynt* success. His gutter-style anti-Semitic pamphlets began appearing more regularly, becoming a Jew-baiting opinion journal called *Auf gut Deutsch* ("In Plain German"), which was later subsumed into the Nazi party paper. Politically, Eckart promoted a pan-German union consisting of Germany and the German-speaking parts of the Austrian empire. He also composed the first Nazi marching song, *Sturm, sturm, sturm!* (Storm, storm, storm!), which evoked the image of the German assault infantrymen who had nearly won the war on the Western Front in the spring of 1918. The lyrics could be remembered easily enough, in plain German. It was Eckart too who thought up the Nazi watchword, *"Deutschland, erwache!"*

Germany, wake up! Hitler met this glib personality about a year after the bandages from his war injuries were removed from his eyes. He could see again after a short but traumatic impairment; the return of vision would be used, metaphorically, in Hitler's words at a later date. The new Armistice-era German republic offered no long-term counseling or psychological therapy to its millions of war veterans. Instead of support groups, Hitler stumbled across the newly founded German Workers' Party. And Dietrich Eckart. The playwright and theater fan took a liking to each other. They met sometime in the winter of 1919–20. Corporal Hitler, still on the military payroll, had been detailed to observe meetings of the group on behalf of the Bavarian Army. This was no silent observer, however. When Hitler piped up, one of the party elders spotted him as a born orator. A bit of flattery got him to sign on. Eckart homed in next.

Eckart was at that time the Nazis' only show-business celebrity; he found in Hitler a sulking loner, a bachelor with no family nearby, a soldier still living in barracks who needed support to rejoin civilian life. But this veteran had never completed school nor held a peacetime job: in civilian life, he would be lost. If nothing else, though, the unemployable Hitler cherished the theater. Eckart, who never had a son, lavished on the adult Adolf the paternal affection that Adolf never got from his father, Alois. To the corporal, Eckart made the ideal surrogate father, being a racy man of letters with a wit that was irresistible—at least to hardcore anti-Semites. In turn, Hitler was promoted by Eckart from a pal to a political Pygmalion project. With that, Eckart shelved writing mere stage plays.

Between his makeovers of *Peer Gynt* and Adolf Hitler, Eckart had turned out two historical dramas. His *Heinrich VI Hohenstaufen*, set in the twelfth century, portrayed the emperor Friedrich Barbarossa's heir in pan-Germanist terms. Eckart thereupon ventured into Renais-sance-era Florence with the rhymed verse play *Lorenzaccio,* about Lorenzino de Medici, a friend of Michelangelo. The plot concerned an intrigue in 1537 to assassinate Lorenzino's companion Duke Alessandro the Moor and seize the Florentine government. Race is a pointed mes-sage in the play. Besides the mulatto Alessandro, there is a character called Ahasver, "the eternal Jew." *Lorenzaccio* marked Eckart's last drama. He completed it in October 1918, just before the Armistice and a series of coups d'etat upset the German political order.

The verdict of public and academic taste has deleted *Lorenzaccio* from literary memory, along with its author. For history, though, at least some of the play's cadenced lines bear recall. It is known that Hitler saw or read the play. Act I contains an appeal to the hero, urg-ing him to be the unwavering, charismatic savior:

> Our redeemer, our Führer
> No one, no one, no one purer.
> (*Unser Führer, unser Retter*
> *Reiner, keiner, keiner, keiner!*)

From political theater, Eckart glided to theatrical politics. Bestowal of "Führer" as the official Nazi title for Adolf Hitler would come in mid-1921, drawing on this play among other sources. Eckart was at that time still the guiding personality in the party's press and public-relations efforts. He took over the editorship of the *Völkischer Beobachter* ("Ethnic Observer") in August 1921. Quasi-religious refer-ences to Hitler as redeemer began appearing then as well. A bond of affinity developed between this man of the theater and his discovery. The two shared as well a mutually reinforcing narcissism, a gift for gab, and a love of portent-laden climactic scenes.

Eckart's switch to practical politics and to nurturing a protégé did not by any means entail dropping his Peer Gynt pose. Contemporaries from the 1920s affirmed that the Nazi publicist really took himself to be Peer Gynt. Alfred Rosenberg, Eckart's co-editor, put it:

> Eckart paralleled his inner life with Peer Gynt.

and:

Eckart declared many times that he saw in Peer Gynt a mirror
of his own form.

Such are the perks of poetic license. How literally Eckart meant
it, only Eckart knew. Emulation had its practical limits. Peer Gynt
traveled far and wide, but Eckart stayed put in central Europe. Even
so, his identity as "Peer Gynt" found its way even to a Nazi-era travel-
ogue volume about the Obersalzberg mountain above Berchtesgaden,
its alpine backdrop looking like the Hall of the Mountain King in
Ibsen's play. Another mystic incidental buttressed Eckart's quirk: He
had been gestating in his mother's womb at the very time Ibsen was
drafting the *Peer Gynt* text in 1867, making Peer Gynt and Eckart a
timely fit, just right for believers in transubstantiation.

Hitler took Eckart as the most formative individual in his life, and
so he must have been. No one else comes close to Eckart's mentoring
role. At Nazi headquarters in Munich, Hitler's reserved place in the
cellar canteen was dominated by a sculpted bust of the playwright.
Time and again for two decades, Hitler would tell Eckart anecdotes
to his staff. Once the Führer put it: "He shone in our eyes like the
polar star." Press aides and secretaries confirmed the enduring hold
of Eckart on their chief. Kurt Lüdecke handled Nazi foreign liaison
tasks in the early 1920s and noted, upon his own reading of Eckart's
works, "He was something of a genius, and to a great degree the
spiritual father of Hitler and grandfather of the Nazi movement."
And again, as Lüdecke revealed his own admiration for the man, "It
was interesting to find that Hitler had also learned from the same
source. Many of his most essential ideas clearly had sprung from the
brain of Eckart."

Eckart's idiosyncrasy and fixation on Peer Gynt would hardly
warrant History's remembering him at all, had he been just another
bygone bard. But this bard had done a bit of gardening: He was the
one who transplanted, pruned, weeded, and watered Adolf Hitler.

Here, then, is the crux: The person whom Hitler declared his
guiding "polar star" was a man who touted himself as a hero from

an Ibsen play. It matters less whether Eckart did this as pretense, pose, or premise. Either way, the operative fact is that he presented himself as an avatar out of Ibsen, who had in turn borrowed Peer Gynt from Norwegian legend. Hitler drew deeply from Eckart, while refining both his act and his own core beliefs. Through several years of bonding, the disciple's emphases shifted toward those of the adept, leaning toward the mystical and theological. It was during their association in the early 1920s that Hitler began stating that he too harbored alter identities.

This marked a new development for the Führer. August Kubizek remembered his friend agog over Wagner's *Rienzi*, but the teenage Adolf did not assert that he was a literal incarnation of Rienzi himself. Neither did Hitler's Vienna acquaintances after Kubizek, nor his trench buddies from the Western Front, observe him discovering any hidden selves—and it is the sort of trait a messmate could be expected to recall. In a combat zone, comradely concern (and the instinct for self-preservation) will be aroused should some corporal in the next dugout announce that he is a character from a play, or a Roman general, or Jesus Christ. All Hitler's known talk to that effect began postwar, during his association with his avowed role model: Dietrich Eckart, a.k.a. Peer Gynt.

These nuances of Eckart and Hitler may be distinguished from other flotsam in the Nazi potpourri. Not all that is Nazi is to be found in Eckart or Hitler. Likewise, the Führer reserved to himself a private area unshared with other Nazis after Eckart. But while he lived, Eckart displayed specific preferences useful for discerning the inner Hitler. Eckart, and Hitler too, held a special regard for the world of antiquity. It shows in the putative transcript of a long conversation between the two men.

THE *DIALOGUES* AND THE ARYAN CHRIST OF GALILEE

Eckart set down a record of their chats to be publicly circulated. "Published" may not be the precise word, for *Bolshevism from Moses to Lenin: Dialogues between Adolf Hitler and Me* ("Der Bolschwismus

von Moses bis Lenin: Zwiegespräch zwischen Adolf Hitler und mir")
appeared first as a kind of mimeographed typescript just after Eckart
had died and as Hitler stood trial, in March 1924. As the title suggests, the main point is that various preceding forms of Communism
supposedly stretched back to ancient times, and that all along they
had really been disguised instruments of Jewry.

Throughout the *Dialogues*, Hitler and Eckart addressed each other
with the intimate pronoun *"du"* in a colloquy of mutual affirmation.
These reconstructed (or perhaps imagined) talks make up Eckart's
defining rationale for hating the Jews, via words imputed to Hitler.
The *Dialogues* proved awkward for Nazism, since it was released while
Hitler was in jail and without his editorial approval. So the document
exists, like the quasi-biblical *Apocrypha*, a fount of information but
not quite canonical. Hitler refrained from emphasizing this text,
but neither did he ever repudiate it. He certainly read it, and its wording
resounds in the "Table Talk" monologues nearly two decades later.
The *Dialogues* thus became part of the genuine, received Hitler. Its
themes reveal an aspect of Hitler that was downplayed in *Mein Kampf*,
but which emerges in other writings, speeches, and talks.

At the very opening of *Bolshevism from Moses to Lenin*, Eckart
has Hitler declaring how the forces in History operate not visibly on
the surface, but instead as an undercurrent. Analysis should identify
the secret force. In the *Dialogues*, Hitler compares the task of discovery to that of an astronomer who must infer a hidden gravitational
pull, given the shifts among objects in the sky from night to night.
By such means, an invisible planet's existence may be calculated.
Having compared his task to that of an empirical scientist, Hitler
says: "Somewhere there must operate a secret power directing all
according to its principle." In the next line, he identifies it.

The hidden power, of course, is Jewry. Individual Jews may appear
to pursue mere everyday tasks. But the manipulation of society by
a collective entity, Jewry at large, operates at a deeper, unseen level.
The concern is not with particular Jews or even with Jews as a force
limited to Germany, since Eckart and Hitler knew that Jews comprised
less than 1 percent of the country's population. No, the Eckart–Hitler
scope transcended Germany both in historic time and geographic

space. At all points, the concern is the malevolent, cosmic threat posed by Jews anywhere and everywhere, Jewry as a whole. It follows that the secret force of Jewry may be effectively opposed only by a counterforce. In the *Dialogues* and in other pamphlets, Eckart vested that power in Christ; to be precise, in Christ "the Galilean."

Many minds have been stirred by diverse images of Jesus, among them an infant in a manger, a miraculous healer, a hilltop preacher, a Passover celebrant, an agonized victim suspended on the cross. The Jesus Christ of modern German neo-paganism made another. He was de-Judaized, a trend that went back to Johan Fichte at the start of the nineteenth century. By the time of Dietrich Eckart, a system had been worked out alleging that this Christ had sprung from gentile, not Jewish, forebears. "Galilean" became far more in this rubric than just an incidental reference to a district of northern Israel. What made this Christ Aryan, to Eckart and Hitler, was his very derivation from Galilee. Eckart cited the words of a Jew in the Gospel of St. John 7:52: "Out of Galilee arises no prophet." Thus, Eckart argued, the Jews disparaged all Galileans as being outside the chosen people from among whom a prophet might arise.

Eckart thereby took "Jew" and "Galilean" to mean separate ethnic groups. Eckart's further Bible study (2 Kings 15:29) had Jews disappearing from Galilee by 750 B.C.E. Matthew 26:73 describes a distinctive Galilean accent, and Isaiah 9:1 alludes to the district as "Galilee (from the Hebrew *galil*, meaning circle) of the nations," seemingly noting gentiles present there alongside Jews. That was supposed to underscore a gentile Galilean identity, even though Jewish worship was again the Galilean norm by the second century B.C.E. But Eckart had little use for historical facts. A Jesus from Galilee was an Aryan Jesus, notwithstanding the Jewish Jesus that pervades the Gospels.

Ibsen knew better. In *Emperor and Galilean*, the Norwegian's use of "Galilean" for Christ derived directly from Julian the Apostate in the mid-fourth century. Neither Julian in antiquity nor Ibsen in his play ever expressed any doubts about the Jewish genealogy of Jesus. Yet as the idea of a gentile, "Aryan" Christ gained currency after World War I, the term "Galilean" became a code word among racial nationalists. They directed ire not only toward the Jews but against the mainstream churches, both Catholic and Protestant, which accepted Jesus' Jewish origins. That long-accepted fact was awkward. An Aryanized Jesus could make anti-Semitism more palatable among the millions of nominal Christians ready to be swayed by the radical racists.

Eckart followed neo-pagan precedent in denying Christ's Jewishness. Among those then current, Paul de Lagarde, Ernst Haeckel, Houston Stewart Chamberlain, Eugen Diederichs, Julius Langbehn, Artur Dinter, and Friedrich Döllinger wrote along similar lines. The gentile Jesus comprised a basic tenet of Nazism from its inception, as in the article "War Jesus ein Jude?" ("Was Jesus a Jew?") by Widar Wälsung, serialized in the party paper *Völkischer Beobachter* in the early months of 1920, where it doubtless formed part of Hitler's daily booster shot of misinformation. Hitler had also read Chamberlain and Lagarde, and had at least a secondhand exposure to Haeckel and Langbehn during this time. Moreover, he owned a copy of Döllinger's illustrated book *Baldur und Bibel* ("Baldur and the Bible," published in 1920) with its sketches of Christ as a Germanic fighter out to liberate the Holy Land from the Jews.

In addition to construing stray passages from the Bible their way, German racialists also drew upon the late-classical Christian writer Origen, who had passed on a tale alleging that the biological sire of Jesus was a Roman soldier named Pantheros (this name is also given as Panthera, Pantera, or Pandera). The Talmud incidentally refers to Jesus in several places as the son of Pandera. Archaeology provided inadvertent support. It so happened that the gravestone of a Roman soldier called Julius Abdes Pantera, dating from the reign of the emperor Tiberius (r. 14–37 C.E.), had been unearthed at Bingerbrück, Germany in 1859. According to the inscription, this man, an archer, came from Sidon on the Lebanese coast. The place was reasonably close to Galilee. That clinched it for those ready to be convinced, and the circumstance of a German connection was serendipity to the racialists.

The point here, though, specifically concerns the fuss over Christ as a "Galilean." Artur Dinter, a Nazi pamphlet writer, drew an equivalence of Aryan with Galilean in a 1921 polemic, *The War on Spiritual Teaching*. Here again, an Aryan was taken *ipso facto* as an opponent of the Jews, and Christ was foremost a Galilean. Hitler had caught on by April 21, 1921, if not before. On that date, he concluded his harangue to a Nazi rally at Rosenheim, Bavaria with these words:

> We are surely minute, but once a man rose up in Galilee, and today his teaching rules the whole world. I can't imagine Christ as anything other than blond, with blue eyes, the very mug of the devil to Jews.

To oppose the Jews was to take up the ageless battle of this blond Galilean Christ, as drawn in the Döllinger book. The fight was an eternal mission, because the Jews were identified as an eternal, deadly foe, genetically dedicated to subversion and the murder of gentiles. The Hitler of the *Dialogues* with Eckart offers an illustrative example from the reign of the Roman emperor Trajan. It is the year 115 C.E. Trajan has managed for a fleeting time to occupy the entire Euphrates and Tigris valleys southward to the Persian Gulf. Had Rome held this zone, it would have secured the eastern frontiers of its empire. There is no telling how long the empire might then have lasted.

But Trajan's gains proved untenable. A scattered but massive Jewish revolt disrupted the Roman rear. The Jews rebelled all around the eastern Mediterranean and throughout Mesopotamia in the Roman army's wake. Massacres of gentiles by Jews claimed untold lives, according to the *Dialogue*, where Eckart and Hitler compete in pulling statistics out of the clear blue. Eckart says Jews slew 75,000 Persians centuries before, during the events recounted in the "Bolshevik" Old Testament's Book of Esther. Hitler outbids him. A mere 75,000 was:

> ...so much fewer than under emperor Trajan when half the Roman empire endured a bloodletting. Hundreds of thousands and still more hundreds of thousands of non-Jews of the noblest blood slaughtered like cattle in Babylon, in Cyrenaica, in Egypt, on

> Cyprus; the most horrific martyrdom! And today the Jews still
> rejoice over it. The Jew Graetz exults that if the various sparks
> of the revolt had only been coordinated, it would have given the
> coup de grace to the Roman colossus.

"The Jew Graetz" referred to Heinrich Hirsch Graetz (1817–91), author of a magisterial *History of the Jews* in eleven German volumes. As related by Hitler in the *Dialogues,* the Trajan story showed the effect of Jewish perfidy. Coping with the Jews diverted so much Roman effort that the hard-won gains against Persia were lost. Trajan's successor Hadrian had to withdraw, consolidate, and quell the internal foe. Meanwhile, the Persian menace revived. So the Jews constituted a security risk during wartime when an army was hotly engaged on an eastern front. It follows that preemptively suppressing the threat would be justified should analogous conditions arise.

After Trajan, the next Roman emperor to campaign that far to the east was Julian. He was in turn undermined not directly by the Jews, but by Christians in his own ranks. And Christianity was, in the Eckart–Hitler *Dialogues* scheme, nothing but a Jewish warping of what the Aryan, Galilean Christ had set out to achieve.

FOLLOWING IBSEN TO BERCHTESGADEN

The intellectual endowment of Eckart to Hitler did not end with a warped Christology. There was as well a counter-cabala, a doting on the mystic significance of names. Ibsen had shown this penchant too, as Eckart probably knew from his reworking of *Peer Gynt.* Ibsen's usage of names, self-evident to Norwegian audiences, imparts a parable-like quality to his scripts. Hitler readily took to this sort of game for himself and for those around him. One of his pseudonyms was "Rolf Eidhalt," an anagram formed from the eleven letters in Adolf Hitler. It translates as "Rolf upholds the oath." The name game went further. One Führer headquarters was known as "Adlerhorst" after the eagle, *Adler* in German, as in the first two letters of "Adolf" and the last three of "Hitler."

Here too in Hitler was a non-driver who later chose as his favorite chauffeur a man surnamed Schreck, meaning "fright," from whom Hitler would demand top speed on narrow country roads in their supercharged Mercedes. He chose as his master builder a named Fritz Todt, whose surname could mean "death." This tarot-card quality among the names of people in the Hitler entourage smacks of Eckart. It was Eckart who bestowed the alias "Herr Wolf" on Hitler when registering him at a Berchtesgaden inn. Hitler welcomed the name, since Adolf itself connotes "noble wolf" in old Germanic. Eckart further abetted the penchant by hiring as the Führer's first clerical secretary a woman named Johanna Wolf. Around the office she was nicknamed Wolfchen, or "Little Wolf," to distinguish her from the big bad Herr Wolf. Later the Führer designated several command sites for this beast, such as the Wolf's Lair (*Wolfsschanze*).

Eckart did little to discourage the Hitlerian merging of symbol with substance. That is the very essence of theater, and of the politics construed as theater that launched Hitler. Work accomplished, Eckart's exit arrived on cue since, in keeping with the dynamic of friendships, the two men had begun to grate on one another.

Herr Wolf's pup days were over. By early 1923, Eckart, the tipsy former playwright, found himself honorably put out to pasture. His other protégé, Alfred Rosenberg, took control of the Nazis' daily organ *Völkischer Beobachter* at the behest of the Führer. Several months later came the Beer Hall putsch debacle. It flopped, and Hitler went to jail. So too did Eckart, by then a mere bystander. He forthwith took ill in his cell and won compassionate release. Eckart died at Berchtesgaden on the day after Christmas that year, aged fifty-five. He had reputedly told associates:

> Follow Hitler! He will dance, but it is I who will call the tune! I have instructed him into the secret doctrine, opened his centers of vision, and given him the means to communicate with the powers. Do not mourn for me; I have influenced history more than any other German.

These sentences ring of folklore and cannot be traced to any primary source. The so-called secret doctrine, if there was one, is not amenable to identification from what Eckart is more reliably quoted to have written and said. Eckart consorted on the fringes of the racist and ritualistic Thule Society in Munich, but he cannot be documented among its initiates. And although the rival mystic and playwright Rudolf Steiner used the term "secret doctrine," Eckart was hostile to Steiner and his cult.

WHAT THEN OF the "secret doctrine"? There does remain a set of statements skirting the occult. Eckart referred to himself as the embodiment of a character from an Ibsen play. Hitler too would initiate moves paralleling the scripted actions of several identifiable Ibsen characters, and would paraphrase their words in his own writings and speech. But not everything in Hitler owed to Eckart. The fascination of each man with Ibsen predated their mutual acquaintance, if it be accepted that the Hitler attempt to write a play in 1908 was indeed inspired by a reading of *Emperor and Galilean*. A cultural current of Ibsen-as-prophet flowed all during those years. It swirled during Hitler's Vienna period, and it had moved Eckart to adapt and adopt *Peer Gynt*. The Ibsen current continued strong at the time of the special Eckart–Hitler friendship in 1920–23.

Hitler attended a performance of *Peer Gynt* at the Staatliche Schauspielhaus in Berlin in company with Eckart himself in March 1920. However, not until October 1921 did Eckart present Hitler a copy of the script. It bears only a terse inscription. The binding of this volume is intact, its pages pristine with few overt signs of readership: no dog-ears, no marginalia, no coffee stains or smudges. Either Hitler handled his books with a surgeon's fastidiousness or, among Ibsen's works, *Peer Gynt* held but a low priority for him. It does not seem to have figured in Hitler's own magical game. As the paraphrased lines from *An Enemy of the People* show, he evidently preferred other Ibsen plays. Whatever their tastes, Eckart's "fatherly friendship" (Hitler's words) counted a lot. He was the Führer's *éminence grise* at least through much of 1922. Hitler might have stayed cocooned for life had not Eckart taught him how to dress, speak, and behave. Eckart coached his pupil how to star at a speaker's rostrum and in the genteel salons of moneyed backers. He bestowed on Hitler a public persona.

NO ECKART, NO Hitler. Without the former, there would not and could not have been the man who came to be known in the world as the Nazi Führer. The latter said as much and concluded *Mein Kampf*'s Volume II (1926) with a tribute to his mentor and patron, appending him to the list of fallen heroes to whom he had dedicated Volume I:

> And among them I want also to count that man, one of the best, who devoted his life to the awakening of his, our people, in his writings and his thoughts and finally in his deeds:
> DIETRICH ECKART

The above typography is set apart, as in many Nazi editions. Such special homage may have reflected just a twinge of regret, considering how Hitler had sidelined his coach during 1923. Their last personal leave-taking went unrecorded.

Ensnared by pre-trial detention, the Führer missed Eckart's death and funeral, thereby getting off easy yet again. He was spared composing a eulogy and the dilemma of whether to call the deceased "Dietrich Eckart" or "Peer Gynt." Later on, Hitler would confer lavish tributes. During the Third Reich, the playwright's rented cottage (Göll-Häusl) at Berchtesgaden became a Nazi pilgrimage site. A new amphitheater was also named for him near Berlin, albeit tamely, as the Dietrich Eckart Memorial Stage.

4

THE IMITATION OF CHRIST, ET AL.

JULIAN: The Galilean, the carpenter's son, reigns
as the king of love in the warm believing hearts
of men.

—IBSEN, *EMPEROR AND GALILEAN,*
PART TWO, ACT V

... the Jewish drones, these money changers which
our religious teacher, the carpenter's son from
Nazareth, drove out with a whip from the Temple of
their fathers.

—ADOLF HITLER IN A SPEECH, AUGUST 31, 1920

SOMETHING IN GERMAN culture, going back at least to Goethe, accommodated the notion that a person might harbor an alter self. *Faust* (Part One, Act I) states: "Two souls live in my breast." Countless novels and stories explored the theme of the Doppelgänger. Thus Dietrich Eckart could go about claiming to be Peer Gynt without being returned to custodial care. Less openly, Hitler could purloin a persona as he did with Dr. Stockmann. But *An Enemy of the People* had its limitations. The good doctor discovers germs, annoys his town, and winds up a pariah: The End. A politician of grandiose ambition would need to fantasize on a role model more substantive than Stockmann.

THE LEAGUE OF YOUTH

Of all the characters in Ibsen's many plays, there is one whose externals approach the Adolf Hitler of the early Nazi years. He is the aspiring demagogue Stensgaard, from *The League of Youth* (Norwegian: *Unges forbund;* German: *Der Bund der Jugend).* Ibsen wrote this drama in 1868, just after *Peer Gynt* and just before *Emperor and Galilean. The League of Youth* was the first play Ibsen wrote while living in Germany.

Stensgaard is a small-town lawyer, thirtyish in age. He still thinks young, like Hitler did when at age thirty he quit the army to join the German Workers' Party, spout a mishmash called "national socialism," and set up the Nazis' strong-arm squads. Stensgaard is a sworn rebel. In Act I, he vows to mobilize and overthrow vested interests:

> We are the young ones. The times are ours; but we also belong to the times. Our right is our duty! We demand opportunities for initiative, for drive, for vigor! We'll found a league. The money bags are no longer in command in this district. . . . Neither thanks nor threats matter for him who knows his own will.

Stensgaard claims a divine commission. So did Hitler. He forms a league to combat the "money-bags." So did Hitler, with the Nazis' stormtroopers. Stensgaard is even ready to decide who has forfeited the right to exist:

> God has favored me more than he has them. . . . The man who feels no sense of dedication at such an hour does not deserve to live upon God's earth.

In Act I, Stensgaard relates a dream:

> So vivid! I thought the Day of Judgment had arrived. . . . A gale arose; it swept in from the west, and swept all things before it. First it swept the withered leaves, then it swept people. Yet still they stayed on their feet. . . . At first they looked like ordinary

> people running after their hats in a high wind. But when they got
> nearer, they turned out to be kings and emperors; and the things
> they were running after and grabbing, and which they always
> seemed to be on the point of reaching but never did, were crowns
> and scepters.... Many of them cried out and asked "Where has
> it come from, this terrible storm?" And the answer came: "One
> Voice spoke, and the Echo from that one Voice was such as to
> create the storm!"

Looking back after World War I, this certainly seemed prescient. The czar, two kaisers, and a sultan had just lost their crowns. The images ring like Hitler's own; but alas, the storm, the voice, the echo, the wind-tossed crowns and scepters never come together in any known Hitler speech. Demonstrable paraphrase must be the ironclad criterion in confirming a Hitler debt to an Ibsen script; no lesser standard can suffice.

Other incidentals from the play are suggestive, though. In *The League of Youth*, Act I, Stensgaard's associate suggests a practical agenda issue: public roads.

> Who's had the job of building the roads, especially these last two
> years? It's gone to foreigners, well, strangers anyway, to people
> nobody knows anything about!

Those words seem to presage a Hitler who would emulate Mussolini's autostrada with an Autobahn of his own once he came to power. As German chancellor in 1933, he immediately proceeded to usurp the existing Autobahn plans from a pre-Nazi consortium of engineering firms and municipal governments. That body had been headed by the Jewish mayor of Frankfurt, who was by Nazi criteria a "foreigner." Once Nazified, the Autobahn became a symbol of the new regime.

SO THE LEAGUE of Youth does offer enticements. Yet the Führer's early style recalls Stensgaard in only a general sort of way. If Hitler steered clear of filching Stensgaard's words outright, it soon becomes understandable why: Ibsen's very purpose was to lampoon a certain type of populist firebrand. Stensgaard comes off eventually not as a hero but a dubious, conniving, self-deceiving windbag. A critic calls him a split personality. His parentage is derided. Even his surname is sterile, meaning "stony garden." The point could hardly be lost on a Hitler who liked to ponder what's-in-a-name.

Stensgaard furthermore has to be talked into standing for parliament, in Act II. He is steered by manipulators. He aims to succeed by marrying the daughter of a wealthy and influential patron. And he compromises principle. By the end of the play, an associate predicts:

> Mark my words, gentlemen! Ten or fifteen years from now and Stensgaard will be in parliament or the Privy Council or something, perhaps both at once.

Parliament and an advisory job spelled a humdrum career for the dreamer from Linz. Railing steadily against parliaments, Hitler had more radical tasks for his own "league of youth," as the Nazi stormtroopers showed in their 1923 putsch attempt. Far from being steered into a conventional political slot, he maintained headier goals.

At his treason trial the next spring, Hitler rang out:

> How trivial are small men's thoughts! My own goal, from Day One, was a thousand times grander than to just be a state minister. ... The man who is born to be a dictator is not forced; he wants it. He doesn't let himself be pushed. It is he who moves himself forward.

So even if the Führer knew *The League of Youth,* as seems reasonable for one who had read Ibsen's plays, he had to reject Stensgaard as a lifetime model. There were other possibilities, more suited, from other sources. Hitler did take these as models; that much is known. Because he said so.

The record from 1923 shows the Führer declaring identity with:

* the fictional king in a recent drama entitled *Der König;*
* Jesus Christ;
* the Roman consul Marius.

THE KING AND I

Der König ("The King") by Hanns Johst (1890–1978) was written for the stage in 1920 and performed at the Kammerspiele Theater in Munich for a few months during that year and the next. Playwright and Führer made acquaintance in 1923, according to German literary historians. With *Der König,* Johst turned from subjective "expressionist" theater toward a more political drama style. He found an avid fan in the Nazi leader. Years later, Johst recalled what Hitler said at their chat:

> He had seen *König* seventeen times; it was his favorite work, and more: So would he, Hitler, one day meet his fate.

The fate of the scripted king in *Der König* incidentally happened to have been death by a self-inflicted bullet.

When the Führer spoke to Johst in 1923, the last production of this play was already two years past, but it was still on Hitler's mind. Later, as newly appointed German chancellor in April 1933, he designated Johst to lead the German Academy of Literature (*Deutsche Akademie der Dichtung*) and subsequently to be president of the National Socialist Writers Guild (*Reichsschriftumskammer*). Johst thus became the poet laureate of Nazi Germany, official successor to Dietrich Eckart.

Der König offered thin fare for a mass cult. It lacks quotable lines. Where normal folk are concerned, a couple of viewings would already overdo it for this minor play, soon forgotten by all except its author and a lone groupie. But something in it appealed to Adolf Hitler.

Johst's drama of moderate length is divided into ten short scenes. Its tragic hero stays nameless throughout. He's a generic: "the king" of a land someplace, sometime. Action starts on the day the king ascends to his late father's throne. He reigns as an iconoclast from the outset. Canceling the honored rites of coronation, the new monarch tells the palace protocol lackeys that they are redundant. Next, His Majesty meddles in the legal system. He elbows aside the judges and oversees the law courts, dispensing with pompous judicial robes. Out as well go statute and precedent. Honesty alone will do, states the ruler.

One of the court cases he hears involves a whore of the streets. She catches his eye. In short order, the king makes her a countess and his royal consort. That compromises regal decorum. Titled aristocrats and officials are scandalized. Support for the crown weakens. Meanwhile, the king goes on alienating everyone else he can. He offends the clergy with impious talk. He commissions grand architectural works and bankrupts the treasury. Creditors mob the palace. Commoners grow restive. A regicide attempt one night is narrowly thwarted. The king's own mother is aghast. Even she deserts. His courtesan finally walks out too, along with what's left of the royal cash.

Wholly isolated, the king meets his fate in a noisy final scene. Angry enemies close in on the palace. Offstage, the rumble of their approach grows louder. Meanwhile, onstage, his majesty laments his lot to his chamber attendants. They are worldly-wise and have suspected all along what has to happen. The inevitable moment arrives. At last the servants depart, leaving their king alone in the royal rooms. His door shuts. A shot resounds from within. The curtain rings down.

Was the April 1945 drama in the Führer's Berlin bunker influenced by this script, or does it only seem that way?

Hitler saw the final curtain descend on *Der König* no fewer than seventeen (!) times, or so he said. Seventeen sittings through the same play, or film, is the sort of behavior expected of an addled preteen, but hardly that of a mature politician eyeing high office. It smacks of the incredible. Yet with Hitler it fits. Attending *Der König* multiple times conforms in habit with his seeing the same Wagnerian operas dozens of times each, as attested by himself and confirmed by his friends. There is thus no cause to gainsay Johst on this point. Even if the figure of seventeen stretched literal truth by a bit, Hitler had stated thereby how he could contemplate seeing *Der König* as many times.

The script of *Der König* was printed on some eighty-five pages. Only about two hours or so are required to present it. Sitting through seventeen performances adds up to a normal working week, and that is the point. To the politician who kept coming back for more, this play was not light diversion, but instead the essence of his work. He had reverted to type, the schoolboy of Linz who called idling in the theater his real education, as opposed to taking notes and doing his homework.

Seventeen times. His purpose in seeing the same show repeatedly thus had to be deliberate self-inculcation. It can hardly have been the popcorn at the Kammerspiele Theater. It cannot have been suspense either, since after a few performances it must surely have dawned on Hitler that the ending would not change. Furthermore, to take in seventeen recitals of this one play entailed paying attention to the theater's schedule, since the Kammerspiele program varied from night to night. So the one-man fan club went to see this skit by design. Presumably he slunk off solo most of those evenings; no contemporary harked back in print about attending *Der König* with Hitler. He was in this way preparing for power, absorbing Johst's *Der König* in the way other aspirant rulers have read and re-read Machiavelli's *The Prince*.

Had the Führer not gushed his esteem to Johst, this factoid of seventeen trips to the Kammerspiele might have entirely slipped past history. That is, it was quite possible for Hitler, the man who would be der König, to fixate on a dramatic work and to do so in a private manner, deigning only to tell the playwright. It was Adolf Hitler and none other who volunteered that his own mortal fate had been scripted for the stage.

That guy always in the *Der König* audience, the one sporting the little moustache, saw many more plays after his romance with this one. *Der König* proved but a passing fling, however intense. What endured was Hitler's love of the stage. The special function of theatrical role-play showed at length in his own act. Sooner or later, some of those around him perceived the act to be just that. Among the disillusioned was Otto Strasser, a Nazi from a leftist faction wary of Hitler. When the Führer lashed out to massacre his rivals in the party, Strasser escaped into exile. Eventually Strasser wrote:

He [Hitler] never ceases from watching himself and playing a conscious part.... He discovered that his lachrymatory glands were obliging and could be turned on at will. After that, he wept to the point of excess. Next he was St. John the Baptist, preparing for the coming of the Messiah; then the Messiah himself, pending his appearance in the role of Caesar.

MIRACLE WHIP

Strasser had gotten onto the right track. As he saw it, Hitler did not invent new personas, but instead picked existing characters for his role-playing. One of those characters would combine attributes of "the Messiah" and "Caesar." All that remained was to identify some script where these two were combined as one. The Führer moreover played "a conscious part," with enough footing on terra firma to present himself, to outsiders, as the person named on his baptismal certificate. That fact should not degrade the power and persistence of the role-playing. It was no once-per-year donning of a Mardi Gras mask, but an oft-observed, recurrent personality feature. At least some who well knew Adolf Hitler thus saw role-play as the key to comprehending the man.

If so, then the historian's main task ought to be following documentary clues to fix as precisely as possible who the assumed characters were, from what sources, and at which points they become evident in the Führer's career—or repertoire. By 1923 (if not earlier), he had sated himself for the time being with Hanns Johst's suicidal king and begun browsing around for another part to play.

The Nazi chief then found Christ—or at least an Aryan take on the imitation of Christ. Hitler's Christ was neither the gentle healer nor the pathetic sufferer on the cross. The Führer selected instead the irate figure cracking a whip portrayed in the Gospel of St. John 2:14–15. This was an Eckart favorite too. Hitler and Eckart's Christ had journeyed from (allegedly) Aryan Galilee to Jewish Jerusalem with flagellation in mind. But in empathizing with this lash-flailing Christ taken from St. John, the Führer could get carried away. Even Eckart is said to have fretted.

Something has gone completely wrong with Adolf. The man is developing an incurable case of *folie de grandeur*. Last week he was striding up and down in the courtyard here with that damned whip of his and shouting, "I must enter Berlin like Christ in the Temple of Jerusalem and scourge out the moneylenders" and more nonsense of that sort. I tell you, if he lets this Messiah complex run away with him, he will ruin us all.

This quotation attributed to Eckart is not the only reported instance of Hitler posing as Christ-of-the-Whip. His press aide Ernst Hanfstaengl recalled another on similar lines. Again Berlin stands in for Jerusalem. Hanfstaengl quoted Hitler:

When I came to Berlin a few weeks ago and looked at the traffic in the Kurfürstendamm, the luxury, the perversion, the iniquity, the wanton display, and the Jewish materialism disgusted me so thoroughly that I was almost beside myself. I nearly imagined myself to be Jesus Christ when he came to his Father's temple and found it taken by the money changers. I can well imagine how he felt when he seized the whip and scourged them out.

Hitler's "nearly" imagining the scene is discountable; if he said it, he indeed *well* imagined it. There is tangible reason to believe that he consistently fantasized himself on a daily basis as the whip-wielding Christ, since for years he toted about a whip of his own, a tough one made of rhinoceros hide. This whip was with Hitler at least as early as the autumn of 1922. Later, it occasionally appears in photographs through the 1920s and into the 1930s. The idea of lugging the thing around need not be thought a Hitler original. Julius Streicher, the Nazi propagandist, tabloid pornographer, and onetime child molester, also had a whip. Streicher's whip may well have signified a more conventional sexual deviance. For Hitler, however, it had to be otherwise.

It served der Führer as a costume accessory. He was not an equestrian, not a rodeo star. Pets did not feel this lash; he schlepped it even when his dog stayed home. And, salacious rumor aside, there are no accounts of S&M bouts with a Dominatrix Adolpha. The whip was rather a consciously intended talisman, like the traditional attributes marking one saint off from the next on holy statues and icons. So what did Hitler say? He said the knout sustained his irate Christ role. He was chastising those (Jewish) moneylenders.

Even so, he considered other personas.

MARIUS AND RIENZI

From Jesus, the Führer briefly retrogressed chronologically to the late Roman Republic. In September 1923, he told his retinue:

> Do you know Roman history? I am Marius and Kahr is Sulla. I am the leader of the people, but he represents the ruling class. This time, however, Marius will win.

Gustav Kahr—Hitler's proxy for Sulla—headed the Bavarian regime that the Nazis tried to oust in their November 1923 putsch.

Dropping the name of Marius does not make Hitler a learned classicist. But what he said does imply a cyclical view of history, wherein leading characters may get a second chance. The wording of the Marius allusion also shows, again, a tendency to role-play. Hitler did not say that he was *like* Marius, but that he *was* Marius, the Roman consul of the second and first centuries B.C.E., a champion of the plebians who welcomed men without property to join his legions. In 1923, Hitler maintained a similar force in the Nazi stormtroopers, who were about to confront the standing regime. And so Marius might fit, although only for a short while. Then, having tried on Marius, Hitler dropped him as a persona after the putsch debacle. Chameleon that he was, Hitler could even liken himself on other occasions to Sulla. He would repeatedly assert that once he had gained power and instituted his program, he intended to abdicate and live quietly by himself, painting and designing buildings.

Der König, Christ, and Marius had much in common. All could be seen as heroic, tragic losers in this-worldly terms. So too was Dr. Stockmann, whose words so inspired Hitler in *Mein Kampf.*

Meanwhile, operas were still Hitler's staple fare. He went to an opera house at least once or twice a week and saw Wagner favorites many more times than Johst's *Der König.* As for the Rienzi so hallowed by the youthful Hitler, that Wagner character well fits the paradigm of the tragic political loser along with der König, Christ, Marius, and Stockmann.

Yet Hitler came to judge Rienzi in critical perspective. This emerges from the memoirs of a day-to-day companion during 1930–32, Otto Wagener. Wagener served as a stormtroop official and concurrently as a counselor on economic matters. He traveled with Hitler on speaking tours. Wagener later recalled how the itinerary of Führer appearances in various cities could be decided based on what happened to be showing in local opera houses. At one point, for example, Hitler had a gofer telephone ahead to learn what was playing in Dresden and in Weimar. The latter town featured a performance of *Rienzi* on a certain day.

That did it. The Führer opted for Weimar, and *Rienzi.*

The choice astonished Wagener. He surmised aloud to his chief, "I thought it might make you uncomfortable to be in the audience while onstage the action shows a man of the people, who has risen to be leader, falling victim in the end to intrigues."

"On the contrary," Hitler replied. "Perhaps I always see the mistakes that can be made, so I can avoid them later on."

The aide doubtless knew nothing of how closely Hitler had studied *Der König.* Wagener pressed on: "Rienzi was betrayed by conservatives, by aristocrats, by the important owners of land and industry, to whom he had extended the hand of friendship."

The Führer had a ready retort: "But he lacked the backing of a party of his own."

So *Rienzi* it would be that night, as a political-science lesson for the Nazi party brass. A seminar of sorts followed. After the show, Hitler lectured his boon companions on the need for strengthening the party apparatus against reactionary intriguers. He credited his insights to the opera they had just seen.

"It"—meaning Hitler's career—had begun at that earlier soirée in 1906 when he first beheld *Rienzi,* or so his friend August Kubizek recalled Hitler having said. Hitler's reported words check out well. Rienzi indeed marked just the start of a pattern. As a tragic hero type, Rienzi the failed rebel is repeated in the Hitlerian character array by Johst's king, then by Marius, and then by Dr. Thomas Stockmann. Three of these four characters adopted in the early 1920s came from drama.

From Wagener's account, it is apparent that in about 1930 or 1931, Hitler on the threshold of power still viewed politics through the medium of the stage. He would literally go out of his way to attend a given show. But he could discuss Wagner's *Rienzi* with analytical detachment. He had by then seen or read enough plays to avoid the mistakes of scripted sovereigns and of others he knew from popular history. What he said of Rienzi also held true of Marius, of Johst's king, and of Stockmann. All of them lacked support from a disciplined political party. In instructing Wagener, Hitler might have added that the other role models had neglected as well to inject their movements with quasi-religious zeal.

Coming to power in 1933 proved no brake on this inveterate borrower from literature and the stage.

A COPYCAT PERICLES AND HIS SURROGATE "PARTHENON"

The author of *Mein Kampf*, it will be recalled, expressed his admiration for Pericles, the great Athenian ruler who had commissioned the Parthenon. Hitler did not quite state in so many words that he was Pericles. But he hardly had to; the self-flattering comparison was implied. If there are any doubts, however, they may be dispelled by Joachim Fest, a biographer both of Hitler and of the architect Albert Speer. Fest was also reputedly the ghostwriter, or at least the rewrite man, on the latter's memoirs. Fest worked closely with Speer and preserved this observation:

> Hitler regarded his artistic and political ideas as a unity and was fond of repeating that his regime had at last reconciled art and politics. He considered himself a ruler in the mold of Pericles and

> was wont to draw parallels; Albert Speer recalls that he regarded
> the Autobahn as his Parthenon.

In a published interview, Speer confirmed that "When he [Hitler] compared himself to Pericles, it was the great builder image." Albert Speer, he of the bloated ego, was being unusually candid, for Speer did not build the Nazi Autobahn. Rather, it was constructed under the direction of Speer's predecessor as Master Builder of the Third Reich, Fritz Todt. But how would Todt's boss, the latter-day Pericles wanna-be himself, get it into his head to compare a modern highway system to the Parthenon, that nonpareil of classical structures?

The Führer felt some special connection to the Parthenon, to the point of commissioning a set of special silverware bearing its embossed image. But to declare a highway his "Parthenon" takes some explaining. The bizarre metaphor begs close scrutiny under the historian's loupe. From whence could it have come? And what does it signify?

A likely source appears in a best-seller of 1923–24 by the architect Le Corbusier, entitled *Vers une architecture*. The book was widely reviewed in most European languages and came to be regarded as essential reading for anyone professing interest in the field. Page upon page of *Vers une architecture* features pictures of the Parthenon. There are foreground views with tumbled-down columns and chunks of loose rubble. And juxtaposed below the Parthenon, on several pages, are showroom shots of cars, all racy roadsters of the day.

Le Corbusier's point was that the Parthenon had, in an earlier age, achieved an apotheosis in design. It set a model for millennia. Now, like the Parthenon, cars too had reached perfection. Architecture would perforce adapt. The challenge was to style something new, worthy of what the Parthenon once was, worthy of the cars, and worthy of future ages. Le Corbusier tossed the gauntlet:

> It remains to use the motor car as a challenge to our houses and
> our great buildings. It is here that we come to a dead stop. "Rien
> ne va plus." Here we have no Parthenon.

None yet. Somebody would have to build one. Le Corbusier proclaimed himself the apostle of the automobile age in building. At hand, he said, lay the greatest architectural moment for the past two thousand and more years of human civilization. As caption for a photograph showing a 1921 Voisin Sports Torpedo convertible, he wrote:

> It is certain that Phidias was at the side of Ictinos and Kallicrates in building the Parthenon, and that he dominated them.

Dominating Phidias in turn was Pericles, Athens's dictator, maestro in art appreciation—and in strong-arm tactics, if that is what it took to get buildings built. For Hitler, the Parthenon symbolized his own personal affinity for Pericles. The joining of the Parthenon visual cliché to automobiles is so singular, however, that a Hitler derivation from the contemporary book by Le Corbusier must be strongly suspected, even if it cannot actually be confirmed with total certainty.

A SCENE FROM *FAUST*?

The "Parthenon" remark preserved via Speer does not complete Hitler's eclectic mix of metaphors. More visuals may be noted with reference to the Autobahn, on the very occasion of the groundbreaking for the highway. That event took place at Frankfurt-am-Main on September 23, 1933. Nazi luminaries stood by alongside seven hundred workmen, each equipped with a spade. It was the road engineer Fritz Todt's public debut. But Hitler himself starred. The Führer spoke, then took shovel in hand to inaugurate the project.

Several decades later, the scholar Max Domarus prepared an annotated selection of Hitler's speeches as historical reference material. It was Domarus who observed the striking visual and thematic likenesses between this ceremony and a digging scene from Goethe's *Faust*, Part Two, Act V, "In the Forecourt of the Palace." There too, a crowd of laborers is standing by, each one holding a shovel. They are in fact souls damned to perdition, rounded up by Mephistopheles to excavate Faust's grave. Faust happens by and mistakes their activity for a public-works project. Taking charge, he usurps Mephistopheles's purpose.

So, did Domarus guess correctly? There can be no doubt of Hitler's main role in the choreography for the Autobahn groundbreaking. What remains for relating *Faust*, Part Two in particular, to the events at Frankfurt-am-Main is some word confirming that Hitler had, indeed, been impressed by this play.

On this account, August Kubizek once again supplies the word. He recalled their days together in Linz, before the 1908 move to Vienna:

> Of Goethe's *Faust*, he [Hitler] once remarked that it contained more than the human mind could grasp. Once we saw, at the Burg Theater, the rarely performed second part, with Joseph Kainz in the title role. Adolf was very moved and spoke of it for a long time.

The play was performed again in Vienna on April 25, 1908 at the Hofburg Theater during one of Hitler's theater sprees. So, a quarter century later, did the Nazi leader stage-manage a groundbreaking out of a stage play he adored? Domarus offered the comparison of the Autobahn ceremonies to *Faust*, Part Two without any reference to Kubizek's recollections of the youthful Hitler, while Kubizek for his part never tied the *Faust* imagery to the Frankfurt Autobahn setting. There can be no definite assurance that Hitler retained *Faust* consciously in mind on this particular occasion. Domarus speculated on *Faust* as the source because Hitler's theatricality, and his mimicry, were both taken as givens.

What is certain, though, is Hitler's abiding concern on September 23, 1933 for the appearance of the Autobahn ceremony. Joseph Goebbels, the Nazi propaganda minister, supervised the lining up of newsreel footage and still photographs. And the likeness to *Faust* at Frankfurt-am-Main goes beyond externals. The scene Domarus cited is about immortality and cheating the devil. Hitler at the Autobahn groundbreaking was beginning work on the monument by which he wished to be forever remembered, his "Parthenon."

HITLER'S *HOUND OF THE BASKERVILLES*

The Führer's bent for refracting reality through a literary lens contin-ued into the World War II years. His evening monologue of February 3–4, 1942 holds a telling instance:

> You know the story of the hound of the Baskervilles. On a sinister, stormy night I was going to Bayreuth through the Fichtelgebirge. I'd just been saying to Maurice: "Look out on the bend!" I'd scarcely spoken when a huge black dog hurled itself on our car. The col-lision knocked it into the distance. For a long time we could still hear it howling in the night.

Car had met cur about ten years before, since that is when Emil Maurice was chauffeuring Hitler. The point here is not just Hitler's prodigious memory, but his equating the hit-and-run victim with the monstrous "hound of the Baskervilles" from the Sherlock Hol-mes novel by Arthur Conan Doyle. For Hitler, fiction made the facts more real. How he knew the tale, he did not say. There are five likely sources. A play in five acts titled *Der Hund von Baskerville* was cur-rent in 1907, at the height of the adolescent Adolf's drama feeding frenzy. It reached the German silent screen in 1914 and again in 1929. A German sound-film version was released in 1936. That prompted the publication of the Doyle novel in German in the following year.

In *The Hound of the Baskervilles,* Sherlock Holmes and Dr. Watson are called to investigate at the centuries-old castle of the Baskerville clan, set on a desolate moor. Weeks before, a huge mastiff had liter-ally scared to death the lord of the manor. The beast is still afoot somewhere on the moor. It is feared that the Baskerville heir may fall next to the animal—and its handler.

An old portrait helps reveal who has let loose the deadly hound. Images of the Baskerville ancestors for generations past adorn the gloomy castle hall. All are shown wearing the garb of their day. Holmes mentally subtracts the period costume. A face is left, of a cruel Baskerville lord from long ago. But he has a lookalike among the modern nearby neighbors. The resemblance is unmistakable.

Records on the living man prove him a Baskerville scion. Under a pseudonym, he is scheming to eliminate his kinsmen, then reassume his family name and inherit the whole estate. Telltale physiognomy alerts the detective in time. Sherlock Holmes sums up the miscreant as "an interesting case of a throwback, which appears to be both physical and spiritual."

So bad-guy genetic throwbacks could be discerned in faces. The idea intrigued Hitler. Of course, he felt constrained to add an anti-Semitic twist while speaking at dinner on May 12, 1942, some three months after he adduced the Baskerville tale.

> There are plenty of Jews with blue eyes and blond hair, and not a few of them have the appearance which strikingly supports the idea of the Germanization of their kind. It has, however, been indisputably established that, in the case of the Jews, if the physical characteristics of the race are sometimes absent for a generation or two, they will inevitably appear in the next generation.

Here was a genetics lesson quite like that of Sherlock Holmes, rendered just as the Führer was acting to suppress all Jewish genes—forever, he hoped. His next sentence broadly hints at his mental scene. Logically it makes a non-sequitur. Visually, however, his stream of consciousness evokes that Baskerville castle interior scene.

> One thing struck me when I visited the arsenal at Graz. It is that among the thousand suits of armor to be seen there, not one could be worn by a present-day Styrian, for they are all too small.

The "thousand suits of armor" are nothing if not stock props for a manor hall, as in the film versions of *Baskerville,* juxtaposed here with the idea of genetic throwbacks perceived in facial features, as in the story. Hitler alluded to the arsenal at Graz, but the moral of the Sherlock Holmes tale stayed fresh in his mind.

That is where it ends. After citing the suits of armor, Hitler veered off on another tangent. There are no more avowed allusions from Conan

Doyle. The point to be taken is the Führer's use of borrowed imagery to animate doctrine. He sets a stage. There are main characters and bit parts, but the logic of drama prevails. Real life has a story line like a play or a film. The plots move to a climax and a resolution.

TAKING STOCK

Some people are driven to mimic what they see onstage or in a film, or read in a book. If such a person gains absolute power, then their mimicry replays as History. One such mimic in power was Adolf Hitler, who borrowed personas, plagiarized words, and restaged scenes at will. His sources therefore become a valid historical issue. One demonstrable source, on textual grounds, was Ibsen's *An Enemy of the People.* Hitler may also have read Le Corbusier, whose book was then current, and adapted its metaphor for the superhighway he dubbed his "Parthenon." Hitler was moreover suspected of adapting a scene from *Faust*—which he adored—when he choreographed the Autobahn groundbreaking. It is fair to theorize too that he adapted the message of *The Hound of the Baskervilles* for his own racist program. Hitler said outright that he was the Roman consul Marius and then launched a coup to overthrow the Bavarian government, headed by a stand-in for Sulla. He saw his fate in the person of *Der König* and proceeded to exit the mortal stage in accordance with that script.

And he imagined himself like Jesus Christ scourging the moneylenders, then proceeded to carry a whip for years, adding that Providence had ordained his mission. As assumed personas go, Christ inevitably trumped all others. Hitler underscored the divinity of his purpose at the close of *Mein Kampf,* chapter 2: "I believe that I am acting in accordance with the will of the Almighty Creator. By defending myself against the Jew, I am fighting for the work of the Lord." There was, as it happened, another Ibsen character said to embody the persona of Christ, reborn once as a Roman emperor, and destined to come again. In Hitler's world, a cult had formed around that very Ibsen play.

5

CONNECTING THE DOTS:
FROM THE IBSEN CULT TO HITLER

It is a part of my own spiritual life which I am putting
into this book [*Emperor and Galilean*]; what I depict I
have, under different conditions, gone through myself;
and the historical subject chosen has a much more
intimate connection with the movements of our own
time than one might at first imagine. The establishment of such a connection I regard as imperative
in any modern poetical treatment of such a remote
subject, if it is to arouse interest at all.

—HENRIK IBSEN, IN A LETTER
DATED OCTOBER 14, 1872

FEW COULD STAY neutral about Ibsen. His every play mocked
hypocrisy and flouted taboo. By the 1890s, conservatives
deplored "Ibsenites" and their "Ibscene" style. Clergymen, politi-
cians, and feminists either took heart or felt the playwright's sting.
Ibsenism as a cult was no tightly ordered sect, but instead a loose
potpourri. Expounders, apostles, and a few outright fanatics vied
for the master's mantle. Even before Dietrich Eckart, their number
already included a few swastika-flaunting anti-Semites. One such
was Alfred Schuler.

ALFRED SCHULER'S THREE IBSEN FAVORITES

An Enemy of the People had its Munich premiere at the Residenz Theater on September 7, 1889. It played to good reviews. One article noted the special appeal to young people and the boisterous applause they accorded Dr. Stockmann's tirade in Act IV—the very act that would echo in *Mein Kampf.* Among the first-night crowd sat an aspiring writer, aged twenty-four.

"This was a storm to clear the air," Alfred Schuler scrawled in notes to himself that day. "A lightning bolt has flashed through the decrepit, dying world of prevailing ideas." Schuler felt uncommonly moved and sure that a societal revolution would follow soon. "I feel so free today." Ibsen was to him a "powerful fighter for truth" and "a writer for the future." Ecstatic, Schuler quoted from memory those very Stockmann lines that the Führer would paraphrase at table over a half century later:

> All those who live by lies should be exterminated like harmful beasts! Let the whole land be razed, let all its people be exterminated!

Fans in 1889 saw this play as more than a tiff about polluted water. To Schuler, Ibsen was the symbol of values in an emerging post-Christian world, re-imbued by the paganism of ancient Rome. Schuler evidently also knew *Emperor and Galilean,* which was just out in a German translation. Later in 1889, he introduced himself to Ibsen in a letter. The fan hailed the playwright as "the warm, throbbing pulse of our life" and defined his own creative literary future in terms of "your Julian," referring to *Emperor and Galilean.* Getting no response, Schuler tried again in April 1890. Ibsen then granted him a meeting. No account of it survives; but Schuler's literary collaborator, Ludwig Klages, later credited Ibsen—and particularly Ibsen's portrayal of Julian the Apostate—as exerting a formative and enduring grip on Schuler. Emperor Julian's fourth-century neo-pagan struggle suggested the same motif for Schuler's own never-finished opus, a drama about the first-century emperor Nero.

Some three years after their talk, Schuler again felt moved to write to Ibsen. This time the stimulus was *The Master Builder,* just performed in Germany. Schuler interpreted the work as the struggle of the new to supplant the old. His review of the play in the monthly *Die Gesellschaft* ("Society") for January 1893 incidentally comprised one of just two Schuler pieces published while he lived, the other being a sonnet in 1904. The essay posited master builder Halvard Solness as standing for transition from the outmoded to the modern. Solness's forlorn middle-aged wife stood for the haggard past. The ruthless young conniver Hilde Wangel represented the spirit of the future.

Schuler completed no major works. His published output was laughably meager. He never earned a degree, never held a steady academic or publishing job. And yet scholars agree that he exerted a catalytic influence via his presence on the Munich literary scene. The homosexuality he shared with others of that milieu widened his social set. For a while he belonged to a poetry circle centered on the anti-Semite Stefan Georg. Later on, he broke with Georg but formed a liaison of sorts with Ludwig Klages, who edited Schuler's papers. Despite an interest in archaeology, Schuler never conducted a dig—although he did wear togas to costume parties. Otherwise, he wrote fragments of would-be opuses on antiquity and eroticism, occasionally gave lectures, and styled himself "the last Roman."

And he became a leading light in the anti-Christian, increasingly anti-Semitic neo-pagan movement. Also among his papers are notes on the mystical sway of the swastika. This enthrallment with a previously arcane symbol began as early as 1895 and continued until Schuler's death in 1923. By then, Hitler and his storm troopers were wearing the twisted cross on their sleeves.

Ibsen had sparked Alfred Schuler's career, to the extent that one drama review and one sonnet in print can be called a career. Most noteworthy is that while Ibsen wrote some twenty-six dramas, three particularly transfixed Schuler by his own account. They were *An Enemy of the People, Emperor and Galilean,* and *The Master Builder.* For Schuler, this trio of plays outlined the world to come. They happen also to be the same three plays exhibiting literary pentimenti in the writings and remarks of Adolf Hitler.

EGOISTS AND OTHERS

The idolizing of Ibsen had promotional worth. Cults boost box-office sales and turn books into bestsellers. Ibsen's contemporaries Victor Hugo and Leo Tolstoy also won a kind of secular sainthood, to the benefit of sales. Aspects vary from author to author, cult to cult. Most literary cults remain little more than avid reading groups, though some spawn sects with agendas, and a few ripen into full-blown movements. The early faddish adulation over Ibsen owed much to William Archer (1856–1924), his translator and agent in Britain. For five decades, Archer promoted Ibsen as a guru. In America, the critic and essayist John Gibbons Huneker (1857–1921) served as Archer did in England. Huneker successively elevated Ibsen from "iconoclast" (1905) to "superman" (1909), perceiving in the plays an outlook trendy among German intellectuals: egoism. Egoist tenets anticipate the philosophy Ayn Rand would call "objectivism," which thrives on heroes who transcend the mundane. Ibsen supplied plenty of these in his plays—plus one more in his own person.

Throughout the English-speaking world, Ibsen gained support from no less a figure than George Bernard Shaw. Shaw's 1891 book *The Quintessence of Ibsenism* came out in German in 1908, the same year that Hitler read the plays. When Shaw beatified Ibsen as a "prophet" in 1913, he echoed the faith of a cult he had helped foster. It grew despite the waning of the frequency of Ibsen productions on the German stage. The cultists drew on prior movements, including the psychologist and founder of egoism, Max Stirner (1806–56), whose followers saw Ibsen as a successor saint.

It made some sense. Ibsen himself had read Stirner. When Ibsen wrote, in a letter, "Away with the state!" he expressed a thought Stirner shared. Some might label Stirner an anarchist, but the twentieth-century word "libertarian" better fits Stirner's elitist plea for an unfettered individualism of the talented few. Libertarians of the Stirner type admired Ibsen heroes like Peer Gynt, Dr. Thomas Stockmann, Halvard Solness, and Julian the Apostate, as well as the Ibsen heroines Hedda Gabler and Hilde Wangel. Each defied convention.

Egoists held that rebel geniuses must shape their own destiny. In the process, they mold the destiny of the world.

BUT EGOISTS NEVER monopolized Ibsen. His works were, after all, not tracts but dramas: psychological, enigmatic, and often unresolved. The various scripts could be used by disparate sorts, from free-market libertarians to Christian ethicists to women's rights activists. And, in time, by proto-Nazis too. Ibsen himself kept silent about all this. Felled by a stroke in 1900, the playwright was beyond either blessing or damning any of the manifestos proclaimed in the name of his works.

Despite his Norwegian nationality, during the first decade of the twentieth century Ibsen came to be discussed in German as much as, if not more than, any other writer since Goethe. Ibsen's appeal transcended borders, although his personal presence in Germany for much of his career had made him virtually a German literary figure—albeit in translation, since he still wrote in his native language. Egoists kept the interest fresh after the master's passing in May 1906. Debate tended toward the political. Even the brooding dramas of Ibsen's later years, like *The Master Builder*, were included in his "political legacy." But those who cited Ibsen often blurred mysticism with their politics.

In 1908, along with Shaw's book, the German reading and book-buying public could come across or read reviews of such current titles as *Ibsen als Erzieher* ("Ibsen as Teacher") by Bernhard Münz. Shelved nearby would be Paul Schulze-Berghof's *Die Kulturmission unserer Dichtkunst* ("The Cultural Mission of Our Literature") with its essay on "The Ethical Spirit of the Times in Ibsen's Works." Schulze-Berghof saw in Ibsen a new Goethe for a new age. A playwright, novelist, and critic, Schulze-Berghof later also contributed a long, effusive, and political review of Dietrich Eckart's Germanized *Peer Gynt.*

If readers missed Schulze-Berghof's 1908 piece, a 400-page title beckoned. Bold print embossed on the cover and the spine trumpeted *Ibsen als Prophet* ("Ibsen as Prophet") by Eugen Heinrich Schmitt (1851–1916). It bore the subtitle *Grundgedanken zu einer neuen Ästhetik* ("Basic Ideas toward a New Aesthetic"). There were synopses and apt comments on every play. Before tackling Ibsen, Schmitt had produced analyses of gnostic Christian texts and of utopian societies in literature. Not surprisingly, he discerned hidden meaning in Ibsen's work and saw *The Master Builder* (written and translated in 1892) according to terms set in *Emperor and Galilean* (1873; translated into German in 1888). It mattered not that the plays' own author never connected the two dramas in such a way.

In these years, while Hitler was reading Ibsen, no other living or recent author enjoyed equivalent status in the German-speaking world. Ibsen would be called "the great magus of the north" by Johann Mayrhofer (in *Henrik Ibsen: Ein literarisches Charakterbild*, in English *Henrik Ibsen: A Literary Portrait*), who also wrote a critical book about Emperor Julian. Mayrhofer aimed, unsuccessfully, to thwart neo-pagans from grabbing Ibsen's legacy with their all-out emphasis on the Julian play. The problem was that Ibsen had declared that play to have been his crowning masterpiece, and in terms subsequently useful to German chauvinists. He had even called its message "racial." That remark stemmed from a prevalent nineteenth-century belief that a clash of belief systems, in this case paganism versus Christianity, amounted to the projected attributes of different ancient cultures that were construed as "races." Ibsen's comment, although meant innocently enough in his own day, would in a later generation feed into Nazi genocidal racism.

The debate went on. All told, in the period between the death of Ibsen and the rise of Hitler there were probably about two dozen major books on Ibsen published in German, along with many more short tracts and articles in newspapers and literary journals. To read Ibsen, and about Ibsen, and particularly about Ibsen's Julian was to keep current. Dietrich Eckart's pamphlet war against the translator Christian Morgenstern and Ibsen's executor Georg Brandes fit within this ongoing debate on how to interpret Ibsen. Enough people cared to read such diatribes; otherwise, the venom would hardly have been worth the spitting.

To be sure, not all German Ibsenists were egoists, gnostics, utopians, or Jew-baiting schemers. There were also learned academics, the Catholic layman Mayrhofer, and even a cleric, all ready to parse what Ibsen really meant. The clergyman was Emil Felden (1874–1959), a Lutheran pastor in Bremen who at one time held an elected seat in the German Reichstag. Felden adroitly combined staunch faith, left-wing Social Democratic politics, and a stalwart ethic. Ibsen served as his moral exemplar. Felden titled his book on the playwright *Alles oder Nichts!* ("All or Nothing!"), echoing Ibsen's contempt for moral ambiguity. But the pastor's book avoided discussing one key, controversial play: *Emperor and Galilean.* Others felt no such constraint. In 1913, Alfred Markowitz (following Schmitt; *contra* Mayrhofer) made the Julian saga central in *Die Weltanschauung Henrik Ibsens* ("The Worldview of Henrik Ibsen"). Markowitz fit all the other plays into a first, a second, and a coming "third Reich," a concept Ibsen had borrowed from the medieval thinker Joachim of Fiore. Markowitz thus treated Ibsen's lifetime output as an organic entity pivoted on *Emperor and Galilean.* By the eve of the Great War, many shared this approach to Ibsen.

Ordinarily, bohemian belletristic games catch hold in the campus and coffeehouse world. And there they stay. But then came 1914 and a wider tumult. Nothing would ever again be the same. So utterly disrupted was Europe's old order that pieces of literary cant, churned out by a dead dramatist's devotees, could be welcomed more widely as blueprints for the brutal new age.

HENRIK IBSEN AS "HERALD OF THE THIRD REICH"

Rolf Engert (1889–1962) also took *Emperor and Galilean* as central, and at a time when "third Reich" took on more of a political nuance. Engert was a doctoral student in literature, exempted from the German army on health grounds. He wrote undisturbed while Europe tore itself apart. Engert's dissertation on Ibsen was published in 1917. Even then, a year before the collapse of Kaiser Wilhelm's imperial second Reich, Engert chose *Herald of the Third Reich* as the working title for a projected book on the topic to appear sometime after the war. But a preliminary 1917 work asserted that Ibsen's thought was a unitary creed. Engert included Ibsen's letters and plays in the egoist canon. His Ibsenist dogma was hostile to the state, exalting instead genius, the will of the transcendent man.

In addition to the Julian play, Engert also granted a special status to *Peer Gynt*. He relied on the authorized Morgenstern text. The choice of translation marked one's loyalties on a hardening political battlefront. In the next year, 1918, Paul Schulze-Berghof countered by extolling Eckart's *Peer Gynt*. Ibsenism was polarizing into a contest for the prophet's legacy in a "revolutionization of the human spirit." It spilled out into the streets. Engert and Schulze-Berghof articulated radical left and right extremes. On one thing they concurred: The future had been cast by the message of the prophet Ibsen. By late 1918, the Kaiser state and its army had collapsed. Near-chaos reigned in Berlin and elsewhere. The audacious saw their moment. Radical Ibsenists gravitated to public champions within a rapidly churning mix of assassinations, mutinies, strikes, and coups d'etat.

Rolf Engert attached himself as publicist to an Argentine-born economic thinker, Silvio Gesell. Gesell had formulated a free-market doctrine of monetary and land reform. His tracts are mostly forgotten, but they drew serious attention at the time. He commanded enough respect to be cited favorably by John Maynard Keynes. Gesell promoted a brand of individualism and anarchism congruent with what Rolf Engert saw in Ibsen. The Gesell theory taught that social inequality resulted when money was misused, not as a medium of exchange but as an instrument of dominance. Simply put, usury was to blame for strife. No particular group of usurers was singled out, but that mattered little in the Germany of 1918–20. Given the hoary belief linking money-lending with Jewry, Gesell's theory could attract anti-Semites. Gottfried Feder, the house economist of the early Nazi party, was a doctrinaire anti-Semite who took notice.

In the spring of 1919, Gesell saw practical chances in the German Communists' short-lived Munich "Soviet" (*Räterepublic*). Although not himself a Communist, Gesell's theory and his evident talents appealed to this leftist regime. He held the title of Bavarian finance minister. When militarists staged a counter-coup that May, Gesell was arrested and tried, yet acquitted. He went on professing his brand of agricultural and financial reform.

Rolf Engert published Gesell's treatises via his own Dresden-based outfit, calling itself Third Reich Publishers (*Verlag des dritten Reiches*). The term "Third Reich" had a bit of history behind it, going far back beyond Ibsen to the visionary Joachim of Fiore (c. 1135–1202), who had cast all of history into three great ages. The first two divisions were the pre-Christian era and then the period of Christianity. Yet to come was an age of fulfillment, harmony, and bliss. In his play, Ibsen projected the origin of this tripartite scheme much further back than Joachim of Fiore, all the way to the fourth century, when he has the character Maximus expounding it to Julian the Apostate. The three ages in this Ibsen version are paganism, Christianity, and a third era in which the best of Christianity and paganism are synthesized. "Third Reich" had a double meaning in Germany since the Kaiser's state had called itself the Second Reich (while referring to Charlemagne's empire as the First Reich). By seizing on the term "Third Reich," Engert combined New-Age millenarianism with the political ideas of the Stirner–Gesell egoists.

Engert continued his own writing on Ibsen as well, expanding the academic thesis text of 1917 into a popular book called *Ibsen als Verkünder des dritten Reiches* ("Ibsen as Herald of the Third Reich"; Leipzig: R. Voigtländer, 1921). Thus the label "third Reich" remained identified for a while with the Stirnerite wing of Ibsenism. The 300-page, well-annotated study went beyond the 1917 book in idolizing Ibsen as the harbinger of a libertarian utopia. Engert again classed all Ibsen's plays within the *Emperor and Galilean* "three-Reich" scheme. The prophesied "third Reich" was at hand. Yet Engert evinced no animus toward the Jews.

EMPEROR AND GALILEAN AS "ALLEGORY"

Paul Schulze-Berghof added the ingredient of anti-Semitism that was missing from Engert but fulsome in what Alfred Schuler taught. Between 1918 and 1923, Schulze-Berghof shifted his own emphasis away from *Peer Gynt,* to cite *Emperor and Galilean* as the most prophetic, most profound of the Ibsen plays. His booklet appeared in 1923 under the title *Ibsens Kaiser und Galiläer als Zeitsinnbild* ("Ibsen's 'Emperor and Galilean' as Allegory"). It makes no mention of Engert's book but was surely intended as a polemic response to that work. Although no match for Engert in literary erudition, Schulze-Berghof fed freely on what the egoists made of Ibsen, twisting it his own way.

Schulze-Berghof took *Emperor and Galilean* as "a prophetic world view in the mirror of history" and Julian the Apostate as "a parable for the character of the German cultural soul." But Julian failed in the play: His synthesis of emperor with Galilean had aborted short of founding the prophesied third Reich. Now another opportunity loomed: Schulze-Berghof pronounced Ibsen's drama "a warning and admonition of the writer–prophet for our German people as the leader of Germanic mankind and a bright torch of spiritual awareness for the achievement of our will and for our way through the darkness and the chaos of the times." He cited Ibsen's own words from 1888, looking back on the time he wrote the play:

> I experienced the great time in Germany, the year [1870–71] of the [Franco–Prussian] war and the development afterward. To me, all this had in many ways a transforming power. My view of the history of the world and of human life had been until then a national view. Now it broadened to a racial view, and I could write *Emperor and Galilean*.

It helped that Ibsen had written the entire two-part, ten-act Julian play in Germany and published it in 1873, the year Schulze-Berghof was born. Schulze-Berghof's book *Ibsen's 'Emperor and Galilean' as Allegory* summarized the play in a couple of chapters, then looked at what the allegory portended for the times ahead. Germans had to learn from Julian's failure by building on *Emperor and Galilean.* As in his book about *Peer Gynt,* Schulze-Berghof again suggested Nietzsche's *Thus Spake Zarathustra* as a fortifying supplement to be fused with Ibsen. The amoral Nietzschean superman ideal supplied those transcendent qualities that Julian had lacked in the Ibsen play.

Thus spake Schulze-Berghof. *Emperor and Galilean* was for him not merely a script; it was scripture, The Book for the salvation of Germanic mankind. Just as Goethe's *Faust* had dramatized the German folk soul of the seventeenth and eighteenth centuries, so too did Ibsen's *Emperor and Galilean* embody the Germanic spiritual and cultural will in the nineteenth and twentieth. Ibsen had been especially attuned to this will, like "a fine seismic apparatus," as Schulze-Berghof rhapsodized. Norwegians were then idealized as paragons of Nordic racial purity. But to transform prophecy into praxis would next require an instrument to mobilize the Germanic will.

THE DOTS CONVERGE

Henrik Ibsen's parody of a would-be demagogue in *The League of Youth* indicates clearly enough how the playwright might have scorned Adolf Hitler. Ibsen (d. 1906) cannot be blamed for what anti-Semitic cultists, proto-Nazis, outright Nazis, or the Nazi Führer himself wrought with Ibsen scripts in mind. No playwright, and still less a famed immortal, can direct what is done in his name once he has left the mortal stage. But it is a fact: When selected Ibsen plays became "prophecy," Jew-hating, swastika-sporting cultists glimpsed their own third Reich written in the scripts.

It remains to be seen how close the cultist dots connect to the theater maven who would lord over the historical Third Reich. Are the dogmas of Alfred Schuler, Rolf Engert, and Paul Schulze-Berghof mere figments on the literary fringe? Or did they feed with consequence into History? Adolf Hitler, it appears, was well primed for Ibsen via his own youthful reading and again via Peer "Dietrich Eckart" Gynt. He had co-opted Dr. Stockmann's *Enemy* Act IV harangue into *Mein Kampf.* The question then is whether Hitler was swayed by others besides Eckart on the Ibsen cultist fringe, particularly those touting *Emperor and Galilean* as a trumpet call for a "third Reich."

Alfred Schuler is an intriguing figure whose patron, the publisher Hugo Bruckmann, also donated funds to Eckart and to the newborn Nazi party. Bruckmann's wife Elsa hosted literary lights at the Bruckmanns' Munich salon. It was there, in 1922, that Schuler gave a series of lectures about the mystique and force of the swastika. From the documentary evidence, however, Hitler himself cannot be counted among those attending. On the contrary, in later years Hugo Bruckmann took the trouble to draft a memoir dating Hitler's first visit to the Bruckmann address as December 23, 1924, immediately upon the Führer's release from prison. Schuler had meanwhile died, on April 8, 1923. But that negative evidence does not rule out a Schuler–Hitler meeting at some earlier date.

Whether or not they actually met, the impression Hitler made on the older man was not good. A spare, disparaging mention of the Nazi party Führer in Schuler's writings notes "with growing horror" how the party was "profaning" the swastika symbol. "Who really is this Herr Hitler?" Schuler asked. "I hear he was an officer in the war. This doesn't sound good to me." It certainly doesn't sound like a close acquaintance either, given the fact that Hitler only advanced to corporal, a far cry from officership. Suspicious of the fast-growing nationalistic "tumor" in Munich, Schuler moreover feared that Hitler might be insincere, merely using anti-Semitism as a ploy to rally support. He so stated in a letter written on January 6, 1923, just three months before his death. Schuler thus cannot be deemed Hitler's mentor in any direct, personal sense. Yet a Schuler distaste for the Nazis and their star performer does not by any means rule out Schuler's influence—via reputation, via Eckart, or via some other means. The Schuler dots veer near.

And what of Rolf Engert? Is there reason to suspect that Hitler knew of his book about Ibsen? Hitler did read political material about the plays, as shown by his knowledge of Per Hallström's pamphlet using *An Enemy of the People* as allegory. In the case of Engert, though, there is yet another likely connection, via Silvio Gesell. Despite Gesell's cameo role in the Munich "Soviet" republic, the economist's writings did offer a respected, anti-plutocratic, and sufficiently radical alternative to Marxism. Early Nazidom lacked the intellectual resources to devise such a system on its own. The Nazis had at best among their founding members the engineer Gottfried Feder, a crank who lacked any credential in economic theory but who posed as an economist nonetheless. Feder proceeded to rest his theory of "interest slavery" upon elements all too obviously drawn from Gesell. Indeed, Feder the National Socialist and Gesell the free marketeer co-authored at least one pamphlet, published in 1921, by the Nazis.

What Feder took from the writings of Silvio Gesell thus formed the scarcely disguised basis for the Nazi economic platform, insofar as the party had any in its first few years. There was, to be sure, a skewed emphasis. Singling out what suited him from the breadth of Gesell's work, Feder was preoccupied mainly with attacks on the traditional scapegoat of alleged Jewish usury. Here lay the nexus to the primary Nazi tenet, blaming all worldly woe upon the Jews.

Hitler knew enough about Gesell to decry him in 1922 as one who "worked with the Jews," presumably a reference to the Munich Soviet. But it is also hard to imagine a Hitler unaware of Engert's "Third Reich Publishers" as long as the Nazis coveted the "third Reich" label for themselves. Given these associations on the political scene as well as the keen interest in Ibsen displayed by both Hitler and Eckart, it seems fair to postulate a Hitler aware that Engert had incidentally also written a book on Ibsen as the "herald of the Third Reich." It may not be demonstrable that Hitler actually read this book; but, via Gesell and Feder, a line of dots from Rolf Engert intersects the Hitler orbit.

What then of Hitler and Paul Schulze-Berghof? Can any dots link them?

Schulze-Berghof had written a glowing review of Eckart's *Peer Gynt* and its import for changing times. Given human vanity, Eckart could not have remained oblivious to Schulze-Berghof, and he could hardly have failed to mention the review to his protégé. That would presumably also have raised the visibility of Schulze-Berghof's book about *Emperor and Galilean* as an allegory. Or maybe Hitler found that Schulze-Berghof piece first, on his own. Beyond presumption, though, *Mein Kampf* offers some internal evidence hinting that Hitler had read Schulze-Berghof's book about the Julian play, in 1924. There are no explicit references to Ibsen in *Mein Kampf*, nor anywhere else in the extant Hitler corpus. But a passage in the Hitler memoir does appear to parallel a passage from *Ibsens Kaiser und Galiläer als Zeitsinnbild.* Both passages concern Hitler's most fervid topic, the Jews.

The Schulze-Berghof selection recites this litany: The classical Greeks were creative, the Jews parasitic. The institution of the state represented the apotheosis of Greek and Roman political creativity. The Jews, by contrast, obeyed a Torah injunction to feed off of other peoples. For support, Schulze-Berghof adduced a passage from Deuteronomy 7:16: "You shall consume all the people which the Lord God delivers unto you." Anti-Semites savor this sentence like manna.

After losing their own state, the exiled Jews dispersed throughout the lands of other peoples but maintained an exclusive racial identity while pursuing their innate tribal "gold lust" for almost two thousand years. Schulze-Berghof deemed this a "categorical imperative" determined by the "*Mosaic* will to power" [italics added]. He continued: "Jewish history teaches us like no other what national character, springing from race and formed through spirit, means for the life of a people in conflict with its surroundings."

These thoughts were commonplace to Nazis and those of like sympathies. Of concern here, though, is not just the contents but the vocabulary. A passage of paragraph length some four fifths of the way through Volume I, chapter 4 of *Mein Kampf* betrays just enough resemblance to suggest that Hitler had read the then-current *Ibsen's 'Emperor and Galilean' as an Allegory of the Times.*

The Schulze-Berghof and Hitler texts cover the same distinct ideological points:

- Jews constitute a parasitic race.
- Their religion "is nothing but a doctrine for the preservation of the Jewish race" (Hitler).
- Judaism is quaintly referred to—by both authors—as the "Mosaic" faith.

"Mosaic" serves as a tracer by dint of its near-total absence from the Führer's lexicon before 1924, then its appearance during that year like a shooting star, only to disappear again thereafter.

Given his obsession with Jewry, Hitler was pressed for synonyms connoting the people he loved to hate. He orated almost daily on the topic; anti-Semitism defined the basis of Nazism, as Hitler proudly stated. Ruling out gutter epithets, among the available adjectives were "Jewish" (*jüdisch*), "Semitic," "Hebraic," "Israelite," "Talmudic"—and also the antiquated form "Mosaic," denoting the religious laws transmitted by Moses. The word "Mosaic" might be stretched from there to mean the broader Jewish faith and the alleged characteristics of the Jews—for example, as Schulze-Berghof used the term, postulating a "Mosaic will to power."

"Germans of Mosaic faith" was actually a formula favored by those German Jews eager to assimilate. For them, it was not in any sense a derogatory term. The stilted oddness of "Mosaic" thus lends a bit of sarcasm if uttered by an anti-Semitic demagogue at the rostrum. Hitler had done just that on occasion with "kosher." Enunciated with a sardonic emphasis on each syllable, "Mosaic" too might vary the nuance of a tirade, elicit snickers, and so establish a bond between the Jew-baiting speaker and a like-minded crowd. The Führer always spoke at friendly rallies, but even he occasionally needed to spice up his lines to rouse a crowd.

Yet until 1924, when he dictated *Mein Kampf* while relaxing at Landsberg, the adjective "Mosaic" is almost lacking from his mental thesaurus. Over a thousand pages in the definitive, complete edition of Hitler's articles, interviews, speeches, and letters from his boyhood up to 1924 yield but one solitary instance, in a letter written in September 1919. And despite the title *Bolshevism from Moses to Lenin*, the adjectival form "Mosaic" (*mosaisch*) is absent too from the fifty pages of purported talks between Eckart and Hitler that Eckart set down in 1923.

Then at Landsberg in the spring of 1924, Hitler began composing *Mein Kampf*. As seen, he had to have had beside him a volume of Ibsen, since he reworked a passage from *An Enemy of the People*, Act IV into chapter 3 of his political testament. A contemporary work of Ibsen criticism by a Nazi-inclined dramatist would be fully in keeping among items on hand with the Führer at that time. And Hitler uses "Mosaic" amidst the very same skein of ideas as did

Schulze-Berghof in his book. Schulze-Berghof in his pages also condemned the "Mosaic-Christian tyranny of Sinai."

No absolute proof exists that Hitler read Ibsens 'Kaiser und Galiläer' als Zeitsinnbild. But the close similarity of thoughts from this passage on the Jews, expressed with the occurrence of "Mosaic," otherwise so rarely used by Hitler, does lead to the strong suspicion that Hitler had picked up the word and reactivated its use in his lexicon from a recent reading of Schulze-Berghof before setting down his own formulation of similar thoughts. "Mosaic" would then be a literary pentimento in Mein Kampf, from a book positing Ibsen's play about Julian as allegory, or parable, for the times to come. This time the dots all but connect.

There is more, though. Schulze-Berghof next wrote a political novel, published in 1924.

Its strange title, Wettersteinmächte, means "Thunder Stone Powers." Etymologically, it referred to a fossilized prehistoric shellfish that tapered to a sharp point, called belemnite (Wetterstein). Popular superstition attributed the shape to thunderbolts. The novel's contents matched the imagery. As in previous works, Schulze-Berghof drew on Nietzsche's unyielding, amoral Zarathustra figure as well as on Ibsen. So much for background. What counts is what's in the book.

By way of substance, this novel called for a savior to resurrect Germany and the world from the postwar chaos. Schulze-Berghof identified that savior as follows:

> The Roman Caesar with the soul of Christ as leader (Führer) and tyrant (Zwingherr) of the world flame and world revolution—that is what we lack, that is what mankind lacks.

But the predicted savior would—indeed must—appear. The union of Caesar and Christ is precisely the role to which Julian was appointed in Emperor and Galilean. As "people's leader" (Volkes Führer), the one destined to carry on Julian's task would grasp how church Christianity as practiced hitherto had been tainted by Judaism, the doctrine of "a foreign, black-blooded people." And, as is written in Wettersteinmächte, he would be the one saluted with this very call:

Heil!—Heil!—Heil!

"Heil! Heil! Heil!" was an exclusively Nazi greeting by the time Schulze-Berghof wrote in 1923–24. There can thus be no doubt as to who he had in mind. The one so described was to succeed Emperor Julian, found the Third Reich, and destroy Christianity by extirpating its Jewish roots. That would bring about the worldwide pagan triumph.

A MATRIX OF DOTS

Paraphrased lines from a few selected works by Henrik Ibsen turn up, it seems, in the words of Adolf Hitler. They turn up over many years to indicate a deep, sustained interest. That fact long escaped notice, but it should otherwise hardly astound. Ibsen's plays were neither esoteric nor exotic. Their presence was familiar and thus accountable in the place where Hitler lived and in the circles where he moved. More than merely commonplace or accountable, Ibsen was—as "herald of the third Reich"—all the rage, at least to some in those circles.

There is thus no one line of dots from Hitler to Dietrich Eckart, Rolf Engert, Paul Schulze-Berghof, and Alfred Schuler, not to omit Johann Mayrhofer, Alfred Markowitz, or Eugen Heinrich Schmitt. Instead, there is a matrix of dots that shades the background of Germany and Munich on the eve of Hitler's rise. Hitler—avowed theater fan, pupil of Dietrich Eckart, and borrower of Ibsen lines for his own memoir—could not have been unaware of at least some of these writers on Ibsen.

All these men stated or wrote that Ibsen was a "prophet." Some meant it in an occult sense. This is not how literature professors would later think of Ibsen, but it was certainly a popular trend then, not one loner's raving but a full-blown literary cult that thrived for over a decade with ample publications as evidence. Modest minions bought these cultist books, which kept coming, selling, and swaying at least some who read them. The cult had its nuances and schisms, although most cultists agreed on the centrality of Ibsen's own favorite script. *Emperor and Galilean* was an "allegory" of the past for modern times. It told the life of Julian the Apostate. The play posed a paradox: that Julian, who struggled against Christians, was himself Christ incarnate. *Emperor and Galilean* foretold his return, someday, to found a "third Reich."

6

FROM BERCHTESGADEN, A WORLD DRAMA

The work which I am now bringing out will be my chief work. It is entitled *Emperor and Galilean*, and consists of: 1. *Caesar's Apostasy*, 2. *Emperor Julian*. Each of those parts is a long, five-act drama. The play deals with a struggle between two irreconcilable powers in the life of the world—a struggle which will always repeat itself; and because of this universality, I call the book "A World-Drama."
—IBSEN IN A LETTER, FEBRUARY 23, 1873

I T IS ONE thing for a critic to dub a play "prophetic" and evoke a politician to enact its message. It is quite another thing for the politician to heed that call. Hitler did not name his source when he extolled Julian to guests on several occasions in 1941–42. A merely passing Hitler interest in the emperor Julian would scarcely rate a footnote. But should Hitler's Julian prove to have been Ibsen's Julian—an "allegory" and "harbinger of the third Reich"—then a more frightful prospect stares History in the face. Determining whether that was so demands a careful scrutiny of *Emperor and Galilean* for how the play's distinct features set it apart from all other treatments of Rome's last pagan ruler.

THE MANY TAKES ON JULIAN

Julian the Apostate reigned for less than two years during 361–363 C.E., but he was never forgotten. He remained one of those contentious men of mission who are both admired and despised during their own lives, then remolded by remembrance. Literature recast him repeatedly. Well before Ibsen, Lorenzo de Medici had penned a play. Diderot, Voltaire, and Gibbon had all shown interest. Friedrich Schiller once told Goethe of his own plans for a drama about Julian. Nothing came of that, but Schiller's published letter of 1798 challenged others to give the subject a try.

Julian attracted sympathy in the eighteenth- and nineteenth-century societies of Europe and America. Some writers were commenting as much on their own times as on the doomed attempt by a mid-fourth-century Roman ruler to revive the pagan rites. In this way, Macaulay's *History of England* had couched criticism of King James II in the form of a comment on Julian. Likewise, an essay of 1847 by David Friedrich Strauss depicting Julian as "the romantic on the throne" was widely considered to be a disguised critique of the Prussian king Friedrich Wilhelm IV. Julian had his uses on modern agendas.

With greater historical fidelity, the German theologian August Neander focused on Julian in his own right with a monograph first appearing in 1812. Resurgent public interest occasioned a revised printing in 1867. Another respectable biography of Julian was by J. F. Alphons Mücke, *Flavius Claudius Julianus.* J. E. Auer had meanwhile written a major tome, also in German, on Julian's stance toward the church. The best account in French was that of Albert de Broglie, published in 1864. When Ibsen came in turn to conduct research for *Emperor and Galilean,* he widened his limited classical grounding by recourse to Neander, Mücke, Auer, de Broglie—and his own fancy.

Others before Ibsen had taken up Schiller's notion for a drama about Julian. In 1812, as Napoleon's armies struggled in Russia, Kuno von der Kettenburg's *Julianus Apostata: Tragödie* was published in Berlin. An English-language play in 1831 by the Pennsylvania politician Charles Jared Ingersoll (1782–1862) followed, setting five acts on the marches outside the Persian capital of Ctesiphon. Contemporary with Ibsen, several other European playwrights interpreted Julian. William Molitor damned the apostate in a German Catholic version of 1866 while a Dane, Carsten Hauch, attempted a character study that appealed for religious tolerance. Ibsen said he refused to read this work of his fellow Scandinavian, so as to keep an original voice. Meanwhile, more rival Julians kept coming. Hermann Riotte released a five-act German tragedy in 1870. Four years later, there was yet another, this time in verses rhymed by one P. Seeberg.

The figure of Julian beckoned, virtually made for theater. Here was a young man who had set out to reinvigorate a passing classical epoch. Seven centuries separated him from Alexander the Great. Seeing himself as Alexander's spiritual heir, Julian managed to perish while campaigning at a place in Mesopotamia not very far from where Alexander had met his end. Each man had lived a mere thirty-two years. Julian's life and the polemics directed against him ensured historical immortality. Ample source material was around for historians, novelists, and playwrights to consult. Julian is known far better than any antecedent or subsequent Roman ruler during the period of the empire's decline.

THE JULIAN OF HISTORY

The quest for Hitler's Julian among all other literary Julians requires summarizing the life of the historical personage. Born in 331 C.E. during the reign of his uncle Constantine, he was the first Roman emperor to adopt Christianity, though paganism still remained respectable. Many throughout the empire observed heathen rites. Christianity itself was split among squabbling sects. Young Julian's tutorial curriculum featured classical philosophical texts alongside Christian scriptures. He was an eager student. The empire was then ruled by his cousin Constantius II, son of the great Constantine. Yet Julian and his brother Gallus distrusted Constantius. While Julian immersed himself in books, Gallus and his wife governed far-off Gaul, where they contended with border incursions by German tribes.

Julian continued to study, secretly embracing paganism in 351.

He fell under the influence of a neo-Platonist savant known as Maximus the Mystic. As of that year, 351, information on Julian's life becomes more detailed, owing to an historical narrative by Ammianus Marcellinus. This lucid account emphasizes military and political developments. It depicts Gallus as ambitious and cruel, with Julian as bookish and ascetic but also superstitious.

The year 355 marked a turning point. Julian read classics at Athens and wed an imperial cousin named Helena, the sister of Constantius, in a purely political marriage. Helena's sister, shortly to die of a fever, was likewise the wife of Julian's brother Gallus. By marrying his sisters to the brothers Gallus and Julian, Emperor Constantius sought to secure the loyalty of his brothers-in-law. Despite that goal, he failed, twice.

Gallus himself was soon seized and executed for treason on the orders of Constantius. Julian kept mute about his brother's death, whereupon the emperor appointed him to succeed Gallus as Caesar in Gaul. That suddenly thrust him from a contemplative scholar's life into battle along the Gallic frontiers. Julian surprised all by proving a fearless, capable soldier. He defeated the German tribes and restored the Roman forts along the Rhine.

Ammianus, the chronicler, was an officer in Julian's army. He observed Julian in person but wrote after Julian was gone, lending credibility to his book: He no longer needed to please his chief, which makes the narrative more than the mere sycophancy of a courtier. According to Ammianus, Julian won respect, from veteran officers down to the rank-and-file troops. At this point he still outwardly observed Christian rites. He concealed his private paganism, and it is accordingly downplayed by Ammianus, who was himself a pagan. Ammianus did note the presence of Maximus at Julian's court but offered only limited detail on this mystic, magician, and philosopher. There is even less about Princess Helena, except to note her Christian piety. Ammianus supplies no cause for her death, but another ancient source states that she and a fetus died during childbirth. Julian then ordered her mortal remains carried to Rome for burial. Rome is clearly stated as the place. (The importance of this will be seen later.)

A sharp internal crisis in Rome then ensued upon an order by

Constantius that Julian detach troops to serve with the emperor, whose war against Persia was going poorly. Julian's reluctance escalated into revolt. The army in Gaul hailed Julian as emperor and so compelled events. Julian marched against the ailing Constantius, who ceded the empire to him, then promptly died. Taking the throne, the new Emperor Julian shortly revealed his pagan sympathies, although he urged general religious toleration. His policies included rebuilding the Jewish Temple in Jerusalem. There were significant Jewish communities in the region. Placating them made political sense, given the ongoing Roman struggle against Persia. But mishaps plagued the Temple project. The failure hurt the emperor's stature as he prepared to invade Persia via the Euphrates valley.

At first, the military effort went well: Julian scattered the Persian armies. Leaving the Euphrates, the Roman troops trekked toward the enemy capital of Ctesiphon, situated on the Tigris. Julian ordered most of his supply ships on the Euphrates burned to keep them out of hostile hands as he marched overland. A question then arose of whether or not to beleaguer Ctesiphon. In a council of war, his generals advised him to refrain from a siege. Persia's king Sapor still maintained a mobile field force that could hurt the Romans should they settle into static warfare.

And so Julian turned his men north, away from Ctesiphon. Persian troops harassed them on their way. During one such skirmish near a small place called Phrygia, Julian incurred a mortal wound. It had been prophesied that a king would die at Phrygia, by which Julian had assumed was meant the larger province of that name. But upon learning he was at a "Phrygia," he accepted his fate and expired. He had reigned as emperor for only nineteen months. The surviving Romans bought safe passage out of danger, ceding border lands to Persia. Julian's grandiose dreams had ended in disaster. A resurgent Christianity now made his name anathema.

Ammianus gave a sympathetic yet still believable assessment of Julian. It accords with some other contemporary accounts. In battle, he was brave and level-headed. He eschewed luxury, contenting himself with simple field rations while on campaign. As a magistrate judging cases of official corruption, he was stern but astute and fair.

Julian showed no interest in sex after the princess Helena's death, and so the record is bare of the scandals by which certain other Roman sovereigns are remembered.

Where Ammianus faulted Julian, it was for excessive reliance on portent and prophecy. That was quite a significant censure, since in Roman times rulers normally consulted signs and soothsayers. To Ammianus, Julian took it too far, the appointment of Maximus to his staff being part of that excess. Even so, as Ammianus also records, Julian could show impatience with portents and strike out resolutely once he had made up his mind.

Hitler's affinity for Julian owes both to circumstance and to shared character traits. A widely accepted German tenet postulated the ancient Hellenes to have been of Germanic stock, and Julian self-identified as a Greek. That made him racially acceptable. Both Julian and Hitler announced epoch-making goals and both pursued risky, grandiose plans. Both actively looked to omens for guidance. Both cultivated an image of self-denial. Neither showed much libido and neither sired children, at least none that survived outside the womb. Both gabbed too much, yet both were capable of keeping vital secrets over time. Both men thought they were world redeemers, chosen by Providence. Both rejected Christianity and its clergy, the apostate Adolf while still in junior middle school.

Julian seemed made to mimic, save for one major contrasting point: his handling of the Jews. As emperor, he had tried to rebuild the Temple in Jerusalem so as to attract Jewish support. He thus thwarted the admonition of Christ that the temple would be ruined and remain accursed rubble. The reconstruction effort proved disastrous, however, and presaged the greater disaster in Persia. A Hitler blessed with hindsight could correct these errors. Ibsen, in his own way, had already done so.

IBSEN'S EPIC

The concept for *Emperor and Galilean* first came to Ibsen at Rome in the summer of 1864. He attended a talk by the visiting young

Norwegian historian Lorentz Dietrichson (1834–1917) about Ammianus Marcellinus's book. Dietrichson spoke vibrantly, and Ibsen
glimpsed epic potential in a heady historical play. Writing it demanded
much research, however. Ibsen began to delve into the ancient history,
although he shortly turned to work on *Peer Gynt* and *The League of
Youth.* Those two dramas were completed in Germany, where the
playwright had moved, drawn by the cultural attractions. Then in
1871, events rekindled his resolve. Prussia won a war with France and
united most of the German-speaking lands as a new state. Ibsen saw a
country infused by euphoria as one age passed and another began.

The era of the Second Reich had dawned, and with it came the
Kulturkampf. This struggle for cultural control between the Catholic
church and Germany's chancellor Otto von Bismarck resembled
Julian's battle against Christianity. A papal message of 1864 had
condemned civil marriage and civil education as "errors." Then the
Vatican Council of 1870 asserted a doctrine of papal infallibility,
a challenge to state control in any largely Catholic country. Soon
thereafter, Germany's seizure of Alsace and Lorraine brought major
Catholic populations within the new Reich borders. The Catholic-
affiliated Center party won 58 percent of the German vote in the
Reichstag elections of March 1871. It set a course of church–state
confrontation. Bismarck responded with a decree in 1872 aimed at
wresting German schools out of Catholic control.

Ibsen's Julian project was resumed in mid-1871 against the background of these events. Seeking authenticity, Ibsen consulted Ammianus in a German translation but rejected an essay on Julian by David
Friedrich Strauss as presenting an overly "romantic" Julian. He set
pen to paper on July 24, writing with a new friend, the Danish scholar
Georg Brandes, as an imagined reader. Ibsen liked to ask himself, as he
wrote, "What would G.B. say to this?" But a year later, just three acts
were complete, a low output for the time spent. A refreshing lift came
again in mid-1872 as Ibsen inhaled the alpine air at Berchtesgaden.
It had become a project of fits and starts. That summer, he sent his
publisher an outline of a three-part drama. The first part, comprising
the three acts already done, showed Julian's love for classical learning. The second part, in another three acts, was then being written;

it examined his renunciation of Christianity. The third part was planned for five acts, to dramatize his brief reign as emperor. Then, during the autumn, the writer had a change of heart. He combined the first and second parts into a single five-act play, *Caesar's Apostasy* (Norwegian: *Caesars Frafald*). Left to be written in the new scheme were the five acts of what would be the final part, *The Emperor Julian* (Norwegian: *Kejser Julian*). Ibsen rushed this to completion during the three months from November 1872 to February 1873, and revised no further.

Most roles came out as stereotypes. Only two characters stood forth, these being Julian the Apostate and Maximus the Mystic. As of early February 1873, Ibsen still sought details on Maximus. On February 4, he addressed a letter to the Norwegian professor Ludwig Daae asking for further information.

> There exists a work by a certain Eunapius on Maximus the Mystic.... Can you give me a short account of the contents of the book, which I know is not a classical work? What I especially want are facts relating to the life and career of Maximus. Ammianus does not give many, and there are no other sources available to me.

This was really well past the time for basic fact-checking. Ibsen had depicted Maximus as the greatest single influence on Julian without having consulted the biographical source he now sought. He revealed uncertainty too on whether Eunapius had written in Latin or in Greek. Two days later, without waiting for Daae's answer, Ibsen went ahead and told his publisher:

> I have the great pleasure of being able to inform you that my long work is finished—and more to my satisfaction than any of my earlier works. The title is *Emperor and Galilean*.

Obviously relieved near the end of a long project, he was ready to stick with what he had on paper, whether or not Daae could assist on sources for Maximus. Hand-copying of the entire manuscript lay ahead—a dreary task. In the meantime, Ibsen assured the English critic Edmund Gosse on February 20 that "I have held rigorously to history." But he had not. Within days, Ibsen wrote a chagrined letter to Daae, whose prompt reply had come with a specially prepared seventeen-page translation from Greek to Norwegian of Eunapius's account of Maximus. It was expressly done for Ibsen's reference, yet in vain. Ibsen had let show his ignorance of this main source about a character second only to Julian in his all-but-completed historical drama. To recover from the fumble, he told the helpful Daae,

> I am glad to see that the biography contains nothing that conflicts with what I had read before, and made use of.

But the playwright dissembled. Having used Ammianus, who offered very little on Maximus, Ibsen felt emboldened to maximize the mystic for dramatic effect. That was that. Ibsen's customized Maximus departs significantly from the philosopher described in Eunapius's *Lives of the Sophists*. The Maximus in Ibsen's play is instead a fanciful concoction who incorporates material from Joachim of Fiore, the twelfth-century Christian thinker. Nothing Daae supplied led to any Ibsen revisions. Apart from creative effort, the sheer drudgery of time-consuming hand-recopying doubtless deterred Ibsen from doing much emendation at this late stage. Dialogues between Julian and Maximus form the heart of the play, but they were concocted without reference to the most informative ancient source.

As it turned out, fictionalizing in *Emperor and Galilean* went far beyond the portrayal of Maximus. Ibsen, untrained as an historian, had for all his adult life enjoyed the liberties of a scriptwriter. His mastery lay in shaping plots to develop character. He had achieved success at that craft, but now ventured into something very different. The falsehood lay in promoting a drama as virtual history and getting others to vouch for him. Ibsen's authorized English translator William Archer even risked the superlative: "Of all historical plays it is perhaps the most strictly historical . . . reproduced with extraordinary fidelity."

Not really. Besides Ammianus Marcellinus's account, Ibsen seems to have made only minimal direct resort to other ancient texts. Lines from an essay by Julian do wind up in the play at one point, although mouthed instead by Maximus the Mystic. A valid character study of a figure whose writings are largely extant might be expected to reflect that figure's actual words. Julian's offered authentic grist for dialogue conveying the protagonist's own thoughts. But again, Ibsen substituted wholly imaginary sentences, depriving Julian of his authentic voice.

Ibsen could have referred too to an ancient panegyric on Julian by Libanius, a Roman chronicler, but he appears to have known this work only via a secondary source, that of the nineteenth-century Frenchman Albert de Broglie. Also available in modern translation were relevant writings by Julian's antagonists, principally Gregory of Nazianzus. However, the play text and Ibsen's letters do not confirm direct resort to these materials, even though Ibsen insisted on giving the impression that he had based *Emperor and Galilean* mainly upon ancient sources. Decades after the opus was done, a biographer asked him about his methodology. Ibsen claimed: "I went through and made extracts from a whole series of writers of ecclesiastical history," relying on the holdings of a German library in Rome. These writers went unspecified, but they followed Ibsen's allusion to Ammianus, implying that they were likewise ancient.

Again Ibsen shaded facts. He had read on Julian during the autumn of 1864 after hearing Dietrichson speak, but then became immersed in competing projects. After he left Rome, there is no more evidence of his using library resources for the Julian play, let alone poring through ancient ecclesiastical tomes. His knowledge of fourth-century theology remained sketchy and contains some anachronisms. Elsewhere, he did as schoolboys do:

He cribbed.

Textual analysis has revealed the main Ibsen sources. Chief among them was *L'Eglise et l'Empire romain au IVème siècle* by de Broglie, published in 1864. As one leading Ibsen critic put it, *Emperor and Galilean* amounted to, in large part, a "translation from French." Paraphrase would be a fairer judgment; but the evidence of passages lined up for comparison makes inescapable the finding that Ibsen took from de Broglie consistently and substantially. He adapted de Broglie's narrative prose to spoken dialogue while still claiming to have used primary sources, and without duly acknowledging the extensive resort he had made to the French scholar's recently published book on fourth-century church history.

Ibsen did confirm reading August Neander, who wrote a general history of the church as well as a biography of Julian. Instances of overt copying from Neander's two books and the ones by Auer and Mücke were less frequent than from de Broglie. Ibsen would have been remiss had he not consulted these secondary works while reading for *Emperor and Galilean*. Perhaps he should have consulted, cribbed, and plagiarized more. From the standpoint of accuracy, the problems in his play occur less at places where he copied from informed sources than where he did not. Left on his own, he again did like a schoolboy:

He fibbed.

Emperor and Galilean is history insofar as Ibsen folded in the works of historians. But it is historical fiction, the imaginative often getting significantly beyond the facts as these are known from primary and secondary sources. To be sure, Ibsen had poetic license, although he did insist in private correspondence that he was using his subjective affinity for the Julian character to write historical truth. He wanted to have it both ways.

Precisely how and where Ibsen deviated from the documentary historical record has heretofore mattered only to a tiny circle of Scandinavian literature professors who care about one of the playwright's least-studied works. And even to these learned authorities, the issues of fact versus fiction have been at best very minor concerns. Here, though, they matter.

IBSEN FICTIONS, HITLER FACTS

The fine points matter because Hitler raised the stakes. By borrowing other material from Ibsen, by his penchant for emulative role-play, and then by voicing an interest in Emperor Julian, the Nazi Führer raised the prospect that *Emperor and Galilean* was his motivational source and action blueprint. That makes the particulars of Ibsen's Julian more than an academic quibble. Upping the ante are the cult books touting *Emperor and Galilean* as an "allegory" and anointing Adolf Hitler as the man to make the allegory real in the flesh. The instances where Ibsen fudged or shaded facts give his Julian identifiable features. These serve as litmus tests to differentiate Ibsen's Julian from all other treatments, whether historical, novelistic, or theatrical.

The goal here is to determine whether the Julian of the Ibsen play was the Julian that Hitler had in mind when he compared his own enterprise to that of the apostate Roman emperor. Among the aspects of the Julian story where Ibsen embroidered or invented, there are some that foreshadow the words and deeds of Hitler.

OVERCOMING "BLINDNESS"

Early in *Caesar's Apostasy,* Ibsen's Julian refers repeatedly to Christianity as blindness. Counterposed to the blindness is paganism, likened to the recovery of eyesight. This Ibsen usage reduces to a simplistic duality what was actually a pluralistic religious situation in the Roman empire. It downplays what Julian copied from Christianity, such as his attempt to establish a state-sponsored paganism under the discipline of a churchlike hierarchical organization. With regard too to Julian, the metaphoric apposition of blindness and sight has the effect of dating his private turn away from Christian belief to a time earlier in his career than the historical sources can support.

MAXIMUS THE MYSTIC

Maximus was a mystical neo-Platonist, as Eunapius made clear in *Lives of the Sophists.* Yet instead of giving him neo-Platonic lines, Ibsen had his Maximus quoting the Bible. A pivotal instance is a speech reciting the First Commandment from Exodus followed quickly by an allusion to the initial sentence from the Gospel of St. John. This odd, telltale scriptural juxtaposition eventually found its way into ramblings by Hitler.

Ibsen also scripted his Maximus to conduct a séance, to doctor Julian's wine with a hallucinogenic substance, and to utter prophecies that are found nowhere in the historical sources. It is this fictional Maximus who vainly tries to get Julian to comprehend the great paradox of the Ibsen play: that Julian is simultaneously a reincarnation of Jesus and also the one ordained to take humanity beyond a corrupted Christian religion. He whom Christian clergymen would condemn as the Anti-Christ is therefore none other Christ himself, returned to earth.

A THIRD REICH

Ibsen's Maximus foresaw a third Reich in world history, combining the first Reich of pagan Hellenistic learning together with the second Reich of Christ. Julian was supposed to be the one to seal this synthesis by the upcoming year 365. Then a Great Year would have passed, in length the same number of years since Jesus' putative birth year as there are days in a year. But this "third Reich" does not occur anywhere in sources from Julian's times. Of all the many literary productions about the apostate emperor, only one—the play by Ibsen—projected the third-Reich idea back onto the Julian story.

"Third Reich" is actually a medieval term tracing back to Joachim of Fiore in the twelfth century. Even then, it was permeated with the idea of a world-altering new age. A few decades before Ibsen wrote this play, the term "third Reich" also turned up in a literary essay by Ludolf Wienbarg. Ibsen's usage cast the "third Reich" within a Hegelian historical dialectic of thesis, antithesis, and synthesis, which took on political shading for Germans. Readers of *Emperor and Galilean* during the German Second Reich, from 1871 to 1918, could hardly miss inferring that some grand transformation still loomed.

THE DEATH OF PRINCESS HELENA

Julian's wife Helena is known dimly from fourth-century historical sources. She was the sister of the Caesar Gallus's wife who had earlier died of a fever before Gallus was executed for treason, as Ammianus related in his Book XIV.11. The passing of these two women was merely incidental. Yet Ibsen goes far beyond Ammianus to make their deaths a major plot element. After Helena departs, the Julian of *Caesar's Apostasy* discerns a pattern, construing the death of his wife as a prerequisite for the attempt by Julian, the Caesar, to become emperor. He concludes that she was murdered and that he could be next. With Helena gone, Julian overcomes his hesitation and resolves to overthrow the emperor Constantius.

The Ibsen play resorts to pure embroidery. Ancient sources agree that Julian had no deep emotional attachment to Helena, but for Ibsen's Julian she was the love of his life. In Ammianus's text, Book XXI.1.5, the death of Helena was reported without any suspicion of foul play; Ibsen had Helena succumb after tasting a gift of poisoned fruit. Ammianus stated nothing about infidelity; Ibsen had her bearing a child sired by someone other than Julian. Ammianus had Julian send Helena's body off to Rome for burial, and he did not escort her remains; Ibsen arbitrarily changed the burial place to Vienne (in Gaul), and had Julian accompany her corpse there for a dramatic scene of soul-searching.

JULIAN'S SHIELD BREAKS OFF FROM ITS HANDLE

In Book XXI.3.1 of his history, Ammianus recounted an incident on the drilling field of a military camp while Julian still only bore the rank of Caesar. He was practicing swordplay when the joints of his shield gave way, which left him holding just the handle. The accident dismayed those present, who saw an adverse omen. A quick-witted Julian reassured them, saying:

> Let no one be alarmed. I shall hold firmly on to what I had before.

Not content with this narrative, Ibsen reworked the mishap. The venue becomes a tournament: that is, a public spectacle more fraught with symbolism, should anything go awry. Whereas Julian's defensive words as given by Ammianus were resolute, those in Part II of the play *Caesar's Apostasy* show Julian's aggressive ambition. Rebounding from the broken-shield mishap, Julian leaps impulsively onto his horse, in the process jostling a retainer who falls to the ground. Julian takes this as a sign of the end of Emperor Constantius.

> I knocked over the man who was helping me into the saddle; that seems to point to a sudden fall for Constantius, to whom I owe my elevation.

REBUILDING THE TEMPLE AT JERUSALEM

Ammianus in his Book XXIII.1.2 gave a simple motive for why Julian ordered the Temple at Jerusalem rebuilt: The emperor wanted "a great monument to perpetuate the memory of his reign." But fires forced abandonment of the project. That is all. Ammianus drew no great significance from this.

Ibsen, however, places the episode squarely in a context of religious confrontation. Recalling how Christ stated that "no stone would stand upon another," Ibsen presents Emperor Julian's attempt to rebuild the structure as a calculated taunt against Christ "the Galilean," who had hexed the Temple site. Faithful Christians in the play then attribute the mysterious explosions and fires at the Temple to a higher wrath, which was directed against Julian. The building effort and Julian's whole enterprise are thus ill-fated. The clear implication is that instead of trying to restore the Jews' Temple, he should have accepted the divine will for its destruction. The Temple episode marks a fateful omen for the disastrous war that shortly follows.

WAR AND PEACE WITH PERSIA

In the account by Ammianus, Persia made ceaseless war against Rome through the reigns of Constantius and then Julian. The Romans had been losing until Julian took over as emperor and launched an attack down the Euphrates valley. There was no recorded peace treaty, no cessation of hostilities. But Ibsen invented a non-aggression pact in *Emperor and Galilean,* Part Two. The playwright had the Persian king Sapor propose peace to Julian, who accepted. Shortly thereafter, Ibsen's Julian annulled their agreement and invaded the Persian lands.

VEERING AWAY FROM THE ENEMY CAPITAL

The contemporary accounts of Ammanius and Libanius both relate how Julian turned northward away from the Persian capital of Ctesiphon after reaching its outskirts. Here are the circumstances from these historical accounts: False defectors tricked the Romans into burning their boats and marching toward Ctesiphon, where the city was said to be ready to surrender and hand over its supplies. But Persian scorched-earth and guerrilla tactics placed Julian's army at risk. It was the Roman generals in a council of war who then advised Julian to march away from Ctesiphon, to the north.

Ibsen changed the nuance: Julian is at first tempted to march against Ctesiphon but then recognizes the Persian trap. The historical fact that the Roman army actually reached and circumvented Ctesiphon is not at all clear from *Emperor and Galilean.* To Ibsen, the decision to veer northward away from Ctesiphon is undertaken by Julian alone. Even so, Julian confidently declares that Ctesiphon can wait; he will eventually conquer it. He commands the Roman army by inspired intuition.

ANTI-CHRISTIAN MEASURES

For all Julian's anti-Christian invective, his own writings are devoid of violent threats against the faithful for their religion alone. He proselytized, propagandized, and satirized. Yet nothing in the historical record shows Julian initiating any slaughter of Christians solely because of their faith. Even church historians at the time conceded that Julian had not launched any violent persecution. The very denial of martyrdom galled Julian's severest contemporary Christian critic, Gregory of Nazianzus. Gregory complained how the emperor might look the other way when pagan mobs attacked Christians, but that he himself preferred argument to physical repression.

> Besides his other motives, he begrudged the honor of martyrdom to our combatants, and for this reason he contrives now to use compulsion, and yet not [let us] gain honor as though suffering for Christ's sake.

The real Julian had cheated the Christians out of their martyrdom. Ibsen, however, wanted a bloodthirsty Julian for dramatic effect. In Part Two, he had the emperor order executions and vow to exterminate the Christians after his Persian war, win or lose. Christianity is rescued only by the Apostate's death at the end of the final act. Maximus then vows: "The third Reich will come!"

THE DEATH OF JULIAN

Ammianus was present with the Roman army in Persia. In his Book XXV.3.6, he stated the uncertainty prevailing at the time about who had delivered Julian's mortal wound. "Suddenly a cavalry spear, directed by no one knows whom, grazed his arm, pierced his ribs, and lodged in the lower part of his liver."

Ibsen, as a dramatist, added drama. Shortly before Julian is wounded (Part Two, Act V), he thinks he hears singing in the air. It comes from the "Galileans" (i.e., Christians) in Julian's own army. Then Ibsen adduces a Christian soldier among the Romans, Agathon, who hurls a spear at Julian. Agathon shouts "With Christ, for Christ! The Roman's spear from Golgotha!" But it cannot be just any spear. In the play, Julian's wound is inflicted by the relic spear of Longinus, the centurion who delivered the coup de grace to an agonized Jesus on the cross.

IBSEN'S JULIAN/CHRIST

In the Ibsen version, Julian's end thus becomes an act of Christian vengeance. It comes in a manner, though, that connects the person of Julian with that of Christ. The essential paradox of the play is thus mystically maintained.

When all was done, the playwright realized that his belabored product had come out awkwardly suited for stage production. It was meant for reading, as Ibsen stated in a letter to Edmund Gosse: "I wished to produce the impression on the reader that what he was reading was something that actually had happened." Imagination would best substitute for performance. *Emperor and Galilean* remained longish even when truncated to two parts. Its cast was large and costly. Producing *The Emperor Julian* presumed that audiences of *Caesar's Apostasy* would want to sit through a second round of five acts.

The first German translation of the script came in 1888, although there were no German stage recitals until 1896, in Leipzig, and two years later in Berlin. A decade later, the first part played for a month, again in Berlin. As Ibsen's popularity gained among Germans, there were more performances: at Riga in 1910, Düsseldorf in 1911, and Hamburg in 1915.

But Adolf Hitler saw none of these. He seems never to have been present in a city where the play was being performed. And since *Emperor and Galilean* never had a film version, the only possible medium by which Hitler could know of it had to be through reading—and in German, as he had no reading facility in Norwegian.

Still, can it be firmly ascertained that a reading of this work by

Ibsen was what sparked and sustained Hitler's interest in Julian? After the Ibsen play, a spate of materials continued to gush forth on the subject. Johan B. Fastenau wrote a novel published in 1888. From the pen of Marie Tyrol came a three-volume novel in 1889. Felix Dahn went on to fictionalize Julian as the naïve tool of evil advisers in yet another three-volume novel, in 1893. Nikolaus Heim wrote a book in 1902 applauding the victory of the church over Julian. Julian's own works, translated to German, became available in an affordably priced multi-volume series titled *Kaiser Julians Philosophische Werke.* Wilhelm Vollert offered a treatise on the Apostate's theology. And there were still more plays by minor German dramatists in 1876, 1881, 1894, 1904, and 1905.

When Ibsen died in 1906, August Strindberg paid tribute with a short prose piece on Julian called "Apostata." This followed *Emperor and Galilean* in the emphasis given to Maximus the Mystic and to the attempted rebuilding of the Temple in Jerusalem. Strindberg included a line attributed to the churchman Eusebius, who says of Julian: "He lived like a Christ and taught himself as did Christ, yet he is a despiser of Christ."

In Zürich about 1910, the psychoanalyst and neo-pagan Carl Jung was drawn in his turn to Julian. And broad interest continued to pick up. Stories by Adam Josef Cüppers, Gerhard Hennes, and Therese Kellner were set against the background of Julian's era. A balanced scholarly biography, the first in German for a half-century since Auer and Neander, was that of Johannes Geffcken, whose *Kaiser Julianus* came out in 1914. The Catholic writer Johannes Mayrhofer novelized Julian the sun-worshiper in 1918, as did the Germano-Christian propagandist Friedrich Doldinger in 1926. As of 1918, German readers moreover had a translation of an 1894 Russian novel on Julian by Dmitry S. Merezhkovsky, which appeared as part of a trilogy titled *Christ and Anti-Christ.*

Yet another of Julian's (and Hitler's) admirers was Savitri Devi (née Maximiani Portas), a Greco-French convert to Hinduism who preached an Aryan racialist reaction against Judeo-Christianity. Her 1939 book, *A Warning to the Hindus*, bore a dedication: "To Divine Julian, Emperor of the Greeks and Romans. May future India make his impossible dream a living reality, from one ocean to the other."

So Julian was hot stuff, and especially so in the German-speaking lands of the late nineteenth and early twentieth centuries. This was the time of a new, self-conscious pagan revival and of unresolved debate about whether Christianity could ever be made sufficiently Germanic. Adolf Hitler had no lack of choices for reading fare on Julian, pro and con.

Nevertheless, the Führer squarely discounts himself from having read any of Julian's own works prior to October 1941:

> I really hadn't known how clearly a man like Julian had judged the Christians and Christianity. One must read this.

These remarks are of a man in the flush of enthusiasm, only just acquainted with a sampling of the emperor's prose. He had known well enough about Julian, but had not hitherto been aware of Julian's clarity as a writer against Christianity. Therefore, Hitler cannot have read too deeply, either, among the many prose works that mention Julian as a cogent stylist. Of all the abundant secondary items on Julian, Hitler could conceivably have had some glancing acquaintance with the novel by Felix Dahn since on February 17, 1942, he did mention Dahn as among those who "reach a fairly high level," but without specifying any of his titles.

Narrowing the field still further, the only other piece to flag as Hitler's likely principal source about Julian is the two-part Ibsen drama. It is explicitly known on the word of Hitler's roommate, August Kubizek, that he did read Ibsen's plays in the spring of 1908. Also known from the same informant is that he then chose pagan defiance of Christianity as the theme for a playwriting try of his own. Both bits of information from 1908 must be deemed credible. Kubizek maintained no special agenda to associate Hitler with the author of *Emperor and Galilean*.

But besides explicitly admiring Julian in his remarks of 1941 and going so far as to identify his own earthly mission with that of Julian,

Hitler is also on record as identifying himself too with Jesus Christ. The Führer embraced an Aryanized Christ even as he forswore Judeo-Christianity and strove to uproot the faith as propounded by all established churches, Catholic and Protestant alike. That rejection of Christianity while nevertheless aligning his own person both with Julian and with Christ makes a bizarre and hopelessly contradictory mix—unless some factor operated to resolve the paradox.

Resolution may be had through just one literary piece. Only one portrayal amongst all the works of history and literature describes Jesus the Christ and Julian the Antichrist as the very same soul in successive human incarnations—and bound to return to earth. Such a figure derives neither from Julian as he saw himself nor as told by any historian, any novelist, nor any dramatist besides Ibsen. It is not the Julian of Ammianus Marcellinus, Libanius, or Gregory of Nazianzus among the emperor's ancient friends, chroniclers, and foes. Among moderns available for Hitler to have read in German, such a figure is incompatible with Julian the Apostate as interpreted by the scholars Neander or Auer. It is not the emperor Julian made animate by more than half a dozen minor dramatists besides Ibsen, and not the Julian narrated by the prose authors Lübker, Mücke, Geffcken, Vollert, Merezhkovsky, Fastenau, Dahn, Cüppers, Hennes, Kellner, Doldinger, Mayrhofer, Heim, or Marie Tyrol. The dual figure of Jesus-cum-Julian—that is, of Christ and Antichrist portrayed as united in one human body—appeared in no work other than the Julian from Henrik Ibsen's two-part play, *Emperor and Galilean.*

As with *An Enemy of the People,* Hitler would indeed come to paraphrase telltale lines out of *Emperor and Galilean.* But he did not recite them verbatim. Which translation he read thus remains guess-work. Several editions were available. The Reclam publishing house in Leipzig and the S. Fischer firm in Berlin each put out the complete plays of Ibsen in multi-volume sets, the translations respectively by Ernst Brausewetter and Paul Hermann. Reclam was a nineteenth-century pioneer in economically priced paperback books. There were several Reclam editions of Ibsen over the years with various plays bound together. An 1889 printing had combined three plays in one volume, these being *The League of Youth, An Enemy of the People,* and *Emperor and Galilean.* Unfortunately, it cannot be determined if Hitler read this edition. But that he did read *Emperor and Galilean* seems all but certain, on the same sort of evidence that shows him to have read *An Enemy of the People.*

7

AN ALLEGORY OF THE TIMES

I have seen the characters before my eyes in the
light of their age, and I hope that my readers will do
the same.

—IBSEN DISCUSSING *EMPEROR AND GALILEAN*,
IN A LETTER, FEBRUARY 23, 1873

I T IS CLEAR that Hitler felt more than mere nostalgia for Julian's pagan last stand. Visitors sometimes noticed. Leon Degrelle, leader of the Belgian Nazis, observed:

> He knew Julian the Apostate as if he had been his contemporary.

Degrelle had made but passing mention of Hitler's alleged (and mostly dubious) readings of Aristotle, Plato, Nietzsche, Tacitus, Mommsen, Clausewitz, the Bible, the Talmud, Thomist philosophy, Homer, Sophocles, Livy, and Cicero. Julian, however, was singled out. If Degrelle had any clue about the Führer's source(s) for the Apostate, he kept it to himself. He probably had not troubled to ask.

Here the asking and the testing must finally be done, with probable cause to suspect Ibsen's "prophetic" play. Given the Ibsen associations already shown for Hitler, it becomes germane—no, urgent—to determine what (if anything) he knew of *Emperor and Galilean;* and, if he knew it well, what impact (if any) the play had on his plans. The unique features of that play should assist in solving whether it was truly Hitler's fount.

This is not a footnote, not a sideshow, not a bookish fluke. A lot of big-ticket History hangs in the balance if the Führer was following a script. The inquiry should therefore be rigorously empirical. To be credible and significant, specifics of the play must correlate to specific Hitler actions. Distant vibes do not suffice. A direct impact is what counts, demonstrable by a sustained pattern of matching words and deeds. Either the Führer knew this Ibsen script, or he did not. Either it demonstrably swayed the moves he made, or it did not. Only hard textual and historical data will do. Since the inquiry gauges the practical impact on a murderous despot of a provocative literary work, the idiom of literary criticism comes up.

PARAPHRASE, PLAGIARISM, CRYPTAMNESIA, INFLUENCE, INTERTEXTUALITY, IMITATION

Verbatim quotations from *Emperor and Galilean* are lacking among Hitler's extant words. If they were present, the task would be no task at all. Instead, what may be sought consists of reworked *paraphrase*, like those pentimenti of *An Enemy of the People* discernible in *Mein Kampf.* Such adapted paraphrases indicate not only that Hitler knew a particular play, but that he had subsumed its message into his own thoughts. Separate instances of paraphrasing occurring over time show those thoughts to be not transient, but embedded. Ad-lib paraphrase actually reveals more than quotation, precisely because it is extemporaneous. As such, it offers a deeper glimpse into the mind of the man. Quotation, by contrast, is contrived, a product of deliberation. To render a quote accurately entails consulting the source text and mulling over where to begin quoting and where to stop. Quotation can thus mask or mislead as much as it reveals. But Hitler paraphrased, adapting as he did so for his own needs of the moment. If *Emperor and Galilean* resonated from time to time over the years in the form of off-the-cuff paraphrases, that circumstance indicates that the play had taken up permanent residency status in the Führer's psyche, warped to his reading of the text.

In a technical sense, it is accurate to state that the Hitler paraphrase from *An Enemy of the People,* Act IV, in *Mein Kampf,* chapter 3 amounts to plagiarism. That is because *Mein Kampf* was dished up purportedly as a book: written, edited, printed, bound, and distributed for sale by a publishing house. Enough of the play showed up in the Hitler memoir to confidently state that a copy of the Ibsen script had to have been present, pages open, in the Führer's cell at Landsberg fortress prison. But *Mein Kampf* made no real pretension to be literature; it is basically a rambling spoken harangue dictated to a scribe, Rudolf Hess. The trace of *An Enemy of the People* in *Mein Kampf* thus has similar value to the subsequent shorter trace of that same act, same play, in Hitler's "Table Talk" eighteen years later. Both were morsels ingested and regurgitated in speech. That is their real worth. With eight decades having elapsed now, it may be impractical to sue Hitler for theft of intellectual property. But far more consequentially, it is never too late to show how his thorough absorption of a playwright's works replayed as historical events.

For present purposes, the further paraphrases from *Emperor and Galilean* will also serve as markers, like a chalked "Kilroy was here," showing that Hitler knew the play about Julian and knew it well. Such paraphrases may occur only rarely over the years. Taken together, they constitute but a tiny fraction of all that Hitler ever said. But if they occur at all, solid and unambiguous, then that fact is significant. Some phrases are more equal than others. A few convincing, close-enough paraphrased lines from Ibsen plays are sufficient to show that the theatrically absorbed leader of the Third Reich had these dramas in mind, either consciously or stirring below in the depths of his memory.

Conscious borrowing is usually the decisive factor in cases of literary plagiarism when one author has sought to profit from the work of another without proper attribution. Yet a subtler form of purloining occurs as well. The term *cryptamnesia* covers the phenomenon where borrowed material is absorbed so fully that the source is not recalled when a thought comes to mind or emerges in speech. A speaker may mistake such a thought for his or her own. Whole literary works have occasionally been inspired in this less-than-original way, a well-known example being that of Vladimir Nabokov's novel *Lolita*, published in 1955, which followed a very similar story of the same title by Heinz von Eschwege-Lichberg, published in 1916. Similarly, a study of recurrent keywords and approximate phrases has shown Albert Camus's novel *La Chute* (*The Fall*) to have drawn heavily on an eighteenth-century work by Denis Diderot, *Le Neveu de Rameau* (*Rameau's Nephew*). Camus even has his narrator wondering whether his ideas were original or picked up from an elusive source, read or heard somewhere. After the instance cited in *Mein Kampf*, Hitler's spoken paraphrases to Ibsen's plays may likewise be attributed to cryptamnesia. The hold of these scripts on the dictator was all the more compelling given his easy, uncontrived recall of certain passages. Hitler had doubtless read the scripts more than once, for their lines to so thoroughly mesh with the web of his own thoughts.

Along with unconsciously paraphrased words in Hitler's case come parallel deeds—i.e., things he did that match episodes in the suspected source script. These repeated deeds, unlike the paraphrased words, can only have been the product of conscious calculation. Such occurrences of parallel actions work in tandem with the verbal paraphrases, so that word and deed mutually reinforce one another to pinpoint the source text. Taken alone, of course, no single matching instance can be judged conclusive. Each pair in isolation might be attributed to mere random chance. Only when an Ibsen script matches Hitler's deeds in a sequential, sustained pattern can it be said that the limits of randomness have been surpassed. Every Hitler-initiated deed having consistent particulars recalling an episode in the suspect text may thus be treated as a de facto, non-verbal allusion to the text. What narrowed the focus onto this suspect text, *Emperor and Galilean*, for this writer was the thrice-explicated Hitler allusion to emperor Julian in 1941–42.

Is it accurate then to say that Ibsen "influenced" Hitler?

No. The term woefully understates. If mere *influence* were the issue, there would be no issue. Literary influence is soft, easy to allege but often too vague to yield definite proof. A case in point involves

Nietzsche's oft-supposed influence on Hitler. There exists no confirming evidence that Hitler ever read anything Nietzsche wrote. That lack has not dispelled a persistent belief in some Nietzschean sway, since influence can be filtered via other writers or diffused through the culture at large. Paul Schulze-Berghof formulated a synthesis of Nietzsche and Ibsen; that by itself makes a case for second-hand Nietzschean "influence" on Hitler; but like most claimed influence, it is too nonspecific to be of practical use. By contrast, this present inquest on Ibsen's *Emperor and Galilean* far transcends amorphous influence or, for that matter, intertextuality.

A hallmark of postmodern critical thought, *intertextuality* has sometimes been loosely applied to quotation, plagiarism, allusion, and conscious or subconscious influence. When first coined in the 1960s, however, the term introduced something subtler in nuance—the deeper relations of texts within a culture. By this view, no text's meaning should be considered in isolation from other texts. All texts are derivative and contingent, via their shared language. Intertextual theory downplays authorship, demoting authors to mere conduits for cultural currents existing among texts and outside of texts as well. Events too are part of intertextual discourse, since events are textually conditioned; and, in turn, events act to shape texts. That aspect of intertextual theory recalls Hitler's actions patterned on a particular text, which was in turn but one node on a web of texts about Julian the Apostate. Lest Hitler be promoted to postmodern guru, however, it need be remembered that although intertextuality was only articulated as such in the 1960s and 1970s, the workings described by the term were around all along. Thus, if the phenomenon known as "Adolf Hitler" was postmodern or intertextual, then so too were others in his milieu. Anyway, "intertextuality" (like "influence") is just too airy to be of practical help.

"Supratextual" or "metahistorical" *imitation* may more aptly cover Hitler's preposterous private program. Here was a psychopathically contrived, item-by-item adaptation of a drama script onto the world stage, complete with real blood and a cast of (unwitting) millions. The present, no-frills sleuthing task is to lay out the evidence that this is what occurred: The facts, ma'am, just the facts.

An inspirational (if not indeed instructional) prompt was Schulze-Berghof's 1923 book calling the suspected source play "an allegory [of the times]," followed by his novel the next year that all but named Hitler as Julian the Apostate's modern heir. The German for "allegory" is *Zeitsinnbild*, a compound built of words respectively meaning "time," "mind," and "picture." That is, in German the idea of history recycled over time is suggested more strongly than by the prosaic English word "allegory." Schulze-Berghof's essay and subsequent novel conveyed an invitation to a literal-minded Hitler for taking up Julian's cause as told by Henrik Ibsen. But a minor figure like Paul Schulze-Berghof does not conceive such notions out of the clear blue. They fit a contemporary context.

"Life imitates Art" comes up as more than mere cliché. The aphorism appeared in an essay by Oscar Wilde published first in 1889. Wilde continued, "Life is in fact the mirror and Art the reality. . . . Life imitates art far more than Art imitates life." This, along with Wilde's idea of life itself as an art form, was known in the German-speaking world by the time Hitler came of age. And in 1922 another Irishman offered an ancient fable recast as modern novel. It existed as a consciously contrived masterpiece of intertextuality before anyone coined the term. Some call it the most profound fictional work of the twentieth century: James Joyce's *Ulysses* reset Homer's *Odyssey* onto the streets of Dublin with the whole tale's action compressed into just one day. Odysseus is Leopold Bloom on June 16, 1904. Joycean incidents stalk Homeric episodes in faithful sequence. Allusions to the Greek tale crop up in Dublin dialogue. *Ulysses* was at once derivative yet original, parody yet homage. Its concept generated comment among Germans well before it appeared in their language in 1927, *Ulysses'* first translation. To know of *Ulysses'* existence was (and is) to know the book's premise. On extant evidence it cannot be determined whether Hitler read reviews of *Ulysses* before 1927 or, eventually, the work itself in three hefty German volumes. *Ulysses* figured at the least in the 1920s background.

Anyway, whether the Führer was knowing or not, here is an analogy on analogies to put the issue in perspective: The *Odyssey* is to Leopold Bloom as *Emperor and Galilean* is to Adolf Hitler. What remains is to provide documentary evidence for the latter. Ibsen lightened the task by those peculiarities that distinguish his play from all other treatments of Julian the Apostate. Selected episodes reappear in a Hitlerian ritual guise.

To mime the plot of a literary work over the course of years is to conduct a form of ritual, the essence of ritual practice being its analogy to the sacred. If Hitler restaged *Emperor and Galilean* as allegory, then signpost events can be expected to crop up. Considered in isolation, they will puzzle an observer as seemingly irrational, accidental, even helter-skelter. But as rituals in a series keyed to the script, they become explicable. One set of examples involves Hitler's choice of his niece as a putative consort, followed by the bizarre circumstances of her death and then of her burial. Another example is the breakage of a ceremonial silver hammer as the Führer affixed a plaque to dedicate an art museum. Such small events seem to have no larger ramifications. Yet when taken in series along with Hitler's paraphrases from the script, these seeming incidentals substantiate the script's guiding role. The ritual character of more consequential actions then becomes apparent. One example is *Reichskristallnacht* ("Crystal Night"), the demonstrative torching of synagogues throughout the Reich in November 1938. Here was a timed destruction of Jewish temples having its own analog in the Ibsen script, both events being preludes to a looming war. Another example is the Hitler–Stalin pact of August 1939. As a purely diplomatic move it stunned the world, although anyone plotting Hitler's progress through the script of *Emperor and Galilean* would not have been surprised. The short-lived pact came right on cue. So too did its rupture, by Hitler.

In this scripted game, the shooting of a niece, the breaking of a hammer, the burning of temples, the signing of a treaty, and the launching of a war are events of a common denominator. Notwithstanding their disparity in magnitude, all were of ritual character since they all came on cue, matching episodes in a script. Moves of wider consequence—e.g., the war—may exhibit some features of compromise that facilitated their practical implementation. They fulfilled a dual purpose, being diplomatic or strategic as well as merely ritual. Yet their underlying imitative, ritual nature in an overall series is borne out precisely by the more trivial, meticulously staged events with analogies in the script. The features of these, too particular to replicate by chance, offer proof of the game. The devil, as always, is in the details. Had the fact of a guiding script been realized at the time, then its predictive value would have been incalculable. If only. Intelligence analysts spend their lifetimes hoping for such breaks. As it happened, the pettier ritual acts went unnoticed, at least as patterned events. No one (or almost no one) suspected any pattern, let alone where that guiding pattern might have originated. Time passed and war came. With the world in flames, no one was disposed to study the dictator's petty bygone foibles for anything so far-fetched as a pattern matching a theatrical script. And, to be fair to the intelligence analysts, the record of Hitler's spoken words substantiating what he knew of *Emperor and Galilean* became available only after the end of the largest mimetic deeds: the invasion of Russia during World War II, and the Holocaust.

Ritual mimicry may best describe the artful reenacting of a scripted set of deeds, but the exercise could hardly have been art for art's sake. So why do it? Whip in hand, Hitler spelled out a motive at the very start. This same motive is expounded in the pseudo-*Dialogues* Eckart wrote. It was about Christ—and, inevitably, about the Jews. The earthly mission of Christ "the Galilean" (thereby Aryan, thereby pagan) savior had been resistance to the Jews. St. Paul, née Saul, a Jew, then usurped Christ's message and devised Christianity as a cynical Jewish ploy. But Christ will return again, to take up the struggle in some revamped guise. Maximus the Mystic explained in *Emperor and Galilean:*

> There is one who always reappears at certain intervals in the life of the human species.... Who knows how often he has walked among us, unrecognized by any man?

He—i.e. the chosen one, i.e. the great soul—was Christ returned as Julian the Apostate. Maximus the Mystic again, addressing his pupil:

Are you sure, Julian, that you were not in him whom you now persecute?

Most casual readers of *Emperor and Galilean,* being people with families, jobs, and normal lives to live, would variously find this message provocative, heretical, or insane. Casual readers plow through such stuff, then set it down and get back to their families, jobs, and lives. The phrases of the play do not trip from their lips. Adolf Hitler was not such a casual reader, however. The play's phrases do echo in his words, again and again. He likened his mission to Julian's own. But Julian had gotten it wrong on at least three counts. First, the emperor failed to realize that he was the latest incarnation of the great soul that successively reappears on earth. Second, Julian had attacked the wrong foe, namely Christ—i.e., his own former avatar. And third, as a Hitler tutored by Eckart had to believe, Julian had aligned with the falsest of friends, namely the Jews. Hence Julian's "third Reich" was doomed to abort. While Julian was correct to repudiate Christianity, he had gone about it all wrong. The proper path was to run through the script again, but this time to embrace "the Galilean" and uproot the Jewish pest.

A man whose casual speech repeats phrases from such a play has evidently taken its message to heart. A rootless man who is truly convinced that he is the "one who always reappears at certain intervals in the life of the human species" is, however, faced with an existential imperative. Setting the script aside is simply not an option. He cannot walk away. He must take up the cause, learn from past errors, apply the lessons learned, and strive to persist where his predecessor failed. It is all there, in *Emperor and Galilean,* the script itself supplying the life's mission to such an imbued reader. Thus is decreed the purpose in adapting, updating, and restaging this "prophetic" play. The effort cannot have been blindly imitative. Rather, it represents a deliberate pacing through the acts and scenes, choosing the key parts, gliding over the rest, righting the wrongs and correcting the mistakes until a point has been reached when the success that eluded Julian can, finally, be grasped.

For whom would Hitler do it? Not for an audience of mortals, his peers in this world of mere flesh. If he were convinced, truly convinced of his ordained role, then he could only have done it for the higher Power dispatching the "one who always reappears." The motivation issues from a cosmic plane, as Hitler hinted more than once.

What follows is an inquest into the evidentiary grounds for such a finding. Only hard evidence can demonstrate whether this psychotic theater maven literally construed the script of *Emperor and Galilean* as a quasi-scriptural "allegory" with himself cast by Providence to make the allegory real. If he did so, then the madman's actions should match episodes from the play. To be sure, not every episode from the Ibsen epic correlates to something Hitler wrought. But quite a few seemingly do. The first such action of life imitating art dates to 1924. It is Hitler's narrative, in *Mein Kampf,* of his temporary blindness near the end of World War I. This evolved *Mein Kampf* account of 1924 must be distinguished from Hitler's actual war wound sustained in 1918.

BLIND MAN'S BUFF

Part One, Act I of *Emperor and Galilean* introduces Julian's quest for truth. Craving enlightenment, he figuratively refers to himself as blind. Ibsen underscores the metaphor when Julian happens to jostle a genuinely sightless beggar on the street. Julian scolds the man:

> JULIAN: Look where you're going, friend!
> BLIND MAN: Who are you, making fun of a blind brother?
> JULIAN: Your brother in unbelief and blindness.

In subsequent instances, blindness is again used rhetorically to lambaste Christian belief. Seeking truth beyond church dogma, Julian approaches a pagan philosopher:

> JULIAN: I'm as much in the dark as ever.
> PHILOSOPHER: There exists a whole world of splendor which you
>   Galileans are blind to.... You Galileans have banished truth. See how

we [pagans] bear the blows of fate. See how, with wreaths upon our brow, we hold our heads erect.

Pagans proudly wear wreaths even as they bear the blows of fate. While still vacillating between Christianity and paganism, Julian is then moved to exclaim "How blind I have been!" Later, as a confirmed pagan, he looks back to his days as a Christian and tells a friend:

I was blind then, as you are now. I only knew the way which stops at doctrine.

In Part Two, Ibsen confirms the contrast with a sharp disputation between Julian and a bishop named Maris. The bishop is old, frail—and blind. Blindness is Julian's consistent metaphor for Christianity, starting at the initial phase of the two-part, ten-act drama. He embarks on a quest first for mystical vision and then for political power.

Hitler duly followed, working with the same metaphor, one that held a deeply personal meaning for him. While still a soldier, he underwent treatment as an ocular patient after exposure to searing gas on the battlefield. According to his military service record, he became incapacitated at La Montagne, near Ypres, on October 14, 1918. A casualty-clearing station tagged him for evacuation to Germany.

Corporal Hitler was relatively lucky among the gas casualties of the Great War, having neither incurred respiratory complications nor endured damage to his retinal tissue. Within a few days he recovered full vision, convalescing at a military hospital in Pasewalk. By his own account, he was able to read books there, in the last month of the war, while fighting still raged in France and Flanders. Many a gas victim from the trenches would have envied him that. Patient Hitler had suffered some sharp physical pain in the short term, and had faced the racking trauma of uncertainty, but he had escaped lasting impairment.

Three years after the event, Hitler alluded to his wounding in an autobiographical statement (dated November 29, 1921) confirming that he had regained his eyesight within a short time. He had been fit for duty by November 9, 1918, just as revolution broke out in Germany and the war came to a halt. The corporal soon rejoined his unit at its base in Munich. In his account, Hitler offers up this incident cut and dried, without any special significance, as just one episode in his life. Nothing he says in this 1921 statement hints of a recovery followed by a relapse. His release from Pasewalk on November 13, 1918 is consistent with recuperation, but not at all with a recurrence of sightlessness on November 9 or 10, as he subsequently alleged. Not until 1923 does any printed record of the story attach the battlefield trauma to any Hitlerian epiphany. Thereafter, Hitler would connect his week of eye inflammation with his subsequently learning about the German revolution and the armistice a month later. That is, sometime between late 1921 and early 1923, the Führer decided to capitalize on the 1918 wound and treat it with allegorical weight.

He is said to have begun an autobiography during 1922, then postponed the effort. If it is true that he embarked then on writing his life story, then how he could best present the brief interlude of discomfort obviously comprised a narrative challenge. A frontline brush with poison gas would inevitably be refracted through the prism of a politician's needs. The 1918 episode fermented as he kept it consciously in mind. His actual autobiography was delayed, although a journalist's report in early 1923 described a Hitler resolving, while (allegedly) blind again in 1918, to make saving the country his life's mission.

Later in 1923 came the botched putsch, followed by the Führer's arrest and indictment. Hitler as trial defendant developed the blindness story further, in his opening statement to a Bavarian court on February 26, 1924. It was becoming the fulcrum event of a personal legend. The decision for a public career was made to coincide with the struggle for sight.

> My life's great dilemma, as to whether I ought to turn to politics or remain a master builder, met its end. During that night I decided, upon recovering light, to turn to politics.

The night referred to in this testimony was that of November 9–10,

1918. He told the court that he heard about the German collapse from a delegation of mutinous sailors who visited the patients at Pasewalk on November 9, seeking recruits for the revolutionary ranks.

In *Mein Kampf,* the tale was further reworked. The sailors are gone. Instead Hitler wrote how his sight had returned to normal until news of Germany's defeat was announced at the hospital on November 10. This time a pastor delivers the bad tidings. The psychological shock makes everything go dark. Hitler stumbles back to his bed just as he had groped his way rearward to the medical-aid post after the frontline gas attack a month earlier. He did not attribute this second, putatively sightless bout to any tangible external cause.

This supposed relapse is anyway physiologically preposterous. Reconciling the *Mein Kampf* passage to medical reality has long baffled biographers. Hitler as chancellor contributed to the obfuscation, since his hospital records from Pasewalk disappeared—somehow— once he had risen to power. His time as a Pasewalk patient then became grist for an anti-Nazi propaganda novel that further skewed historical understanding, since some historians have chosen to grant factual credence to the fictional account.

Hitler's army physician at Pasewalk, a Dr. Edmund Robert Forster, is said to have assembled his private notes of the case and deposited them in Paris during 1933, the year of the Nazi takeover. There they were supposedly drawn upon for a *roman à cléf* by a German refugee author, Ernst Weiss, who titled his story *The Eyewitness* (*Der Augenzeuge*). It was first published in 1939. Written with overt political intent and evidently informed by *Mein Kampf,* the novel falls far short as bona fide evidence. Forster's own notes on Hitler from 1918 would be of great historical interest, but they have never surfaced. The doctor committed suicide in 1933, supposedly under Gestapo pressure, after having returned to Germany from France.

Discounting *The Eyewitness* as slanted hearsay, what remains on Hitler's blindness is a confirmed bout of brief impairment and a full recovery. This was followed by the undocumented, medically inexplicable claim of a relapse without any external physical cause. Hitler the Western Front veteran had no need to invent a war wound. Yet he waited over four years after events until he began to evolve a tale slanted toward the dubious return of blindness. That story's successive renderings are more than suspiciously inconsistent in matters of detail. Its variants rule out taking the *Mein Kampf* account at face value. Even so, the very revisions offer clues for identifying what raw grist went into the refined product.

When committed to a leisurely crafted version and set down in *Mein Kampf*, the relapse into sightlessness was alleged to have been brought on by the words of a Christian clergyman. That is the key. *Mein Kampf* thus sealed the mature legend of blindness. Hitler himself offered no further elaboration.

By keeping mum on the issue for the next two decades, he avoided accounting for a tale only too obviously cobbled from off-the-shelf components. The classic case of temporary blindness accompanying a conversion is of course the experience of St. Paul in the New Testament, Acts of the Apostles, chapter 9. Paul has been persecuting Christians when, on the road to Damascus, he is rendered sightless for three days when struck by a celestial light. The spirit of Christ speaks to him, whereupon Paul becomes a disciple. Like every boy raised as a Catholic, Hitler was familiar with the story.

A born-again commitment while incapacitated and delirious also comprises the turning point in the life of Ignatius Loyola, the sixteenth-century Spanish soldier who overcame a nasty leg wound and proceeded to found the quasi-military Jesuit order. He had been struck by a cannon shot during the siege of Pamplona in 1521, a battle the Spaniards lost to France. It is worth noting that in 1916 Hitler took a hit in the thigh while in action on the Somme front and spent a few months recovering. Hitler knew the basics of the Loyola story. Like the St. Paul conversion episode, Ignatius Loyola was standard fare for every European Catholic lad. Dietrich Eckart even has Hitler allude to it in *Bolshevism from Moses to Lenin*.

It so happened that an account of blindness overcome, with shamanistic qualities, figured as well in the personal legend of Guido von List, a Vienna-based neo-pagan pamphleteer whose writings reached their peak of popularity just during Hitler's own Vienna years, 1908–13. The idle young artist has been suspected on reasonable grounds to have read List's works then. If he did, he could have encountered the self-made List legend. In 1902, List (by his own account) had supposedly undergone a temporary loss of sight during which he claimed hallucinations revealing to him the secrets of runic writing and the old Germanic sagas. The Paul story from Acts 9 still imparted an aura of sanctity, retaining its structural essentials while being reworked to pagan advantage by List.

Whether or not he knew List's story, Hitler came in turn to recycle the tale yet again. The trouble was that his own moderate exposure to an irritating gas compound on October 14, 1918 took place rather too early to stretch its all-too-transient disabling effects on his vision so as to encompass the Armistice in the second week of November 1918. Creativity had to jibe with credibility in the Germany of 1924. The Pasewalk medical records were still extant, subject to being checked.

He accordingly acknowledged regaining vision at some juncture before the Armistice, while combat still raged. However, the sighted Corporal Hitler did not bolt from a hospital bed to rejoin his unit. He went on convalescing in relative comfort at the seaside sanatorium, just another mildly injured frontline grunt, hardly a superhero. A relapse thus served more than one purpose for the jailed agitator five and a half years later, in 1924.

Hitler as politician and autobiographer imposed on himself an agenda of requisites. He wished, foremost, to grant centrality to the trauma of blindness and to metaphorically link the recovery of his eyesight to a dawning political and religious mission. He sought also to denigrate the hapless Pasewalk chaplain as a defeatist. All of it had to be timed to occur precisely at Germany's darkest hour. Yet as a matter of clinical fact, he could not tenably profess blindness from mid-October all the way to mid-November 1918.

Only a relapse while in hospital fit the time frame. For plausibility, the *Mein Kampf* account of a relapse drew on the notions of hysteria that were then pervasive, owing at least partly to Sigmund Freud. Much of the public was ready to believe that hysteria can induce blindness. Hitler uttered a trial version of this story during his courtroom defense in February 1924. But it could hardly be left dangling thereafter. Sustained credibility for the reshaped anecdote mandated its prominent billing in whatever memoir might emerge from Hitler's confinement at Landsberg. The author could only hope that readers would not look too hard at how his tale had evolved through stages before culminating in *Mein Kampf.*

With tropes reminiscent of St. Paul, Ignatius Loyola, and Guido von List, what Hitler adduced fit a transparent allegorical intent at the time it appeared. This fable's published pre-*Mein Kampf* versions of 1923 were capably traced by the psychohistorian Rudolf Binion. The focus of attention should be cast still further back to Hitler's November 1921 version that omits—and so for all intents obviates—the Pasewalk relapse episode of *Mein Kampf.*

To that *Mein Kampf* fable must be added the identification of a framework for a real-life metanarrative provided by a piece of theatrical literature. Hitler the reader knew it in German as *Kaiser und Galiläer,* having been inspired by the play as early as 1908, perhaps, on the evidence of his then-roommate August Kubizek. The Ibsen play equated blindness with Christianity, a circumstance consonant with Hitler's needs. In the script, the metaphoric regaining of sight is the rejection of Christian belief. Julian is only a nominal Christian; he cannot bring himself to true belief and is thus the blind man's "brother in unbelief and blindness." Later, Julian will see through the Christian dogma. *Mein Kampf* in its turn imports a Christian clergyman to spread the damnable word of a German national defeat, triggering blindness anew in the distraught corporal. Thereupon Hitler as well, by his account, will proceed to grope through falsehood toward truth and thence to spread that truth far and wide. Adolf the Apostate, like Julian, would pull a switch on St. Paul.

Hitler's enigmatic narrative of his blindness in 1918 has never been fully explicable when standing alone. It can now be seen to initiate a series of episodes that shadow scripted lines from *Emperor and Galilean* in a broad sequential conformity.

WREATHED IN MYSTERY

At Landsberg fortress in 1924, the Nazi prisoners read books and snacked on delicacies brought by visitors from outside. One inmate took the liberty of adorning the premises: A stark decoration appears in his photographs. The object is not a swastika but instead a leafy wreath. It was affixed to a whitewashed wall in the shared dayroom, prominent against a bright background. Someone wanted that wreath to appear, on the record.

Who else? The wreath is seen only in photographs showing Hitler. When other convicts are present, it is he who poses closest to the wreath. Care went into composing these pictures. They feature a dapper Führer. In one picture set he sports an open-necked Bavarian alpine costume. In another shot he goes formal by prison dress codes, in shirtsleeves with a knotted tie and neat collar, perusing a newspaper just beneath the wreath.

So too does the garland change, its configuration of leaves distinct from one picture set to another. The wreath or wreaths apparently went up, down, and back again, but the motif always had to be there in the dayroom with Hitler for the camera. His photographer, Heinrich Hoffmann, visited on several occasions. Hoffmann shot a fair number of portraits resembling not so much jailhouse scenes as vignettes from a high-school yearbook, with the conspicuous wreath on the wall looking like an award for some varsity triumph.

Hoffmann also recalled that when Hitler had finished drafting *Mein Kampf,* he set up a still-life composition on the desk in his cell consisting of the book manuscript framed by just such a wreath. It is thus all but confirmed that the object, there and on the wall, was Hitler's own touch. He followed no usual norm in choosing the symbol. First-time authors, however proud, do not ordinarily festoon their to-be-published product with laurels for the camera. Since Hitler had so pointedly dragooned the wreath into the pictorial record from Landsberg, and since he had included material from Ibsen in *Mein Kampf,* the question arises, whether an Ibsen stimulus might likewise account for the wreath.

Two possibilities emerge from the Ibsen corpus. In *Emperor and Galilean,* the wreath specifies the pagan orientation of a character, early in Part One, who entices Julian to renounce Christianity. And later on in the play, Julian himself appears wearing a wreath after he has openly acknowledged his pagan convictions. Such a wreath as the one on the Landsberg prison wall would also be a suitable stage property for the finale of *The Master Builder.* In that play, the builder renounces churches. He then ascends to crown the spire of his own newly built home, with a wreath.

But that all constitutes intriguing circumstance, not proof. In photographs, the wreath must hang on the whitewashed Landsberg wall, unexplained by the decorator and bound to tease, forever. It cannot be said for certain whether Hitler mentally linked this prop with either Ibsen play; we only know that he was responsible for the wall display, that he read Ibsen and seemingly also Schulze-Berghof's book about Ibsen while imprisoned, and that he later revealed a familiarity with *The Master Builder* and *Emperor and Galilean* by clues no less firm than his earlier textual snatch from *An Enemy of the People.*

FORSWEARING AMBITION TO RULE

Part One, Act I of *Emperor and Galilean* depicts a regime facing the recurrent Roman problem of imperial succession. Julian is still but a philosophically minded nephew in the dynastic clan. He confers with his brother, Gallus:

> GALLUS: The emperor is thinking of making you his successor.
> JULIAN: Never! I swear, my dear Gallus, that will never happen! I won't.... That is not where I am going, I tell you.... I on the imperial throne? No, no, no!
> GALLUS: Ha! Ha! Well acted for an amateur!

Julian later changes his mind, or his act. After Julius Caesar thrice refused the top job in the first century B.C.E., it became political etiquette for an heir-designate to abjure such ambition. As protocol, the feigned modesty fits some systems and not others. It became customary in the Roman dynastic state, which selected de facto monarchs by the soldiers' acclamation, then deferred ratification to vestigial organs of the old republic.

By contrast, a protocol of coy self-abnegation is grossly inappropriate for the head of a political party in a modern constitutional republic. A party's chief is by common consent its candidate to head the government, not to play a charade of placeholder for someone else still to come. Yet that is just what Adolf Hitler did in his early years as head of the Nazi party. He called himself but a "drummer," marking time until the right leader appeared. On its own merit, the pose would make real sense only for the head of an avowed party of monarchical restoration. The Nazis were not formally such a party; they rejected the Hohenzollern dynasty. Neither did Hitler actually woo anyone else. The former general Erich Ludendorff held the best credentials for proclamation as a new Caesar, but the Nazis exploited him shamelessly as a mere figurehead.

Among the profusion of contending party leaders in early Weimar Germany, only Hitler put on an act of forswearing personal ambition. He did so repeatedly and ceremoniously, thus hewing to some other agenda. By mid-1923, he had drummed up enough support to gradually drop the drummer-boy act. The point here, again, is that the act corresponded more to a script than it did to the norms accepted by all other political contenders in Hitler's own time and place.

AN INTOXICATED MYSTIC INSTRUCTS THE ASPIRING LEADER

Having embarked upon a quest for truth, Julian resolves to seek counsel from the famed eccentric Maximus the Mystic. Part One, Act III of *Emperor and Galilean* reveals that Maximus gains better insights through chemistry. It is at a party that Julian and Maximus confer. Maximus tells his visitor: "Wine is the soul of the grape. Free yet willingly enslaved. Logos in Pan!" And: "Intoxication is your marriage with the soul of nature." And: "In vino veritas."

The evening's refreshment had been specially fortified, since Julian was moved to exclaim, in a phrase anticipating psychedelics, "My senses are transposed, I hear the light and I see sounds." He inquires: "Ah, what was in the wine?" Julian then hallucinates that he hears someone speaking to him. An offstage voice proclaims at this point that he is destined to establish an empire.

It is not known what additives found their way into the wine quaffed by Julian or, for that matter, by Henrik Ibsen. Hitler spent his lifetime as a virtual teetotaler. But a Hitler intent on casting himself as Julian requires an analog of Maximus the Mystic. The certifiably alcoholic, substance-abusing Dietrich Eckart fits the bill.

DIVINING A THIRD REICH

Captivated by Maximus in *Caesar's Apostasy*, Act III, Julian overcomes his self-abnegation and pleads to learn which empire he will found. Maximus obliges. He lists the three "empires," his term for successive epochs in the growth of the human spirit. First came the Reich founded on the tree of knowledge, meaning the world of pagan antiquity. It was succeeded by the Reich founded on the cross, meaning Christianity. Finally there shall come a third Reich. This third Reich, the "Reich of great mystery," is destined to supersede the previous two, yet combine aspects of each. Maximus tells Julian how the third Reich is at hand according to his calendar reckoning.

The Hohenzollern dynasty's Second Reich collapsed in November 1918. But the succeeding Weimar Republic studiously refrained from counting itself a "Reich" prefaced by an ordinal number. A Reich, per se, seemed too imperial. Orphaned by the German government, the term "Third Reich" was adopted by others—though not, at the outset, by Nazis. First came the egoists with Rolf Engert, his book on Ibsen, and the imprint "Third Reich Publishers" in Dresden, which lasted from 1921 to 1923. Not until 1923 was the egoists' exclusive clamp on the term loosened, with the appearance of another book under the title *Das dritte Reich,* written by Arthur Moeller van den Bruck (1876–1925). This item helped to align a "third Reich" with an anti-Semitic, anti-Bolshevik brand of German chauvinism. Moeller had been a literary critic and the editor of novels by Dostoevsky in German translation. His Russian ties dated to a sojourn in Paris from 1902 to 1906 when Moeller associated closely with the mystic Dmitri

Merezhkovsky, also author of a novel about Julian the Apostate. Moeller was also incidentally a reader of Ibsen. The Moeller vision of a so-called third Reich was a millenarian regime quite like the one Hitler proposed—albeit minus its stellar attraction: Hitler.

But Moeller, a troubled man, had lapsed into a personal depression by late 1924. He ended his own life the next May. With both Moeller and the egoists having faded from the scene, "Third Reich" again came up for adoption. By this time the term was tainted, and by more than just the hoary mystical notions stretching back to Joachim of Fiore. After 1924, any political group touting a third Reich also had to be aware that much of the public would associate the label either with the late Moeller or with the egoists and their leader Rolf Engert's bizarre idea of Henrik Ibsen as herald of the coming age. Despite—or because of—those strange associations, the Nazi Führer latched onto the term in the years after his release from Landsberg prison. By the end of the 1920s, German newspapers treated "Third Reich" as an exclusively Nazi patent. The advent of a third Reich in *Emperor and Galilean* hinged on certain prior conditions. He who would usher in the new era had to combine within himself the nature of Christ plus a resolve to overcome the false doctrine of Judeo-Christianity. Hitler met those seemingly paradoxical criteria. He had abandoned the church during his teenage years, and he had already whipped up a self-image as an avatar of Christ.

In 1931 came the meeting of another criterion: Rule over a "third Reich" required the mortal sacrifice of the only woman he said he loved. It was so scripted, in *Emperor and Galilean.*

8

DEATH IMITATES ART:
THE SACRIFICE OF GELI RAUBAL

JULIAN THE APOSTATE: Inscrutable retribu-
tion, you great leveler! That is why she had
to go.
—IBSEN, *EMPEROR AND GALILEAN*, PART ONE, ACT V

IN *EMPEROR AND GALILEAN*, Julian takes his cousin Helena as a consort during the years before his ascension to the imperial throne. When she passes away prematurely, her demise is viewed as a precondition for Julian's rise.

A DEATH IN THE FAMILY

In mid-morning on September 19, 1931, members of Hitler's staff in his Munich residence entered the room occupied by his twenty-three-year-old niece, Angelika Maria "Geli" Raubal. Rapping on the door and loud calls of her name had brought only silence. Something was wrong. It proved to be a fatal gunshot wound to the lung. Near Geli's corpse lay a 6.35-mm Walther pistol belonging to her uncle Adolf.

Munich policemen shortly arrived at No. 16 Prinzregenten Strasse. They were told that the young woman's room had been locked from the inside. That circumstance backed a facile official finding of suicide.

Without conducting any autopsy, a Munich police physician, Dr. Müller, estimated the time of death as early in the evening of the preceding day, September 18, somewhere between 5:00 and 6:00 P.M.

Word was sent to Hitler, who had left town on the afternoon of the 18th for a speaking tour and spent the night of September 18–19 in Nuremberg. He returned by car with the members of his traveling party. The Führer appeared suitably grief-stricken at the loss of his half-sister's daughter. Despite the implications of incest, some people beyond the inner circle of friends and relatives believed Geli to have been his mistress. Since 1929, she had stayed alternately at the Munich address and at Hitler's Berchtesgaden villa, where her mother was the housekeeper. The true nature of the Hitler–Geli relationship even baffled associates in the Führer's entourage. As his aide Kurt Lüdecke put it, "The special quality of Hitler's affection [for Geli] is still a mystery to those closest to him."

But among ordinary people, there is no inexplicable "special quality" in the usual drive attracting a fortyish man to a woman in her early twenties. It poses no "mystery." If all were still the same old story between Hitler and Geli, then Lüdecke would hardly have resorted to such delicate phrasing after the pair had cohabited for two years. Yet sex—or its absence—is here just an ancillary factor: Here the concern is an appearance of events correlating to an Ibsen play, *Emperor and Galilean.*

At the end of Part One, Act III in *Emperor and Galilean,* Julian takes his engagement to his half-cousin Helena as a sign fulfilling a destiny, a necessary precondition for his rise to emperor. An aide brings word to Julian that she is on her way to meet him for their wedding. "The pure woman!" proclaims Julian. "Everything is miraculously fulfilled. Robe me in the purple!" She would die, though, before he gained the imperial throne. The death fulfilled another necessary precondition.

Hitler and Geli were neither married nor engaged, but their affinity looked—at least to many—like an affair. Social censure had not swayed Germany's most eligible bachelor. Had he been so inclined, he had his pick of females, including actresses and society women. In fact, while he was living with Geli, he did keep company of sorts with Eva Braun and Erna Hanfstaengl. Geli maintained a separate bedroom at their large Munich flat. Gossips could only guess whether they actually made love. Even if not, the very appearance of the arrangement risked offending Hitler's backers in staunchly Catholic Bavaria. Hitler was thoroughly versed in the morals and mores of that culture. Therefore, some compelling private agenda of the Führer had to outweigh the inherent scandal of keeping a nubile niece so publicly attached to him.

Over the two years of her living with Hitler, Geli took up and dropped a medical-school program. Then came singing lessons, but she was no chanteuse. She never practiced, either medicine or arias. While her voice rated little notice, her death rang out loudly. Nazi-leaning Bavarian officialdom ruled Geli Raubal's death a suicide at the time, although murder at Hitler's instigation was widely supposed. The shooting came on a night when the Hitler household help all happened to be off duty save for one Frau Dachs, who was deaf.

Geli Raubal has been variously described as a young woman of compelling allure and "an empty-headed little slut, with the coarse sort of bloom of a servant girl, without either brains or character," the latter words coming from Hitler's German-American confidant, Ernst "Putzi" Hanfstaengl, following his own estrangement from the Führer in 1937. Her photographs show a girl of average looks, not a classic beauty. Yet her girlish mannerisms evidently held some appeal to Hitler, who even traipsed along on her shopping rounds, leading some to think him smitten. Their private, sexual life together has been variously guessed to have been normal (although incestuous), or unspeakably grotesque, or nonexistent. Guesswork is the only possibility on that score, but it matters little in the present context.

Here the question is whether Angelika Maria "Geli" Raubal was set up to die in a ritual reenactment based on a playwright's script.

SUICIDE OR MURDER?

Until September 16 of that year, Geli had been enjoying some carefree time in the mountains with her mother at Hitler's Berchtesgaden estate. An account by her brother, Leo, stated that she was her usual happy self during these days. Uncle Adolf meanwhile remained in the Munich flat. He telephoned her on the 16th or 17th, bidding her to return there despite his own plans to leave on the 18th on a scheduled speaking tour. There were no plans for her to accompany him on the trip; Geli nonetheless complied with the order. Then Hitler left town himself on the afternoon of the 18th, bound for Hamburg, with Geli remaining as commanded at the Munich apartment.

The Walther pistol stayed put as well, in an exceptional departure from Hitler's usual routine. According to the Führer's valet, Heinz Linge, he always toted this gun and had done so since 1919. Each pair of his trousers was tailored with a special leather pocket to holster it. The pistol offered ready self-defense, which is why he always carried it on tour. To pack the pistol was only prudent for a controversial politician. To leave it behind on this sole occasion in 1931 was unaccountable.

According to Heinrich Hoffmann, the Nazi photographer, Hitler appeared to be on friendly terms with his niece just hours before she met her end. Hoffmann observed him bidding goodbye to Geli on the overcast, drizzly afternoon of September 18. She called out to the departing travelers, "Auf Wiedersehen, Uncle Adolf! Auf Wiedersehen, Herr Hoffmann!" Hitler hesitated on the stairs, then returned to be alone with her for a moment before proceeding to the car. The Nazis drove off, Hitler keeping silent. While heading out of the city, he turned to face Hoffmann and remarked "I don't know why I feel so uneasy."

Hoffmann suggested that it might be the weather. The drive continued in silence to the Deutscher Hof hotel in Nuremberg, run by a pro-Nazi management. This was where Hitler liked to stay in case he had to be reached, although why he halted there just two hours out of Munich on a Hamburg-bound itinerary of about 380 miles was a question Hoffmann left unasked. The Führer and his aides were at the Deutscher Hof when Geli took a bullet in her chest that night. But her demise was not noted at the apartment until the next morning. By then, the Nazis were already on the road again, driving north toward Hamburg. The hotel had to send a messenger in a chase car to catch up. Hitler ordered a U-turn back to Munich, the chauffeur incurring a speeding ticket en route, at 1:37 P.M. in the vicinity of Reichertshofen. That, of course, further substantiated Hitler's personal alibi.

In Munich, Hitler got his pistol back without ado. The gun was not impounded for any forensic inquest, with no systematic ballistics examination or fingerprint test conducted on the putative death weapon. Furthermore, it is not definitively known whether Geli's body exhibited traces of an exiting projectile or of powder burns from a close-up, self-inflicted wound. The hasty official closure of this case thus failed to put it to rest. Apart from the millions of Nazi victims in Germany and Europe, the violent end of Geli Raubal has lingered as an unsolved mystery. Hitler is certainly responsible for a myriad of murders. Geli, though, figures as one of those few persons in his own personal circle whose deaths he is widely suspected of arranging. Since 1931, various theories about Raubal have made the rounds.

Suicide hypotheses surmise that Geli shot herself in a jealous fit after learning that Hitler had some other lady friend; or in apprehension over a singing audition; or from disgust at Hitler's sexual demands: or because she had become pregnant either by Hitler, by one of his chauffeurs (the aforementioned part-Jew Emil Maurice), by a student boyfriend, or by her art tutor, also said to be Jewish. The profusion of contradictory suicide motives dampens the credibility of each. Murder hypotheses attribute the deed to Hitler because Geli was about to leave him, or because she was pregnant, or because she was about to tattle regarding their conjectured offbeat sex life.

But chronic discord alone could hardly compel suicide, as the uncle doubtless sensed. Young adults routinely flout the wishes of parents and familial guardians without shooting themselves. The housekeeper at Hitler's Munich apartment, Frau Annie Winter, observed later that Geli seemed "depressed"; yet she left no suicide note. To the contrary, on her desk was found a very ordinary letter to a girlfriend in Linz, broken off in midsentence.

Upon returning to Munich, Hitler was interviewed by an Officer Sauer, who required something to bolster the suicide story and wrap up the case. A presumption of suicide dominated both what Hitler said and what the detective wrote down. Their shared task was to record a plausible scenario meeting the respective needs of Uncle Adolf as the on-scene next-of-kin, and of Sauer as a cop on the spot. Hitler duly provided.

Sauer's report notes: "She [Geli] had previously belonged to a society that had séances where tables moved, and she had said to Hitler how she had learned [that] one day she would die an unnatural death." That consigned the young woman and her death to the status of a dumb-blonde joke. Hitler indeed had a cooperative medium who conducted such séances, the Nazi-leaning Jan Erik Hanussen. But Sauer pursued neither the date of the reputed séance, nor the name of the occult society, nor the identity of any medium. Pursuing the thread was relevant with likely leads forthcoming from a diary, friends, or correspondence—that is, if she had attended a séance. If she had not, then the ascription of her death to an occult suggestion would have been suspect. It was a thread eminently worth pursuing. But the inspector, Sauer, let it all pass.

The reported circumstance of Geli's room being locked from inside would appear to support suicide. However, the locked-door story was vitiated by no fewer than four conflicting statements on who broke the door down. A hasty conference of Nazi henchmen held at the apartment prior to summoning the police had failed to come up with a consistent account.

One spin tried out at first by Nazi spokesmen had the deceased merely playing with the Walther pistol when it went off accidentally. This again placed her in the ditzy-blonde category. Another—contradictory—excuse made the death a purposeful self-immolation, with Geli an aspiring songstress who supposedly acted from desperation over her "unsatisfied artistic achievement." Worse than unconvincing, this was inane. Geli had taken voice lessons for only a year, giving them a lackadaisical effort at best. There were no rejection notices, no failed tryouts, no diagnoses of clinical depression, no suicide threats, no failed prior attempts.

An account of a broken nose on the corpse is inconclusive, although it has been most believably explained as the result of Geli's head hitting the floor after she was shot. With or without additional injuries, any case of death by gunshot wound warrants an autopsy. Here the procedure was waived on the orders of Franz Gürtner, the pro-Nazi Bavarian minister of justice. Gürtner had arranged leniency for Hitler back in 1924. In 1931 he again short-circuited due process by squelching the Raubal investigation. His solicitude for the Nazi leader expedited the removal of Geli's remains to Vienna on September 21.

There, notwithstanding the official Bavarian ruling of suicide, Catholic church authorities disputed the verdict that she had taken her own life. A priest, Father Johannes Pant, approved interment in a consecrated Catholic cemetery plot to which a suicide would be ineligible. Hitler responded to a hostile story that appeared in the anti-Nazi *Münchener Post* when his niece's death became public. He denied having had a violent spat with Geli. The newspaper printed a letter in which the Führer seemed to be protesting too much. Supposedly overwrought, he then withdrew from public life for three days to a cottage on the Tegernsee, a lake resort.

PARALLELS TO *EMPEROR AND GALILEAN*

The known facts of Geli Raubal's death support neither a finding of suicide nor of impulsive murder by the hand of Hitler himself in the course of a spat. But the circumstances in 1931 do eerily parallel *Emperor and Galilean*.

Salient elements in the case include the following:

⊕ Geli Raubal was a blood relative of Hitler: the daughter of his half-sister, i.e., his half-niece.

⊕ Hitler would state his desire to marry her, as the only woman he ever loved.

⊕ She died unexpectedly, in otherwise good health.

⊕ The objective circumstances of her death suggest homicide.

⊕ She was rumored to have been pregnant at the time of her death, although this was never confirmed.

⊕ Hitler arranged for her body to be buried in Vienna.

- Raubal was buried with proper Catholic rites, notwithstanding an official verdict of suicide and Hitler's own expressed animus toward the Catholic church.
- Hitler attributed her death to a confused state of mind after she attended séances predicting her early demise.
- Hitler wrote a defensive letter to a newspaper, which had the effect of casting suspicion on himself.
- Hitler became reclusive for a few days after Raubal's death, then resumed his speaking engagements with a rally at Hamburg five days after Geli was pronounced dead.
- In *Emperor and Galilean,* the death of the princess is interpreted as a precondition before Julian can rise to the imperial throne; after Geli's death, Hitler shortly afterward challenged Hindenburg for the German presidency.

The relevant portions from Ibsen's *Emperor and Galilean* consist mainly of brief, neighboring passages in Part One, Acts IV and V. In Act III, Julian had attended a séance where he heard the seer, Maximus, foretell the advent of a third Reich. The Maximus prophecy came with the broad hint that Julian was destined to rise from the rank of Caesar to that of full emperor and bring this third Reich to fruition.

First, however, Julian's consort would have to die in fulfillment of a prophetic precedent. Once death removes her, Julian embarks upon the quest for full power. His consort is his half-cousin, Princess Helena. In Act IV, Julian proclaims to her: "You are the only woman I have ever loved, the only one who has ever loved me." Shortly thereafter, she dies unexpectedly from apparent poisoning. She was said to have been pregnant, as Julian belatedly discovers, the fruit of an infidelity. Helena's death comes when her brother, the emperor, is enfeebled and expected to die soon, leaving the way open for Julian to succeed as emperor. A bereaved Julian secludes himself for five days in the catacombs at a place called Vienna, where Helena's body has been taken after her passing, at Lutetia.

The following dialogue ensues in the Vienna catacombs at the start of Act V between Julian and an aide, Sallust:

SALLUST: Many think it is not grief so much as remorse which has driven you underground in this strange way.

JULIAN: They think I killed her?

SALLUST: The whole thing was so mysterious that they must be forgiven if they—

JULIAN: No one killed her, Sallust! She was too pure for this sinful world, that is why an angel came down each night to her room and called to her. You don't believe it! Didn't you know that is how the priests in Lutetia explained her death? And the priests must know. Wasn't her funeral procession here like a victory procession through the land? Didn't all the women of Vienna stream forth to meet her coffin outside the gates. . . .

Yes, she certainly was a truly Christian woman. She kept the commandment. She gave unto Caesar what was Caesar's, and to the other she gave—but that is not what we wanted to talk about; you have not been initiated into the mysteries of the faith, Sallust!

The "mysteries of the faith" referred to arcane teaching. Julian had studied neo-Platonism in an Athenian academy. At the time of Helena's death he still wavered between Christianity and paganism. He would restore the latter after becoming emperor.

As for "Vienna," the place by that name in the play refers to a town in southern Gaul, Vienne, in what is now France, not Austria, although that geographic fact is not clearly spelled out in the script. It would be possible for a reader with limited geographic knowledge to presume that Vienna, Austria was meant. Even if a reader was aware of the difference between the two Viennas, there is a similar discrepancy elsewhere in *Emperor and Galilean* when the shared name of two separate places proves decisive in a prophetic sense. In Part Two, Julian is warned by a soothsayer that danger awaits him in "Phrygia." He takes this to mean the large province by that name in Asia Minor. Circumstances then bring him to meet his fate at another Phrygia, a mere village of the same name located much farther east. The prophecy proved true. Seemingly, what had counted was the name of the place.

If events ensuing upon the death of Geli Raubal appear to track closely to the death of Julian's Helena in the Ibsen text, the accounting for those events in no way depends on happenstance. Every salient aspect congruent with *Emperor and Galilean* may be documented or reasonably surmised as a machination by Geli's uncle Adolf.

Some six months following Raubal's death, Hitler chose to run against the aged incumbent Hindenburg for the German presidency, in a national ballot. The challenger lost that contest in the spring of 1932. Here, though, the point concerns developments during the latter half of 1931, when Hitler prepared for the election.

Within Ibsen's play, a precedent actually mandates Helena's end as precondition for Julian's ascent to the imperial throne. It repeats a formula recounted in Part One, Act III. An earlier emperor candidate, Julian's brother Gallus, made his bid for the highest office only after his wife, Constantina, was removed by death. She had been identified in the text as a spiritual impediment to Gallus's reign. Once she died, Gallus unsuccessfully attempted a coup d'etat, but he paid for disloyalty with his life.

Julian and his friend Gregor debate the value of portents in assessing these events. Gregor is skeptical. Julian insists, however: "Should I not believe suspicious signs which have already been proved true? I can tell you, my friends, that a great upheaval is at hand." He goes on to relate how just before the rise of Gallus Caesar, a citizen in the town of Sidon reported a vision commanding him to prepare a purple robe for Gallus, such as newly elected emperors wear.

> GREGOR: Was that the sign you just said had been proved true?
> JULIAN: Seven days later, [Gallus] Caesar's wife died in Bithynia. Constantina had always been his evil spirit, so she had to go, because of the change in the divine will.

She had to go. The death of Constantina presaged her husband's attempt to become sovereign. Where Gregor voices doubts, Julian sees portents:

> GREGOR: That's strange. In Athens there were different rumors going about.

JULIAN: I know for a fact. The purple robe will be needed very soon, Gregor! And should I doubt then what Maximus has prophesied as imminent for me?

Julian will reach for the purple, convinced of his divine favor. The signs are there. As the man in Sidon foresaw a purple robe for Gallus Caesar, so too did Maximus the Mystic envision a third Reich brought forth by Julian. And as Gallus Caesar attempted to gain the purple upon shedding his consort, so too in his turn must Julian. Fate commands no less.

A FUNERAL IN VIENNA

Princess Helena died after eating some tainted fruit that had been presented as a gift. She too had to go. Julian had her body moved from northern Gaul to a town in southern Gaul—Vienna (also called Vienne).

Geli Raubal's burial at another Vienna serves as one more tip-off, rather like "leather merchants" in *Mein Kampf* confirmed the Hitler debt to *An Enemy of the People*. With *Emperor and Galilean* seen as possible subtext for the whole Raubal episode, the funeral arrangements take on another dimension.

The interment at Vienna, so far away from Munich where Raubal died, presents a problem—and points to the solution. Transporting the cadaver there cannot have been merely a ploy to dodge an autopsy and a coroner's inquest since the very same official empowered to waive those procedures, Franz Gürtner, was the one who approved removing the body outside Bavaria. He did so, moreover, after the corpse had been cleaned and embalmed, thereby altering data of forensic value. Sending the embalmed remains abroad was thus redundant as an action taken to legally insulate the Führer. If anything, burial beyond Gürtner's jurisdiction exposed Hitler—and Gürtner as well—to potential jeopardy, should Austrian authorities be induced to exhume the body and conduct tests. And sending the corpse *to Vienna*, of all destinations, again waves a flag. This last journey of Geli to Vienna had to have another purpose than escaping the coroner's scalpel.

The decision regarding where to bury Geli lay with the one leading family member on the scene with her remains: Adolf Hitler. Yet he felt sensitive enough about the curious choice of Vienna to attempt a dodge. The memoirs of Heinrich Hoffmann relate how Geli's mother Angela Raubal received word of the tragedy and her alleged reaction:

> Frau Winter [the Prinzregenten Strasse housekeeper] immediately alerted Geli's mother [at Berchtesgaden], then Rudolf Hess and Mr. Schwartz, a state treasury official. The perplexed [*fassungslos*] Frau [Angela] Raubal decided that her daughter should be transported to Vienna and buried there.

Perplexed. That is, the choice of Vienna was viewed as perplexing at the time. From his account, it is evident that Hoffmann did not speak directly to Angela Raubal. His knowledge of her response was hearsay, coming to him via an unspecified third party. The decision on where to bury Geli seemed perplexing, hence the "perplexed" Frau Raubal, Geli's mother and next-of-kin. The woman was distraught with shock and grief.

But she was distraught and residing at Berchtesgaden, not Vienna. Her "perplexed" state of mind was stated in the context of where her daughter would be laid to rest. There is not the slightest indication, however, that the mightily strong family member on the scene with the corpse in Munich tried to dissuade Frau Raubal from the particularly perplexing and logistically inconvenient decision to bury Geli in Vienna. Hoffmann's account serves to convey a point: that the idea of sending the dead Geli off on a journey to Vienna was indeed devoid of external rationale, so much so as to require attributing the decision to someone other than Hitler. That person happened also to be someone not only off-scene, but securely buffered by Hitler. Angela Raubal was isolated on a mountain at Hitler's other home and surrounded by his goons. In Munich, Hitler could represent himself as speaking for his "perplexed" half-sister while dealing with the municipal police, with Bavarian justice authorities, with Austrian consular officials, and with family friends like Heinrich Hoffmann.

And so Geli Raubal's body was conveyed to the Austrian capital from Munich on the orders of Adolf Hitler. But Vienna had been neither her abode when she died, nor her family home, nor her birthplace, nor the Raubals' traditional burial ground. There were no reserved tomb vaults or family plots for the Raubals at Vienna, only an ordinary grave hastily designated for Geli, alone. She got plebian treatment, albeit in consecrated ground.

The Raubals and the Hitlers were upper Austrians hailing from Linz and its environs, 160 kilometers west of Vienna and closer to Germany. As a young girl, Geli had lived in Vienna, where her mother worked at the time. They had no property and lived a straitened existence, an impoverished single mother and her daughter occupying rented quarters. Eventually, the pair left to keep house for Hitler at his Berchtesgaden villa. Then Geli moved in with Uncle Adolf in Munich. Burying Geli either at Munich or Berchtesgaden would have been reasonable for accommodating family visits to her gravesite. Burial at Linz, near the crypt of her father Leo Raubal, would have had a sentimental rationale. Burial still farther away at Vienna made no family sense at all.

Actually, it made for a nuisance. As a stateless person and still *persona non grata* in his homeland, Hitler needed special permission to enter Austria. This was granted only on a one-time basis for a graveside visit. Hitler moreover disliked polyglot Vienna. He had stated so in *Mein Kampf* for all the world to read. Notwithstanding his distaste for the city and the travel complication, he countenanced and indeed ordered that the woman he called the sole love of his life should be interred in Vienna.

Burial with proper Catholic rites also accorded with the script. *Emperor and Galilean,* Part One, Acts IV and V emphasized the piety of the dead Helena: "She certainly was a truly Christian woman. She kept the commandment. She gave unto Caesar what was Caesar's."

SALACIOUS RUMORS

Burying the body failed to bury discussion of the death, or the scandal of Geli's reputed life with Hitler. Rumor had it that he had coerced her into odious acts. One third-hand story quotes Geli calling him a "monster," adding: "You would never believe the things he makes me do." There are no reliable details, and so some form of sexual perversion has usually been guessed at.

Once again, *Emperor and Galilean* bears consulting. Ibsen places the scene not in bed but in the bath. Shortly before her death in Part One, Act IV, the princess Helena indulges in a ritual ablution, infusing her Christianity with a ritual drawn from paganism:

> HELENA: Like sweet incense, their blood shall rise up to Him, the Blessed One. We will magnify His glory. His fame shall be proclaimed by us. I shall take part myself. The Alemannic women shall be mine! If they do not bow, they shall be sacrificed! And then, my Julian, when you see me again [I'll be] young and rejuvenated! Give me their womenfolk, my dearest! Blood. It isn't murder, and I'm told the remedy is infallible. A bath in the blood of young virgins.
>
> JULIAN: Helena, what criminal idea is this!
>
> HELENA: Is it sinful to do wrong for your sake?

Emperor and Galilean cannot tell what Hitler and Geli did in bed, if anything. But if Hitler mimed this script, the script offers some clues beyond kinky sex about those unspecified "things he makes me do." In a similar way, *Emperor and Galilean* also offers a precedent for Hitler's casting suspicion on himself in connection with her death. No naïf in public relations, Hitler surely knew that he had done just that with his letter to the *Münchener Post* newspaper denying a quarrel with Raubal.

The words spoken by Sallust in Part One, Act V likewise stipulated suspicion, on Julian the Apostate: "Many think it is not grief so much as remorse which has driven you underground in this strange way." Helena's passing did seem dubious. Julian then seemingly undergoes an epiphany. He explains to Sallust that Helena was murdered as part of a political plot to frame and discredit him. "That is why she had to go."

She had to go. As Julian would have it, enemies arranged Helena's death to make it appear that he wanted her eliminated in fulfillment of a ritual prerequisite assuring his rise to the imperial throne. That would follow the precedent of Gallus Caesar. But Gallus was himself slain after his wife died. Julian intimates that his foes have planned the same fate for him. The ultimate culprits are those who would thwart his succession. Undaunted by evil omens, Julian thus surmounts the crisis of Helena's death in Part One, Act V. He will ascend as emperor after all when the dying incumbent Constantius accepts the inevitable and, reluctantly, appoints Julian in his stead. Casting Geli Raubal as Princess Helena makes President Hindenburg the obvious analog to Emperor Constantius, if indeed Hitler read and ritually restaged portions of this play.

MOSES AND MONOTHEISM, *PAN IN LOGOS*

An analogy between real life and a stage drama may be due either to chance or to deliberate intent. And to convincingly allege intent on Hitler's part, it is necessary to uncover evidence that he actually had the script of Ibsen's play in mind just then, in September 1931.

In this, the Führer duly obliged. It was his custom to ramble aloud to his staff. During the period 1929–31, an aide, Otto Wagener, served as sounding board. He kept notes that eventually found their way into the archival record. Wagener was a businessman who also held an honorary academic doctorate. Hitler employed him as an economic adviser and concurrent administrator of the stormtrooper organization. Wagener had more education than anyone else in the Nazi inner circle as of 1931, and is believed to have kept a diary or journal then.

During World War II, Wagener became a German Army general. After the war, while a prisoner under investigation by an Allied war-crimes investigation, he found enough time to set down from memory what Hitler had said in their informal chats. Some fifteen years had passed, yet Wagener recalled enough to fill thirty-six standard British Army exercise notebooks. Posterity thus owes this Nazi a debt, if only for his scribal service. Wagener reconstructed direct quotations and keyed his recollections to events, although rarely supplying exact dates. But Geli's demise had made a highly memorable, milestone episode during Wagener's daily work at the side of the Führer during the years from 1930 to 1932.

A week after Geli died came these theological ruminations by Hitler, as told to Wagener, in the left column [italics added for emphasis]. Hitler uncharacteristically employed the Greek word *Logos* referring to *pan in logos, logos in pan*—"all is in the Word, the Word is in all." The right column gives the text of an Ibsen passage from *Emperor and Galilean*, Part Two, Act III.

For me, ***God is the Logos of St. John, which has become flesh and lives in this world, interwoven with it and pervading it, conferring on it drives and driving force, and constituting the actual meaning and content of this world.*** Perhaps the adherents of the Roman Church would call this paganism. That may well be so. In that case, Christ was a pagan. I call pagan their distortions of Christ's ideas and teachings, their cults, their conception of hell and purgatory and heaven, and their worship of saints. None of the religions of antiquity, no Negroid idolatry, not even the most primitive sects of the Mohammedan, Indian, or Chinese religions has created so many gods and auxiliary	MAXIMUS THE MYSTIC: Somewhere it is written ***"Thou shalt have no other gods before me."*** JULIAN: Yes, yes, yes! MAXIMUS: The seer of Galilee did not proclaim this god or that god; he said "God is I. I am God." JULIAN: Yes, this thing outside me? That is why the emperor is powerless. The third Reich? The Messiah? Not that of the Jews, but the Messiah of the empire of the spirit and the empire of the world? MAXIMUS: The god-emperor. JULIAN: The emperor-god. MAXIMUS: ***Logos in Pan—Pan in Logos.*** JULIAN: Maximus—what will he be?

deities as the Roman Church. And yet their choirs join in singing from the book of Moses: *"Thou shalt have no other gods before me."* But let's drop it; it's too stupid.

MAXIMUS: He will be as he himself so wills.

Here is a verbal smoking gun.

✦ Both quotations contain allusions to the same biblical passages, these being the First Commandment as revealed to Moses in Exodus 20:3, and the first line of the New Testament Gospel of St. John. The two passages are not customarily juxtaposed. As a unit composed of paired phrases not ordinarily uttered together, it is no less traceable than identical strands of DNA or striations on a spent slug found at a murder scene.

✦ The Ibsen passage from *Emperor and Galilean* moreover uses the Greek *logos*, meaning "word." So too did Hitler, although his speech was usually devoid of foreign terms. Ordinarily, Germans use a term from their own language, *Wort*, when quoting the first line of the Gospel of St. John.

IT MAY ALSO be noted that the Hitler identification of Christ as a pagan is fully in keeping with what Hitler would say, repeatedly, in his "Table Talk" monologues a decade later, 1941–42. This consistency on an eccentric point regarding Christ argues for the fidelity of what Otto Wagener wrote down. Wagener had no access to the "Table Talk" transcripts while in British internment during 1945–46.

Hitler's statement of *logos*, i.e., word, becoming flesh and imparting a driving force explicates incidentally the very mechanism at work if a text, in this case *Emperor and Galilean*, had been taken as an action blueprint, with Hitler himself playing the role of a reincarnated Julian. Ibsen loosely constructed the speech in his play from a mid-fourth-century tract by the historical Julian, *Against the Galileans* (*Kata Galilaion*). Julian wrote:

> "*See that I am and there is no God save me.*" These then are
> the words of Moses when he insists that there is only one God.
> But perhaps the Galileans will reply: "But we do not assert that
> there are two gods or three." But I will show that they do assert
> this also, and I call John to witness, who says: "*In the beginning
> was the Word (Logos), and the word was with God and the Word
> was God.*"

So, could Hitler have bypassed *Emperor and Galilean* and gone directly to Julian's own writing? No, not yet at this stage, in 1931. For one thing, Moses' monotheistic affirmation is given by Ibsen (and by Hitler) in the imperative, as the First Commandment, that is, from the book of Exodus. The version Julian used comes instead from the book of Deuteronomy 32:39.

Then there is the matter of when Hitler gained direct familiarity with Julian's own works. The Führer himself ruled out his having read Julian's tract *Against the Galileans* by 1931. He did so in a remark ten years and one month later, on October 21, 1941. On that date, he brandished a copy of *Against the Galileans* and exclaimed to his dinner companions:

> I really hadn't known how clearly a man like Julian had judged
> the Christians and Christianity. One must read this.

So Hitler did not know *Against the Galileans* in 1931, meaning that there had to be some other source for the paired biblical allusions. Common sense rules out Otto Wagener's having consulted Julian while scrawling his original journal entries or later, while writing his memories of Hitler when he sat in a British prison camp after the war. He was, moreover, by training an economist and a businessman, not a dramatist or a classical scholar. It is plausible that he guilelessly scribbled down what he recalled. And if Hitler's own remarks to Wagener in September 1931 did not derive at first hand from the writings of Julian the Apostate, then the only thing that remains as the suspect source for what Wagener wrote as scribe is Ibsen's *Emperor and Galilean*.

BY DRAWING ON this passage, Hitler had incidentally zeroed in on the very quintessence of *Emperor and Galilean,* selected as such by no less than George Bernard Shaw, who quoted it in *The Quintessence of Ibsenism.*

Besides his interpretation of this passage as he related it to Otto Wagener, Hitler showed particular regard elsewhere for the Gospel of St. John. Wagener recalled an exegesis of it on another occasion. The Führer even quibbled about the standard translation of *logos* as "the word." He told Wagener:

> Here is where I see the *logos* of St. John, which Luther unfortunately translated as "word." Goethe tried to rectify the error with the critical lines: "I cannot possibly place such a high value on the word, I must translate it differently," and he said: "In the beginning was the deed." But I say: "In the beginning was the urge! And the urge existed from eternity! And the urge was a creation of God, and God himself was this urge." And the urge was the spark of life, which resides in us as well. And though it rose to consciousness in man, we pass it by, as Christ already bemoaned. The peace on earth Christ wanted to bring is the very same socialism of nations! It is the new great religion, and it will come because it is divine! It awaits the Messiah!

The National Socialist Führer hastened to add that he was not the Messiah. St. John in his gospel, verse 1:20, had after all denied being the Christ. Modesty notwithstanding on this occasion, though, Hitler had already commissioned a painting by the artist H. O. Hoyer that depicts him haranguing an early Nazi assembly. It bears the title "In the Beginning Was the Word." He was, in a word, bewitched by the phrase. The *logos* phrase also turns up in a mystical tract on rebirth among items in Hitler's personal library.

For Hitler to favor St. John's gospel is hardly surprising. It counterposes Jesus to the Jews, who are depicted as collectively set on obstructing Christ. The Christ of John is portrayed as a figure working apart from the Jews in contrast with the synoptic gospels of Matthew,

Mark, and Luke, all of which take for granted the preaching of Jesus within a Jewish social and religious milieu.

Here the specific issue is the idiosyncratic pairing of St. John's *logos* from the first line of his gospel along with the First Commandment, as in the Ibsen play. Particularly noteworthy too is the Führer's timing for this idiosyncratic pairing of the two biblical allusions, reminiscent of their pairing in the Ibsen play. It came in the immediate wake of Geli Raubal's violent death, a death replete with even more features analogous to specific elements in *Emperor and Galilean*.

It may be presumed that Otto Wagener maintained no private agenda to falsely salt the historical record with paraphrases taken out of *Emperor and Galilean* and that Wagener as a scribe remained clueless of any derivation from Ibsen. So, barring a mathematically infinitesimal chance recurrence, the words Wagener quoted may be used to substantiate Hitler's active interest in the Ibsen script just around the time his niece died. She had lived under his control for the final two years of her life. Features of their life, and then her death, conformed to the role of Julian's consort: a blood relative fated to perish before the imperial pretender can ascend to the throne. And on the drive back to the Obersalzberg from Vienna, Hitler declared: "So, now begins the battle, a battle which we must pursue to its end!"

"PERHAPS IT WAS MEANT TO BE THIS WAY."

A voluble Hitler summed it up in this revealing talk to Wagener on or about September 26, 1931:

> Now I am altogether free, inwardly and outwardly. Perhaps it was meant to be this way. Now I belong only to the German Volk and to my mission. But poor Geli! She had to sacrifice herself for this.

With these words, Hitler explicitly linked "poor Geli" to his political mission—that is, to the establishment of the prophesied third Reich. Present in what Wagener set down are the themes of ordained fate—"it was meant to be this way"—and of required sacrifice. The Führer hereby hinted to Wagener—as far as he could, short of outright self-incrimination—that Geli's passing a week earlier had been a scripted ritual act that removed an impediment. Wagener could not be told of any hastening nudge poor Geli received when "she had to sacrifice herself for this." Even so, the heir apparent had said quite enough.

9

FÜHRER AND GALILEAN

JULIAN: What would the Galilean say if he were here, invisible among us?
MAXIMUS: He would say, "The third Reich is at hand."

—IBSEN, *EMPEROR AND GALILEAN*,
PART TWO, ACT IV

BY NOW IT should not occasion much surprise if Hitlerian parallels to *Emperor and Galilean* were to continue beyond the burial of Geli Raubal. And so they do. Some parallel events manifest a ritual character. Others involve the very substance of statecraft.

TIMING A BID FOR POWER

A mood of now-or-never prevails in *Emperor and Galilean,* Part One, Act V. Emperor Constantius, although ill, has been trying to detach portions of Julian's army to weaken him. Some troop units waver in their loyalty. Julian must reassert control over his men or lose all. Near the end of Act V, he confers once more with Maximus the Mystic. A heartened Julian declares: "The empire for me!"

He then smears himself with sacrificial blood. He will proceed to

march on the capital. Before he arrives, Emperor Constantius bows
to the inevitable, capitulates, and dies.

> GREGORY: It was said that Constantius had died of fright at what you
> were doing, and had made you his heir. Hailed as a superman, and
> with the reports of your victories racing on ahead, you, the hero of
> Gaul and Germany, had ascended the throne of Constantine without
> striking a blow.

Here is the modern parallel: In the winter of 1931–32, Hitler agonized over whether he should oppose the octogenarian incumbent
Hindenburg in the presidential election set for March 1932. Running
for the post made no sense in practical terms, since victory for the
popular Hindenburg was virtually certain. He kept putting a decision
off. But in February he at last entered the race.

The ballot produced the expected Hindenburg landslide. Notwithstanding the president's increasing infirmity, his 49.6 percent
of the vote swamped Hitler's 30.1 percent in a four-candidate field. A
runoff then brought Hindenburg 53 percent to Hitler's 36.8 percent.
These results confirmed pre-electoral forecasts of a Hitler setback.
Nazi rhetoric in the two electoral rounds had resorted to heavy
mudslinging against a venerable hero who did not need to actively
campaign at all. The Nazis' own prestige was tarnished in the process.
Hitler knew all along that standing for election made more sense in
actuarial than political terms, amounting to a wager on mortality.
Should Hindenburg die during the campaign, the upstart stood to
win by default, but the president had not quite reached death's door.
Running against Hindenburg flouted common sense in the spring of
1932, nearly bankrupted the Nazi treasury, and disrupted the Nazi
ranks. Part of the SA stormtroops seceded from Hitler's control, and
an anti-Hitler faction in the party gained ground.

Given the circumstances, some other factor besides cool political
calculation may reasonably be suspected of motivating Hitler. Such
a factor presents itself at the appropriate juncture in *Emperor and
Galilean,* where a lunge for the top job is scripted in the immediate

wake of the death of the Caesar's consort. Failure in the 1932 election provided a dose of reality.

But then fate favored Hitler, notwithstanding the electoral drubbing, when Hindenburg chose him to be chancellor just ten months later. If the Führer were following *Emperor and Galilean* as an allegory and a blueprint, that stroke of fortune could only reinforce faith in the script.

IF I HAD A HAMMER. . . . FRACTURED IMPLEMENTS AND OMENS OF SUCCESSION

Appointed chancellor in late January 1933 by a debilitated President Hindenburg, Hitler yet again found himself in a position analogous to that of Julian waiting for the sickly emperor Constantius to die. As German chancellor, Hitler still lacked the formal trappings of a head of state. But that formality did not deter him from conducting ceremonies in the grand style of a reigning sovereign.

One such public rite came in Munich on October 15, 1933: the cornerstone dedication for the House of German Art. It would occupy the former site of a museum, the Glass Palace, razed by arson two years before. The replacement was to be a massive neoclassical stone building according to Hitler's suggestion and a blueprint by a Nazi architect, Paul Ludwig Troost.

Fine weather blessed the open-air event. A block of cut stone measuring about a cubic meter had already been set in place. Dignitaries, artists, and thousands of citizens attended. Hitler was to affix a plaque. All looked ready for a predictable public observance free of hitches, glitches, or mishaps. Munich artisans had prepared a special silver hammer for the task. Resembling a pickaxe, it was wrought according to a design by Troost himself. The Bavarian state interior minister formally presented the implement. Hitler intoned the hope that it would be used in all future building dedications. Then he raised the hammer for the customary three taps.

Never a dull moment. At the very first stroke, haft and head separated. The head of the implement clanked on the ground. The chancellor still grasped the handle. He managed to look disconcerted, according to an account by his photographer, Heinrich Hoffmann. On the spot, Hitler told Hoffmann,

> The people are superstitious, and might well see in this ridiculous little misfortune an omen of evil.

Indeed. "Hitler Breaks Hammer; Germans See Evil Omen," ran a foreign headline. The German press, already under tight Nazi control, was more upbeat. The leader's unflustered speech saved the day. Taking the hammer as metaphor, he assured everyone how Germany would mend that which had been destroyed and rebuild itself as a nation with a proud national art.

Ordinarily, for an ordinary politician, a broken tool is a broken tool. Hitler's hammer might be dismissed as such, were it not for the prior pattern of events that pantomimed episodes from *Emperor and Galilean*, along with Hitler's words that matched those in the script. The play offered a ritual formula for creating his Third Reich. Yet on that October 1933 day, the task remained incomplete. The Führer remained only Reich chancellor, Number Two in the official hierarchy. Back again then to the script, *Emperor and Galilean*, Part One, Act V. Julian is still ranked as a mere Caesar—that is, Number Two in the Empire. He and his aide Sallust confer in the spooky setting of the catacombs. The talk turns to omens.

> JULIAN: The time is not auspicious, Sallust! Didn't you know that in the war games before we left Lutetia, my shield broke in pieces and I was left holding only the handle? And didn't you know that when I was about to mount my horse, the servant stumbled as I swung myself up on his folded hands?
> SALLUST: Still, you got into the saddle, my lord!
> JULIAN: But the man fell.

Hitler's reenactment required updated props, since he was neither swordsman nor equestrian. If not at a tournament, the breakage needed to occur at another public event. Two themes are conjoined: 1) steadfastness despite an evil omen; and 2) a portent of impending succession. The rupture of a ceremonial object provided the scripted omen. Such an omen might deter a leader of faint resolve but not Julian, and not the German chancellor set on becoming Reich president once the post was vacant.

A man had to fall. *Emperor and Galilean,* Part One, Act V proceeds.

> **JULIAN:** We certainly shouldn't be put off by those omens. The fact that I was left holding the handle when my shield was shattered in the tournament could, I think, quite reasonably be interpreted as meaning that I shall succeed in retaining what I seize. And if, when jumping on my horse, I knocked over the man who was helping me into the saddle, that seems to point to a sudden fall for Constantius, to whom I owe my elevation.

President Hindenburg died in August 1934, two months short of his eighty-seventh birthday. If the breakage of the hammer by Hitler amounted to sorcery, it seemed to have worked. Upon Hindenburg's passing, Hitler fused the German presidency with the chancellorship and dispensed with both titles to rule henceforth as "Führer," not just of the Nazis but of the whole Reich. As Heinrich Hoffmann stated of the hammer incident: "During the course of our twenty-five years of association, I had numberless opportunities of seeing how prone he was to premonitions."

Premonition or pantomime? To Hitler in 1933, the upcoming consecration of the new art-museum site evidently meant more than just a chore. He even commissioned an artist to sketch the scene, weeks in advance. And given all the parallels to *Emperor and Galilean* preceding the breakage of the hammer, there is every reason to suspect the "premonition" of October 15, 1933 as another charade. As for that oddly brittle hammer itself, German metal craftsmanship is not usually known for such shoddiness. An implement designed for decorous function must pass all reasonable tensile tests before being placed in a bigwig's hands. Yet this one somehow broke, as if on cue.

LULLING THE CHURCHMEN

Maximus the Mystic advises Julian, in Part One, Act V: "With victory in your heart, like a rider on his fiery steed, you must surmount the Galilean if you are to reach the imperial throne." Not repudiate, but surmount.

That same act concludes with a symbolic ritual of Christianity counterposed to paganism. A church choir intones the Lord's Prayer. Julian meanwhile daubs himself with blood from an animal sacrifice, consecrating his decision to seize the highest office. He has regained his soldiers' backing. They hail him as emperor although he is formally still just Caesar, one rank below the top spot. The choir continues its chanting in the background. Julian chimes in when it suits him.

> SOLDIERS: Long live the Emperor Julian!
>
> JULIAN: We will not look back; all ways lie open before us. Up into the daylight. Through the church! The liars shall be silenced! My army, my treasure, my throne!
>
> CHOIR: Lead us not into temptation, but deliver us from evil!
>
> JULIAN: Free, free! Mine is the kingdom!
>
> SALLUST: And the power and the glory!
>
> CHOIR: Thine is the kingdom, and the power, and the glory.
>
> JULIAN: Ah!
>
> MAXIMUS: Victory!
>
> CHOIR: For ever and ever, Amen!

This is the only place in the Ibsen text where the Lord's Prayer is recited. Julian is now a confirmed pagan, yet he wishes to appear tolerant of Christian observance, at least for the time being. When he has assumed the throne as emperor in Part Two, Act I, he quickly reassures the faithful:

> I mean that all citizens are to enjoy complete freedom. Cling to the Christians' God, those of you who find it desirable for your peace of mind. . . . I will in no way tolerate malicious attacks on the churches of the Christians, nor shall their burial grounds

> be desecrated, nor other places which, through some strange
> delusion, they have come to hold sacred.

At the analogous juncture in Hitler's ascent, religion was foremost on the chancellor's mind. Merely two days after taking office, on February 1, 1933, he assured the country in a radio address that his new government would "regard Christianity as the foundation of our national morality." Nine days later, he closed a speech in Berlin with "the new German kingdom of greatness and power and glory and justice," phrasing adapted from the Lord's Prayer. He even closed with "Amen." These occasions were the only instances during the Third Reich when he drew phrases from the Lord's Prayer, or concluded a public speech like a holy supplication.

Five days later, Hitler spoke at Stuttgart, a city still run by the Catholic Center party. He assured his hosts, "I confess I will never ally myself with the parties which aim to destroy Christianity," and elaborated his tolerance of the faith despite his disdain for the churches. Hitler took pains to show that he was not renouncing Christ. That February and March 1933, he larded phrases like "Man cannot live by bread alone," "our daily bread," and "peace on earth" into speeches.

On July 20, 1933, he concluded a concordat with the Holy See. Under its terms, the Catholic church acceded to dismantling the Center party. The Vatican's secretary of state, Cardinal Eugenio Pacelli, conducted these negotiations. Pacelli, the future Pope Pius XII, had previously been papal nuncio at Munich and Berlin. Having witnessed the Marxist uprisings in Germany after World War I, he combined a reflexive hatred of Communism with an anti-democratic streak. Pacelli regarded the neo-pagan Hitler as the lesser evil, compared to the specter of Communism. As the chief papal diplomat, he preferred reaching Vatican concordats with authoritarian states to reliance on national Catholic parliamentary parties resistant to the papacy. By sacrificing the Center party, Pacelli actually achieved several items on his agenda. He also renounced the rights of church-run organizations to dabble in politics. That left the German clergy a right to pray, but little else. Moreover, the Catholic church in Germany all but abandoned converts from Judaism. By Nazi standards, such converts were still Jews.

The respective assurances of Julian and Hitler to Christians each proved a sham. The latter never had any intention of respecting the faith for long. Sometime in 1932, shortly before taking the reins of government, Hitler told his aide Kurt Lüdecke: "Once we hold the power, Christianity will be overcome and the German church established." He added: "Jesus was Judaized, distorted, falsified, and an alien Asiatic spirit was forced upon us. That is a crime we must repair." These sentiments had not changed by the time the new chancellor spouted phrases from the Lord's Prayer and signed the Vatican concordat. Religion held a high place on his agenda; he paid attention to timing. First the opposition had to be lulled.

In the Third Reich, church-affiliated newspapers, youth groups, women's societies, and other associations were dissolved and replaced by Nazified organs. The crackdown should have come as no surprise: As early as March 1933, even while speaking sanctimonious words, Hitler had refused to take a reserved seat in the Potsdam parish church for rites to bless the Reichstag.

Impiety would not end with mere snubs, however. By 1935, the drive quickened to denigrate the churches and end their hold on the populace. The Führer frankly told a Reich students' league leader that his attack on Christianity was aimed at the faith as a whole, not against any particular branch or sect:

> We are not out against the hundred and one different kinds of Christianity, but against Christianity itself. All people who profess creeds are smugglers in foreign coin and traitors to the people. Even those Christians who really want to serve the people—and there are such—will have to be suppressed.

Hitler had betrayed the concordat. Foreign-based Catholic sources for 1936 published the names of some 220 priests, nuns, chaplains, and lay church officials who had been arrested and fined by the authorities. All had either spoken out against Nazi policies or defied the curtailing of church organizations. Catholic youth groups and sports clubs ceased to exist, their members being persecuted or coerced into joining the neo-pagan Hitler Youth and Nazi sport leagues. An encyclical of protest in 1937 by the reigning Pope Pius XI came too little, too late.

None of it should have surprised observers, had the pattern of likenesses to *Emperor and Galilean* been discerned at the time. The withdrawal of Nazi toleration recapitulated Emperor Julian's reversal of course toward the church, beginning in Part Two, Act II. Julian imposes a state cult of pagan worship. To Christians it is blasphemous. There follow riots and a crackdown. The emperor decrees arrests and executions, but faithful clergymen dare the emperor to make them martyrs.

AUTO DA FÉ

In *Emperor and Galilean,* Part Two, Act III, Julian orders Christian literature consigned to flame. A woman laments: "The emperor has ordered all our holy scriptures to be burned!" A man confirms: "The slightest thing written about Christ is to be wiped out of existence, and from the memory of the faithful."

Julian goes on, berating the believers:

> By Apollo, no true Greek would recite your verses. . . . As for those books you are moaning and howling about losing, I can tell you that before long you will grow to think less highly of them, when Jesus of Nazareth is shown up as a liar and an impostor.

Hitler too staged a book-burning on May 10, 1933, just three and a half months after he took power. It was a nationwide coordinated gesture consisting of giant bonfires lit on campuses and stoked by Nazi student activists. As an analogous item in sequence, the event comes in proper order. Once again, though, it differs from its scripted counterpart in a way consistent with other analogous events. Instead of consigning Christian scriptures to flames, as in *Emperor and Galilean,* the Nazi demonstration targeted secular works by Jews and a few selected anti-Nazis.

SECURING THE RHINE *LIMES*

Imperial Romans called their fortified German frontier the *limes,* cognate with "limit." The defense works consisted of wooden palisades, signal posts, and watchtowers in a swath cut through present-day western Germany. These were built in the imperial heyday to keep barbarian tribes at bay. When Julian in his time pushed back the Germans, he restored the *limes.* Part One, Act IV of *Emperor and Galilean* has Julian, as Caesar, demanding due credit from the emperor.

> Did I rebuild Trajan's fortress when we advanced into German territory?

and,

> Did I in fact drive the barbarians away from the islands in the Rhine? Did I build up the defenses of the ruined town of Tres Tabernae for the greater security of the empire?

The emperor grudgingly confirms,

> The Rhine frontier has been made secure.

Here is the Third Reich parallel event: In the spring of 1938, Hitler suddenly ordered a massive defense construction along the Rhine and its western approaches. These works consisted mainly of concrete pillboxes and anti-tank traps in a line stretching north from the Swiss border to cover much of the Dutch frontier. The accelerated project would eventually absorb about 51 percent of German cement output and the labor of half a million workers. Like the Roman *limes,* the purpose was to substitute fortification for military manpower in the west so as to release soldiers to fight in the east. Beginning in late 1938, ordinary Germans called this system the Westwall. The British dubbed it the Siegfried Line. But there was yet another, official name, a curious reversal of geography: From the outset, Hitler himself referred to this project as the *limes.* That is how it appears in Wehrmacht orders, as the *limes* project of the spring and summer of 1938. The Führer clearly had Roman precedent in mind, but no officials chanced to ask why.

Among significant, Hitler-initiated episodes paralleling *Emperor and Galilean*, this is the sole departure from the sequence of events as scripted by Ibsen in his play.

A SMOKE SIGNAL: *REICHSKRISTALLNACHT*

In Part Two, Act II of *Emperor and Galilean*, Julian sets out to rebuild the Jewish Temple at Jerusalem despite a Christian belief that Christ had placed a curse on the rubble. Julian rashly accepts a dare from a Christian cleric.

> BISHOP MARIS: Try, powerless as you are. Who has had the power to raise up the temple of Jerusalem again since the Prince of Golgotha decreed its destruction?
>
> JULIAN: I have the power! The emperor has! Your God shall be shown up as a liar. Stone by stone, I shall build up the temple of Jerusalem in all its glory, as it was in the days of Solomon.
>
> MARIS: You shall not lay one stone on another; for it is cursed of the Lord.
>
> JULIAN: Wait, wait; you shall see.

In Part Two, Act III, Julian sneers: "Did the crucified Jew not prophesy that the Temple should lie in ruins to the end of time?" This emperor accepts Christ's dare. Julian sends his general Jovian to command two thousand construction workers and predicts: "Before a year is up, the Temple of the Jews shall stand again on Mount Zion. Its golden roof shall shine in splendor over the lands and bear witness, liar, liar, liar!"

Jovian's men benefit from unseen assistance as they tear down remnants of the former Temple's walls. But the actual reconstruction is thereafter stymied. Winds blow away heaps of lime from the job site. Earthquakes occur just as workers carrying torches descend into the old subterranean vaults. And, as Jovian reports to Julian, "A tremendous stream of fire shot out of the caves. A noise like thunder shook the whole town." Julian had miscalculated by trying to restore the divinely accursed Jewish structure, and hundreds of men are killed in an explosion. The obliteration of the Temple was indeed willed for all time. This foiled attempt marks the critical pivot of *Emperor and Galilean,* Part Two, and is a harbinger of Julian's own eventual downfall. He must pay the ultimate price for defying Christ and ally-ing both himself and the empire with the Jews. A crowd murmurs, "The Galilean has conquered the Emperor! The Galilean is greater than Julian!" A churchman, Cyrillus, confronts Julian:

> It's you, Emperor, who are mistaken in this. It was you who renounced Christ the moment he granted you dominion over the world. Therefore, I declare in his name that he soon will take from you both your dominion and your life, and then, too late, you shall recognize the strength of him whom you despise in your blindness.

Hitler's analogous action, occurring in proper sequence, was *Reichs-kristallnacht* ("Crystal Night"), the coordinated assault on synagogues all over Germany on November 9–10, 1938. The date itself hints of a contrived anniversary event: November 9 marked both the German revolution of 1918 and the abortive Nazi putsch of 1923. Ostensibly, the destruction of synagogues was in reprisal for the shooting two days earlier of a German diplomat posted to Paris, by a Polish Jewish youth. The assassin had somehow gotten hold of a pistol.

But the actual implementation of *Kristallnacht* made clear that it had long been in the planning. Synagogues were the high-profile symbolic target. SA men set fire to one hundred ninety-one and demolished another seventy-six by other means across the country. Hitler—the "sole instigator," according to his press aide—ordered Goebbels to implement this deed. The Führer flew into a rage upon hearing a report of SA hesitation.

The common denominators of the two signal events bear noting:

- Each action by the respective ruler (Julian, Hitler) was intentionally symbolic.
- Whatever the ruler's stated wish, each episode ended in the destruction of a Jewish temple, or temples.
- In each episode, the obliteration was ostensibly willed either by Christ (as in *Emperor and Galilean*) or by a figure who had personally identified himself with Christ (as Hitler had notably done at an earlier juncture).
- Each episode was followed shortly by the initiation of a war of territorial expansion to the east.

These paired events should be seen in the light of previous and subsequent Hitlerian actions also having parallels to the script. If the observed parallels may be deemed significant, then Hitler's *Kristallnacht* assault against the synagogues assumes the nature of a corrective to Julian's mistake. Whereas Julian had taken a move favorable to Judaism, Hitler omitted that step and proceeded straight to the result, the reduction of Jewish temples to rubble. The Führer moreover followed this demonstrative act forthwith by issuing a threat, which he called a "prophecy": In a speech to Reichstag deputies delivered on January 30, 1939, he prophesied that the Jews would be exterminated if a new world war were to break out. Whereupon he set about initiating the steps to ensure the eruption of that world war.

NON-AGGRESSION PACT WITH A LARGE EASTERN EMPIRE

To the east of Julian's Roman state was the Persian empire. Rome and Persia had long alternated between periods of war and détente. In *Emperor and Galilean,* Part Two, Act III, Julian reports the latest Persian offer of peaceful coexistence. He addresses his subjects:

> The king of Persia, alarmed at my approach, has made me an offer of peace. I am thinking of accepting.

The Hitler analogy is, of course, his pact with Stalin in 1939. If there were to be a Berlin–Moscow rapprochement, the initiative would have to come from the German side. Moves toward that goal began with Hitler's Reichstag speech of January 30, 1939, which for once neglected the Red menace while still attacking Western democracy. More hints followed. In April, the SS propaganda organ ceased running anti-Soviet cartoons. The Führer omitted his customary anti-Soviet tirade in a speech of April 28. By early May, a significant shift in tone was becoming clear.

Stalin responded to the German overtures. Following a summer of negotiations, Hitler sent his foreign minister, Joachim von Ribbentrop, to the Kremlin in August. A non-aggression pact was signed on August 24, 1939. World War II followed a week later when Germany attacked Poland and shortly thereafter partitioned that country with the Soviet Union.

Hitler achieved his pact, and his war, with bold moves that once again matched those in a script about Julian the Apostate. The sequence of episodes paralleling Ibsen's play thereby passed beyond the merely nominal and ritual to the substantive, on an international scale. But in August 1939, a stunned world missed the analogy to *Emperor and Galilean.*

RUPTURE OF THE PEACE PACT AND ADVANCE EASTWARD

In Part Two, Act III of *Emperor and Galilean,* Julian annuls a non-aggression pact in short order.

> **JULIAN:** The king of Persia has offered me tenders of peace, which I over-hastily agreed to. My envoys are already on their way. They must be overtaken and recalled.
>
> **MAXIMUS:** You mean to reopen the war with King Sapor?
>
> **JULIAN:** I will do what Cyrus dreamed of and what Alexander tried to do.

As early as November 23, 1939, Hitler confided to a military adjutant his intention to betray Stalin. He hoped to attack in 1940, but the logistics of redeploying an entire army from western Europe forced a postponement. Wehrmacht General Günther Blumentritt sensed something dreamlike in the whole endeavor:

> This, as I say, was his [Hitler's] attitude during the winter of 1939–40. It must be realized that Hitler was not a realistic statesman. He never regarded politics as the sober pursuit of a definite end. For him politics was a dream, and he the dreamer; ignoring alike time, space, and the fact that German power was limited and Germany herself only a small patch on a large globe. Shortly after the Polish campaign, we may assume, his dream became preoccupied with the East.

Finally, on June 22, 1941, Hitler broke the Nazi–Soviet pact. The dreamlike détente had lasted twenty-two months. Axis armies crossed the frontier, with the main armored force echeloned on the central section of the front, poised to advance toward Moscow. The largest military campaign in all history had begun.

A TURN NORTHWARD AWAY FROM THE ENEMY CAPITAL

When action resumes in *Emperor and Galilean,* Part Two, Act IV, after Julian's decision to abort the non-aggression pact, the Roman armies push into Persian territory, headed for the capital at Ctesiphon. Julian's mood is upbeat. But the Roman thrust slows. Supply becomes a problem, once the advancing force moves away from the Euphrates. Julian and his staff interrogate a Persian defector:

> NEVITA [*to the Persian*] : Do you know whether they have stocks of grain and oil in Ctesiphon?
> THE PERSIAN: In Ctesiphon, there is more than enough of everything.
> JULIAN: And once we've taken the city, the whole rich province will lie open before us.

THE PERSIAN: The people will open their gates to you, my lord! I am
not the only one who hates King Sapor. They will rise against him
and surrender to you if you take them by surprise and strike terror
with all your concentrated might.

It sounded reasonable. The whole empire must yield with the fall
of its capital city. So the offensive slogs east toward Ctesiphon. But
again, in Part Two, Act V, it founders. The Persian defector absconds.
He had been a spy sent to lure the Romans eastward to their doom.
Julian should really have veered away from Ctesiphon earlier. Now
as his army pauses, he must decide where to march next. Many of
his men yearn to withdraw westward, but that option is ruled out
when Julian orders the burning of the Roman convoy ships on the
Euphrates. Supplies would no longer be brought up by water.

JULIAN: We are going to modify slightly our line of advance.
PRISCUS: Oh, praise to your wisdom!
JULIAN: This expedition to the east, it's not leading anywhere.
CHYTRON: No, no, that is certain!
JULIAN: Now we are going north, Chytron!
CHYTRON: What, my lord? North?
PRISCUS: Not west, then?
JULIAN: Not west. Far from west. That would be difficult because of
the rivers. And Ctesiphon we shall have to leave till later.

Ibsen had contrived Julian's optimism about capturing the Persian
capital after a mere postponement. In history, the turn northward
cannot realistically be called an advance, but rather a retreat via an
alternate route. At this point, both in the historical sources and the
Ibsen version, the Romans consult auguries. Although the signs have
turned inauspicious, Julian remains dazzled by the prospects of triumph.
A turn northward will help them avoid being drawn into an enemy
trap, he believes. A delay in capturing the enemy capital is tolerable
since the capital will eventually fall anyway; that is, in the play.
     Again the play presaged policy nearly sixteen centuries later.
Hitler scripted a northward turn into his basic plan for the attack on

Russia: Directive No. 21, issued on December 18, 1940. He had initially deployed the bulk of the German armor and motorized formations on the central axis of advance, facing Moscow. However, once these troops had smashed Soviet resistance in Byelorussia on the central front, he predicted:

> This will create a situation that will enable strong formations of mobile troops to swing north.

The stated rationale for shifting the panzers away from the central front was to assist in isolating Leningrad. Once that had been achieved,

> The offensive operation is to continue with the objective of occupying the important center of communications and armaments manufacture, Moscow.

So went the Hitler scenario. This northward shift and the deferral of advance on Moscow were robustly opposed by the German Army general staff, which was counting on the fall of Moscow to trigger a wholesale Soviet disintegration and thus deliver all of European Russia and the Ukraine into German hands. The two opposing concepts remained unresolved throughout the planning stage. Tension emerged in the high command once operations had begun.

Hitler stuck to his plan. On July 17, 1941, he bid a pause on the central line of advance and diverted Panzer Group 3 of Army Group Center, under General Hermann Hoth, away from Moscow to head northeastward, ostensibly to cut enemy road and railway links from Moscow to Leningrad. That might have made sense if the Führer had planned to occupy Leningrad and make use of its Baltic port. But he did not; instead, he stated an intention to destroy the city along with its wharves, overriding the misgivings of German naval officers. Meanwhile, Army Group North had made satisfactory progress on its own and had not requested Hoth's extra panzers. Detaching tanks away from the central vector of advance thus lacked any military rationale in the operational context of July 1941.

Over the next few days of July, Hitler reiterated his queasiness about Moscow in Führer Directive No. 33 and a supplementary decree, downplaying the Red capital as an objective and shelving it for the whole summer. In addition to Hoth's detour northeastward, Panzer Group 2 of Army Group Center under General Heinz Guderian was also deflected, southward to the Ukraine. This twofold diversion of the Wehrmacht tank force effectively put off Moscow as a military goal for months, until autumn.

OKH (Oberkommando des Heeres: Army High Command; that is, the general staff) chief Franz Halder recorded his dismay in a war diary. On July 21, he speculated that the Führer might have been swayed by the head of the rival armed forces general staff (OKW: Oberkommando der Wehrmacht: Armed Forces High Command), a body more under Hitler's sway.

> Someone, apparently [Field Marshal Wilhelm] Keitel, is constantly pushing the Führer that armor should be shifted from Center to Army Group North... but further north [Wilhelm Ritter] von Leeb [the Army Group North commander] has all he can use.

The next day, Halder recorded that Hitler was "again in a state over Army Group North," although its movements were "developing according to plan" and thus required no more tanks. Halder soon realized that Keitel had not encouraged Hitler to detach Hoth's armor northward; it was entirely the dictator's own notion.

A Führer conference of July 26 decreed "no hurry" on Moscow. Halder confided to his diary that the plan "indicates a complete break with the strategy of large operational conceptions." Then on July 30 the diary states: "Plan of thrust to cut the Moscow–Leningrad railroad is dropped." Yet that was the stated pretext for steering Hoth north. The detoured army was sidetracked from the Moscow vector of advance, without commensurate gain. Halder rued "the Führer's obstinacy," which seemed inexplicable.

The Army general staff still remonstrated, yet Hitler held firm. On August 4, Halder summed up the chief's priorities: "Emphasis is on Leningrad and control of the south (coal, iron, elimination of the enemy air base in the Crimea), with Moscow being brushed aside." Halder's diary for August 7 reveals:

> Commander of Army Group South also raises points of great strategy and emphasizes the importance of Moscow. The Führer again showed himself absolutely deaf to these arguments. He still harps on his old themes. Leningrad, with Hoth brought into the picture.... Moscow comes last.

Hitler's war teetered at this pivot in time. Half a century later, the military historian R. H. S. Stolfi judged: "But for one fateful decision, Germany could have won World War II in the summer of 1941." Most, probably all, other military historians agree. The logic puzzled scholars and generals alike. John Lukacs confessed his bafflement in 1976: "We do not know why Hitler ordered the halt of Army Group Center. We know that many months earlier, during the planning of Barbarossa, he kept repeating that too much importance must not be attributed to the capture of Moscow."

The well known, much discussed southward move of Guderian's tanks did at least respond to genuine opportunities arising in the Ukraine. It has been rationalized for eliminating a large Red Army force around Kiev and for seizing resources useful in a protracted war. But the latter attrition strategy flouts the blitzkrieg idea. Blizkrieg presumed a solar-plexus blow against the Red capital for maximum psychological and political shock. As of mid-July 1941, OKH felt sanguine about a knockout, that is, a total Soviet collapse coming upon the fall of Moscow.

By contrast, no matching economic or military reasons can explain the northward turn of the Wehrmacht armor. It has always mystified observers, then and since. As planned in Directive 21 of December 1940, it would have made sense, on paper, if the port of Leningrad, as mentioned above, were to be seized and used for German logistics. Rational utility was not the Führer's plan, however. What is left? Like certain other inexplicable items in the overall Hitler program, this scripted turn of the panzers came on cue. In sequence, it matched a move of Julian the Apostate in *Emperor and Galilean*.

REFUSAL TO PARLEY AND RESUMPTION OF
ADVANCE AGAINST THE ENEMY CAPITAL

Peace feelers from a shaken Stalin in summer and autumn 1941 hinted at ceding the Baltic states, Byelorussia, and part of the Ukraine. Hitler refused. Once again, the Nazi tyrant had scriptual sanction, from *Emperor and Galilean*, Part Two, Act V.

> AMMIAN: Three high-ranking envoys from King Sapor have just arrived in camp to sue for an armistice....
>
> JULIAN: I will not receive the Persian king's envoys today. They only want to waste my time. But I shall not negotiate a settlement. I will follow up my victory with utmost vigor. The army shall turn against Ctesiphon again.

Had Hitler actually been engrossed in reenacting this play, the Soviet offer of a battlefield truce came once more on cue. It could only abet Hitler in following a private script. The Führer duly turned to march on Moscow again in October 1941. At first, the Germans did well. But now their timing was off. The drenching rains of a Russian autumn soon transformed the ground to a miring, all-but-impassable muddy glue. Next, Arctic winds chilled the invaders, who had come clothed for a balmier clime. Finally, fresh Siberian troops appeared on the opposite side, warmly clad in fur-lined boots and sheepskin jackets, driving tanks and firing guns all made to work in the numbing frost. The Wehrmacht barely survived. Three and a half years later, in February 1945, Hitler looked back and lamented 1941: "We should have been able to conclude the campaign before winter came. How differently everything has turned out!"

EARLY CHRISTIAN ASSAULTS ON PAGAN SHRINES

As of October 19, 1941, a Nazi victory in Russia had still looked attainable. The Führer waxed buoyant at dinner that day as he updated

HENRIK IBSEN as he appeared in the mid-1860s, when he began the research that resulted in his epic, *Emperor and Galilean*, about Julian the Apostate, the last pagan ruler of the Roman Empire. *Courtesy of the author*

HENRIK IBSEN (1828–1906) in later life. The Norwegian playwright befriended Jews and despised demagogues, yet three of his plays were adapted as scripture by Hitler. *Courtesy of the author*

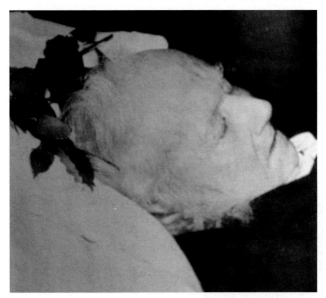

IBSEN on his deathbed, May 1906. In the wake of the playwright's passing, a cult arose in Germany hailing him as a "prophet" and treating certain of his plays as neo-pagan scripture. *Courtesy of the author*

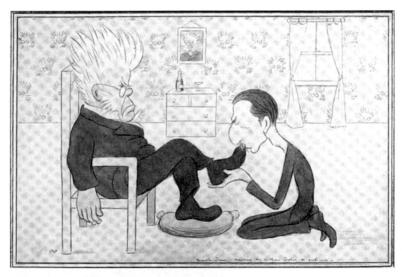

IBSEN'S ENGLISH TRANSLATOR William Archer pays homage to the master in a cartoon by Max Beerbohm, satirizing the exaltation of the playwright late in life. German devotees would subsequently fashion their cult around the "prophetic" Ibsen with an occult interpretation. *Courtesy of the author*

Franz Eher Nachf. G. m. b. H.
Deutschvölkische Verlagsbuchhandlung
Fernruf 20047 • München • Thierschstraße 15

Postscheck-Konto: Nr. 11540 München
Bank-Konto: Deutsche Hansabank A.G., München

Kommissionär:
Herr Robert Hoffmann, Leipzig

4½ Jahre Kampf
gegen Lüge, Dummheit und Feigheit
Eine Abrechnung von Adolf Hitler

Leitspruch

„Sie müssen sich ge-
genseitig wieder achten
lernen, der Arbeiter der
Stirne den Arbeiter der
Faust und umgekehrt.
Keiner von beiden be-
stünde ohne den ande-
ren. Aus ihnen her-
aus muß sich ein neuer
Mensch kristallisieren:
Der Mensch des kom-
menden Deutschen
Reiches!"   Adolf Hitler.

Der Eher-Verlag kündigt „Mein Kampf" an. 1924
Die kürzere Fassung des endgültigen Titels ist wesentlich schlagkräftiger!

AN EARLY ADVERTISEMENT FOR MEIN KAMPF, first published in 1925. Part of chapter 3 was modeled upon Act IV of Ibsen's drama, *An Enemy of the People*, although critics and historians long failed to note this instance of plagiarism. *United States Holocaust Memorial Museum (USHMM), courtesy of Library of Congress*

In a 1937 Berlin stage version, EUGEN KLÖPFER starred as Dr. Stockmann in *An Enemy of the People*, giving the impassioned harangue against complacency which Hitler had earlier plagiarized in chapter 3 of *Mein Kampf*. Nazis took Stockmann's warning about noxious germs as a metaphor for the alleged danger posed by Jews. *Theater collection of Cologne University*

DIETRICH ECKART (1867–1923) was a Nazi poet, playwright, and pamphleteer whom Hitler often acknowledged as his most significant mentor. *USHMM, courtesy of Stadtarchiv Muenchen*

NAZIS REVERED ECKART as a spiritual founder of their movement. *Bavarian State Library*

Besides adapting Ibsen's *PEER GYNT* to the German stage, Eckart insisted that he embodied the Peer Gynt character in his own person. But Hitler favored other Ibsen plays. *Courtesy of the author*

HANNS JOHST, successor to Dietrich Eckart as Nazi poet laureate. In 1923, Hitler confided he had seen Johst's drama *Der König* ("The King") seventeen times, and that his own mortal fate was foretold by the king's suicide at the conclusion. This prophecy was self-fulfilled in 1945. *Courtesy of the author*

In prison at Landsberg in 1924, HITLER posed for photos several times beneath a conspicuously displayed wreath. A wreath figures as a symbol for paganism in Ibsen's *Emperor and Galilean* and as an ominous prop in *The Master Builder*; both plays were emulated by Hitler in word and deed. *USHMM, courtesy of Richard Freimark*

BERCHTESGADEN in Bavaria, the alpine resort where Ibsen wrote much of *Emperor and Galilean,* subsequently became Hitler's favorite mountain retreat. *Credit: Jennifer L. Rodgers*

JULIAN THE APOSTATE (reigned 361–363) attempted to restore paganism to the Roman empire. In Ibsen's play *Emperor and Galilean,* Julian strives to found a "third Reich" to repudiate the Christian church. Phrases derived from the play turn up in Hitler's transcribed talks, wherein Hitler also explicitly likened his own mission to that of Julian. The Nazi dictator believed he could succeed where Julian had failed and eliminate Christianity by first exterminating the Jews. *Courtesy of the author*

JULIAN as portrayed on
a coin struck during his
brief reign. *Courtesy of the
author*

In this novel published in
1921, the Lutheran pastor
and Ibsen scholar EMIL
FELDEN lampooned a
Hitler-like politician who
misconstrues the phrasing
of Ibsen's *Emperor and
Galilean*. His novel, translated as *The Sin Against the
People*, assailed the Nazi
dogma that stated Jesus
Christ had not been a Jew.
Courtesy of the author

In the novel *Thunderstone*, published in 1924, the pro-Nazi Ibsen cultist PAUL SCHULZE-BERGHOF hailed Hitler as the one anointed to resurrect Julian's neo-pagan "third Reich" as foretold in *Emperor and Galilean. Courtesy of the author*

Having immersed himself in *Emperor and Galilean*, Hitler extolled Julian's sayings as presented in this short digest prepared by a Nazi writer, KURT EGGERS, under the title *The Emperor of Rome Against the King of the Jews. Courtesy of the author*

OTTO WAGENER, a Hitler aide during 1929–1932, kept a record of what Hitler said. In a crucial instance, the phrasing he transcribed matches lines from *Emperor and Galilean*, substantiating that play as the Führer's secret script. *Ullstein Bilderdienst*

Hitler's twenty-three-year-old niece and consort, GELI RAUBAL. Key particulars of their relationship mirror that of Julian the Apostate and his wife in *Emperor and Galilean*. Geli was fatally shot by Hitler's pistol on the night of September 18–19, 1931. The timing of her death matches the September 19 appearance of Hilde Wangel, aged twenty-three, in Ibsen's play *The Master Builder*. Hitler spoke lines derived from both Ibsen plays and initiated a series of actions paralleling highlights of their plots. *Courtesy of the author*

The REICHSTAG building in Berlin, shown burning in late February 1933. Having eliminated the Reichstag's legislative obstruction, Hitler proceeded to decree the Autobahn project under Fritz Todt, who served as master builder of the Third Reich until his death in 1942. *USHMM, courtesy of Bildarchiv Preussischer Kulturbesitz*

Hitler's master builder, FRITZ TODT (1891–1942), engineered the Autobahn. In this photo he wears the insignia of a Luftwaffe general. The rank was awarded by Hitler although Todt exercised no air war responsibilities. In November 1941 Hitler hinted at Todt's impending demise. *USHMM, courtesy of Nederlands Instituut voor Oorlogsdocumentatie*

TODT DISTRIBUTING MEDALS to Westwall workers. Hitler initially referred to the fortification as the *limes*, following ancient Roman usage. *USHMM, courtesy of of Anne Gentry Burgess Dyess*

ALBERT SPEER, subordinate and eventual successor to Fritz Todt as Nazi master builder after Todt's airplane blew up in February 1942 at the Führer's wartime headquarters. *USHMM*

HANS BAUR, Hitler's personal pilot, wrote that Todt's fatal air crash in February 1942 had been caused by an explosive devise aboard the plane. *Courtesy of the author*

After daring the Master Builder to climb
too high, HILDE WANGEL points as
he topples to his death in an early 20th
century Norwegian production of Ibsen's
play. The record of Hitler's transcribed talks
substantiates his familiarity with Hilde's
lines in the German version of the script.
Courtesy of the author

guests on an obscure theme that he had long cherished, the pagan shrines of antiquity:

Rome [i.e., the Vatican] wants to reproach Bolshevism for having destroyed the Christian churches. *As if Christianity hadn't done the same with pagan temples!* [italics added]

Didn't he know there was a war on? Of course; he had started it. In retrospect, the germane question should be: Which war was he in fact waging? The issue had already preoccupied him in *Mein Kampf,* Volume II, chapter 5: "Christianity also could not be content with building its own altars, and felt compelled to proceed with destroying the pagan altars." During 1941, though, it is safe to say that the over-zealous Christian pillage of Greco–Roman shrines preoccupied the Führer alone among his entourage, busy in their chilly wartime bunkers. The impulse to at last redress this monstrous historic wrong arose from some impetus within their chief. What matters to the chief, though, matters to History. Long ago, in February 1908, he had seen these pious abominations portrayed onstage in a Viennese production of Wilbrandt's *Der Meister von Palmyra.* Still more vivid images could be had from *Emperor and Galilean.*

In Part Two, Act II of Ibsen's play, the churchman Gregory of Nazianzus informs emperor Julian of communal religious strife in the city of Caesarea. Doctrinaire Christians there:

demanded that the authorities should bear palpable witness to Christ by razing to the ground any monument still standing to the former might of paganism in Caesarea.

Julian seeks details, and Gregory continues:

We Christians in Caesarea have decided that the temple in which the pagans in their day worshipped a false deity, under the name of Fortuna, shall be demolished and razed to the ground.

An alarmed Julian warns the cleric against such wanton waste:

> You shall feel how far the emperor's arm can reach! . . . Ah, you
> Galileans, you rely on my patience. Don't count on it.

A disheveled pagan named Eunapius bursts in, just back from Caesarea.

> I left the town this morning to visit the little temple of Venus
> which you recently restored. When I arrived, I was met by songs
> and the sound of flutes. Women were dancing gracefully in the
> forecourt, and inside I found the whole place filled with a joyous
> crowd, while the priests at the altar offered the sacrifices you
> have prescribed.

But Christian bigots were about to dampen that joyous mood. Eunapius continued:

> A great swarm of young men forced their way into the temple. . . .
> What a scene there was! With these hooligans hurling abuse and
> beating them up, the dancing girls ran weeping from the forecourt
> to us inside. The Galileans fell on us all, molested us, and insulted
> us in a most disgraceful manner. . . . The brutes went further. Yes,
> your most gracious Majesty. In short, the altar has been pulled
> down, the statue of the goddess smashed.

Still indignant in Part Two, Act III, Julian vows:

> Wait, just wait! The Galileans in Caesarea shall pay with their
> blood, and the whole city shall go up in flames, as soon as I can
> find the time.

He could never fit it into his schedule, although slaughtering "Galileans" in just one town would have been to no avail. Had Julian only known what Hitler grasped, about who subverted the teaching of Christ! Four months later, on the night of February 20–21, 1942, the Führer rehashed:

> Christianity is the worst of the regressions that mankind can ever have undergone, and it's the Jew who, thanks to this diabolic invention, has thrown him [mankind] back a millennium and a half.

Not nineteen centuries, back to the time of Christ, but just a millennium and a half. Which, plus a few decades, goes back to Julian's pagan restoration. Hitler continued:

> The only thing that would be still worse would be victory for the Jew through Bolshevism. If Bolshevism triumphed, mankind would lose the gift of laughter and joy. It would become merely a shapeless mass, doomed to grayness and despair.

Then once more, as on October 19, a jab at Christianity for ending the pagan idyll:

> The priests of antiquity were closer to nature, and they sought modestly for the meaning of things. Instead of that, Christianity promulgates its inconsistent dogmas and imposes them by force. Such a religion carries within it intolerance and persecution. It's the bloodiest conceivable.

Amidst the laughter, love of nature, search for truth, and partying with the dancing girls, Rome's pagan priests and rulers let a deadly threat slip by. Their empire collapsed. But the lost joy of antiquity might yet be restored. Once "the Jew" has been revealed as the source for spreading Christianity, then:

> all Jews will be struck down. This time, the Jews will disappear from Europe. An unburdened, free laughter will come again to our world, when this mountain is removed!

10

FINALLY, A SOLUTION TO
THE "FINAL SOLUTION"

JULIAN: The third Reich has come, Maximus!
I feel the Messiah of the world is alive in me.
The spirit has become flesh, and the flesh
spirit. All created things are within my will and
my power.

—IBSEN, *EMPEROR AND GALILEAN*,

PART TWO, ACT IV

AT THE END of *Emperor and Galilean,* a Christian in Julian's army aims his javelin at the emperor who falls, mortally wounded. The assassin yells, "The Roman's spear from Golgotha!" Julian dies by the very weapon used three centuries before to end Christ's agony on the cross. A persistent legend, albeit one eluding reliable documentation, has it that Hitler maintained a fetish over a relic purported to be this same spear. When he annexed Austria in March 1938, the Führer supposedly ordered it transferred from Vienna's Hofburg Museum to Nuremberg. If true, any number of factors could have stimulated his interest in this object. One factor that can be documented is Hitler's focus on Julian the Apostate.

A NEW JULIAN FOR A NEW THIRD REICH

In 1941, Hitler took special care to avoid mortal peril in the enemy's land. He kept his visits to the Eastern Front few and brief. Perhaps he recalled a joke line from *Peer Gynt*: "One cannot die in the middle of Act V." Instead, the Führer hunkered down and read his concern for Julian into the historical record. The task here is to substantiate whether Ibsen's nineteenth-century historical drama about a fourth-century Roman emperor really provided the basic blueprint for Hitler's twentieth-century neo-pagan quest, the German Third Reich. If so, he revised the replay to make amends for Julian's big mistake of antagonizing Christ. Having thumbed through to the end like some impatient reader of a mystery thriller, Hitler knew who the real culprit was and adapted accordingly. Where Julian trifled with a Christ he mistook for a Jew, Hitler paid respect to a divine Aryan guru. Where Julian burned Christian books, Hitler put the match to books by Jews. Julian had flouted Christ by trying to rebuild the Temple at Jerusalem, only to face divine wrath in rubble and flames. Hitler, duly taking heed, instead torched the synagogues of the Reich.

Mutatis mutandis, by October 1941 the Nazi dictator had at last discovered Julian's own polemics. The Julian of *Emperor and Galilean* mentions these treatises in Part Two, Act III. But not until 1941 are there any hints of Hitler reading what the real Julian wrote. When he got around to doing so, it was probably late at night in his private lodgings. Most of the Führer's daytime work hours were spent with generals and maps, plotting brutal war against Stalin's resilient troops. A break would come at mealtimes. The Führer's fare—a vegetarian porridge heavy on legumes—would be followed by sessions where he loosed himself from the pressures of . . . command. Stenographers jotted down his anecdotes, opinions, tirades, and laments. The etiquette had guests at most assenting politely while their relaxed chief vented at will. More so even than *Mein Kampf,* which was edited for publication, these private "Table Talk" monologues offer the most genuine inner glimpse of a messianic mind. Hitler aide Martin Bormann did some limited editing, but the source still stands.

Two days after he fulminated over the Christian trashing of pagan shrines, Hitler at last put the name of Julian on record. His words of midday, October 21, 1941, bear repeating:

> I really hadn't known how clearly a man like Julian had judged the Christians and Christianity. One must read this. (*Ich habe gar nicht gewusst, wie klar ein Mann wie Julian die Christen und das Christentum beurteilte. Man muss das einmal lesen.*)

He was addressing the SS lords, Heinrich Himmler and Reinhard Heydrich. Himmler incidentally pursued his own historical hero cult over an odd, non-Aryan and "Asiatic" choice: Genghis Khan. The Reichsführer-SS had been inspired after reading a biography of the medieval Mongol ruler by one Michael Prawdin. Several years earlier, Himmler had pushed this volume on his boss, who now returned the favor by commending an item that Julian wrote.

Hitler continued, on Christianity and Christ:

> Christianity was destructive Bolshevism. Nevertheless, the Galilean, who later was called the Christ, meant something quite different. He was a popular leader (*ein Volksführer*) who took a stand against Jewry. Galilee was a colony where the Romans had probably settled Gallic legionaries, and Jesus was certainly no Jew. The Jews incidentally called him the son of a whore: the son of a whore and a Roman soldier.

No philologist, he had wrongly conflated the Hebraic "Galilee" and "Galilean" with the linguistically totally unrelated Celtic terms "Gaul" and "Gallic," in a bid to convince himself about the gentile makeup of Jesus' homeland. The Führer went on:

> The decisive falsification of Jesus' doctrine was the work of St. Paul. He gave himself to this work with subtlety and for purposes of personal exploitation. For the Galilean's object was to liberate his country from Jewish oppression. He set himself against Jewish capitalism, and that's why the Jews liquidated him. Paul of

Tarsus—his name was Saul, before the road to Damascus—was
one of those who persecuted Jesus most savagely.

Hitler thus finally specified his own mission as a replay of Julian's
anti-Christian quest and the culmination of a metahistorical epoch.
The present war was intended to reverse the millennial chicanery
of St. Paul, a.k.a. Saul, as he reminded himself and anyone listening.
Again the fall of Rome crops up:

> If the Jew has succeeded in destroying the Roman empire,
> that's because St. Paul transformed a local movement of Aryan
> opposition to Jewry into a supra-temporal religion, which pos-
> tulates the equality of all men amongst themselves, and their
> obedience to an only god. This is what caused the death of the
> Roman empire.
>
> It's striking to observe that Christian ideas, despite all St.
> Paul's efforts, had no success in Athens. The philosophy of the
> Greeks was so much superior to this poverty-stricken rubbish
> that the Athenians burst out laughing when they listened to the
> apostle's teaching.

Hitler continued the analogy:

> Of old, it was in the name of Christianity. Today, it's in the name
> of Bolshevism. Yesterday, the instigator was Saul; the instigator
> today, Mordechai. Saul has changed into St. Paul, and Mordechai
> into Karl Marx. By exterminating this pest, we shall do humanity
> a service of which our soldiers can have no idea.

This is the very kernel of *Bolshevism from Moses to Lenin,* the
dialogue with Dietrich Eckart from eighteen years before. The analogy to Bolshevism incorporating the "spirit of Judas" (*Judasgeist*) also
occurred in Paul Schulze-Berghof's treatise on *Emperor and Galilean*
as an allegory. But Hitler had more recently been reading another
source. Four days later, on October 25, he returned to the topic and
invoked a work written by Julian.

The book with the sayings of Emperor Julian should be distributed by the millions. Such wonderful insight! Ancient wisdom! Such perception! It's fantastic!

SAYINGS OF THE EMPEROR JULIAN

Fantastic it was, indeed. On October 21, Hitler had pushed the book on Himmler and Heydrich. In the four days since then, it had grown in his esteem, enough to propose circulation en masse. By way of prior example, Himmler had once ordered a large-scale printing for SS men of Prawdin's life of Genghis Khan. But another, more immediate prompt is at hand in *Emperor and Galilean,* Part Two, Act IV. There Julian relates a dream he has had while campaigning in Persia, and written a record down on a scroll.

Do you see this, Jovian? This morning in bed, I wrote down my dream. Take it, have a lot of copies made, and get it read out to the regiments. I believe it's important that on a dangerous campaign fraught with hardship and peril, that the soldiers should place their fate with confidence in the hands of their leader, accepting him as infallible in matters affecting the war's outcome.

Julian was more than the ephemeral stuff of which dreams are made. Three months later, on January 27, 1942, Hitler ruminated at the midday meal. After a poke at Emperor Constantine for adopting Christianity, he turned again to Julian:

It would be better to speak of Constantine the Traitor and Julian the Loyal than of Constantine the Great and Julian the Apostate. What Christianity wrote against Julian is the same drivel as the stuff the Jews pour forth about us, while the writings of Julian are the pure truth.

The analogy could not be more explicit: The Jews are to Hitler what the Christians were to Julian.

But it does not end with the Jews or "Judeo-Bolshevism." All the while, the annihilation of the Jews comprised merely a necessary first phase for the eventual expunging of Christianity. Toward that end, the Julian scenario lurked in his thoughts through the autumn and winter of 1941–42. It remains to clarify as far as possible the function of Julian the Apostate in Hitler's mind as of 1941–42, with particular regard to his sources. Amidst pursuing strategies of war and genocide in October 1941, the Führer singled out "the book with the sayings of Emperor Julian." He spoke those words while dining with the two top-ranked SS implementers of the Jewish extermination. It is thus of weighty material importance to identify what particular book was meant by the initiator of the Final Solution, and, above all, what led him to read it.

A postwar German editor of the "Table Talk" transcripts guessed—and only guessed—that Hitler's interest owed to a biography by the Belgian scholar Joseph Bidez, originally published in 1930 as *La vie de l'empereur Julian;* it then appeared in German translation in 1940 as *Julian der Abtrünnige,* with reissues in subsequent years. The problem is, this biography does not include excerpts of the emperor's essays and therefore cannot meet the criterion of "the book with the sayings of Emperor Julian"; that had to be some book containing the words of Julian himself.

Which book, then? Julian composed more than one book. His surviving corpus fills over seven hundred pages of text in Greek as reprinted in modern editions. There were two lengthy essays in praise of Emperor Constantius that together comprise a book, and another long panegyric to the empress Eusebia. Julian formulated a form of sun-worshipping paganism in a "Hymn to King Helios" and a "Hymn to the Mother of the Gods," each of which is also regarded as a book. He spewed more religious invective against the Christian clergy in the satire *Misopogon,* translated as "Beard Hater," and he evaluated preceding Roman rulers at book length in "The Caesars." There is also Julian's consolation to himself upon the departure of Sallust. There are orations and letters of essay length addressed to Cynics, to Themistius the philosopher, and to the senate and people of Athens. There are fifty-eight dated shorter letters and another fifteen undated ones, various fragments, and collected epigrams. And there is an anti-Christian diatribe of moderate length, lost in the full-text original but reassembled from quotations as they were recorded in a response to Julian by a Christian critic. This is titled *Kata Galilaion*, or "Against the Galileans."

Of all these, what book by Julian did Hitler read while turning the Final Solution from a breezy concept to lethal Zyklon-B? It would have to be a book wherein "Julian had judged the Christians and Christianity," as the Führer stated on October 21, 1941. Given Hitler's animus toward Moses and St. Paul, each of those villains could be expected to feature prominently in this book. Also, the book had to be compact enough in size and simple enough in text to prompt his whim that it be "circulated in millions." Moreover, the book had to take the form of "sayings" (dictums, maxims—*Ausspruchen*), as stated on October 25.

At the Wolfsschanze headquarters, the compiler of Hitler's transcribed utterances prefaced the entry for October 21 with: "The chief spoke with reference to a book, *Der Scheiterhaufen.*" This is not quite Julian's sayings, but it offers a valuable clue. Hardly a memorable literary work, *Der Scheiterhaufen* ("The Funeral Pyre") turns out to be a thin, large-print volume only seven inches high, the size of a prayer missal. Outwardly it seems to be an item from the knick-knack book rack between the floral bouquets and get-well cards in a hospital gift shop. Inside, *Der Scheiterhaufen* amounts to an anti-religious Nazi breviary. An enlarged version published the following year was indeed titled just that: "A Heretic Breviary." The subtitle of *Der Scheiterhaufen* is *Worte grosser Ketzer*, "Words of Great Heretics." Its text was compiled in 1941 by one Kurt Eggers (1905–43), a failed Nazi playwright who shortly went to his own mortal fate on the Russian front, serving as a war correspondent for the Waffen-SS. While tossing together *Der Scheiterhaufen*, he had plucked quotes from the words of Nietzsche, Schopenhauer, Kant, and Frederick the Great to fill most of his funeral pyre's 107 dainty pages.

Hitler remarked on *Der Scheiterhaufen:*

When one sees how clear were the opinions of our best men toward Christianity already a hundred and two hundred years ago, it's a shame how we haven't come any further.

Kant, Frederick, Schopenhauer, and Nietzsche were this book's best men of "a hundred and two hundred years ago." Hitler then glided into Julian: "I really hadn't known how clearly a man like Julian had judged the Christians and Christianity. One must read this." And four days later: "The book with the sayings of Emperor Julian should be distributed by the millions. Such wonderful insight! Ancient wisdom!"

Hitler thereby singled out Julian, not Kant, Schopenhauer, Nietzsche, or Frederick the Great. But *Der Scheiterhaufen* contained only two pages of Julian's ancient wisdom among the dozens more pages each from the "great heretics" of the eighteenth and nineteenth centuries. Seven short Julian quotes comprise under two percent of *Der Scheiterhaufen*. By its overall contents, the breviary hardly qualifies as "the book with the sayings of Emperor Julian."

There had to be some other volume; and the clue that Kurt Eggers was involved quickly turns up another of his petite books of sayings. From the criteria Hitler uttered, only one item fits, a sixty-four-page popular edition of reworked excerpts that also appeared in 1941 under the attention-grabbing title *Der Kaiser der Römer gegen den König der Juden: Aus den Schriften Julians des "Abtrünnigen"* ("The Caesar of the Romans against the King of the Jews: From the Writings of Julian the 'Apostate'"). This one bore a twelve-page preface by Eggers, who had visited a library and drawn from a translation of Julian's *Against the Galileans*, adding introductory remarks to present the work of Julian as a parable for the rise of Hitler.

Eggers struck at St. Paul, as in "the unholy work of the Jewish rabbi, Paul" (p. 6), Hitler's own bugaboo in his October 21 talk. The Eggers preface disdained the theoretical equality of believers in Christianity (p. 8), grousing about how baptism raises black Africans to the level of white men in God's esteem. Eggers went on: The Jewish priests were political agitators, through which they prepared the ground for

Jewish world domination. Christianity, spread by Jews such as Paul, appealed to slave instincts. Eggers (p. 9) described how:

> Not only did "heathen" temples crumble, not only were images of the gods defiled by the crazed Christian mobs, but all that the strong, hearty, and brave held sacred in those days was trampled in the dirt.

Taken alone, Eggers's preface might seem a candidate source for triggering Hitler's remarks on the night of October 19, 1941 about Christians rampaging through pagan temples, as well as for what Hitler said at midday on October 21. But there was nothing at all in the passages Eggers had excerpted from Julian's *Against the Galileans* about Christian attacks against pagan houses of worship. The SS bard had to have grabbed that allusion from somewhere else. *Emperor and Galilean*, Part Two, Act II offered a natural recourse for Eggers, himself an erstwhile playwright. Or perhaps, whoever commissioned Eggers to compile the sayings of Julian as a booklet could conceivably have recommended the Ibsen play for reference. Eggers drew an analogy to Hitler as he wound up his prefacing dirge on Roman decline:

> Then came in the greatest need a savior! Emperor Julian!

Passages in this version of Julian's sayings had been selected for easy reading and set in large type. That made it most convenient for a Führer whose staff routinely recopied memoranda to him on a special big-print typewriter to accommodate his myopia. Because of his eye problems, he couldn't go through as much written material as in his younger days; what he did read thus had a relatively greater impact. At only sixty-four pages including blank sheets and a twelve-page preface, Eggers's digest reduced Julian's *Against the Galileans* from treatise to tract, a bedtime reading snack well suited to Hitler's impaired vision, his limited patience for abstractions, and the busy schedule of a man running a war.

Nearly all the quotes Eggers selected from Julian hewed to two
simple themes. These hit Moses' Judaism for naming the Jews as
the spiritually chosen people, and attacked Christianity as Paul's
structure atop this Jewish basis. The Judeo–Christian monotheist
intolerance toward other faiths had offended Julian. Relativizing
Christ himself, Eggers presented this quotation (p. 63):

> Jesus Christ is but one of a series of miracle workers and religious
> founders who from time to time become manifest according to
> a certain progression.

The notion fits perfectly with Maximus's teaching about the reincarnated great soul in *Emperor and Galilean,* Part Two, Act IV:

> He had to fall as the god-begotten man in the Garden of Eden;
> he had to fall as founder of the world empire; he had to fall as
> the Prince of God's Kingdom. Who knows how many times he's
> wandered among us without anyone recognizing him? Can you
> know, Julian, that you weren't once in him you now persecute?

Lest anyone doubt the presence of this recurring figure in the
world of 1941, Eggers added a line:

> For soldiers in battle, the most exalted sight is a wise leader
> (*Führer*).

One reader at least may have sighed, his self-image lovingly
spoonfed. But the Julian encountered via Eggers's *The Caesar of the
Romans against the King of the Jews* cannot have been that reader's first
introduction to the Apostate. Some prior acquaintance is implicit in
Hitler's remark of October 21, 1941: "I really hadn't known how clearly
a man like Julian had judged the Christians and Christianity." These
are the words of a man surprised to learn an unanticipated aspect
of something already familiar, at least in part. From the nuance it is
evident that Hitler knew well enough of Julian's existence in history;
had had more than a passing interest in Julian prior to October 1941;

but had hitherto been unacquainted with Julian's own writings. It is impossible for his expressed interest toward Julian during 1941–42 to have emerged full-grown like Pallas Athene from the brow of Zeus. What specific prompting had steered Hitler to the Kurt Eggers version of the sayings of Julian the Apostate?

The Hitler phrase "how clearly a man like Julian had judged the Christians and Christianity" (*wie klar ein Mann wie Julian die Christen und das Christentum beurteilte*) yields a lexical link between *Against the Galileans* and Hitler's choice to place it on his reading syllabus. A "clear judgment" (*ein klares Urteil*) regarding the Jewish conception of deity was precisely how the German academic classicist Joseph Vogt had characterized *Against the Galileans* in a short book published in 1939. That monograph carried the title *Kaiser Julian und das Judentum* ("Emperor Julian and Jewry").

Two areas of Hitlerian interest are united in Vogt's title. Textual evidence suggests that before 1939, Hitler had already known Ibsen's play about Julian. In 1939, there then came along an item specifically discussing Julian and Jewry. Vogt's treatise on Julian and the Jews thus presents the most readily available bridge in the Führer's reading. Its phrasing and that of Hitler coincide with specific reference to *Against the Galileans.* The due appearance of Eggers's shortened version of that very tract in 1941 may therefore be suspected of having been initiated by an outright commission or an informal word of encouragement from on high. Then, having read what Eggers dished up by the autumn of 1941, Hitler would be in a position to exclaim: "I really hadn't known how clearly a man like Julian had judged the Christians and Christianity."

Vogt had incidentally absolved Julian of harboring any pro-Jewish principles. The professor interpreted Julian's attempted rebuilding of the Temple at Jerusalem as no more than a tactical propaganda measure on the eve of the Roman offensive against Persia. Vogt also dismissed as apocryphal a conciliatory letter by Julian to Jewish communities. Vogt's Julian was therefore not at heart a philo-Semite. That could only reassure Hitler. It remained for the Führer to obtain and to absorb some accessible, reader-friendly version of the Julian book. And one was duly published.

In sum, *Against the Galileans* as simplified by Kurt Eggers makes the only realistic candidate for the "book by Julian" that Hitler pressed on Himmler and Heydrich in October 1941. Looking back in turn, Joseph Vogt's book about Julian and the Jews (1939) provided a strong recommendation that readers seeking further knowledge on the topic should proceed to *Against the Galileans.* Vogt's "clear judgment" wording is echoed by Hitler, and *Against the Galileans,* repackaged as "The Caesar of the Romans against the King of the Jews," meets the other criteria for determining it as Hitler's "book with the sayings of Emperor Julian."

But if Hitler read Julian via Kurt Eggers's excerpts, as seems all but certain, and if he also glanced at Vogt's tome on Julian and the Jews, do those works obviate or supplant a hypothetical Hitler fixation on Ibsen's *Emperor and Galilean?* No. Further traces of the play appear, like the pentimenti of underlying brush strokes, in the transcripts of Hitler's spoken words during 1941–42. They substantiate *Emperor and Galilean* as the dictator's principal source on Julian the Apostate, and as the Ur-text for the basic Hitlerian program.

CONSTANTINE THE UN-GREAT

The stenographic record for early 1942 yields a cluster of Hitler locutions resonating with items in the last three acts of *Emperor and Galilean.* On January 27, 1942, the Führer's itch about Christianity had gotten to him. It was Emperor Constantine who began the ruin of the Roman empire after he adopted the faith in the early fourth century. Julian had made that very point in Part Two, Act III. Julian's words are in the left column, addressed to Maximus; Hitler's remarks are on the right.

Constantine extended the boundaries of the realm. But didn't he narrowly restrict the boundaries of the spirit and will? You overestimate the man when you call him "the Great."	It would be better to speak of Constantine the Traitor and Julian the Loyal, instead of naming one as the Great and the other as the Apostate.

Hitler then followed this judgment with his earlier quoted words: "What Christianity wrote against Julian is the same drivel as the stuff the Jews pour forth about us, while the writings of Julian are the pure truth." Comparing the two passages above:

* Both passages pit the same two historical figures: In *Emperor and Galilean,* Julian himself speaks scathingly of Constantine, whereas Hitler compares Julian and Constantine by name.
* In both passages, the title of Constantine as "the Great" is called into doubt.

Taken alone, this set of paired quotations cannot be deemed definitive. But this pair did not occur alone.

ASCENDING MT. OLYMPUS

In Part Two, Act IV, Emperor Julian awakens from his remarkable dream, the same one he recorded on a scroll to be read aloud to the troops. The dream narrative needs recounting in full, in the left column. On the right is Hitler's brief echo, spoken at midday on February 27, 1942, and including the German text of his remarks.

I dreamt I beheld a child pursued by a rich man who owned herds of cattle but who derided the worship of the gods. This evil man wiped out the child's entire family. But Zeus pitied the child and extended a hand of protection over him. I then observed the child grow into a youth protected by Minerva and Apollo.	I feel fine in the historical company I am in if there is an Olympus. Where I'm going will be found the most enlightened spirits of all times.
	[Ich fühle mich wohl in der geschichtlichen Gesellschaft, in der ich mich befinde, wenn es einen Olymp gibt. In dem, in den ich eingehe, werden sich die erleuchtetsten Geister aller Zeiten finden.]
I then dreamt that the youth fell asleep upon a stone under the open sky. Hermes then descended to earth in the form of a young man and said	

"Come, I'll show you the way to the abode of the highest god!" He led the youth to the foot of a very steep mountain, and left him there.

The youth then cried and lamented, calling loudly to Zeus, whereupon Minerva and the Sun King, who rules over the earth, came down beside him, lifted him up to the peak of the mountain, and showed him the inheritance of his family. This inheritance was the whole globe, from ocean to ocean and beyond the ocean.

They told the youth that all of it should be his, and issued three warnings: He should maintain alertness, unlike his kinsmen; he should not listen to the advice of hypocrites; and lastly, he should pay divine honor to those who resemble the gods. "And don't forget," they said as they took leave, "that your soul is immortal and of divine origin. If you follow our advice, you shall see our father and become a god, like us."

To compare:

* Greco–Roman mythology provides the referential setting for both passages.
* The dominant image in both passages is a mountain, left unnamed by Julian but referred to by Hitler as "an Olympus."
* In Julian's dream, the residents of the mountain are gods given by name, including Minerva, the goddess of wisdom (a.k.a. Pallas

Athene); Hitler refers to the mountain's inhabitants as "the most enlightened spirits."

⊕ For both speakers, the mortal who is ascending to an afterlife on the mountain is the ruler or heir of a vast earthly domain.

⊕ Both speakers attain their exalted position after great struggle against adversity and injustice, narrated by Julian in his dream and elsewhere by Hitler.

Just a few sentences later in Julian's speech comes the part where he commands that the dream be copied and read to out to the regiments of his army.

THE PROMISED LAND

Hitler's verbalized thoughts at midday, February 27, 1942, again drifted to his divinely appointed rule. And again, the remarks parallel *Emperor and Galilean,* this time Part Two, Act V, the final act of the two-part epic. Emperor Julian's dying words from near the drama's final scene are in the left column, faced by the German Führer's on the right:

I have nothing to regret. The power which destiny placed in my hand, and which is a divine emanation, I know I have used to the best of my ability. I have never intentionally mistreated anyone.	I am here due to a higher power, if I am necessary for anything. Leave aside that she is too cruel for me, the beatifying Church! I have never found pleasure in maltreating others even if I know it isn't possible to stand your ground in the world without force.

The tone of each speaker is that of a man looking back and surveying his life's work. Conjoined are the following distinct thoughts. In each of the brief paired passages, the ruler:

⊕ claims to hold a divine commission;

⊕ implicitly acknowledges that his rule had incurred harm to some;

⊕ but states how that harm had not brought him gratification.

Hitler's subsequent remarks again paraphrase Julian, from a portion in the opening scene of *Emperor and Galilean,* Part II, Act V. In the script, the emperor has just been reminded by an aide of how he killed Christians who placed their faith in Christ above loyalty to him. Julian then reaffirms his mission against the Christians via a signal metaphor. Julian's words appear in the left column, those of Hitler on the right:

The Hebrews had to wander forty years in the wilderness. All the old ones had to die off. A new generation had to mature, but that generation— you should note—that generation entered the land that had been promised to them all.	The time in which we live is a phenomenon of the collapse of this thing [Christianity]. It may still endure a hundred or two hundred years. I'm sorry that, like Moses, I'll only glimpse the promised land from afar.

Here are the specific contents common to the two passages:

⊕ "Promised land" is defined or clearly understood in both texts as a world without Christianity.
⊕ Both passages specify a long period of time elapsed and the passing of human generations.
⊕ In both passages, the leader of the present anti-Christian movement likens his mission to that of Moses. Hitler made the allusion specific, whereas with Julian it remained implicit but undeniable in his reference to wandering in the wilderness and to the old ones dying off.

Given Hitler's reflexive repugnance toward everything Jewish, his self-analogy to Moses even in this limited instance is nothing short of astounding. An external stimulus is required to account for such an egregious departure from his personal norm. *Emperor and Galilean,* Part Two, Act V provides that prompt. The date of Hitler's talk came just a month after a Hitler reference to Julian by name. Here Hitler's metaphoric parallels to the play's last act include one from near the end of the act, then leap back to near its beginning. This circumstance should demonstrate, as on earlier occasions, that the Führer did not memorize the Ibsen script per se; rather, he had recently read this act of the play, gaining a vivid, active impression. In the extemporaneous speech of his "Table Talk," he then casually jumbled Ibsen snippets. While speaking, he need not have been consciously trying to quote the literary source for his remarks.

However, Hitler stayed fully aware of his self-identity as heir to Julian. As such, his expressed long-term goal was to wipe out the Christianity of the churches. He continued without pause:

> We are developing toward a sunny, truly tolerant world outlook.
> *(Wir wachsen in eine sonnige, wirklich tolerante Weltanschauung hinein).*

Throughout *Emperor and Galilean,* Julian equates the teachings of the church with blindness and darkness, to which he opposes vision and light. Here the question concerns the particular source in the play for the use here of the adjective "sunny," otherwise a rarity in the Hitler lexicon. *Emperor and Galilean* offers several possibilities.

One occurs at the very moment when Julian succumbs to his mortal wound. His dying words are: "Beautiful earth, beautiful life on earth. Oh sun, sun, why have you deceived me?"

Part One, Act I offers another possibility. A prophetic pagan philosopher speaks with the young student Julian. They have observed the vicious, intolerant squabbling so endemic among various Christian sects.

The shared context between the play and the Hitler monologue is Christian intolerance contrasted to pagan tolerance. Within that context, each speaker brightens paganism with solar imagery. And each promises a neo-pagan world to come. The philosopher's words are in the left column, Hitler's in the right:

I know One who could be ruler of this great and sunlit kingdom.	We are developing toward a sunny, truly tolerant world outlook.

The pagan philosopher adds that he is "awaiting the arrival of

Helios"—the solar god. *Emperor and Galilean,* Part Two, Acts II, IV, and V all contain further references to Julian's worship of Helios, the solar disk. By contrast, the solar metaphor for tolerance is lacking from the Eggers book of Julian sayings, eliminating it as the direct stimulus. What remains, again, is *Emperor and Galilean.*

This has not been a scavenger hunt after verbal pentimenti for the sake of a literary game. At stake are the historical actions initiated by Hitler, paralleling the plot action of the Ibsen play. Accounting for those actions with reference to the play requires demonstrating that Hitler knew this drama. It appears that he knew it so well that its phrasing emanated quite freely from his lips, interspersed with the rest of his chatter. Ample confirming paraphrases to the concluding acts of the play occur in early 1942, as do Hitler's explicit allusions to Julian from the months October 1941 to January 1942. Why are there not more paraphrases for previous years? It should be noted that for those prior times there are fewer records of Hitler speaking off the cuff. When such records are available, they again yield an occasional metaphoric parallel to this two-part play. It constituted a lens through which the Führer viewed the world, set goals, and made big plans.

What matters for History is less Hitler's prattle than his plans and commands. His moves during the rise to power, his stance toward the church, his relations with his niece and her death, the book-burnings, *limes* building, synagogue torching, peace pact, pact betrayal, and invasion of Russia all have their sequential parallels in this Ibsen drama. The Führer adjusted where necessary. Practical compromise meant transposing geography—a northward shift of latitude, an exchange of Germany for the Roman Empire, of Persia for Russia, of Ctesiphon for Moscow. This was nothing new. In a 1923 raving, he had substituted Berlin for Jerusalem as the place from which he, in his guise as Christ-of-the-Whip, would scourge the Jewish moneychangers.

In Hitler's sunny, tolerant pagan utopia, humanity could develop its God-given potential (*Der Mensch soll in der Lage sein, die ihm von Gott gegebenen Fähigkeiten zu entwickeln*). To realize the goal, it was necessary to destroy "a yet greater lie [than Christianity], the

Jewish–Bolshevik world." Since the Jews were defined as the propagating vector of Christianity, exterminating them constituted but a means to an historic end, the goal of Julian, to achieve the end of Christian intolerance.

EXTERMINATING "PARTISANS" / "A HOSTILE ARMY IN THE REAR"

Heinrich Himmler kept a daily log during 1941–42. Seized by Soviet forces in 1945 along with much else, this document disappeared into a secret Moscow archive, where it remained throughout the Cold War, finally coming to light in 1991 when the USSR collapsed. One entry has since attracted particular interest. It is the notation from December 18, 1941. The SS leader spent that day at supreme headquarters in East Prussia, meeting the Führer for lunch and again at four o'clock in the afternoon. At the latter session, Hitler spoke and Himmler scrawled notes in a brief outline form. The top item on the agenda concerned the "Jewish question." Himmler's notation reads simply:

Judenfrage. / als Partisanen auszurotten.

meaning:

Jewish question. / to be exterminated as partisans.

The spare note might reasonably be interpreted as an outright command to kill, or as an instruction on how to word orders for the killing of Jews, or as the public-relations spin for those killings. Either way, it is a Hitler order conveyed to a responsible subordinate.

But a further question involves which Jews the Führer meant in this context. Were they Soviet Jews, who on the flimsy pretext of being "partisans" had already been shot in droves since the invasion in June? Or did the broader term "Jewish question" here indicate the extension of the murder campaign to include Jews throughout the Nazi-occupied lands, stretching westward to the English Channel?

The former explanation, limited to Soviet Jews, would hardly require either mention by Hitler or notation by Himmler, since Hitler had been examining action reports of the Einsatzgruppen murder squads since early August. These reports often referred to Jewish victims in general as "partisans," although that term was not meant to be taken literally. The usage was rather a euphemism to preserve nicety within official circles, via the pretense that the massacres accorded with martial-law procedures for pacifying military rear zones. At any rate, by mid-December 1941 this cosmetic vocabulary was old hat, well established for Nazi-occupied Soviet territory and therefore not a point worth explicating again or jotting down, especially in relation to Russia, the Ukraine, or the Baltic states. Furthermore, the surviving Soviet Jews under German control were not all shot forthwith. They were instead confined, for the time being, to ghettos.

So the putative "partisans" in the Himmler log cannot reasonably mean Soviet Jews. The solution to what it does mean comes with the encompassing term "Jewish question." Without limiting geographic qualifiers, this locution had invariably been reserved in Nazi usage to indicate Jewry at large, Jewry as a global menace. Therefore "Jewish question"—*Judenfrage*—expands the reference beyond the Soviet sphere onto the grander scale. The pretext for murder was to be extended to Jews in Europe at large. Hitler had at last referred, on the record, to a generalized Final Solution. Substantiating that interpretation was an entry from Joseph Goebbels's diary just six days earlier. The Nazi propaganda minister recorded that Hitler addressed an assembly of Nazi party regional bosses on December 12 and hinted at how a "clean sweep" of the "Jewish question," meaning annihilation, was drawing near. Even so, the mention of "partisans" in central and western Europe where no active war was then under way presents a riddle unless it can be explained by some other prompt.

And again, the script of *Emperor and Galilean* (Part Two) provides an answer to the riddle. Hitler's words as transcribed for October 1941–February 1942 have already shown on several instances that he had this play recurrently in mind. The date December 18, 1941, occurs about halfway within this demonstrable five-month-long upsurge in Hitlerian enthusiasm for Ibsen's epic. Part Two, Act IV of *Emperor and Galilean* yields an apt analogy to Himmler's logbook scribble for that day. Here is the dramatic scene: A Roman column is marching eastward, its ranks composed of favored, pagan troops alongside sullen Christian levies. Two Christian civilians observe. They suspect that Julian's war against Persia is really cover for a blow directed at their faith.

> BASIL: A curse upon the emperor Julian! This is more cruelly conceived than all the agonies of the torture chamber. Who is he leading his armies against? Not so much against the king of Persia as against Christ.
>
> MACRINA: Do you think he could do such a dreadful thing?
>
> BASIL: Yes, Macrina, it is becoming clearer and clearer to me that it is us the blow is aimed at.

Basil has surmised correctly. The soldiers tread onward. Deep in Persia, far from his supply base, Julian fails to bring the enemy main force to heel. Meanwhile, disloyal elements are spreading unease.

> NEVITA: Don't worry, my lord; the expedition shall proceed with the utmost vigor.
>
> JULIAN: It certainly needs to. . . . The lunacy of the Galileans has exceeded all bounds since my departure. Every day the nuisance is getting worse. They can see that my victory in Persia will lead to their extermination . . . they are like a hostile army in my rear.

Again, Julian's words via Ibsen are in the left column below. On the right are those from Himmler's December 18, 1941 logbook entry, recording Hitler's wishes.

They can see that my victory in Persia will lead to their extermination . . . they are like a hostile army in my rear.	Jewish question / to be exterminated as partisans

The match fits, sequentially, among the practical allegories to *Emperor and Galilean,* Part Two that have already been observed:

- Both quotations employ hyperbolic usage. In each case, the victims dubbed "partisans" (i.e., a hostile army in the rear) consisted of a peaceful religious community who cannot realistically be construed as a military threat. Julian is referring here to Christians back in the Roman Empire.
- The respective regular armies of Julian and Hitler were each hotly engaged on the territory of an enemy eastern empire.
- The respective leaders (Julian, Hitler) had each first concluded non-aggression pacts with their eastern neighbors, only to shortly betray these treaties and invade.
- Julian and then Hitler respectively forswore an attack on the eastern enemy capital, opting to postpone that operational phase.
- At a critical point in each respective military campaign, the chief of the invading force vowed to exterminate the suspect religious community.

But Julian identified the Christians ("Galileans") as the potential partisan foe, whereas Hitler specified the Jews. That might pose a problem were it not for Hitler's having stated clearly enough during these same months that his ultimate goal was to extirpate Judeo–Christianity. He would inaugurate the process by the physical elimination of the Jews, the propagators of Christianity in his view, as he had stressed often enough. Here it is also germane to recall a passage from Dietrich Eckart's pseudo-dialogue with Hitler published in 1924, referring to Emperor Trajan's earlier campaign against Persia during the second century C.E. A Jewish uprising in the Roman provinces destabilized the empire then, forcing curtailment of the military effort in Persia. The Roman armies had been stabbed in the back. The tract *Bolshevism from Moses to Lenin* must be considered along with these passages from *Emperor and Galilean,* Part Two, the Hitler "Table Talk," and Himmler's log entry if Hitler's mindset at this time is to be understood as fully as the documentary record permits.

An operational order, or at least an order on how to "spin" the genocide of the Jews, was recorded by Himmler at a meeting with Hitler in December 1941. A continent-wide final solution to the "Jewish question" would soon commence. New here is the finding that the murderous program and an order confirming Hitler as initiator have counterparts in a stage script that Hitler knew well, and whose protagonist he had pronounced as his model.

Yet there is more. It appears that another Ibsen play ran concurrently in the Hitler repertoire along with the big-stage adaptation of *Emperor and Galilean.*

11

THE MASTER BUILDER

An A.H. Features Production
from a Script by Henrik Ibsen

MASTER BUILDER SOLNESS: Today is the
19th of September!
HILDE WANGEL: Exactly.

—IBSEN, *THE MASTER BUILDER*, ACT I

SINCE THE NAZI Führer defined himself as a frustrated would-be architect, it now seems reasonable to inquire whether indications of Ibsen's play *The Master Builder* appear in Hitler's repertoire like the traces of *An Enemy of the People* and *Emperor and Galilean*. *Baumeister Solness*, the German version, played at Linz in 1903, although whether young Adolf saw the play then cannot be confirmed. Yet in *Mein Kampf* (1925), there appeared a hint that he had absorbed and recycled certain images from the script as he had with the other two Ibsen plays. Below left are lines from Act II, opposite a sentence from *Mein Kampf*, chapter 10 on the right:

MASTER BUILDER SOLNESS:
Hilde, there are amazingly many
devils in the world, unseen.

These black parasites of nations [i.e., the Jews] systematically violate our inexperienced young blonde girls

HILDE: Devils too? **SOLNESS:** Auspicious devils and evil ones, blond devils and black-haired. If only one could ever know whether one was under the sway of the blond or the black!	and thereby destroy something that in this world cannot be replaced.

Both quotations pit "black" against "blond." In both passages black is evil or ominous, whereas blond is auspicious or naïve. Solness warns of unseen devils just as Hitler obsesses in *Mein Kampf* over Jews assimilated into mainstream society. While hardly conclusive, this example suggests the likelihood that Hitler knew Ibsen's play. But if he adapted *The Master Builder* to the real-world stage, whom did he cast for the title role? And for the female lead?

MASTER BUILDER OF THE THIRD REICH

If asked to name "Hitler's Master Builder," most historians and general readers would probably grant Albert Speer the title. Well, they get partial credit. Speer, an architect, served as chief of construction and as German armaments chief from February 1942 to the fall of the Third Reich. But even Speer, despite a grossly outsized ego, acknowledged another as his predecessor and boss: Fritz Todt.

Todt (1891–1942) was for ten years Hitler's Master Builder. He had joined the Nazis in early 1923 but forsook activism after the failure of the Beer Hall Putsch, spending the years 1924–31 as a highway engineer and business director of a Munich-based construction firm. Then in the autumn of 1931, he returned to the Nazi fold and began a meteoric rise through the ranks at the party's Munich headquarters. This hitherto unknown specialist in road surfaces had neither been part of any party faction nor of the Führer's household clique, but his rapid ascent was evidently due to some special favor of the leader. In the spring of 1932, Todt was made commander of a stormtroop unit called the "16th List Regiment" after Hitler's World War I Bavarian army outfit. He also headed the Nazi front organization for architects and engineers, as well as a Nazi advisory panel on science and technology for which he lacked the background and formal qualification. Next came the Autobahn.

During the 1920s, a consortium of engineering firms and regional governments in western Germany had envisioned a north–south toll motorway extending from Hamburg to Basel, just over the Swiss border. The idea failed to gain funding, however, and was obstructed by heavy opposition in the Reichstag. By 1931, only a small stretch near Cologne had actually been placed under construction. As yet, the Nazis had had nothing at all to do with the Autobahn. Then in December 1932, Fritz Todt circulated a memorandum among the top Nazi leadership recommending a nationwide system of freeways as a public-works project if the party gained political power.

Hitler became chancellor on January 30, 1933; less than two weeks later, he proclaimed his commitment to the highway endeavor. A fire soon gutted the Reichstag building, and with the ensuing state-of-emergency decree, opposition to the Autobahn from legislators was effectively quashed. Within several months, the Nazis had taken over the Autobahn consortium and greatly expanded the envisioned scope of the road net, with Todt appointed to head the effort. Over the six years from then until the start of World War II, the Autobahn absorbed major funds. But as war approached in 1938, this high-speed road system remained incomplete. By then, though, the Führer had found more diverse tasks for Todt.

Among those projects was overseeing work on a private chalet for Hitler on a peak atop the Obersalzberg mountain above Berchtesgaden in the Bavarian Alps. The engineer was also assigned in 1936 to build the aforementioned *limes* (a.k.a. "Westwall") line of concrete fortifications along the western frontiers of the Reich; the construction of the Westwall took place during the years 1938 through 1940, and Todt was in charge until 1939. For this gigantic task, he mobilized the Autobahn laborers, augmented by several hundred thousand more men. By early 1939, Todt was given yet another concurrent portfolio, General Superintendent for the Building Industry of the Reich. A glossy monthly periodical, *Der Deutsche Baumeister*, indulged in a cult of adulation, making his title of "Master Builder" all but official. When war came, the militarized engineering corps known as Organization Todt operated in support of the German armed forces. But Todt himself did not wear its uniform or insignia. Oddly enough, in October 1939 Hitler awarded him a commission as major general in the Luftwaffe, although Todt exercised no air-war functions. In March 1940 Todt was named to serve concurrently as the Reich minister of armaments and munitions, despite his lack of experience in manufacturing and economic planning.

The air force rank Todt held constituted just one among several anomalies in a career that was personally guided by Adolf Hitler starting in late 1931 or early 1932. Todt was described by one Nazi colleague as a "white raven" among the top Third Reich brass. He meant it to contrast Todt's honesty, earnestness, and clean lifestyle with many high Nazis' cynical hedonism. But this colleague also pointed out that Todt was an amateur in many of his portfolios, hopelessly out of his depth in coping with the many crucial responsibilities that Hitler had heaped upon him.

In another anomaly, Hitler appointed the young architect Albert Speer to serve as understudy to Todt at several stages of the Master Builder's career. When Todt died in an anomalous midair airplane explosion in February 1942, Speer was standing by to take over as the new Master Builder.

One further anomaly, unnoticed at the time, may explain all the others. It is the seeming likeness of sequential milestones of Todt's career—and of the manner of his death—to the script of Ibsen's play. *The Master Builder* was written in 1892. Its basic plot is simple: Halvard Solness is secure in his regional monopoly on construction. Looking back, he traces his success to the time when his wife's ancestral mansion suddenly burned down, after which he demonstrated his virtuosity by erecting a new edifice. Yet Solness's dark secret is that he had secretly yearned for the fire, willing it to happen. Over the years since then, he pursued the building trade and put all his rivals out of business. He even employs two of them, including Ragnar, an ambitious young architect with innovative design ideas. Then one morning on a September 19 comes a knock at the door. In walks Hilde Wangel, age twenty-three, who had met Solness exactly (to the day) ten years earlier when he completed a building in her town. He had teased her then, promising her a kingdom with a castle in the air. Now, grown up and nubile, she has come to collect. Over the course of a day, she charms the middle-aged builder. Solness confides to her his guilty secret over the mysterious fire long ago. He even agrees to dedicate his latest structure just for her. He will climb to the top of the new building and crown its spire with a wreath. In the last scene, the Master Builder falls from the roof to his death as Ragnar stands by. The End.

Those episodes replicated in the time of Hitler and Todt were:

- the special significance of the date September 19, involving a twenty-three-year-old girl;
- an earnestly sought and all-too-convenient fire that razes a symbolic structure, heralding the rise of the Master Builder;
- the planning of a "castle in the air" with a view for miles around;
- the subordination of all rival contractors to the Master Builder;
- the grooming of the Master Builder's apprentice and heir;
- a premonition of doom for the Master Builder;
- the Master Builder's ascent, carrying a wreath, before his deadly fall;
- the fatal plummet of the Master Builder after a ten-year acquaintance with Hilde Wangel;
- the succession to the Master Builder by a young architect notably adept at design.

SEPTEMBER 19: *FEMME FATALE*

The corpse of Hitler's niece Geli Raubal, aged twenty-three years, was found sometime around noon on September 19, 1931. In *The Master Builder,* the female lead Hilde Wangel is also age twenty-three when she arrives unbidden at Solness's studio, in Act I, scene 8. It is a September 19, of no particular year. Hilde's entrance inaugurates the flirtation between her and Solness that comprises the main focus of the play.

One exits, one enters; same age, same date. As noted, other features of Geli Raubal's passing fit the part of princess Helena in *Emperor and Galilean,* but that play did not stipulate a death date. The suspicion that Hitler had Raubal murdered is a reasonable one, shared by many investigators who have weighed the evidence over the years. Yet despite the closely fit timing, Raubal's demise seems to make little sense in the context of a madman's adaptation of *The Master Builder.* That is, it makes no sense unless the exit via death also marks an entrance, as Hilde Wangel, of someone cast to absorb the spirit of the just departed twenty-three-year-old girl found dead on a September 19.

When Hilde turns up at Solness's door, it is established that they are already acquainted. Ten years have passed, to the day, since his visit to her home town. On that occasion the Master Builder kidded the little girl, calling her his princess and promising her a kingdom. "You were just a child then," recalls Solness. She retorts "Twelve, or thirteen." The German reads *Immerhin so zwölf, dreizehn Jahre alt* in both editions available to Hitler. Women, even younger women, sometimes prefer ambiguity as to matters of age. Twelve or, well, maybe thirteen years, plus ten. But as to the date they met, Hilde harbors no doubt. It was, she reminds Solness, on the 19th of September. Hilde has arrived on cue to demand her kingdom.

What then of the September 19th in 1931? When the Munich police arrived on scene that morning, they officially logged the twenty-three-year-old Geli's death to the evening of the previous day. But no one saw Raubal die—save for her killer(s). The quibble amounts to a matter of hours one way or another. Autopsies can at best approximate the time of death in cases of sudden, suspicious mortality; but in this instance, a proper autopsy was waived. Without a full-fledged postmortem forensic inquest, the date entry on the death certificate may be judged but a guess. It thus remains uncertain whether this young woman departed life late during the waning hours of the 18th, or early on the 19th, or, for that matter, at the stroke of midnight. No dogma need attach to the official date of the 18th. What counts is the finding, achieved about midday on the 19th, that Geli had died of a recent bullet wound sustained during the night. Even presuming that Hitler had ordered a hit by one of his goons, he would have had to leave the exact timing of the shot to circumstances and to the gunman's discretion.

Yet the Führer could be reasonably sure that Geli's body would be found on the 19th of September. The significance of September 19 in the Ibsen playtext is the metamorphosis of Hilde, now grown up. Either late on the 18th or early on the 19th would do for purposes of death and rebirth in a new form. That is, if Hitler's object was to liberate the *Geist* of a twenty-three-year-old woman on a September 19 in adapting the Ibsen script, then Geli Raubal was pronounced dead precisely at the appointed day. The random probability for an event to occur on a given calendar date is, of course, just one in 365. It was Hitler and no other who called Geli's death a "sacrifice" in conversation with his aide, Otto Wagener, soon after the event. And it may be worth noting, incidentally, that twenty-three years had passed since the young Adolf read Ibsen's plays, or so his roommate of 1908 later recalled.

OCCULT FACTORS

If a sacrifice on a set date hints of the occult, then none other than the bereaved uncle himself cast this death in an occult dimension. He began doing so while Geli still breathed, having just bid her goodbye. The Führer was seated in his automobile, riding away out of Munich toward Nuremberg on the afternoon of the 18th, when he remarked to Heinrich Hoffmann about some inexplicable unease. That set the tone of premonition so typical of Hitler moves in many another context.

Back in Munich on the 19th, Hitler elaborated during an interrogation by a Munich policeman, detective Sauer. Pending was the need to arrange a funeral. The investigator probed gently, dealing with the uncle as bereaved kin, not as a murder suspect. Hitler adduced an occult factor, conjuring up the story that Geli had participated in séances that addled her mind and induced her to shoot herself—on purpose. This fabrication intrinsically vitiated that other Nazi spin, whereby a doltish Geli had accidentally discharged the Führer's pistol while idly fingering the piece.

The séance tale rests on Hitler's word alone. For that reason alone it demands attention for what it conveys, not as truth but as a patent fib. The story lacks corroboration from Raubal's remarks as remembered by her friends, or from any testimony by her mother or the household staff at Prinzregenten Strasse. To subtract Hitler's unsubstantiated séance story as an evident untruth leaves Hitler ascribing the premature death to prophesied fate, foreordained and inevitable. The mystic aspect to the event is thus a gratuitous artifact offered up by Hitler and no one else.

It was a week after speaking with Sauer that Hitler recited to Otto Wagener his sermon on pagan theology with its paired biblical allusions traceable to Ibsen's *Emperor and Galilean,* a play laden with omens and prophecies. As determined by his words and deeds, as already noted, Hitler had surely read the play. Casting Geli as Princess Helena, he had apparently reenacted a segment from it. Thus, clues offered up by Hitler himself show that Geli Raubal did double duty with reference to two Ibsen plays. Her outward consort status with Hitler matches *Emperor and Galilean,* while the timing of her death coincides precisely with the key date in *The Master Builder.* Hitler observed the principle of economy in keeping with the practice of many a small theater troupe. Oftentimes players are obliged to perform more than one role, appearing in different scenes of the same production or in more than one sketch of a repertoire cycle.

But why not some other victim? Why Geli neé Angelika Raubal? Besides the blood relationship to Hitler as stipulated by *Emperor and Galilean,* besides her age as required by *The Master Builder,* there is also the circumstance of her very name. Given Hitler's fetish with names no less than with dates, it must be noted that "angel" occurs in both names: Angelika Raubal and Hilde Wangel. Or, as Julian the Apostate had put it of Helena, "No one killed her. She was too pure for this sinful world. That is why an angel (*Engel* in the German) came down each night to her room and called to her."

There is a segue here. Presuming that a set of scripts guided Hitler, then on September 19, 1931 a sequence drawn from *Emperor and Galilean* ended, while another sequence from *The Master Builder* chimed in. It is worth noting that Hitler marked the two subsequent anniversaries of Raubal's death with architectural moves. On September 19, 1932 he signed the papers to acquire title to the Haus Wachenfeld villa on the Obersalzberg above Berchtesgaden. Immediately then he commissioned a major remodeling to turn the property into the luxury chalet he renamed "Berghof."

Another year later, as chancellor on September 19, 1933, Hitler addressed Berlin's mayor and municipal leaders on the topic of constructing a grander Reich capital. The project would inevitably level many homes. The Führer affirmed his resolve:

> What does "heart" mean? One can't get things done with "heart" alone. One needs an ice-cold mind.

Or, as Hilde Wangel had said in Act II,

> If only one had a really brash and hearty conscience! So that one dared to do what one wanted.

If *The Master Builder* truly figured in Hitler's Ibsen repertoire, its casting required at minimum a Halvard Solness and a Hilde Wangel. Hitler would have to concede the Solness part to another and so pursue his declared lifetime building goal through a proxy.

CHERCHEZ LA FEMME

As for the Hilde part, *cherchez la femme.* Her role in a reenactment could be taken by none other than Hitler himself, subsuming the *Geist* of a sacrificed twenty-three-year-old Geli Raubal. That much is hypothesis so far, albeit one founded upon the now demonstrable fact of Hitler's covert ritual obsession with Ibsen, upon his fascination with architecture, and upon the curious coincidence of the September 19 date.

Remaining, however, is the problem of the gender switch. Most men do not fantasize a female persona, let alone privately enact one in protracted role-play. For Hitler to take on the Hilde role required a sex-change operation, literary if not literal. That does not necessarily mean that Hitler was homosexual or bisexual, as some have suspected. The evidence for homosexual tendencies is inconclusive. As Wyndham Lewis put it in 1939 with studied ambiguity, "He is not a homosexual, like most Germans." True or not, allegations of homosexuality are indicative of gender-identity issues although the present context does not require proof of homosexual acts by the Führer. The case here focuses instead on an outwardly expressed effeminacy, displayed often enough, which indicates a female alter persona within the man's private makeup.

Such evidence goes beyond mere rumor or psychiatric conjecture. Observations of effeminacy during Hitler's adulthood are solidly on record from contemporaries. Wyndham Lewis also noted:

> This male Joan of Arc is a strange man.

That was astute, for 1939. Hitler did admire Joan as "a great heroine in the cause of freedom" whose history he knew from the theatrical versions by George Bernard Shaw and Friedrich Schiller. He had indeed either read them or seen them performed. His stated interest in the Joan character falls short of proven identification with her, yet here he was viewed by Lewis as a man with a yen for theater who could identify with favored female as well as male roles.

Well before Lewis wrote, there were the words of Adolf himself during his adolescence. A case of gender reversal is documented in his own handwriting. It is a brief example, but a telling one, from 1906 when young Adolf maintained a crush on a poised young woman of Linz known as Stephanie. He had stalked her from afar for months but never accosted the girl. Apart from one anonymous love letter to Stephanie, he confided his passion for her only to his pal, August Kubizek.

In May 1906, Adolf traveled to Vienna for three weeks. He stayed at his godparents' home there while attending the opera; back in Linz, he entrusted the Stephanie surveillance beat to Kubizek. Hitler kept in touch from Vienna via postcards, wherein he inquired about Stephanie's wellbeing, her comings and goings, and her dates with young men of superior means than the teenaged Adolf. The boys had prearranged that during Adolf's time away from Linz, any mention of Stephanie would hide her identity by the masculine code name "Benkieser."

Hitler could readily have substituted another girl's name. Or he could have abbreviated Stephanie to an initial or adopted some other gender-neutral form. But he made her, the object of his adoration, into a man for this purpose of masking. Boy Hitler had thereby innocently enough demonstrated some inner penchant for gender-switching.

Theater offered a subtle encouragement. "The vital spirit leaps from form to form" was how Adolf Wilbrandt put it in *Der Meister von Palmyra*, which Hitler saw at Vienna's Hofburg in February 1908. This portrayal was of reincarnation across gender lines. An actress played the parts not only of Appelles's successive consorts but also of his grandson, Nymphas. A male body, then, could conceal a female spirit. At least on stage.

But for the grownup Führer, the world was a stage onto which he projected aspects of himself, or selves. The cues were picked up by his foes. On hostile stages, he came to be lampooned as not quite a full man. An account published in 1941 observed:

> In America he is being burlesqued as a she-man, especially in vaudeville, by Jewish comedians who are making him a common laughingstock.

The filmmaker Charlie Chaplin perceived a female side too, parodying him as a ballerina for a celebrated scene in *The Great Dictator*. None other than the great dictator him/herself had divulged enough innuendo through mannerisms of speech and body language to make it plausible comedy.

This ambiguity, of a sort that superficially might be taken as homosexual, persisted through the subject's adulthood. One observer of the mature Hitler was a homoerotically inclined diplomat. After some scrutiny, he came to a verdict of "not gay" after all, although the Führer had apparently broadcast enough behavioral signals to raise the question. A certain departure from heterosexual masculine norms seemed present.

To some, it seemed prominent. An American journalist, Edward Deuss, based his reading on personal contact and interviews while covering Hitler's campaign tours from September 1931 to May 1933. Deuss began a memorandum to Professor Crane Brinton by stating:

> The most obvious thing about Hitler is the blend of inborn feminine and masculine characteristics—a man on the borderline of a woman....

Deuss continued by contrasting the hidden woman with the maniac also present,

> ... an incredible iron will subject to unfathomable fits of depression, a spartan self-disciplinarian who would not kill a fly except in a rage, a mystic-realist, an intuitive warrior, an ascetic adventurer.

The German socialist journal *Das Freie Wort* in November 1932 featured an article titled "The Woman Hitler: Psychology around a Leader," which noted the Führer's "prima donna character . . . his rehearsed gestures, his pathological vanity toward himself and his movement." These were interpreted as essentially feminine characteristics. The article referred to an Italian writer who had stated that there was nothing manly in Hitler, explaining his success in terms of "his feminine side." Also in 1932, the German humor magazine *Simplicissimus* featured a cartoon depicting Hitler as several personas, one of which as a shapely nude Salomé with swastikas for nipples on his/her breasts.

Walter C. Langer headed the wartime effort by the U.S. Office of Strategic Services to compile a psychological profile of Hitler. Two pages in his assessment came under the heading "Femininity," reflecting stereotypical notions of the time. Langer summarized:

Many writers and informants have commented on his feminine characteristics—his gait, his hands, his mannerisms, and his ways of thinking. Hanfstaengl reports that when he showed Dr. Jung a specimen of Hitler's handwriting, the latter immediately exclaimed that it was a typically feminine hand. His choice of art as a profession might also be interpreted as a manifestation of a basic feminine identification.

There are definite indications of such an emotional adjustment later in life. The outstanding of these is perhaps his behavior toward his officers during the last war [World War I]. His comrades report that during the four years he was in service he was not only over submissive to all his officers but frequently volunteered to do their washing and take care of their clothes. This would certainly indicate a strong tendency to assume the feminine role in the presence of a masculine figure whenever this was feasible and could be duly rationalized. His extreme sentimentality, his emotionality, his occasional softness, and his weeping, even after becoming Chancellor, may be regarded as manifestations of a fundamental feminine pattern.

Influenced by the doctrinaire Freudians on the Hitler-profile project, Langer guessed that the personality pattern had its origin in the subject's relationship to his mother. Langer stopped short of labeling Hitler homosexual. What remains is the choice of a quasi-female social role in a group living situation. W. H. D. Vernon of Harvard University also served in 1943 as a consultant to the OSS on the project to evaluate Hitler. His unpublished, long-classified report included these similar observations:

A point of fundamental importance is the large gynic [feminine] component in Hitler's constitution. . . . His movements have been described as womanish—a dainty ladylike way of walking (when not assuming a military carriage in public), effeminate gestures of his arms—a peculiar graceless ineptitude reminiscent of a girl throwing a baseball.

Feminine traits. Hitler's sentimentality, his emotionality, his shrieking at the climax of his speeches, his artistic inclinations, his sudden collapses, his occasional softness—these are all typical not so much of a woman as of a woman in man.

A World War I comrade of Corporal Hitler, Hans Mend, reported that Hitler paid no attention to women during the period 1914–18, despite the presence of many French prostitutes behind the German lines. Posted to rear headquarters areas much of the time, Hitler did not lack opportunities. Instead, Mend states that Hitler formed a close attachment to another soldier, Ernst Schmidt, yet Mend does not firmly venture their bond to have been homosexual. Again, what remains undisputed is an observed effeminacy. A French attempt to psychoanalyze Hitler also looked at his range of behavior and interpreted him not as an active, practicing homosexual, but rather as a man with latent inclinations as based on his effeminacy.

Regarding the effeminate traits, Bertolt Brecht, the leftish playwright, had composed a bit of blank verse:

When the decorator pierces tranquility over the loudspeaker,
The road workers gaze upon the motorways
And see
Knee deep concrete, ideal for
Heavy tanks.

By "the decorator," of course, Brecht indicated Hitler. It was a widely circulated canard among foes that sometime in his twenties Hitler had worked as a wallpaper hanger. Although factually inaccurate, the decorator reference placed him in an occupation pursued by many effeminate men, thereby directing notice to the Führer's traits. Again, an observer has noted the coexistence in one body of a mincing aesthete and a bloodthirsty conquerer.

Where Brecht had Hitler pegged as a "decorator," the fascist-leaning British critic Wyndham Lewis ventured:

He [Hitler] is more like a dreamy-eyed hairdresser whose combative side was manifest as a "German Joan of Arc."

Lewis elaborated:

He is fey;

and,

a paranoiac violet;

and,

The human type to which Herr Hitler belongs is not a tough type, but a soft one;

and,

It is to the 'feminine' order of man that Adolf Hitler belongs;

and,

Hitler is apt to remind people of women rather than men.

Not homosexual, but surely effeminate while yet truculent and other-worldly, a man who "hears voices" and "receives supernatural guidance." Like Joan of Arc, perhaps, but Hitler has not been caught paraphrasing *St. Joan* or *Die Jungfrau von Orleans*. The point here, however, is that a contemporary eyes-on observer with no agenda to connect Hitler to any of Ibsen's female characters had neverthe-less guessed that a female theatrical persona with a vicious aspect resided in the Führer.

For the Berlin-based American correspondent William L. Shirer, it was the Hitler gait. The newsman observed it on September 22, 1938 as the Führer prepared to bargain with British Prime Minister Chamberlain over the fate of Czechoslovakia. Hitler emerged from a hotel in Godesberg and went for a short stroll. A secretly anti-Nazi German journalist nudged Shirer and pointed out, "Look at his walk!" The American scrutinized:

It was very ladylike. Dainty little steps.

This effeminacy, present in the eyes of so many beholders, cannot be denied. Another who saw it was Franz Halder, chief of the German Army general staff for the first fourteen months of the Russian campaign. He dealt with Hitler on virtually a daily basis, matching his professional military reasoning against the Führer's quixotic command style. Looking back, Halder judged Hitler to have been dominated by feminine characteristics. "The intuition that mastered him instead of pure logic was only one of the many proofs of this fact."

Yet another telling account is on record from a diplomat, Dr. Carl Burckhardt, who saw Hitler in action frequently enough in the 1930s. Burckhardt, a Swiss, served as the League of Nations High Commissioner for the free city of Danzig up to September 1939. Some weeks later, a month into World War II, he attended a dinner party in Britain. Present too was the British diplomat Sir Harold Nicolson. Nicolson recorded in his diary:

> I sit next to him [Burckhardt] and find him most intelligent and amusing. He talks a great deal about Hitler. He says that Hitler is the most profoundly feminine man that he has ever met, and that there are moments when he becomes almost effeminate. He imitates the movements of his white flabby hands. He says that Hitler has a dual personality, the first being that of the rather gentle artist, and the second that of the homicidal maniac.

Burckhardt's words supplement those of Lewis, Shirer, and Deuss. The woman in Hitler coexisted with a savage demeanor. Burckhardt had gotten to know the subject even better than the journalists. The League of Nations official was one of the few, male or female, to charm the Führer. Hitler even acclaimed Burckhardt's diplomatic skills before the Reichstag, back on February 20, 1938. Rarely does a head of state laud a foreign envoy. What is more, he did so for the functionary of an international peacemaking body that he despised, and which Germany had quit as one of the initial foreign policy moves of the Third Reich. The two had some rapport. And Burckhardt used that rapport to make this all-too-telling observation.

So others saw a female nature residing within Hitler, and a vicious female at that. No record exists of Hitler himself ever acknowledging this observed effeminacy. The extant verbal clues are oblique. What then of his views on the nature of woman? As always, it is best to let the subject speak for himself. He gave forth to Himmler on the evening of March 1, 1942:

> In the eyes of a woman, the finest of dresses at once loses its charm—if she sees another woman wearing one like it. I've seen a woman suddenly leave the opera at the sight of a rival who had entered a box wearing the same dress as herself. "What cheek!" she said. "I'm going!"
>
> In the pleasure a woman takes in rigging herself out, there is always an admixture of some troublemaking element, something treacherous—to awaken another woman's jealousy by displaying something that the latter doesn't possess. Women have the talent, which is unknown to us males, for giving a kiss to a woman friend and at the same time piercing her heart with a well-sharpened stiletto.

Here he explicitly includes himself among "us males," but again his words speak for themselves. To Hitler the effeminate man, women were vicious.

Still more evidence for Hitler's feminine side came from Frau Elsa Bruckmann, the wife of publisher Hugo Bruckmann and the financial patroness of Nazism in its early days when wealthy contributors kept the party solvent. The Führer long confided in her from time to time, as to a surrogate aunt. In 1942, Hitler called upon the just-widowed Frau Bruckmann to commiserate. She was mourning her husband; Hitler had just recently consecrated and buried the ashes of his Master Builder, Fritz Todt.

As related by Elsa Bruckmann, Hitler's expression of sympathy went:

We all have our graves and grow more and more lonely, but we must prevail and continue living, my dear gracious lady. I also now lack the only two persons around me to whom I was really, inwardly attached (*an denen ich wirklich innerlich gehangen habe*). Dr. Todt is dead and Hess flew away from me!

Here is Hitler naming Rudolf Hess and Fritz Todt not as mere colleagues, but significant others. He placed them in a context analogous to Frau Bruckmann's late husband. The Führer's words were intended to pass for empathy. But Hitler might have mentioned his earlier loss of Geli Raubal, whom Elsa knew well; Geli had stayed with the Bruckmanns for a while. At other times, Hitler had affirmed Geli to have been the only person (apart from his mother) whom he ever loved. To forget her in favor of Hess and Todt when speaking in 1942 sounds preposterous; in the case of Hitler, that is what makes the remark all the more plausible. The source for the remark, Frau Bruckmann, was a long-term confidante of the Führer. To this just-widowed woman, then, he remembered two male associates as those to whom he was really, inwardly attached.

That is as far as it goes. As for any carnal component in what Hitler proclaimed as a real, inward attachment to Todt, nothing on record suggests actual intimacies between them. Todt had a wife, female. Although Elspeth Kramer Todt was eight years her husband's senior, she kept her man busy enough to produce three children. He once confided to a Nazi colleague, "Man is about to divest the sexual impulse—the strongest of all natural impulses—of its mythical and spiritual significance and degrade it to a natural need, so that he can satisfy it in a regulated fashion without making any fuss about it." Frau Elspeth Todt, a German woman, presumably liked the regulated, no-fuss technique. But despite the Todts' degrading of sex to a natural need, and despite a "really, inwardly attached" Hitler, Adolf and Fritz cannot on the evidence be construed as a gay couple.

Adoration is one thing, gratification another. In *The Master Builder*, Hilde Wangel retains physical chastity while casting her spell over Solness. They stay on formal second-person "Sie" terms through the authorized German translation of the play, never lapsing into the lovers' "du." The present issue concerns not sex but whether this theatrical coquette figured among Hitler's own stock of alter personas.

There were ample outward signs of an inner femininity. Over the years, as previously stated, too many persons noticed ladylike flourishes of gesture or gait at too many separate times to dismiss all their reports as some baseless libel. If enough people remark that a man seems effeminate, then he is effeminate, at least on occasion. The question then is hardly whether Adolf Hitler's psyche harbored a woman, but rather who, in particular, she was.

She was Hilde Wangel. We have it on Hitler's word.

TAKING HITLER AT HIS/HER WORD

It remains to substantiate Hilde's presence via a paraphrase out of *The Master Builder.*

Hitler obliged for the record, at table on the night of September 25–26, 1941. Wehrmacht troops had just captured Kiev. Farther to the north, Leningrad [the once and future St. Petersburg] was expected to fall shortly, upon which event Hitler had ordered its total obliteration. The Führer's observations, taken down by an army stenographer, furnish as limpid an insight as any psychotherapist will ever gain from any patient on the couch. It is pure stream-of-consciousness. Hitler has been rambling on about the joy he took in viewing war newsreels:

> I've been thrilled by our contemporary news films. We are experiencing a heroic epic, without precedent.

He groped for some equivalent thrill:

> The revelation that is her encounter with her first man, for a young woman, can be compared with the revelation that a soldier knows when he faces war for the first time. In a few days, a youth becomes a man. If I weren't myself hardened by this experience,

I would have been incapable of undertaking this Cyclopean task
which the building of an empire means for a single man.

Make war, not love. A maiden's yielding her virginity is like a
soldier's baptism of fire, and the soldier envisioned is, of course, none
other than Private Adolf Hitler of the 16th List Regiment of Infantry,
near Ypres in the autumn of 1914. Yet how many male combat veterans are given to such guileless empathy with womankind at the most
intimate rite of passage? He has switched in mid-discourse. Getting
any closer in touch with his feminine side would have required coming out in drag.

Once having sashayed across the gender divide, Hitler recon-
nected in a twinkling with her present war. She spoke to her table
companions, her transcribed words given here in the left column.
Contrast with the original Hilde, stage right.

I suppose that some people today are clutching their heads: "How can the Führer annihilate a city like St. Petersburg?" (*Ich kann mir denken, dass mancher sich heute an den Kopf greift: Wie kann der Führer nur eine Stadt wie Petersburg vernichten?*) By nature I belong to an entirely different genus. (*Gewiss, von Haus bin ich vielleicht ganz anderer Art.*)	**HILDE:** Why shouldn't I go hunting, too? Get the prey I want? If only I can get my claws into it! Bring it to the ground! **SOLNESS:** Hilde—do you know what you are? **HILDE:** Yes, I'm a strange kind of bird. (*Ja, ich bin sicher so eine Art wunderlicher Vogel.*)

Hilde has just spoken for shock effect to Solness in Act II, scene
6. In the standard German rendition of the play, she says she wants
to be not merely a free woodland bird (*Waldvogel*) but a bird of prey
(*Raubvogel*). Here the short paired quotations pack all of four shared
specific points of identity, served up in nearly the same sequence:

⊕ Both excerpts state a craving for wholly gratuitous violence. Captured towns are normally left intact by invading armies, once the
   enemy garrison has fled or surrendered. Hitler declared his/her

urge to violate this convention of warfare, but not from any military need. Likewise, Hilde Wangel was a young lady of civilized nineteenth-century Europe. She did not depend on hunting for survival. Her lines here are intended to reveal a pent-up truculence.

❈ Both threats imply the graphic notion of bringing the victim to earth. In other contexts, Hitler had specified that upon capture, Leningrad was to be razed to the ground.

❈ Both threats pivot on a rhetorical question, wherein an interlocutor expresses dismay at the speaker's bestial savagery.

❈ Both segments end on the speaker's affirming identity with an exotic species.

Thus did the Nazi prima donna echo *The Master Builder,* one week past the tenth anniversary of September 19, 1931. That made an occasion for some sentimental reading, reading that could explain the presence of the script in Hitler's short-term memory. By reciting these lines in September 1941, Hitler/Hilde either performed a prodigious mnemonic feat, or had recently reviewed the script as if to commemorate the death of Geli.

As for the saga of the builder himself, Hitler's suspected game based upon Ibsen's play must be traced step by step through the career of Fritz Todt, Master Builder of the Third Reich.

12

"DER BAUMEISTER IST TOT!"

("THE MASTER BUILDER IS DEAD!")

HALVARD SOLNESS: That fire started me on
my way. As a master builder.
—IBSEN *THE MASTER BUILDER*, ACT II

HILDE WANGEL: My castle must stand high up.
High above everything. Open and free on every
side. So that I can see for miles around.
—IBSEN, *THE MASTER BUILDER*, ACT III

MRS. SOLNESS: He's falling! He's falling!
HILDE: My master builder!
RAGNAR: His head must've been smashed to
pieces. Killed outright.
OFFSTAGE VOICE FROM BELOW: The master
builder is dead! (*Der Baumeister ist tot!*)
—IBSEN, *THE MASTER BUILDER*, CONCLUSION

ITLER'S CANDID WORDS give sufficient reason to proceed on the presumption that he knew the script of *The Master Builder*. His actions paralleling two other Ibsen scripts moreover suggest that he could have included this drama as well in an adaptive repertoire. Of course, not every episode from *The Master Builder* is mirrored in the history of the Third Reich. But reflected incidents do include the fire that launched the builder's career; his subsequent charmed rise to a monopoly in the trade; a castle in the air; the grooming of the builder's apprentice and successor; a premonition of impending doom; and lastly, the Master Builder's fatal fall from a height while carrying aloft a wreath.

TWO ARSON CASES, TWO MASTER BUILDERS

On February 27, 1933, a month after Hitler took office as German chancellor, the interior of the Reichstag building sustained serious fire damage. This act of arson came to be remembered as a Nazi provocation and a cynical pretext for reducing the German parliament to a rubber stamp. But that historical verdict has tended to obscure the most proximate, high-priority Nazi concern during the few weeks immediately preceding the blaze: Hitler's determination to eliminate all bureaucratic and legislative obstacles to an encompassing, nationwide Autobahn. He and Hermann Goering identified a holdover official from the previous government as a key obstacle to the highway plan.

Günther Gereke, a technocratic civil servant, had remained in place as commissioner for jobs creation. He was skeptical of Nazi plans and preferred, on fiscal grounds, to limit the Autobahn to a small pilot project in a country where fewer than five percent of the population owned automobiles as of 1932. Hitler later identified this official as "from the beginning my most persistent opponent." Despite personal harangues from the Führer and Goering during February 1933, Gereke refused to yield. Gereke then found himself framed by the Nazis on embezzlement charges. His postwar account shows that the Autobahn was uppermost in the minds of the Nazi top brass at the outset of the Third Reich.

Within the Reichstag, where the Nazis comprised only a minority, the majority had likewise long blocked the Autobahn. Only drastic measures would suffice to overcome this legislative hurdle. In the context, a significant Nazi internal document helps explain the ensuing fire as a move aimed not just against the parliament's building, but against the Reichstag itself as a political factor. On February 28, 1933, just a day after the blaze, Fritz Todt drafted a confidential proposal on building the motorway network. It was his second such memorandum in two months. In December he had envisioned a huge Autobahn work force of 600,000 men. Emboldened on the day following the Reichstag fire, Todt felt encouraged to up the estimate to a full million, yet he somehow saw no need to mention what had up to then been the Autobahn's main obstacle: parliamentary approval. The Autobahn project was on, with Todt designated to build it. Along the way, a milestone incident in *The Master Builder* had incidentally been parodied, with a mysterious and all-too-convenient fire preceding the rise of the Master Builder.

The incident moreover repeated a Nazi pattern involving an earlier case of arson and an earlier real-life Master Builder. Fritz Todt's predecessor had been the architect Paul Ludwig Troost. And before the well-known, hotly debated Reichstag fire came the soon-forgotten burning of the Glass Palace in Munich: After darkness fell on June 6, 1931, a party or parties unknown entered the large Munich municipal green known as the English Garden and torched a major art museum located at the park's southern edge. This Munich landmark had been constructed with glass walls in a mid-nineteenth-century style. The conflagration reduced it to a total loss along with about three thousand paintings of the German Romantic school.

The blaze hastened civic renewal plans, since the Munich authorities already happened to be contemplating a replacement structure for the Glass Palace. They had a seasoned architect firmly in mind, Adolf Abel of Munich Polytechnic, although pressure had been mounting in the field for a choice via open competition. Then the Glass Palace burned down. There were no named suspects. The crime remained unsolved; not a case of insurance fraud, not traced to any known firebug. Loss of the museum left vacant a significant plot of ground just inside the park alongside Prinzregentenstrasse.

That prime location sat scarcely five minutes' walk from the suite Adolf Hitler then shared with Geli Raubal at Prinzregentenstrasse No. 16. As a neighbor, a sometime painter, and a frequent stroller in the English Garden, the Führer was thoroughly familiar with the Glass Palace. Hardly had the embers cooled when Hitler commissioned a Nazi-affiliated architect to draw a diagram for a new art museum. Paul Ludwig Troost worked in a consulting capacity, according to Hitler's own neoclassical concept. As of 1931–33, Troost had no professional peers among the Nazi ranks. He had remodeled the party's Brown House headquarters on Briennerstrasse and conferred with Hitler on future plans for the Königsplatz in Munich. Hitler even managed to install him on the Munich city council as "First Master Builder of the Führer." But Troost had yet to actually erect a structure on the Führer's behalf.

The loss of the Glass Palace created such a chance. Instead of glass this time, the Hitler–Troost "House of German Art" would be done in stone with a massive hypostyle, a latter-day take on a Hellenic shrine. Hitler was still a private citizen in 1931 at the time he had Troost draw up blueprints. Once in power, he overrode Abel's design, although by then it had passed an open evaluation and been vetted and confirmed by the Munich municipality. When Hitler laid the cornerstone for Troost's structure on October 15, 1933, he had become chancellor of the German state. This was a dream come true, since to Hitler the Glass Palace had long been an eyesore just across the street from his own apartment. As he put it once:

> If the age of Pericles seems embodied in the Parthenon, the Bolshevistic present is embodied in a cubist monstrosity.

As early as 1923, the Nazis' daily press organ had inveighed against the "cubist" Glass Palace and its art holdings. In 1931, this mote in Hitler's eye was at last removed. With the conflagration that struck in February 1933 at the Reichstag, a repeated pattern was established:

◆ Both fires entailed the destruction by arson of symbolic landmarks.
◆ Both acts of arson were shortly followed by Hitler's naming of a Master Builder.
◆ Each fire cleared the way for the respective Master Builder to

work on a specific project: the House of German Art for Troost, the Autobahn for Todt.

⊕ Hitler was an active participant in each building project, with the Führer submitting his personal design ideas.

⊕ In each case, Hitler incidentally also equated the new creation with the Parthenon, either by word or deed. Icons of Athena were on hand for the dedication of the art museum. And Hitler would subsequently refer to the Autobahn as his "Parthenon," in remarks recalled after World War II by Albert Speer.

Speer, the junior successor to both Troost and Todt, recalled another aspect of Hitler that puts these fires in perspective: an apparent pyromaniacal streak. Writing in Spandau Prison in 1947, Speer remembered Hitler's morbid thrill at seeing certain scenes in war newsreels:

> I asked myself whether there are temperaments that belong to a specific element. If so, I would unhesitatingly say that fire was Hitler's proper element. Though what he loved about fire was not its Promethean aspect, but its destructive force. That he set the world aflame and brought fire and sword upon the Continent—such statements may be mere imagery. But fire itself, literally and directly, always stirred a profound excitement in him. I recall his ordering showings in the Chancellery of the films of burning London, of the sea of flames over Warsaw, of exploding convoys, and the rapture with which he watched those films. I never saw him so worked up as toward the end of the war, when in a kind of delirium he pictured for himself and for us the destruction of New York in a hurricane of fire. He described the skyscrapers being turned into gigantic burning torches, collapsing upon one another, the glow of the exploding city illuminating the dark sky.

"Rapture." "Delirium." A pyromaniac tendency is attested, in spades. It is moreover linked to architecture in the mind of the miscreant, and observed by a genuine architect who knew him well.

THE RISE OF MASTER BUILDER TODT

If in the autumn of 1933 someone had asked "Who is Hitler's Master Builder?" the reply would have still been a tossup. The chancellor had presided over groundbreakings at two grand construction sites, in September for Todt's Autobahn and in October for Troost's art museum. In terms of *The Master Builder,* the respective projects were each preceded by a fortuitous and facilitating fire. Of the two project managers though, Troost alone qualified as an architect.

The accolade "Baumeister," or master builder, usually denotes professional mastery, not business monopoly. But the latter is what Ibsen meant, because of Solness's lack of a credential in architecture. In *Baumeister Solness,* he is the sole Master Builder, lording over the qualified experts.

In the Third Reich too, there could be just one, or one at a time. At first it was Paul Ludwig Troost, selected in 1931 to implement the Führer's own sketches for a House of German Art. Hitler, ever the poseur in architecture, beheld Troost with the respect due a virtuoso. It showed in their personal protocol. When the Nazi chief would come calling at his modest Munich studio on Theresien-strasse to review plans, Troost adopted a practice of receiving the exalted guest not out front as formal etiquette decreed, but inside. Hitler deferred, an architectural groupie basking in the maestro's presence.

By mid-1933, a change was under way. The Führer had since decided on the Autobahn as a Third Reich cachet. All other building would be secondary. Todt received a newly created appointment as General Inspector for Roads, if not yet "Master Builder" per se then at least master of the biggest German building job and *primus inter pares* among German construction men. His perquisites and power immediately classed Todt superior to Troost in the Führer's esteem.

Troost's swan song came at the art museum ceremonies in October. Hitler managed to break the small silver hammer Troost had designed to affix a dedication plaque, then take the event as an omen for the death of Troost just three months later. That left Todt, who remained until 1942 the anointed Master Builder above all others, including over Albert Speer. In Ibsen casting terms, why the fresh start? For that matter, why Todt, an engineer but not an architect?

In *The Master Builder,* Solness rules over qualified architects but is not one himself. From Act II:

HILDE: Why don't you call yourself an architect, like all the others?
SOLNESS: I've never really studied it properly. Most of what I know I've found out for myself.

CASTLES IN THE AIR

When Henrik Ibsen relocated from Rome to Germany in 1868, he stayed for a few summer months at a popular Bavarian alpine resort close by the Austrian frontier. The place proved inspirational for writing. It was there, at Berchtesgaden, that he completed much of the work on *Emperor and Galilean* in 1871–73. A half century later, Dietrich Eckart followed, to breathe the mountain air while beholding the incomparable vistas. Eckart's most important creation came in turn. For years, Hitler rented a villa on the slopes of the Obersalzberg above Berchtesgaden, although by the early 1930s he was able to purchase it outright using royalty income from *Mein Kampf.* The Führer took possession on September 19, 1932, the first anniversary of Geli Raubal's death, after which he remodeled the place and renamed it the Berghof. But Hitler soon sought a custom-built hideaway still further up the mountain.

To commission an outright castle risked snickering comparison to the nineteenth-century extravagance of Bavaria's mad King Ludwig. So Hitler settled instead on a "teahouse" atop a crag called the Kehlstein, about a thousand meters' altitude higher than the turrets of Ludwig's Hohenschwangau castle. The Führer laid forth the plan on September 30, 1936, according to a typescript office diary record called the "Führer Tagebuch" ("Führer Daybook"). This document shows that Todt participated from the inception of the project. On November 3, 1936, it says, Todt conferred with Martin Bormann,

Hitler's deputy, about road access to the Kehlstein. A photograph shows Todt and other engineers undertaking a reconnaissance.

The roadbuilding despoiled much of the landscape around the Obersalzberg, for which Bormann was assigned the blame after World War II. But the crews were all Todt's men, pulled off their Autobahn-building assignments to please Hitler and working under the direction of the Master Builder. A pro-Nazi architect, Roderick Fick, was selected to construct the so-called teahouse itself. It consisted of a dining room, a full-sized kitchen, a study, a guardroom, lavatories, a cellar, a balcony, and a fireplace-equipped circular room built to offer a panoramic view. The access road measured some seven kilometers on a difficult uphill grade through a series of tunnels. A special elevator shaft had to be drilled through solid rock. Not surprising, the Kehlstein work lagged; the finished result could not be presented for the Führer's birthday in April 1938, as had been the original hope. It was ready at last on September 16, 1938. An unsubstantiated rumor prevalent among foreign journalists had it that on Hitler's first trip up the elevator, it stalled in the shaft for four hours. Hitler supposedly suspected sabotage until a simple blown fuse was found to be the cause.

Hitler by and by lost interest in the Kehlstein. According to the "Führer Tagebuch," he did visit the teahouse on the 16th, 17th, and 18th of October, 1938, on the last occasion in the company of French ambassador Andre François-Poncet. This invitation to the envoy came during the immediate aftermath of the Sudetenland crisis, in which the British and French had been bluffed into abandoning their Czech ally. Hitler still aimed to impress, but this guided tour proved a Nazi mistake. The diplomat wrote in his memoirs how the eyrie seemed like something dreamed up by an abnormal mind. These remarks were published. After that, the Führer's teahouse trips tapered off.

Other "castles in the air" followed, built by Todt as wartime headquarters for the Führer, who was demanding something more than the already-existing military base complexes with their ready communications facilities. In practical terms, the chief of a mid-twentieth-century armed force did not really need height above a battlefield as was indeed required in Napoleon's day. But that is what

Hitler got, on the Ziegenberg peak and on the Felsennest in the Eifel mountains. Even if altitude were a legitimate consideration—e.g., to accommodate the radio antennas of a command center—plenty of well-appointed chateau structures already existed on high ground in the Rhineland and could have been commandeered. But at Hitler's behest, Todt put up the additional complexes, at great expense, for very temporary and limited use.

GROOMING THE APPRENTICE

In *The Master Builder*, Halvard Solness keeps a tight rein over Ragnar, fearful of the day when the architecturally trained apprentice would inevitably strike out on his own. The real-life analog to Ragnar can be none other than Albert Speer. From early on, the Führer carefully subordinated Speer to Todt on several projects of an engineering nature for which Speer lacked training, and despite Speer's heavy responsibilities in the purely architectural realm. And just as Ragnar is poised to take over the business at the moment of Solness's fatal fall, so too did Hitler position Speer to inherit Todt's mantle of Master Builder immediately upon Todt's fatal airplane crash. There are indeed consistent indications that Hitler always regarded Speer as the eventual successor to Todt, notwithstanding the two men's contrasting professional backgrounds and skills. Present too are indications that Hitler long prepared for Todt's eventual death.

Speer's role as understudy to Todt began in 1934, on the Autobahn, with a task to design workers' barracks. The wretched conditions in road camps were becoming a scandal. Todt saw no problem; miserable accommodations had always been the norm. But the Autobahn was a prestige project, and foreigners were looking on. Hitler commissioned Speer to come up with a standardized layout for sleeping, dining, and recreational facilities.

Why Speer? Speer had only just been appointed to fulfill the duties of the deceased Paul Ludwig Troost. He had to manage the construction of the House of German Art in Munich. Other concurrent Speer jobs were to design new German embassy offices in

London and to handle special lighting effects at Nuremberg for a huge Nazi rally. A standard barracks blueprint could be had off the shelf from the Army. In real-world terms, the tasking was redundant and mundane, a diversion of architectural talent.

But it fit *The Master Builder* script. In Act I, Ragnar has made innovative blueprints for a villa. Solness fears the challenge to his authority. Then in Act II, Hilde Wangel looks over Ragnar's drawings. She urges Solness to approve.

During the Westwall building effort, the Führer informed Speer that the architect would take over from the Master Builder. By then, Speer was commissioned to remake Berlin in grandeur. He had nothing to do with the Westwall that had siphoned off labor and material from his efforts at the capital. Nevertheless, the supreme leader took Speer along on a Westwall inspection trip, evidently to familiarize Speer with Todt's work. As Speer reminisced, "Hitler remarked that if anything should happen to Todt, I would be the one to carry out his construction assignments."

Such concern for succession to relatively young officials was unusual with Hitler. He did not similarly line up heirs to the other top Nazis like Goering, Himmler, or Goebbels in early anticipation of their mortality. Todt moreover enjoyed robust health at the time. At the age of forty-seven, he kept up with an energetic work schedule and was in better trim than many of his debauched colleagues. He looked more hale, for that matter, than the sedentary, fifty-year-old Hitler, whose constitution was steadily weakening due to his famously eccentric diet.

The suitability of Speer to take over from Todt presented another problem. Todt worked through a trusted staff consisting of fellow engineers. Their shared triumphs and travails marked them a clique. Here and there, a few architects had been used, but subordinated to the engineers. The idea of placing an architect on top could only rankle Todt's staff. Yet Hitler had envisioned Speer as inheritor to Todt, come what may, and he stuck to his vision.

Another step came after war broke out. Hitler was lining up Todt to be armaments minister. But he parceled out one armaments program to Speer: the Junkers Ju-88 bomber. By any standard, this made an odd tasking for the architect of the new Berlin. The job is all the more curious since Goering, the Luftwaffe commander, also functioned as Germany's premier industrial manager. Speer had no experience with either plant management or aircraft production.

Amid the wake of the German victory in France in the summer of 1940, Hitler made yet another move to ensure that Speer would eventually step into Todt's position: The Führer offered to place Speer in charge of construction within the enlarged Todt sphere. Todt, Hitler rightly observed, was overburdened. This proposal would have added the building of coastal fortifications to Speer's writ as planner of the new Berlin, and at a time when Hitler was renewing his interest in grandiose plans for Berlin to outdo Paris. Speer declined on this occasion. Despite Todt's genuine burdens, however, no one but Speer was offered the construction job.

The next year, Speer was tapped, and this time given no choice, for the Russian front. Again the anomalies defy explaining this by normal logic. The planner of the German capital and his staff were sent to the Nazi-occupied Ukraine in December 1941 as a unit of Organization Todt, ordered to repair Soviet railways. But Speer lacked training in either railway engineering or military logistics. He frankly conceded his ineffectiveness in the frozen conditions. Nonetheless, through this assignment he was made familiar with the vast Todt bureaucratic enterprise and its work.

A PREMONITION OF DOOM

If the script is *Baumeister Solness,* then the Master Builder is fated to die in a fall from a height, at the peak of his career, having completed an acquaintance with Hilde lasting ten years. Solness confides his forebodings in Act I:

> Day and night, I'm afraid. Because some time my luck must change.... My luck will change. I know it. And I feel it will happen soon.... What of it? Why, that will be the end for master builder Solness.

In late 1941, it was Hitler himself who hinted at his master builder's impending demise. The Führer mused on the night of November 10 about medals for the greatest of heroes:

> The Knight's Cross ought to carry a pension with it—against the event of the holder's no longer being able to earn his living. It's the nation's duty similarly to ensure that the wife and children of a soldier who has distinguished himself do not find themselves in need. One could solve this problem by awarding the Knight's Cross posthumously.

So the Knight's Cross should properly be reserved for dead men. Hitler then contemplated an "Order of the Party"; he clearly had in mind an award for some military man who was also a stalwart Nazi. After four sentences of this, he returned to the Knight's Cross and named a (still living) candidate:

> There are cases in which one no longer knows how to reward a leader who has rendered outstanding services. The exploits of two hundred holders of the Knight's Cross are nothing compared to the services of a man like Todt.

The Führer was already envisioning Todt among the dead.

THE MASTER BUILDER'S FATAL FALL

As scripted by Ibsen, master builder Solness meets his death in a deadly plunge at the site of a new structure he has completed and dedicated to Hilde Wangel. In theater productions, the fall takes place offstage. Onstage, the players point high and narrate Solness's ascent. Then they shout in dismay and lower their heads when he drops.

Adapting the action to real life would present a tough special-effects problem if Hitler was emulating the script. Having Todt shoved off the Kehlstein might only land him in soft snow. That would hardly do; as an accomplished skier, the man knew how to fall. Heaving the

Master Builder down from one of his Autobahn overpasses could add dramatic flair but might merely incur a fractured limb. That would require some messy finishing off. And there was no plausible excuse for a jaunt out to the unused, militarily worthless Autobahn in the winter of 1941–42. An airplane, however, offered possibilities.

The script of *Baumeister Solness* calls for a last emotional meeting between Hilde and her builder before the fatal plummet. At Führer headquarters, Todt bickered with Hitler about the course of the war. For months he had been vainly advising the supreme leader that Germany lacked the resources to win against the combined might of the Allies, now including America. Hitler stood firm in rejecting any peace. Then Todt boarded a Heinkel He-111 aircraft bound for Berlin. It suffered an onboard explosion in midair shortly after takeoff on February 8, 1942, and crashed, killing the Master Builder. He had served Hitler for ten years and a few months.

Todt's final journey was anything but routine. At one point during the evening talks with Todt on February 7, Hitler summoned his Luftwaffe adjutant, Major Nicolaus von Below. He too had clashed with Todt that day, on the issue of travel restrictions. There was a standing instruction from Hitler forbidding top officials from flying in two-engine aircraft. Todt, however, had been using a dual-motor He-111 machine loaned to him by Marshal Hugo Sperrle since Todt's usual plane, a trimotor Ju-52, was being overhauled. That placed Todt in breach of orders. Von Below reminded him of the guideline, whereupon Todt pulled rank to claim an exemption. Only the Führer could decide. Hitler thereupon overrode his own instruction and bid von Below make arrangements for Todt to fly the next morning. The major then contacted the airfield to order a test flight of the He-111 before Todt's takeoff. The plane was found to be fully fit. Departure was set for 9:30 A.M.

Even then, Todt did not really have to fly. He had no state appointments in Berlin, and was expected home at Munich. Berlin and Munich could be reached from Rastenburg by rail. Reserved train seating presented no problem, since officials of Todt's rank had priority rail passes. But the Führer had expedited his flight. As it happened, this particular flight could quite reasonably have been canceled due to weather conditions alone, with cloud cover at 200–300 meters and a snowstorm expected. Air controllers nevertheless cleared a takeoff.

Todt's car pulled up to the airbase at about 9:25 A.M. for the scheduled departure. Just before boarding, the base commander made a request of him. Would Todt accept an extra passenger aboard? The man was a sergeant on leave, also traveling to Berlin and then on to Munich to see his family.

Todt nodded approval just as sergeant Karl Bäuerle arrived at the airfield from the Führer headquarters carrying a wooden box, its contents unknown. The sergeant boarded with the box. Consent for him to ride was pro forma. To refuse would have been contrary both to Todt's own nature and to military courtesy in wartime. Bäuerle anyway had the status of courier from the high command on this flight. That, it seemed, was why he carried the wooden chest. The aircraft lifted up, headed out into the low cloud cover, and radioed back the message that all was in order on board.

But within three minutes the He-111 was returning for an emergency descent back toward the field, landing gear down. A strong tailwind blew. If it touched down, the plane would surely have overshot the end of the short runway. The conditions were not right for landing, but this plane was in dire straits. At this point, when the craft was about a hundred meters from the airfield, witnesses observed blue flames issuing from the rear of the fuselage. That observation should rule out a fuel problem, since He-111s carried their fuel in wing tanks. The plane flipped over on its left wing. It crashed, setting ablaze fully 3,400 liters of aviation gasoline. Incinerated along with Todt were the three-man crew, the hapless furloughed Sergeant Bäuerle, and one more hitchhiker. No one survived. Retrieved from the fire with poles, the charred remains of Todt were identified by shreds of uniform insignia that had not fully burned.

Hans Baur, Hitler's personal pilot, shortly arrived at the scene of the disaster. He helped recover the bodies and then began investigating. Baur wrote down eyewitness accounts. He later stated in his memoirs that he himself saw a smoke plume from the crash while driving toward the base around 9:30 A.M., "as usual," he recalled, although Hitler had no flight travel planned for that day. Baur normally slept at the Wolf's Lair complex situated about seven kilometers from the air base.

That is, from Baur's own statement, he had not been informed of any mishap by telephone at the Wolf's Lair but had already left headquarters and chanced to arrive on the scene just minutes after the He-111 smashed down. There he usurped an investigative function that under any system would be an airfield command prerogative until an inquiry commission was duly constituted. It could only be expected that Baur, like any other chance eyewitness, would assist in dousing the flames. The firefighting had to have taken some time while the airfield staff was also reacting in accordance with procedure. But for Baur to launch an impromptu inquest on his own authority was both unmilitary and presumptuous. Unless he had been cleared to do so.

Baur, who held nominal SS rank, did not figure in the Luftwaffe airfield's chain of command. He was but an aerial chauffeur serving the Third Reich's First Passenger. That gave him a certain license to meddle, albeit selectively and only with higher approval. And here he meddled, apparently unconcerned about bureaucratic turf or consequences, in accounting for a calamity that had just claimed a powerful minister of state.

The cause of the crash was a bomb, of course. Too many witnesses had seen the otherwise inexplicable flames suddenly shooting from the rear of the plane to disguise the fact of an explosion aboard. As Baur noted, some of the witnesses he interviewed lived on a nearby estate. The physical cause of the crash was thus plainly evident on and off the airbase. A bomb carried aboard by an unwitting passenger could quite possibly have been too small to instantly obliterate the aircraft, yet could still have been large enough to cause the flames as observed from the ground prior to the He-111's last plunge on its desperate but futile return to the airfield.

A proper air ministry commission arrived within days to pore over the wreckage. Its results were inconclusive. After the war, Luftwaffe Marshal Erhard Milch testified to his opinion that technical failure, weather conditions, and human error could all be ruled out as factors.

What remained was sabotage, which Milch ventured was "possible, but unproven." In resolving the case, the exploded bomb had to be politically defused, ex post facto.

Again Hans Baur came to the rescue. Of the He-111, he wrote:

> This replacement unit had been at the front, and like all combat-area aircraft, it carried the so-called "destroyer," a small box containing a kilogram of dynamite activated by a pull string with a tiny loop. The "destroyer" was located under the pilot's seat.

There are abundant problems here. "Activated by a pull string" (as opposed to "detonated by a pull string") alludes to the delay mechanism on a military self-destruction device. The delay is set long enough for the crew to don their parachutes and abandon the aircraft. Baur's wording does not and cannot mean a device that, when pulled, brings about the instantaneous, suicidal obliteration of the one who pulled it and his comrades aboard the plane.

Superficially, Baur's analysis might seem objective and professional. But it harbors still further presumptions. Bauer did not know, as an established fact, that this particular airplane carried a legitimate self-destruct charge. He arrived at that point only by placing the plane within the category of "all combat-area aircraft," even though not all combat-area aircraft had self-destruct charges.

Having departed from facts, though, Baur continued in a purely speculative vein:

> Dr. Todt usually sat in the cockpit next to the pilot in the place normally occupied by the flight engineer. Shortly before takeoff, he walked through the little cabin to the pilot's seat. The passage was very narrow, and Dr. Todt, wearing a fur suit, had to squeeze through the opening. He sat and waited until the flight engineer, who also served as the radio operator, had raised the landing gear and could vacate the other seat. In squeezing his way from the passage to the seat, it is possible that the loop on the pull cord caught on one of the buttons of his boot, thereby setting off the timer and detonator.

"It is possible. . . ." But was it? Hitler's pilot indulged in blaming the victim, and of all the victims aboard the plane the one chosen for blame was Todt. Baur hereby choreographed a sequence of events aboard the aircraft not witnessed by himself or any other living person. No one could definitively verify, or refute, a Todt movement forward to the cockpit seats. There is no corroboration whatsoever that the movement imagined by Baur actually occurred. And since Todt traveled as a passenger, his presence in the cockpit would have been an imposition on the crew during the craft's takeoff and ascent.

From the position of the bodies at the time of the crash, it should indeed have been apparent who had sat where, or at least who was and was not in the cockpit when the plane blew up. But Baur physically altered key facts when he pulled the bodies out of the still-burning wreck, obscuring what might be learned of the relative position of the victims upon impact. Having thus tampered with key evidence, Baur proceeded to fabricate further. He insinuated that Todt had gone forward to the cockpit and displaced a crewman from his proper station. This was gratuitous, since Todt had been traveling as a passenger. The conjectural seating of Todt in the cockpit was not stated by anyone on the ground who might have had a last glimpse of Todt up front, through a cockpit window. It is a surmise originating with Baur. If there was a self-destruct charge beneath the pilot's seat, and if it had a pull cord begging to be snagged, then anyone's boot might have done the snagging. Yet Baur felt compelled to blame Todt. That way Todt's own gawkishness—"it is possible"—did him in, along with five unfortunates in the wrong place at the wrong time. The effect was to devalue the most prominent figure among the dead men.

If, if, if, Bauer speculated. If Todt went forward to the cockpit, and if he then turned to leave the cockpit and return to the passenger area, and if his boot button then caught the pull loop of the delayed-action fuse of a dynamite charge, maybe that explains the bomb going off. For those outside the loop, Baur wrote with seeming authority as a German airman and the Führer's own pilot, no less.

Therein lies the problem with Baur's word. By normal procedure he was way, way out of line. His theory of the disaster was circulated at the time, in 1942, offsetting an official inquiry that could not, or would not, promulgate a definitive finding. Again, it would seem naïve to attribute such meddling to the purely private initiative of an aerial limo driver, a man outside the Luftwaffe whose sole job on organization charts was to ferry the supreme commander.

Iffy-est of all is the very existence of the self-destruct charge, Baur's so-called destroyer. If this imagined mishap was really waiting to happen aboard Luftwaffe planes, then with all the dangling loops ready to snag all the boot buttons on all the oafs in all the cockpits of the German air armada, it should have happened more than once, if not regularly. But Luftwaffe records are not replete with planes exploding at random like popcorn kernels in the skies.

Air forces—and that includes the Luftwaffe—keep log books, maintenance records, and equipment manifests for every plane, available to serve as staple reference sources for any crash investigation. The official commission probing this crash had access to the records of this He-111. If Baur's standard-issue explosive charge really existed, it should have been entered onto the equipment manifest as an item for consideration by the duly appointed investigators. But instead of sharing in Baur's convenient conclusion, the official investigators reached no conclusion at all. Baur's surmised self-destruct charge aboard this He-111 turns out not to be a tangible, attested entity. Its presence on board was simply inferred from a general proposition, itself dubious.

Todt's son, Fritz Jr., pursued the matter. He was a newly commissioned Luftwaffe airman, junior in rank, yet with no less a personage than Hitler himself he raised the very issue of the putative self-destruct charge. The young Fritz Todt contended that the He-111 had no such explosive device aboard, at least not as part of its legitimate equipment. To this, the Führer frostily replied: "I wish no more discussion about this matter." Fritz Jr. died in action soon afterwards.

There was a bomb aboard, however. Hans Baur himself admitted that much. He stated that it weighed just a kilogram and, most helpfully, he described its housing as a box. For all Baur's attention to a conjectured box underneath the pilot's seat, there remained the actual box attested to have been carried on board by the last-minute passenger, Sergeant Karl Bäuerle. The sergeant sat not in the cockpit, where Baur strained his imagination to place Todt, but amidships or farther back, where passengers properly sat in an He-111 configured as a courier plane. Any luggage or parcels brought by passengers would also have been in the central or rearward sections of the craft.

The self-appointed crash sleuth Hans Baur had stated, definitively, "The witnesses unanimously agreed that the flames had belched from the plane's rear section." Not from the cockpit. Rarely do eyewitnesses agree on a point. Here, for once, they did. For flames to belch forth requires a hole suddenly forming in a place where none had been before.

Baur breezed past Sergeant Bäuerle in his account with "Besides Todt and the three-man crew, a couple of people on leave had boarded the plane." It was Baur who had sent for long grappling poles to recover the victims' still smoldering remains from the wreck. Baur had the evidence of his eyes and his nostrils to confirm Bäuerle's presence. Whether to preserve delicacy or to skirt around facts inconvenient to his hypothesis, though, Baur gave no exhaustive description of the dismemberment of each corpse. He thereby glossed over forensic data essential in any effort to pinpoint where aboard the plane the blast had occurred. Baur's concern was solely with the plane's most prominent passenger. The other victims amounted to props.

Baur stated only that "Dr. Todt lay head downward, one shoulder touching the earth, and one part of a shoulder that definitely identified the body as Dr. Todt, still recognizable." According to the records of the duly constituted inquiry, Todt had undergone a particularly severe mangling with an opening of the abdominal cavity through which the entrails protruded. Both his legs were broken. The cause of death was attributed to a fracture of the skull. As for Sergeant Bäuerle, his remains were "entirely shattered."

Although all the bodies were badly charred in the fire that ensued upon impact, it appears from the official description of the corpses that Todt and Bäuerle suffered rather more physical trauma than the crewmen who sat forward in the cockpit. That would again conform to an explosive device having gone off closer to the two passenger victims—that is, a bomb exploding either amidship or aft, but not in the crew compartment. On this incongruity, and on the comparative condition of the victims' bodies, Baur offered no comment at all, although such detail would have been of utmost importance in substantiating his speculative case. It was Todt's adjutant, the engineer Haasemann, who conducted a private investigation revealing how Sergeant Bäuerle had boarded bearing a wooden box. The Gestapo then ordered Haasemann to desist from pursuing whether this box was Bäuerle's own property, or an item that had been handed to him that morning for delivery to Munich. Haasemann believed the latter.

So Baur postulated a self-destruct charge under the pilot's seat in the He-111 cockpit, notwithstanding a blast observed from the ground that seemed to emanate from the plane's rear area. The inferred cockpit explosive had an inferred pull cord activating a delay fuse. This was inferentially yanked by an inferentially klutzy Todt. Realizing the disaster afoot, a cool, quick- acting pilot swirled his craft 180 degrees in a race back to base. Bravo, except for the time factor. Such delay fuses are calibrated to give an air crew time to bail out. Therefore, had a delay fuse really been inadvertently triggered, the still cooler, rational (and likely instinctive) course for a quick-thinking military man would have simply been to open a hatch and toss out the activated dynamite charge before it blew up.

The aircraft's sharp reversal of direction once aloft is therefore incompatible both with rational emergency action and with what witnesses on the ground actually saw. It does accord with an explosion from a charge carried on and taken aft, a charge without a delay fuse. As fire raced through the plane from the bomb blast, the pilot realized that his sole survival option was to chance a landing, come what may. Short of the runway, a secondary explosion proved fatal.

The Baur interpretation self-destructs when its inconsistencies are exposed. As in the case of Geli Raubal, the suspicions surrounding this death go back to the time it occurred. When Hitler eulogized "Minister Todt was summoned to a gracious fate at the pinnacle of his success," the Wehrmacht archivist appended his own private note to the files: "For a pretty remarkable fall!"

THE APPRENTICE SUCCEEDS THE MASTER BUILDER

Shocked though the apprentice Ragnar may be when Solness lies smashed to death in the Ibsen play, the young man is the building firm's evident new head. He is on hand and sure to take over the Master Builder's clientele. So too did Albert Speer happen to be on hand on that February 8, 1942. He had returned to Germany from the Nazi-occupied Ukraine at the summons of the Führer, on an aircraft bound for Rastenburg. In fact, as originally scheduled, Speer was also to accompany Todt out of Rastenburg for Berlin on the courier airplane assigned to Todt.

Both men dined at Hitler's table on the evening of February 7, after which they met separately with the Führer. First it was Todt's turn. Then Hitler sent for Speer and detained him to 3:00 A.M. before letting Speer get to bed. Having been thus waylaid by Hitler, Speer canceled his booking on the fatal plane. As Speer explained it in his memoirs, he needed the sleep. Consequently, he sent word ahead stating that he would not be aboard.

But in wartime, transportation is at a premium and everyone suffers fatigue. From 3:00 to about 8:00, which would have allowed ample time for morning ablutions and the short ride to the airfield, Speer could have gotten fully five hours' slumber and supplemented that with a catnap on the plane. Instead, he stayed behind to snooze, then to waken as the new Master Builder. He inherited the job Hitler had long promised to him should something happen to Todt. The "something" had finally happened.

THE LAUREL WREATH BORNE ALOFT

But what, then, of the wreath? At the end of *The Master Builder*, the doomed Solness carries aloft a laurel wreath. He will drape it over the spire of his latest structure, then topple to earth.

An inkling of what would come appeared in a book published in 1939. *Hitler Speaks* related talks with Hermann Rauschning, who had been a Nazi official in Danzig before he defected to the West in

1934. In America, he made a new career of writing about his former Führer. As evidence, Rauschning's memoirs must be used critically; yet it is certain that he met with Hitler on occasion. He summarized one talk with Hitler:

> This Master Builder, this Solness, is himself not immune from dizziness. A whole nation watches anxiously as he climbs to the top of his building to crown it with a wreath. It expects to see him stagger and fall, and lie mangled and lifeless on the ground.

Rauschning thereby likened Solness not to Todt, but to Hitler. Beyond that detail of casting, however, it is worthwhile to note that:

⊕ A clear allusion to the finale of Ibsen's *The Master Builder* appears in a book based upon conversations between Hitler and a sometime Nazi official.

⊕ Rauschning was not usually given to literary flights of fancy. By 1939, well after the peak of Ibsen's popularity, such a reference to Solness would already have been obscure for many readers. The fact that the allusion was nevertheless included in his book suggests a mention of the Ibsen play by Hitler during a private talk with Rauschning.

⊕ If the allusion to *The Master Builder* originated, as suspected, with a Hitler remark to Rauschning, this indicates that the play's final scene and the wreath were vivid images in Hitler's mind.

Wreaths somehow came to Adolf Hitler's mind yet again, just days before fate claimed his own Master Builder. On the night of February 3–4, 1942, the Führer's mind wandered back to laurel wreaths. He recalled out loud how, upon his return to Munich from jail in December 1924, friends had decked out his apartment with garlands and laurel wreaths. And, he noted, "I've preserved one ever since."

That is, with his armies just then retreating on battlefronts in Russia and Libya, the thoughts of the warlord of Europe had somehow strayed to a dried keepsake from decades past. Why? Was a wreath, this particular wreath, slated to be placed in that box sent onto Todt's He-111 with Sergeant Karl Bäuerle on February 8, 1942? A clever parting touch, if it were. We shall never know.

However, Fritz Todt did bring along two other wreaths on the frigid gray morning of his death. The air crew saw those wreaths but paid no heed. Neither Todt nor anyone else watching him board would have deemed them out of place or worthy of remark. All had become accustomed to seeing the wreaths, so accustomed as to screen them out of conscious thought. Albeit unnoticed, they were there, with the Master Builder, for his last ascent. They were wreaths that had been presented to Todt, personally, by Hitler.

The paired wreaths were fashioned of silver braid. They adorned Todt's lapels as the standard insignia of a Luftwaffe major general. Hitler had awarded Todt the rank, although it came with no substantive Luftwaffe responsibilities.

13

FROM SCRIPT TO SCRIPTURE—
A MIMETIC SYNDROME

BASIL: Poetry, poetry; you are confusing fact and fiction.

JULIAN: Aren't the mind and will in fiction subject to the same conditions as those in real life?

—IBSEN, *EMPEROR AND GALILEAN,*
PART ONE, ACT II

The line dividing life and art can be invisible. After seeing enough hypnotizing movies and reading enough magical books, a fantasy life develops which can be either harmless or quite dangerous.

—JOHN W. HINCKLEY JR. IN 1981,
ON HOW SEEING THE FILM *TAXI DRIVER* LED HIM
TO SHOOT PRESIDENT RONALD REAGAN

I don't think there is any difference between fantasy and reality in the way these should be approached in a film. Of course, if you live that way you are clinically insane.

—MARTIN SCORSESE, DIRECTOR OF
TAXI DRIVER, IN 1989

DID THE FÜHRER of the Nazi Third Reich follow a set of Ibsen's scripts? It should hardly cause surprise. If Hitler venerated Julian the Apostate, so too did Heinrich Himmler extol Genghis Khan. But to implement as state policy a drama about Julian takes hero worship to another plane. Is it practically and clinically plausible? And if so, does this mean that the world catastrophe of the mid-twentieth century boils down to a case of murder-by-the-book?

HISTRIONICS AS HISTORY

It doesn't require a rocket scientist to connect the dots. . . .

Contemporaries recalled the youthful Adolf reading Ibsen in 1908–10. Bits of three Ibsen dramas subsequently turn up paraphrased, among Hitler's spoken discourses, in wording close enough to pinpoint the source, in instances noted as late as 1942. Yet besides mere words, there is more. From the 1920s to 1942, Hitler took various actions that correlate, sequentially, to episodes of the same three plays. This is unexpected but explicable. German literary cultists in the early twentieth century had exalted Ibsen as a "prophet" and as the "harbinger of the third Reich." Certain writers in the early 1920s cited the very plays echoed by Hitler's words and deeds, stressing the epic *Emperor and Galilean.* One critic dubbed that work a political "allegory" to be repeated in the near future, and even hailed Hitler as the one ordained to bring it about. The Führer maintained ties to other Ibsen cultists as well, including Dietrich Eckart, his closest mentor. Eckart insisted that he himself was an Ibsen character, incarnate. Hitler's own obsession with the theater is well known. He also had a lifetime penchant for mimicry and would occasionally lampoon the mannerisms of subordinates or other public figures to the amusement of his staff or dinner guests. More seriously, in 1941 he himself compared his work to the mission of Julian the Apostate, the hero of *Emperor and Galilean.* The other two plays, *An Enemy of the People* and *The Master Builder,* also come up by name in contexts specifically involving Hitler or where his presence may be safely inferred.

To be sure, not every plot incident from these three plays has an analog in what Hitler did. There are many characters in all three plays who have no correlative among persons in the Führer's entourage. Practical considerations limit how far any emulation can go, especially when all but the director must be kept unaware. Most of what Hitler did was day-to-day politics. However, there was a prevailing undercurrent replicating the Ibsen drama plots, and that is what may at last be discerned.

The dramas Hitler paraphrased are always accompanied by parallel Hitler deeds, and vice versa. Ibsen wrote twenty-six plays, but Hitler seems to have mimed only these three. A thorough search through the corpus of his monologues, speeches, and writings finds no further pentimenti from Ibsen plays beyond the ones adduced here. And excepting the three Ibsen scripts that were paraphrased on the record by Hitler, none of the twenty-three other drama plots are reflected by Hitler-initiated actions in the same sequential way. For each of the mimed three, there is a set of clearly drawn circumstances connecting the play to an aspect of Hitler's personal identity and aspirations. The three had to have been carefully picked, each on its own particular, methodical grounds.

Hitler's method in this regard resembles that of other factual and fictional killers who have based their deeds on some text. In fact, it makes for a perennial mystery-genre favorite: Deranged criminal follows script, leaves telltale clues; snaring him hangs on finding his script; sleuth spots the game, identifies the script, guesses the perp's moves. Rousing finale; culprit gets cuffed.

In Agatha Christie's *The A.B.C. Murders* (1936), the script is an alphabetically ordered timetable of the British railways. Mrs. A. in town A is the first to be slain, then Miss B. in village B, then Sir C. on an evening stroll at the beach resort of C. In *Club Dumas* (1993) by Arturo Pérez-Reverte, the hero is an antique book dealer hired to authenticate a manuscript of *The Three Musketeers.* Danger lurks when bad guys start behaving like those from the Dumas classic; they've been scripted. Jeffrey Deaver's thriller *The Bone Collector* (1997) revisits the theme. The slayer's script is an old pulp horror novel. A copy surfaces in a used bookstore. That seals the case. The literary factor is also what solves the crime in the novels of Edith Skom, hence *The Mark Twain Murders, The George Eliot Murders,* and *The Charles Dickens Murders.* In the Ira Levin classic *Rosemary's Baby,* the mystery text is titled *All of Them Witches.* Rosemary finds the volume, reads it, and wises up . . . but toooo late.

Whether highbrow or pulp, crime-by-the-book is down to earth, not science fiction. It requires no violations of natural law, no farfetched coincidences. Any resemblance of narrative to a previous plot is purely intentional; that's the whole point. The formula endures as cliché precisely because it is plausible. It is plausible not only because such things *can* happen but because they really *have* happened, sometimes to significant effect. Murderers by the book moreover seem to fit a type, which transcends Hitler's time and milieu.

Four nonfiction names familiar at least to Americans will readily come to mind. Among those who have mimed literature to deadly effect were John Wilkes Booth, John W. Hinckley Jr., Theodore Kaczynski (the "Unabomber"), and Timothy McVeigh.

JOHN WILKES BOOTH AND *JULIUS CAESAR*

On the evening of April 12, 1865, the noted actor John Wilkes Booth entered a VIP box at Ford's Theater in Washington, D.C. and discharged the chamber of a small pistol at short range into the cranium of Abraham Lincoln. After shooting the president, the assassin shouted in Latin, *"Sic semper tyrannis!"* ("Thus always to tyrants!") The death shot was supposed to avenge the Southern defeat in the American Civil War, perhaps even rescue the lost Confederate cause. Booth then jumped down onto the stage before dashing away in a bid to escape. In years previous, he had appeared in over eighty theater recitals of Shakespeare's *Julius Caesar* in Philadelphia and New York. He knew the lines of this play by heart, and was improvising on the role of Brutus, one of Caesar's assassins. His sense of personal connection to the character was rooted in family. Booth's actor father was Junius Brutus Booth, his older brother Junius Brutus Booth Jr.

The younger sibling evidently felt himself at least as deserving of their illustrious middle name.

His own words leave left no doubt that the blow against Lincoln replayed that of Brutus against Caesar. On the road during the days after his last act at Ford's Theater, Booth complained in self-pity to a pocket journal he carried. He dated an entry of April 13–14, 1865 as "the Ides." On April 21 he wrote: "I am here in despair. And why? For doing what Brutus was honored for." Booth's sister expressed the opinion that he was not insane—or, if so, then only during the last few days before he shot Lincoln. He recognized himself to be John Wilkes Booth, but by a decisive stroke he added the alter identity of Brutus. These two, the man and his assumed role, co-existed in one body. John Wilkes Booth died resisting capture. He had carried out his deed in a country that had been at war until just six days earlier, a country likely ill-disposed to a courtroom plea based on Shakespeare-made-me-do-it.

Booth could not restore the Confederacy, but he did alter history's course. Few can doubt that had Lincoln lived, Reconstruction would have played out much differently than it did under Andrew Johnson, Ulysses S. Grant, and Rutherford B. Hayes.

JOHN W. HINCKLEY JR. AND *TAXI DRIVER*

On March 30, 1981, twenty-five-year-old John W. Hinckley Jr. waited with a pistol outside the Hilton Hotel on Connecticut Avenue in Washington, D.C., where President Ronald Reagan was giving a speech. Hinckley, a psychiatric patient, had seen the movie *Taxi Driver* at least fifteen times. He had read the book on which the script was based and owned a tape of the soundtrack, to which he listened again and again. He emulated the title role played by Robert DeNiro, an armed, deranged hackie who stalks a politician. Travis Bickel, the character, drinks peach brandy; Hinckley made peach brandy his booze of choice. Down-and-out Travis wears surplus military fatigues; rich kid Hinckley followed suit. Travis conjures up a make-believe girlfriend and writes home about her; Hinckley did the same, replete with fabricated visits, vacations, even breaking up and making up. He aped Travis's speaking style as well. Hinckley "absorbed the identity of Travis Bickel," an expert witness testified at the trial for the defense.

Notwithstanding the fantasy girlfriend, Hinckley set out to impress the actress Jodie Foster, who plays a teenage whore in the film. He kept her picture in his wallet along with an unsent note asking, "You are a virgin, aren't you?" Foster was in real life a student at Yale. Hinckley traveled to New Haven where he stalked her on campus, telephoned, mailed her letters and poems, but all to no avail as Foster ignored this quirky would-be swain. Unemployed, unnoticed, and chronically unlaid, he dedicated his deed to Jodie like some knight-errant in medieval lore. Reagan emerged from the Hilton, and Hinckley squeezed off his shots.

Had he shifted his aim ever so slightly, the eventual presidency of George H. W. Bush would have begun in the spring of 1981 instead of almost eight years later.

THE UNABOMBER AND JOSEPH CONRAD'S NOVEL
THE SECRET AGENT

Between 1978 and 1993, ex-professor Theodore J. Kaczynski mailed and planted small but lethal homemade bombs in a one-man war against technology. Each device bore the initials "F.C.," for "Freedom Club," incised on a durable part, his signal to the bomb squad. Kaczynski lived in an isolated Montana cabin. Once, in a rare letter sent to family members, he advised them that to understand him they should read a 1907 novel by Joseph Conrad called *The Secret Agent* (inspired by the Greenwich, England observatory bombing of 1894). Chapters 4 and 5 describe a disgruntled ex-academic, "The Professor," who lives alone and crafts bombs. Other dissidents in the book use the initials "F.P." for "Future of the Proletariat." Kaczynski lived for a while on home-grown turnips; an anarchist character in *The Secret Agent* lived on carrots. It goes on.

Kaczynski outlined his copycat goal in an anonymous manifesto blasting modern society. Lawmen code-named him the "Unabomber." He had not only imbibed works by Joseph Conrad, but also used the alias "Conrad." That was how he registered at a hotel in Sacramento on trips there to mail bombs. Joseph Conrad's birth name was Teodore Jozef Konrad Korzeniowski.

The Unabomber's grand aims exceeded his own meager means. However, he did attract considerable FBI resources in the mid-1990s. This was after the first bombing attempt on the World Trade Center, when Al Qaeda was gearing up for a second try. So in an unintended way Kaczynski's efforts arguably proved effective, if only to distract attention from a still deadlier foe.

TIMOTHY McVEIGH AND *THE TURNER DIARIES*

At a few minutes past nine o'clock on the morning of April 19, 1995, an explosive mixture of ammonium nitrate fertilizer and fuel oil was detonated from a truck parked at the Federal Building in Oklahoma City. It killed 168 people, including federal officials, clerical staff, members of the general public, and toddlers in a daycare center. Charged with the crime was Timothy McVeigh, an ex-G.I., in whose car was found a photocopied page of a novel touting white supremacy, *The Turner Diaries* by Andrew MacDonald. It was the sort of incendiary literature sold at gun shows. The xeroxed passage described the ammonium nitrate composition of just such a bomb, for delivery by truck to FBI headquarters at 9:00 one morning. A rebellion of indignant white folks was supposed to follow upon the blast, or so the novel preached. When arrested, McVeigh wore a T-shirt bearing the motto "Sic semper tyrannis!" McVeigh failed to trigger the Aryan uprising of MacDonald's book. Like Kaczynski, though, intended or not, his terrorist deed reverberated to significant effect. FBI agents were detailed by the score to monitor white-power militias.

In each case, those of Booth, Hinckley, Kaczynski, and McVeigh, a text became a personal mantra—that is, a form of scripture. The text provided an identity, a goal, and an overall action guide. In each case, the script was adapted to meet current needs. In each case, the script was selectively mimed, some episodes used, others not. That all holds true for Hitler as well.

A MIMETIC SYNDROME

The Führer moreover shared significant personal traits with the four Americans, enough so to categorize him along with the others in what may be provisionally called a *mimetic syndrome*. This coined term will have to suffice, since formal psychiatry does not seem to have given the phenomenon a distinctive name. The syndrome refers to those who mime a script (novel, film, etc.) in a grandiose bid to alter history. Hitler's success at doing this far outstripped the four Americans, which places him on a pedestal of his own. He furthermore adopted not just one persona, but at least three from Ibsen alone, plus others as required from sundry sources. The result was a longer, more complicated, more destructive game with global scope. His power enabled him as well to cast others in scripted roles, unbeknownst to themselves, then have them killed on cue. The Führer doubled, after all, as producer and director.

Yet strip away a despot's perks, and Hitler seems to fit the type. Again, fiction helps define that basic type. Hercule Poirot, Agatha Christie's sleuth in *The A.B.C. Murders,* profiled the hypothetical suspect as a man . . .

> . . . who is at great needs to express his personality. I see him as a child possibly ignored and passed over—I see him growing up with an inward sense of inferiority—warring with a sense of injustice. I see that inner urge—to assert himself—to focus attention on himself ever becoming stronger, and events, circumstances—crushing it down—heaping, perhaps, more humiliations on him. And inwardly the match is set to the powder train.

"That's all pure conjecture," objects his sidekick foil. But Poirot has the perp perfectly psyched: "You must remember such a type has usually all the outer signs of insignificance—he belongs to the class of person who is usually passed over and ignored or even laughed at!" A suspect emerges. He is single and transient, a muddled, wounded combat veteran, a salesman who peddles ladies' silk stockings, who dotes on the initials of his name (which happen to be A.B.C.), and who sees the same film more than once. The suspect recalls the vagabond Hitler of pre-Führer days before he drifted, like flotsam, into a meeting of the tiny German Workers' Party.

Certain biographical elements buttress the case for a common syndrome among the lethal mimes Booth, Hinckley, Kaczynski, McVeigh, and Hitler. Each lacked regular employment for a protracted time. Of the five, only the actor Booth pursued a normal career, though actors always lived on the margin of social respectability, at once lionized yet unsavory. Hinckley for his part neither worked nor sought a job. Of his own will, Kaczynski left a promising professorship. For Hitler and McVeigh, their only stint at regular work was military service, including a taste of infantry combat and the added psychic havoc it can wreak. Among these men leading unstructured existences, the adoption of a fictive persona and the pursuit of a story line provided an ersatz structure to an otherwise amorphous life.

Also common to each was their marital status: single. Marriage usually provides an anchor, including the elements of a home, meals, affection, and sex. Yet all five mimes were bachelors, discounting Hitler's nuptials with Eva Braun on the last day of their lives. Booth had success with women, perhaps too much since he settled with no one lady. None among the five mimes lived in a stable, long-term, coupled relationship of any sort. At age sixteen, Hitler had stalked a poised young lady of Linz named Stephanie and penned her one anonymous love note—like the outclassed Hinckley stalking Jodie Foster. Their respective objects of desire remained unattainable in the normal sense.

While homosexuality cannot be documented, gender ambiguity can, at least for the Unabomber. After his arrest, Kaczynski revealed to a government psychiatrist a desire he had had during his student days to seek surgical reconstruction as a female. Inhibition at that time had kept him from confiding the plan to a campus counselor. Instead, Kaczynski sublimated his inner conflict by resolving to kill. He wrote,

"Like a phoenix I burst from the ashes of my despair to a glorious new hope. . . . What was entirely new was the fact that I really felt I could kill someone." That turmoil recalls the feminine—albeit vicious—side of Hitler, a side contemporaries observed, and identified here as the aspect fitting Ibsen's Hilde Wangel in *The Master Builder.*

Another feature shared among all five was their impersonal stance toward their chosen targets. Out to kill a president, any president, Hinckley stalked Jimmy Carter but failed to maneuver into shooting range. So he continued, trailing Ronald Reagan in commendable bipartisan spirit. The Unabomber's targets were likewise all symbols of the technological society he despised, rather than people with whom he had any personal gripe. McVeigh too aimed to destroy a symbolic edifice and the federal employees working there. None of his victims had directly caused him harm. Booth, for his part, had never suffered personally at Lincoln's hands. The president was for him more a personification of tyranny, a scripted Caesar cast opposite Booth's own Brutus.

Hitler for his part normally didn't single out and kill particular Jews, but the Jews as a whole, everywhere. He even allowed some minuscule exceptions. A few Jews with whom he had been acquainted fared relatively better than the general lot once the horror began. His World War I Army captain, his boyhood family doctor, and an art dealer he knew in Vienna all left Nazi Germany under special dispensations. A reputedly half-Jewish chauffeur of Hitler's lived out the Third Reich in Munich unmolested by Nazi authorities. It was the mass of European Jews, all but faceless to the Führer, who met the fate he prescribed.

Such a spree of murder-by-the-book goes misunderstood unless the book comes to light. So, did Hitler set deliberate clues? Was he trying to conceal in the short term, yet ensure that the game would be discerned someday? Was he doing as the killer in *The A.B.C. Murders* had done, sending Poirot taunting letters, leaving copies of the ABC rail schedule beside each victim's corpse? There can be no sure answer here, only reference to his counterparts in the game of miming scripts.

Hinckley had to know he would be tackled by Reagan's Secret

Service guards; in fact, that had to be his goal. He wrote Jodie Foster, "There is a definite possibility that I will be killed in my attempt to get Reagan." Without the notoriety of capture, at the least, he stood no chance to wow his lady love. Booth, the star performer, took no pains to conceal his identity after firing the fatal shot. Neither did he plan a viable escape in the wake of Appomattox. When he set out for Virginia, he was fully aware that Lee's army had surrendered. The zone he entered teemed with angry Union troops bent on running Lincoln's known killer to ground. Kaczynski, for his part, could reasonably surmise that the typescript manifesto he mailed to the press would multiply the clues leading his way. It did, his own brother suspecting his authorship and fingering him. Federal agents duly traced the spoor to Kaczynski's cabin in the woods. Last, McVeigh fled the Oklahoma City blast scene in a vehicle lacking license tags, a guarantee to get pulled over by the law. The "Sic semper tyrannis!" T-shirt he wore that day all but screamed, "Search Me."

Was Hitler also yearning to be caught, literally in the act? Trouble is, the Ibsen lines he paraphrased seem mostly ad hoc. Amid free-ranging soliloquies, he would glide into script-derived sequences, then glide out again. Did he do so from some grand design? That grants too much credit. The offhand paraphrased lines appear more like fragments stored in his cerebrum from frequent reading and review, not hints cleverly placed. And so whereas the link to Ibsen appears sound based on Hitler's words and actions, it remains moot whether he intended, or feared, that the source would ever be found.

Next comes the M'Naghton question—i.e., the insanity defense. (Daniel M'Naghton was the first person who successfully used this defense strategy, in 1843.) When a scripted killer kills, who does he think he is? Has he lost his birth identity and, with it, his mind? Does he still know right from wrong? Or has the script conveyed him to a place beyond good and evil? Is murder by script a legally responsible act? In other words, could Hitler have copped a plea?

For each of the five criminals being discussed here, the script-derived role-play made crime inevitable in the fated logic of the game. Hinckley's insanity plea emphasized that the *Taxi Driver* scenario had taken control of his mind. Defense lawyers insisted that Hinckley thought he *was* Travis Bickel. The prosecution countered that he still knew himself to be John W. Hinckley Jr. A federal penal psychiatrist, Dr. Sally C. Johnson, and a hired federal consultant, Dr. Park Dietz, both downplayed the effect of *Taxi Driver* in their expert testimony. They pointed out that Hinckley's own therapist, Dr. John Hopper, had been wholly unaware of his patient's fixation on the film. On the couch, Hinckley had concealed his Bickel role. Scripted mimicry notwithstanding, Hinckley knew full well who he was, according to conventional municipal records. So too did John Wilkes Booth, Theodore Kaczynski, Timothy McVeigh, and also Klara Pölzl Hitler's imaginative son Adolf.

But the syndrome they shared was never described in clinical terms as a condition in its own right, since the practical imperatives of judgment and punishment took precedence in the four American cases. Unlabeled by shrinks, the common features of miming a literary, theatrical, or cinematic work passed mostly unnoticed by the media as well. It appears, though, that the "mimetic syndrome" is at once destructive and self-destructive, but is delusional only to a point. Neither Booth, Hinckley, Kaczynski, McVeigh, nor Hitler ever fully lost sight of their this-world identity. Yet each man sacrificed his life or his lifetime's freedom pursuing role-play actions keyed to scripts. The scripts, all of them, culminate in violent deeds.

AN IBSEN REPERTORY

For Hitler, there are corollary aspects still to explore on how the three Ibsen scripts functioned as scripture:

⊕ The three scripts—*Emperor and Galilean, An Enemy of the People,* and *The Master Builder*—were intricately intertwined in Hitler's awareness. Each gave expression to different adopted personas, and each fulfilled separate functions that sometimes overlapped. The plots intersected at key points, most notably in the murder of Geli Raubal, which combined elements from *Emperor and Galilean* and *The Master Builder.*

* *Emperor and Galilean* occupied a position of primacy in the scheme, while the other two scripts fulfilled ancillary functions.
* Hitler's emulation of *Emperor and Galilean* occurred within the context of a neo-pagan cult active in Germany at that time. But the cultists sought an anti-Christian, anti-Jewish counter gospel. *Emperor and Galilean* filled the void, sanctioned by the elevation of Ibsen to "prophet." Hitler had thus stepped into an arcane neo-pagan creed still in its developmental stage. He offered it an activating component, his own life and career dedicated to fulfilling the third Reich of the script.
* Dietrich Eckart and Paul Schulze-Berghof each exercised pivotal functions in preparing Hitler for this appointment with scripted destiny. Eckart's role was undertaken by his personal mentoring of the young politician and by his own example of mystical identity with an Ibsen character. But Eckart said little or nothing, at least on the extant record, to extol *Emperor and Galilean.*
* After Eckart left the scene, the writings of Schulze-Berghof may be deemed decisive. First came *Ibsen's Emperor and Galilean as Allegory,* published in 1923. It serves as a kind of commentary, synthesizing Nietzsche's doctrine of the "superman" with the neo-pagan quest of Julian. Echoes in Hitler speeches indicate that he knew the script of *Emperor and Galilean* by 1921 and possibly as early as 1908. But a crucial date was reached during his prison year, 1924, which coincided with the appearance of Schulze-Berghof's novel *Wettersteinmächte.* That book all but appointed Hitler as the new Julian for a looming Third Reich.
* *Emperor and Galilean* provided a far more substantial plot line than did *An Enemy of the People,* along with a dual imperial and divine identity in the figure of Julian as an avatar of Christ, to be reborn yet again. It was tailor-made for a megalomaniac deluded under the rubric of a cult. As for the Hitlerian emulation of *The Master Builder,* this must be dated later, starting in 1931. It gave expression both to Hitler's feminine side and to his dreams as a frustrated architect who directed proxies to erect the edifices he would have preferred to construct himself.

* The evidence of the three scripts, when considered together, imparts coherence to a set of hitherto disparate mysteries in Hitler's life and career. These episodes need no longer be considered piecemeal, but instead can be viewed as sequential milestones in a methodically contrived series of emulative steps.

* The Ibsen factor therefore cannot be a mere incidental detail in the life and career of Adolf Hitler and in the history of the Nazi Third Reich he led. That is, the Ibsen factor must be either an element situated at the very crux of things, or else a trivial artifact of mere coincidences, one after the other. If its validity is accepted at all, the Ibsen factor must be taken *in toto,* along with its disturbing historical ramifications.

To address the last consideration first: Coincidences do happen in life. However, a preponderance of circumstances weighs against dismissing the Ibsen evidence as some incredible, recurring string of uncanny, inexplicable, but pointless synchronicities. The resemblances of what Hitler said and did to what Ibsen wrote are credible, canny, explicable, and to the point. To cite a comparable topic in literary sleuthing, there is far more congruence here in word and deed than in the teasing wisps that are often cited to name the seventeenth Earl of Oxford as the hidden author of Shakespeare's plays. When the unrelated background chaff is winnowed out, at least as much evidence emerges linking Hitler to the three Ibsen scripts as that linking John W. Hinckley Jr. to *Taxi Driver.*

Accounting for the evidence requires no paradigm leap. Hitler paraphrased not from some impossibly exotic source—say, *The Tale of Genji,* or *Hypnerotomachia Polyphili,* or the *Book of Mormon,* or the *Popul Vuh*—but from Henrik Ibsen. Works of the playwright were familiar fare on the German stage and a known selection of Hitler's reading. He spoke lines traceable to Ibsen's plays because these plays were in resident memory, ready to blurt out extempore. Hitler's actions matching their plots, episode after episode following Ibsen's scripted sequence, came not by chance. Unlike the offhand paraphrased lines, these emulated actions could only have been planned far in advance with meticulous, obsessive care.

The inclusion of purely ritual steps in the sequence, like the breaking of the silver ceremonial hammer, fits an obsessive pattern. There is a kind of magical thinking reflected here, a notion that some signifying, sanctifying action must be carried out to pave the way for scriptural works of immeasurably greater impact. To what end?

To the desired, corrected end. The purpose of the exercise was not merely a recital of the script, but perfection of the script itself. *Emperor and Galilean*, the main feature, was not by itself flawless. Paul Schulze-Berghof had regarded it rather in the way Christians regard the Hebrew Bible, as an imperfect "Old Testament" in need of rectifying touches and the advent of a prophecy-fulfilling savior. Schulze-Berghof had added the touches in his book on the script as allegory. The savior was nigh, incarcerated at Landsberg fortress when Schulze-Berghof went to press. Schulze-Berghof's call became Hitler's calling. What ensued was not blind emulation for its own sake, but instead a quest to make complete what had been left undone in Ibsen's script. This urge hewed to personal precedent. During Adolf's youth, as his roommate Kubizek recounted, one of his projects had been to try writing an opera. He didn't begin with an original idea, but chose instead a topic left unfinished by Wagner, *Wieland der Schmied* ("Wieland the Smith"). So too with *An Enemy of the People*, *The Master Builder*, and *Emperor and Galilean* where, for each, Hitler's mimetic adaptation brings the story line to a conclusion implied, but unstated, in the script itself.

In *Emperor and Galilean*, Emperor Julian warns of the Christian menace. But Julian failed to end Christianity because instead of extirpating the Jews as the root of the Christian evil, he had even tried to rebuild the accursed Temple in Jerusalem. Hitler, having learned the lesson, took aim instead at the source.

In *An Enemy of the People*, Dr. Stockmann had warned of microbes contaminating the spa waters, but was restrained from taking action. Hitler paraphrased Stockmann's lines, identified himself as the physician who had discovered the Jewish "virus" (or "bacillus," etc.), and proceeded to initiate an extermination campaign while echoing Stockmann.

In *The Master Builder*, the "castle in the air" is only promised by Solness to Hilde Wangel, who had to make do with an already-completed structure, hastily rededicated to her. But Hitler completed the action with a new structure built from scratch. His house high above Berchtesgaden was constructed, at great effort, under the direction of master builder Todt. Also in *The Master Builder* it is evident that Ragnar the apprentice will fill the shoes of Baumeister Solness someday, but the succession is not quite spelled out. In the Hitlerian reenactment, it is. The architect Albert Speer, whose career Hitler had guided as an understudy to Todt, was awarded Todt's portfolios just hours after Todt fell to his death. The date was February 8, 1942.

And around noontime on that same day, with his much-esteemed engineer Todt dead only about three hours, Hitler spoke lines derived from *An Enemy of the People.* How so? Once more the coincidence owes not to chance, but to a coordinated ending of the whole mimetic game. As with the death of Geli Raubal, here again is the intertwining of the three scripts. The finale for the trio of plays had been planned to coincide in the winter of 1941–42, when Axis triumph in the war was expected. That timing was no accident, although victory proved elusive. The magic failed. There was no fallback plan, at least not any derived from Ibsen.

After February 1942, there are no more paraphrased Ibsen lines, no more adapted Ibsen plots. The April 1945 scene in the Berlin bunker recalls another drama, Hanns Johst's *Der König.* Back in 1923, Hitler had said that this play foretold his mortal fate. It did.

DIAGNOSES, DELUSIONS, DUNGEONS & DRAGONS

When a man reverts to a scripted paradigm intermittently over decades, a question must arise about his mental state. Does he control his mind, or does it belong to the scripted persona? Hitler's several scripted roles outdid any mere bomber or assassin, since he rose to greater heights by enacting not one role but several. That circumstance of multiplicity brings up the question of Dissociative Identity Disorder ("DID," a condition known up until 1994 as Multiple Personality Disorder, "MPD"). The diagnosis has been controversial, although a set of traits is found with some frequency among those claiming alternate personas. These include eating disorders, substance abuse, obsession with incest, and gender identity issues. Hitler exhibited them all.

His diet was famously eccentric. He alternated overcooked vegetarian fare with extra helpings of creamy Viennese tarts. He became dependent on revitalizing injections as prescribed by his quack physician, Dr. Theodor Morell. The relationship with Geli Raubal, if they actually met in bed, was certainly incestuous; even if chaste, the liaison *appeared* incestuous. To the point; it fit the scripted requirements in *Emperor and Galilean* on who should be Julian's consort. As it happens, so many MPD/DID patients report breach of the incest taboo that the very term "Osiris Complex" (named after the ancient Egyptian god Osiris, who married his sister Isis) has on occasion been used for MPD/DID. And Hitler's oft-observed effeminacy indicates, at the least, some haziness as to gender.

One crucial MPD/DID diagnostic feature is missing, though, and that is the apparent lack of any memory barrier between Hitler's various roles. Instead of being sealed off from each other, the three Ibsen roles were intertwined. Had Hitler lapsed into a dysfunctional amnesia, his game would have been ended for him much sooner, by the Wehrmacht or other highly ranked Nazis. But the Führer was noted for memory feats, not for forgetting. And the apparent progression through episode after episode of a script like *Emperor and Galilean* took some shrewd planning aforethought.

Whether hypnosis was involved makes another valid concern. Critics skeptical of the MPD/DID diagnosis have dismissed the occurrence of alter personas as artifacts constructed while in a trance, for some patients known to have been hypnotized in therapy. It is in just such a therapeutic context that hypnosis has been ventured for Hitler. The conjectured experience dated to his recuperation at the Pasewalk army hospital in 1918 after being gassed at the front. According to the roman à clef *Der Augenzeuge* ("The Witness"), Dr. Edmund Robert Forster (1878–1933) used hypnosis to get the patient functioning again. The novel describes an obnoxious and obsessively anti-Semitic corporal, "A.H.," who successfully underwent hypnosis at a hospital, "P.," to overcome hysterical blindness. Forster committed suicide during the first year of the Nazi takeover; but he deposited certain papers in Paris that supposedly became the basis for the *Der Augenzeuge*. On this basis, Forster has been called "the man who invented Hitler," vastly overstating the case. There are huge problems with this idea.

For starters, the hospital records disappeared long ago, perhaps even destroyed at the Führer's behest. Forster's papers are also gone. And while the novel by Ernst Weiss clearly refers to Hitler, it is just a work of fiction, crafted years after the event when the subject was already controversial and after the appearance of *Mein Kampf,* which Weiss had no doubt read. So notwithstanding its title, *Der Augenzeuge* must be taken more as a political propaganda piece than a trusted "eyewitness" account. Hypnotism at Pasewalk remains a moot point for the real-life Corporal A.H., interesting but tangential to his later entrancement with a set of theatrical scripts.

Then, a year after leaving Pasewalk, Hitler found Dietrich Eckart, whose own special interest in hypnosis is a matter of record. Yet neither Hitler nor Eckart ever divulged any experimentation with trance states during Hitler's tutelage. Once again, that leaves a spell under hypnosis reasonably suspect but far from proven in accounting for alter personas or scripted roles. Anyway, he did not require hypnosis to do what he wanted to do.

During the next two decades, Hitler occasionally dropped a hint, but no more, alluding to some kind of dazed but still-functional state. In a public speech given on March 14, 1936, he mentioned his messianic mission: "Ordained by Providence, I proceed with the assurance of a sleepwalker." (*Ich gehe mit traumwandlerischer Sicherheit den Weg, den mich die Vorsehung gehen heist.*) The remark was astonishing enough to be echoed in the observations of the Swiss diplomat Carl Burckhardt three and a half years later. Once again, here is Harold Nicolson quoting Burckhardt: "He is convinced that Hitler has no complete confidence in himself and that his actions are really governed by a somnambulist certainty." Had Hitler acknowledged a sort of pre-programming, an inevitability to his course? Exactly so. Does it also mean a hypnotic detachment from the tangible world like, say,

The Manchurian Candidate? No. Because a literal somnambulist or hypnotized subject would divulge no such thing.

Still, it is evident that hypnosis—or an unnamed state akin to it—was taking over Hitler's mind. Another hint came in a conversation on the Obersalzberg on March 12, 1944. He reminisced to his longtime photographer and friend Heinrich Hoffmann about the time when he still hoped to be an architect. "Nowadays, for example, I'm still capable without any trouble of sketching the outline of a theater, but it does not imply that I am in some kind of trance." That is, he could retreat into a blissful reverie, much absorbed but still aware. Then, close to the end of the Third Reich, he made this comment: "I have an unpleasant task to perform today. I have to hypnotize Quisling." That is, he had to buck up the Norwegian puppet's courage with illusions of victory. What counts is the chosen idiom: trances, sleepwalking, hypnosis.

So Hitler displayed an interest in zonked-out mental states, but that does not make him a zombie set up by Forster, Eckart, or anyone else. A sustained fantasy life keyed to a script may operate in the willful retreat to an imagined alter realm. The young Adolf of the years before World War I already liked to ensconce himself in a tower of imagination. He needed neither swamis, drugs, nor drink. The adult Führer's drug dependence deepened only after 1942, at a time when there is no more sign of role-play games from Ibsen.

A non-hypnotic but still altered mental state can coexist—uneasily, perhaps—with a real-world existence. That is so for "Dungeons and Dragons" ("D&D") diehards on many a college campus. D&D is a structured role-play game. Players take on archetype personas like knights, damsels, varlets, and monks, all under a "dungeonmaster." Their intrigues adhere to a set of rules in a realm resembling Tolkien's Middle Earth or the land of the Nibelungen. Some players get carried away, utterly immersed. They miss assignments, cut classes, flunk tests. The fantasy persona takes control. Homicides have struck among the D&D crowd, arising out of conflicts in the game. Yet it all happens in what passes for a normal waking state; and when they do show up for exams, D&D-niks know enough to hand in blue books signed with their own birth names.

Hitler (and Hinckley, et al., for that matter) thus need not have been mesmerized. As in Dungeons & Dragons, their dramatic adaptations required more cunning and bravado than is possible in a passive trance. But to key one's existence to a script is to live a spiraling madness. The player's secret self is cut off from average folks and normal concerns. A part of Hitler was cut off in this way; reviewing the scriptural scripts, plotting from within their plots. Another part of Hitler could give speeches, socialize, and plan this-worldly tactical moves, the everyday stuff that cloaked the master scripts. Which was the real Hitler, which the poseur? That is a question for psychiatry, now that it is known that there were scripts and they've been found. For History, what matters is that three Ibsen scripts were verifiably there, in Hitler's head, in his words, in his deeds.

What propellant drives a marginal man to adopt a novel, a film, or a play as a counter-scriptural mantra? For Hinckley, it was Love ("six trillion times"—his words) for an actress he could never date, kiss, or caress. Rebuffed but undeterred, he would impress her by morphing into Travis Bickel, pistol-packing nut case. What then made *Emperor and Galilean* the most influential play of all time, as gauged by its impact on events? Not some siren of stage or screen and, alas, not love. For Hitler it had to be something else, an even more compelling force he shared with Booth, Kaczynski, and McVeigh.

It was love's ugly twin.

14

JUDENFRAGE: HITLER'S "JEWISH QUESTION"

Take the Jewish people, the aristocracy of the human race—how is it they have kept their place apart, their poetical halo, amid surroundings of coarse cruelty? By having no state to burden them.

—HENRIK IBSEN IN A LETTER, FEBRUARY 17, 1871

The Jew of all times has lived in the states of other peoples, and there formed his own state, which, to be sure, habitually sailed under the disguise of a "religious community" as long as outward circumstances made a complete revelation of his nature seem inadvisable. But as soon as he felt strong enough to do without the protective cloak, he always dropped the veil and suddenly became what so many of the others previously did not want to believe and see: the Jew.

—ADOLF HITLER IN *MEIN KAMPF*, CHAPTER 11

"THE MAIN ENERGY in Hitler is an energy of hatred," Carl Burckhardt observed. The Swiss diplomat had "never met any [other] human being capable of generating so terrific a condensation of envy, vituperation, and malice." Who it was that Hitler hated needs no asking. But to get personal, Why? Did any particular Jew set it off? And how did this foaming rabidity relate to his now-documented miming of theatrical scripts?

AN "X"

It is the mother of all Hitlerian problems, the Big Why, the wherefore behind the zealot's bloodlust for Jews. The Question has long teased. The Answer stayed coy.

Hitler's first postwar biographer, Alan Bullock, deplored "a gap between explanation and event." Lucy Dawidowicz surveyed the literature as of 1981 and concluded: "No work has yet been produced that satisfactorily explains Hitler's obsessive ideas about the Jews." Eberhard Jäckel, the scholarly compiler of Hitler's earliest letters and speeches, saw an enigma at the core of the killer: "The most heinous aspects of Hitler's deeds defy explanation, the murder of Jews"; and "We know much but understand little."

Some grew testy. Arnold Beichman carped: "What is this unfathomable 'mystery' of the Holocaust? A Nexis search, I'm sure, would find hundreds of couplings of 'Holocaust' and 'mystery.' Often a writer on the Holocaust will begin with, 'We will never understand. . . . '" Beichman wanted the perception of a mystery to go away. But it's not so easy. If a mystery is mulled by reasonable minds, then a mystery doth exist, until solved. Again, not an easy task. Holocaust historian Christopher Browning likened the professionals' dilemma to that of the cave denizens in Plato's *Republic:* They try to understand reality but can glimpse only shadows and reflections. Sir Ian Kershaw, the definitive biographer, conceded in a preface that for him, the inner Hitler remained an "enigma," a "black hole." Percy Ernst Schramm, an editor of the "Table Talk" monologues, despaired: "We must be satisfied with the realization that there is about Hitler's . . . anti-Semitism an unknown factor," to which he added: "Psychology and psychiatry . . . are confronted by an 'X.'"

An "X." In 1991, John Lukacs also posited some great unknown beyond historians' ken, and destined to remain so. Lukacs seemed ready to give in. "His main obsession was with Jews. We do not know and will never know the source of that deep obsession." To which the psychiatrist Dr. George Victor added some forlorn hope: "Once Hitler's obsession is understood, many of his acts of state take on a new meaning." And so they do.

The garden-variety anti-Semitism in upper Austria at the turn of the twentieth century cannot by itself suffice to explain. Hitler's hatred, judged by its magnitude, cannot have sprung from mere custom, and still less from a tract or a pamphlet. Adducing a single piece of propaganda recalls the pedantry of geographers who label a trickle as the source of a mighty river that gains its proper tributaries far downstream. There were then multiple hate sheets by a myriad of hacks. Hitler's later wording echoes familiar idioms, but its pervasive vocabulary obscures which tract did the trick, if any. In *Mein Kampf,* he stated how in Linz and then in Vienna he actually rejected anti-Semitism before, as he later put it, he succumbed.

Mein Kampf, chapter 3 narrates this dawning of a life's mission as he discerned a Jewish role in the press, trade unions, and politics. But that narrative still lacks an essential something. What impelled him? This was a wrath beyond Achilles', a globe-embracing monomania dwarfing Ahab's vengeful voyage. But only in fiction does a man sail the world to harpoon a single whale. Real people hate real people, for reasons real to them. What was the personal spur, the offense, the spark that started the smoldering? Should this stimulus be found in the formative years, all the more convincing it will be. As an educator once observed, "You are who you were in junior high school."

What is sought, then, is the life-altering friction that launched a grinding grudge toward someone whom he then magnified to stand in for Jewry-writ-large. The clues come in the form of the attributes Hitler assigned to Jewry. In his soliloquies, he divulges the very particulars that he extrapolated from his personal nemesis onto his view of all Jewry. Parsing his words helps, because the process works both ways. Those same attributes of Jewry can be reduced back to the level of a person, ideally one who relates to the crucial miming of scripts. The individual, Hitler's personal Moby Dick, should then stand out, identified by Hitler's own words.

THE MAN IN THE CAFTAN

Mein Kampf, chapter 3 offers a start, referring to 1908:

> Once, as I was strolling through the Inner City [of Vienna], I sud-
> denly encountered an apparition in a black caftan and black hair
> locks. Is this a Jew? was my first thought. For, to be sure, they
> had not looked like that in Linz.

He goes on to disparage the "smell of these caftan-wearers" who
"were no lovers of water." Adolf, himself no daily bather then, was
likely projecting. More to the point, that single passage comprises the
extent of his distress about overt, traditionally garbed Jews living as a
people apart from modern Europe's social mainstream. He finds the
caftan-wearer distasteful, but does not call him a major menace.

The sight of the man wearing the caftan was not the catalyst for
the Holocaust. This Jew posed no threat to Aryan mankind, precisely
because he could be spotted by his haircut and clothes. Hitler wasted
no ire on the *shtetl* and the ghetto. The rest of his all-too-many
diatribes aim at assimilated Jews who had traded their caftans for
business suits. His consistent plaint from the 1920s onward was about
Jews as manipulators, Jews blending in and dominating. Words like
"disguise," "cloak," and "veil" crop up, along with the bacillus metaphor, to describe an unseen harm.

Going back to his teenage years in Linz and nearby Leonding
before 1908, it bears noting too that Adolf was by then aware of the
existence of Jews, but not yet as an evil other. In middle school, he
already attacked the Christian faith; but the crucial refinement of
blaming Christianity on the Jews came later.

The hatred of Jews as the crafty hidden hand behind Christianity was developed in Dietrich Eckart's quasi-*Dialogue with Hitler,
Bolshevism from Moses to Lenin.* St. Paul (a.k.a. Saul) comes in for
special roasting. Other records are of little help in pinpointing any
particular living Jewish culprit. According to some observers, Hitler
may have expressed anti-Semitic sentiments while in the trenches,
but through World War I his letters and postcards remained free of

remarks about the people he later loved to hate. Like the man in the caftan, Jews posed no dire personal threat, either as individuals or as a collective entity—not, that is, until after the Armistice, during Munich's transient spell of revolutionary rule in the spring of 1919. Then the barracks polarized. Corporal Hitler faced a peril as real as any at the front. Soldiers could be shot for revealing wayward thoughts. The role of a few assimilated Jews among the Munich Red leaders convinced many that Marxism masked a Jewish plot. Even so, that interlude of the Munich "Soviet" never loomed large in the Führer's rhetoric.

The first written word Hitler provided on the topic of anti-Semitism was dated September 16, 1919, in his letter to a Munich Army office. It is malevolent, but the theological aspect is not yet manifest. His thinking ripened through the next few years, gaining fervor and a quasi-religious tone traceable to Dietrich Eckart, whom he met soon after. Eckart shaped Hitler's holy hatred, but was not the one to plant it; the hate was already there. The poet–playwright who thought he was Peer Gynt lent vocabulary and method. Hitler in turn paid Eckart due homage as his tutor, then struck out on his own.

So *Mein Kampf* and the *Dialogues* offer useful data about the matured hate, but still nothing precise on who and what had set it off at an unspecified prior time. The earlier the animus, the more deeply rooted it had to be. But the earlier the date, the scarcer are the sources. There are very few Hitler words on record from before 1919, and not one of them makes mention of Jews. Has a brick wall been reached, a dead end? No, the situation is far from hopeless. One word alone speaks volumes. It is the word most intrinsic to the man himself:

His name.

THE MAD HATTER (OR, WHAT'S IN A NAME?)

Adolf Hittler (that's right, two *t*'s) rests in a cemetery in Bucharest, Romania. An eight-pointed star tops the gravestone. Just below is a symbol of clasped hands, meaning farewell. A circular inscription around the hands identifies this Adolf Hittler as a member of the "Israelite" community of Bucharest. His synagogue name was Abraham, son of Shmuel. Hebrew lettering on the epitaph recalls him as "a dear man" and adds the formula phrase "May his soul be wrapped among the living." A Romanian inscription below adds: "Here lie the mortal remains of Adolf Hittler who departed this life on October 26, 1892, aged 60 years. Pray for him." Adolf Hittler of Bucharest was Jewish, from birth to *brith* to *bar mitzvah* to burial.

Adolf Hitler (one *t*, born April 20, 1889 at Braunau-am-Inn, Austria; suicide April 30, 1945 at Berlin, Germany) was baptized a Roman Catholic in the cradle. All of his stock, so far as is known, consisted of gentiles. Not only were none of them Jews, none of them were Hitlers either, at least not before 1876. Adolf Hitler's father was Alois Schicklgruber. Born out of wedlock, he was finally legitimized in 1876 as Alois Hitler. The surname refracted a family name present in both Alois's maternal and paternal lines: "Hiedler." Why it entered municipal records in 1876 as "Hitler" remains unknown. Alois did not bother to amend the spelling. Perhaps he was unaware or unconcerned that Jewish families bore this name in lands to the east. Soon though, migration would bring many Hungarian and Galician Jews westward to German-speaking Austria. Their arrival would stimulate a greater ethnic awareness, and animosity, among some gentiles.

The most convincing etymology for the surname Hitler (or, more rarely, Hittler) is "hatter." That should cause no surprise, since hat-making was a traditional Jewish trade. And, truth be told, before the Nazi Reich, "Hitler" remained mainly a Jewish name. Of course, no Jew (and few gentiles) cared to keep this name after the rise of Adolf Hitler, one *t*, Führer of the Reich. Yet records prove the point for an earlier time.

From the years 1899 to 1921, a total of fourteen immigrants bearing the surname Hitler (one *t*) arrived at Ellis Island, New York City. The Ellis Island records do not record religion, but their given names tell a lot. Six Hitlers came from the town of Mikulintsy, south of Tarnopol in Austrian eastern Galicia (within the present Ukraine). They were Blima Hitler, Czarne Hitler, Isak Hitler, Leie Hitler, Perla Hitler, and Rosa Hitler; all first names favored by Jews. The Mikulintsy Hitlers hailed from a part of the Habsburg domain where Jews kept traditional ways well into the twentieth century. It was the kind of place where some men still wore caftans and, in keeping with religious dictates, refrained from cutting a lock of hair above each ear.

Cilia Hitler resided in Stanislaw, also in Austrian eastern Galicia. It is a good guess that she too had Jewish roots. That is also the case for Franciska Hitler of Inzenhof, a town on the line between the Habsburg lands of Austria and Hungary. She was aged sixteen and single on arrival at Ellis Island in 1899. Her ethnicity then was entered as "Hungarian," referring really to the language she spoke. However, since Hitler is not a Magyar surname, Franciska Hitler was probably Jewish too.

Gottfried Hitler came to America from Grabin, Russia, in 1912. His ethnicity is listed as "German." Both Jews and gentiles used the given name "Gottfried," so the faith of this immigrant remains unknown from the Ellis Island record. It is also uncertain whether Philip Hitler, a returning resident of New York, was gentile or Jewish. Solomon Hitler and Louis Hitler came from London, respectively in 1903 and 1914. It may be presumed from his name that Solomon was Jewish. If Louis was related to Solomon, then he too would likely have identified as a Jew. There were two Moses Hitlers, one from Tarnopol in eastern Galicia (close to Mikulintsy) and one from an unlisted place. It is a safe bet both were Jewish.

So of the fourteen Hitlers arriving at Ellis Island in the two decades before their surname became anathema, at least ten or twelve would most likely have been Jewish by the criteria the Nazis later used to define a Jew. The Jewishness of the Hitlers of Mikulintsy is established by the memorial (*yizkor*) book for their community. Mikulintsy, part of Poland in 1939, was occupied by the Red Army when war began in September that year. It then fell to the Germans on July 4, 1941. Sporadic pogroms and shootings of Jews continued into the summer of 1942, when the town's surviving Jews were expelled to a ghetto in Tarnopol and later to concentration camps. Among those who perished in the Holocaust were Hinde Hitler, Leib Hitler, and Josef Hitler, likely kin to the luckier Mikulintsy Hitlers who built a new life in America.

The Jewishness of the surname is confirmed, yet again, by the roster of known Holocaust victims at Israel's Yad Vashem institute. Yolan Hitler lived in Ipolysag, Slovakia. Like Franciska Hitler, she probably spoke Hungarian. Other Hungarian-speaking Jewish Hitlers survived the horror. A list of displaced persons in the Dilich forced labor camp, Germany, from the summer of 1945 includes one Rossi Heilerne Hitler. She came from Tapolca, Hungary. Another survivor registered in a Jewish source was one Eva Hitler. Yad Vashem lists still more Jewish Hitlers from Tarnopol, north of Mikulintsy. There were Herman Hitler, Salka Hitler, Toncia Hitler, Bela Hitler, Moses Hitler, Yosef Hitler, and Khana Hitler. Baile Hitler resided in Mikulintsy. Fajcia Hitler was from Zaleszczyki, another nearby town. All of them perished, victims of Adolf Hitler, born at Braunau-am-Inn.

The point is that Adolf Hitler, while not even a scintilla Jewish, had to share a surname with Jews, and eastern Jews at that. This point was taken for granted: e.g., this sentence in a World War II-era U.S. intelligence analysis: "The name Hitler is a common Jewish one." To bear that name in the Austro-Hungarian empire at the turn of the twentieth century meant incurring a quite reasonable presumption of Jewish antecedents. The Hitler family of Braunau and Linz made an odd exception, gentile and Catholic as far back as it could ever matter, according to the genealogical data. And that evidence consists of baptismal records, in churches.

Adolf Hitler, baptized a Catholic, enrolled at age eleven in the church-run Leonding middle school near Linz, in 1900. It was a time of rising anti-Semitism. Into the schoolyard walks a weird kid with an oddball Jewish name. Any schoolyard, anywhere, at any time, is a nasty place for a boy not brutal or big or bold enough to blacken the eyes and bust the jaws of bullies, or at least to make a valiant try. Adolf Hitler was physically and temperamentally not such a boy. Thus it was there, in the Leonding schoolyard, that the greatest hate of all time put forth the foul bud that would blossom as the Holocaust. As the twentieth century dawned, the burden rested on Adolf Hitler to prove he was no Jew: that is, to explain his name. Did he encounter taunts as a suspected Jew? No confirming record exists. In that sense, it is pure speculation. But to get real, Did it happen? Given the circumstances, to imagine it did not is to petition for a repeal of the law of tooth and claw, also known as the school playground.

No certificate in psychiatry is required to make this point: It is beyond doubt that Hitler felt sensitive about the name. The evidence comes later in the form of a phony etymology he supplied. Once, during a meeting at his Berchtesgaden estate, the Führer told Fritz Todt that "Hitler" actually derived from "Hüttler," meaning keepers of salt storage huts on the trans-Alpine trade routes. Todt related this uncritically to a subordinate who put it in a memoir. But the Führer lied. He had to have known that his grandfather was "Hiedler." Why lie, though? One speculation might be that "Hüttler," minus a superfluous t and minus the umlaut from the u, makes an anagram for "Luther"; Hitler liked to regard himself as a reincarnated historical great, and he had elsewhere played Scrabble with his name. More to the present point, why the bizarre etymology? Because a hut keeper in the Alps would be Aryan pure, unlike a Jewish hatter from the east. The actress Whoopi Goldberg's brilliant stage name by itself brings on a smile. At the Leonding middle school, though, the joke was on Adolf Hitler. Overcompensation by him may be safely inferred.

THE USUAL SUSPECTS

However, Adolf's mystery nemesis, a specific Jew, has still not been found. It is time to backtrack and round up the usual suspects. Who was it? What Jew tipped the balance and made him hate them all? And how did the great hate culminate in an adaptive, world-stage performance of *Emperor and Galilean* and two other Ibsen plays?

Time and again, psychohistorians have suggested individual Jews at the inception of the Great Hate. One after another, their pet Jews walked the walk, stood in the lineup. Here is at least a partial list:

- Hitler's biological grandfather, rumored to have been a Jew;
- the philosopher Ludwig Wittgenstein;
- Klara Pölzl Hitler's physician in her dying days, Dr. Eduard Bloch;

- Josef Neumann and Samuel Morgenstern, Viennese art dealers;
- an anonymous, syphilitic Viennese Jewish prostitute;
- Hugo Guttmann, an officer in Hitler's World War I army unit;
- Fritz Haber, Nobel Prize–winning chemist.

It is time to review their cases and to send them home for good.

SUSPECT #1

Hitler's lawyer Hans Frank grasped at straws as he faced the gallows after World War II. In a Nuremberg death-row memoir, he alleged that a search of antecedents ordered by the Führer had hinted at a Jewish forebear. According to Frank, Hitler's paternal grandmother was a housemaid for a Jewish family named Frankenberger or Frankenreither in Graz, Austria. There she got pregnant by one of the family's boys. The baby was baptized in the Hiedler-Schicklgruber-Hitler line, a blot on their escutcheon. From this, the Holocaust becomes an act of obsessive self-hatred toward the stain of Jewish blood. Out, damned spot!

Problems abound. No such family is listed on the Graz civil registers; Jews were legally banned from residing there when Hitler's grandmother was a housemaid; she therefore could not have gotten pregnant then and there, at least not by a Jew. A Nazi genealogical inquiry was indeed conducted. It found feeblemindedness (*Halbidioten*) among some distant Hitler cousins. That is all. Not all halfwits are Jews, and not all Jews are halfwits. Nothing supports the idea that the research found Jewish forebears. Nonetheless, the Führer's alleged fears of a Jewish taint became a staple of pop psychoanalysis; one bogus variant has a Jewish grocer named Sachs ravishing Hitler's mother in the garden one day. The tales took on a life of their own. Hans Frank's, meanwhile, spun out at the end of a rope.

SUSPECT #2

Ludwig Wittgenstein, the philosopher and scion of three Jewish grandparents, was purportedly identified as a schoolmate of Hitler's in a group photo from the Linz middle school. It would be remarkable had these two oh-so-contrasting makers of their times shared classes. It was no less remarkable for an Australian writer, Kimberley Cornish, to surmise, on zero evidence, that the two had some run-in, and to spin the consequences of this non-event into a nearly 300-page book. That is, the author claimed, had there been no logical positivist smartypants Jewboy, there would have been no Holocaust. But documentation of a feud is utterly lacking. And while the boys did overlap at the school for one year, 1903–04, Wittgenstein was two grades ahead. This fact makes doubtful the labeling of Ludwig in a class photo with Adolf. Hitler is there, looking insolent. But the kid taken for Wittgenstein could be any crewcut pupil of the time, whereas Wittgenstein does not belong in that picture due to their age difference.

Furthermore, as Cornish admits, it was Wittgenstein family policy to conceal their Jewish roots. Cornish was correct, though, in judging the Leonding schoolyard years as crucial. That was confirmed by Hitler, who in 1938 permitted the publication of a book about his schoolboy days. It recounted one school feud that really did occur, and resonate, pitting Adolf against Father Franz Sales Schwarz.

SUSPECT #3

Dr. Eduard Bloch treated Hitler's mother for cancer during the painful last year of her life. Professor Rudolf Binion, a non-physician, surmised that it was the medication itself that did in Klara Pölzl Hitler, and that the young Adolf sensed as much. Binion conjectured that it all came back, Proust-like, when Hitler was gassed at Ypres and in hospital he sniffed some ointment like the stuff Bloch used. No botched iodoform antiseptic gauze treatments, no Holocaust. But the medical evidence on Klara Hitler has been disputed as to what was prescribed, in what dosages, and to what effect. Hitler never uttered a single word on the record blaming Bloch. *Au contraire,* as Führer he showed personal consideration for the Bloch family in 1938. Unlike most other Jews, they were permitted to leave Austria with their property shortly after its annexation to the German Reich. It is therefore clear that the animus that grew into the Holocaust was not triggered by the actions of Eduard Bloch, M.D.

SUSPECTS #4 & 5

Josef Neumann, a Jew, lived in a Vienna men's hostel—as did Hitler—in 1910. He reportedly hawked the latter's art work. They would argue politics, including issues of Zionism; but the talk remained congenial, as did their business dealings. A Jewish glazier, Samuel Morgenstern, framed and sold young Hitler's paintings in Vienna during the years 1909–12. Their workaday relations also passed amicably without sign of recriminations at the time. Whatever bugaboo had incited Dietrich Eckart against Christian Morgenstern, the rival poet, Hitler never attacked his very own Morgenstern, the art dealer, in any way. The Führer did later complain of being cheated during his years as a struggling artist, but by a gentile anti-Semite, Reinhold Hanisch.

SUSPECT #6

The Jewish-prostitute figment was given major play in a bogus work of 1941 purporting to be the record of Hitler's psychoanalyst, a "Dr. Kurt Krueger." Trouble was, Hitler never visited a psychoanalyst. The dubious Krueger had produced a piece of wartime *dezinformatsia,* but its message echoed: No harlot, no Holocaust. Hitler did evince an obsession with syphilis. Yet his medical records show no diagnosis of it, ever; and reminiscences by acquaintances of the young Hitler portray him as far from the sort who patronized hookers, any more than he did shrinks. While his gender identity wavered, his sex drive was low if not wholly absent.

SUSPECT #7

Hugo Guttmann, a Jewish native of Nuremberg and a reserve artillery captain, recommended Corporal Hitler for the Iron Cross first class in August 1918. Although it was approved, Hitler only began wearing his medal in 1927. He once said "We had a Jew in the regiment, Guttmann, an unparalleled cowardly person. He wore the Iron Cross first class. It was revolting." They were thus brethren in a military order of heroes. Hitler supplied no further details of the alleged cowardice. This remark of the ex-corporal has led to speculation that some incident between Hitler and Guttmann might just have triggered it all. No Hugo, no Holocaust. But as dictator in 1936, Hitler once chatted with his former captain like two old *Kameraden*. The Führer not only approved Guttmann to emigrate from Germany to America in 1939, but let him continue receiving his German military pension.

SUSPECT #8

Fritz Haber converted from Judaism to a nominal Protestant faith in his student years, as did many an ambitious, non-observant German Jew wishing to dodge anti-Semitism in the professions. It was Haber who devised the nitrogen-fixing process that freed German munition makers from reliance on imported Chilean nitrate. He went on to win a Nobel Prize for chemistry, and then to develop poison gas compounds for combat use. Hitler attributed his brief blinding to "yellow cross gas" (*Gelbkreuzgaz*), a German product that the British captured and used at Ypres. Hence in this hunt for the Jew at the root of it all, Fritz Haber emerges as the culprit *par excellence*. No Haber, no Holocaust. Again, pure conjecture. Hitler blamed the Jews for a host of evils, but not for chemical weaponry. And the extant record shows no mentions of Haber by Hitler. What Hitler did say, again and again and again, was how the Jews emitted something worse than poison gas: They had let loose Christianity.

All rise. Each of the above accused is exonerated, even the nameless whore. One further observation: Neither any of these Jews, nor that fellow in Vienna with the caftan and the ear locks, set Hitler to writing vengeful plays. But someone else did.

NARROWING THE FIELD

Through all his recorded rants, Hitler never mentioned any personal vendetta with a certified, practicing Jew. But the two most prominent Jews whom he did name in hate harangues were actually ex-Jews, men from Jewish stock who had left Judaism, each to found a new faith: St. Paul and Karl Marx. Therein resides a clue.

In *Bolshevism from Moses to Lenin* by Dietrich Eckart, the author had Hitler fume about Saul of Tarsus, that grinch of the first century

C.E., the Jew who stole the Galilean to concoct the Christian faith. Christianity is a Jewish plot, Hitler and Eckart believed. Then in short order in this dialogue, Hitler switched to grousing about popes of alleged Jewish ancestry. His expressed concern is over Christian leaders who are really crypto-Jews. Almost two decades later, while launching the Final Solution, he again named his personal demon as Saul-become-St.-Paul. And again, he kvetches about "Mordechai," a.k.a. Karl Marx, to emphasize the Jewish origins of Marx's forebears, who were converts from Judaism. So a menace deadlier by far than visible Jews came from Jews passing as something else or at least as something less overtly Jewish—i.e., Jews in disguise. But even then, St. Paul fails to fully satisfy as a scapegoat. Too long removed. How could the Führer (or anyone, however deranged) froth venom at a preacher gone for two millennia? Common sense says something was still lacking. Paul needed updating. For a man choking on ire, a personal arch foe is *de rigeur.*

Who, then?

The Führer gave more of it away in those months of 1941–42 when he launched the Final Solution. Thinking aloud, uninterrupted by any response from listeners, his mind could drift at will. And drift it inevitably did, to the one episode that had cut short his chances for a normal, respectable, middle-class life. It is Hitler and no other who spelled it out. The event was the wrecking of his secondary schooling.

On the night of September 27–28, 1941, he put it this way for the benefit of anyone present, and for History. The text is given unexpurgated:

> If my parents had sufficient means to send me to a school of art, I should not have become acquainted with poverty, as I did. Whoever lives outside poverty cannot really see it, except by crashing a gate. The years of experience I owe to poverty—a poverty in its hardest form that I knew in my own flesh—have become a blessing for the German nation. Otherwise today we'd have Bolshevism.
>
> On one point, the environment of want in which I lived left me untouched. At that time I lived in palaces of the spirit (German:

Ich habe während dieser Jahre im Geiste in Palästen gelebt]. And it was at that time that I devised the plans for the new Berlin.

He has incidentally admitted how the architectural mission of a "new Berlin" arose from his fantasy life. Hitler went on:

We must pay attention to two things: 1] That all gifted adolescents are educated at the State's expense; 2] That no door is closed to them. Since I hadn't been able to finish my secondary studies, an officer's career would have been closed to me.

He skewed the tale. Lack of funds had not kept Adolf out of art school: He had applied and been refused for lack of a diploma. Yet along with the poormouth fib of September 1941 came a 24-karat nugget of truth. What still mattered crucially to Hitler, even then, was his truncated schooling. He had been forced out of the Catholic middle school at Leonding by someone. And that someone was a priest.

The Führer never forgot; he extrapolated. Hitler's analogy of Christianity to Bolshevism turned priests into subversive agents against the conduct of legitimate state power. In those evenings of 1941–42, he mused about how churchmen undermined the rule of secular princes during the sixth, seventh, and eighth centuries. Knowing better, the leader of the Third Reich placed his greater trust in specially indoctrinated elite combat troops who dispensed with the spiritual comfort of Catholic or Protestant chaplain-commissars.

I have six SS divisions, entirely free of religion and yet who die with greatest peace of mind.

That is, the absence of chaplains made Waffen-SS troops content. Priests were the problem. Late on the night of January 8–9, 1942, he named the priests he knew best, religion teachers at the Leonding middle school. He misnamed one as Silizko, commenting that "He was our great enemy." Close enough after forty-one years. The school roster lists a Kitlitzko as religion teacher for form IB in 1900–01. Hitler had jumbled the Slavic name.

And he had shown that it could get personal, at least where the Catholic clergy was concerned. Amidst these bitter reveries and having confirmed his mission as a rerun of Julian's, on February 8, 1942 he mused again:

> The evil that's gnawing our vitals is our priests, of both creeds. ... It's all written down in my big book. The time will come when I'll settle my account with them, and I'll go straight to the point. I don't know which should be considered the more dangerous: the minister of religion who play-acts at patriotism, or the man who openly opposes the state.

He would "settle" his "account" with the priests.

Hitler reflexively expected obstruction from the clergy. Sometimes, however, he could be surprised. One avid collaborator with the Nazis was Father Joseph Tiso, a Roman Catholic cleric ruling the puppet Slovak state. Noting Tiso's help, Hitler remarked on August 30, 1942:

> It is interesting how this little priest sends us the Jews.

Why "interesting"? What made Tiso's compliance in genocide mildly interesting was its very deviation from the model of the Jews and the Church as but two sides of the same coin. Hitler then troubled himself no more with this trivial detail. Tiso might be the exception that proved the rule. But the Führer at least kept true, unswerving to his program. As he spoke, the top-priority action was still the Final Solution. And in his spoken thoughts, private pique and public policy are joined throughout.

"I CAN STILL SEE HIM TODAY. . . ."

One noncompliant priest personified all. This time Hitler got the name right. On the night of January 8–9, 1942, the supreme warlord of Europe retold the tale of how schoolboy Adolf had held up those red, gold, and black colored pencils to salute the German state, and how a pro-Habsburg Austrian priest struck back.

Which priest? Which one, indeed! What teacher had shamed him before the class? Who made him sit in detention for thirty-six dreary hours? What priest had wished Adolf to perdition? What priest had effectively expelled him from school? Against what bygone tormenter did the pupil attempt to write blaspheming plays? What memory of a cleric set a grownup tyrant to crumpling all Europe like a cardboard stage set? And how did that crucifix-dangling foe connect to the Jews? Whose face made the Führer grimace, put veins to bulging, molars to gnashing? What face launched a thousand trains bound for Auschwitz and Treblinka?

Hitler wrapped no shroud around his resurrected memory of that face. He kept it with him for life like a mental medallion of a patron saint. The face of Hitler's personal Paul belonged, of course, to Franz Sales Schwarz of the Leonding school, a Catholic cleric and educator, goaded to distress by one snotty, would-be neo-pagan punk. Thirty years buried, Schwarz goaded back. Of a deep winter's night, the class bad boy could drift again to Schwarz's lessons, to those two hours each week, every week, and seethe:

> What I hated was the lying. I can still see him today, with his long nose, and that riled me so that I'd let loose and have at it.

The long-nosed liar. Could the prevaricating, probocid priest, he whose drilling tapped this ever-wrathful geyser of steaming hate, have been a crypto-Jew? *The* Jew? Rumors ran rife in Linz as Adolf made provoking Father Schwarz the capstone of his formal schooling. A faculty colleague (it was the mathematics and science teacher) bandied about a canard alleging that Schwarz had sprung from baptized Galician Jews. He had traded a caftan for a cassock. Or had he?

By the 1930s, Schwarz was a quarter-century dead. His oversized nose was moldering to dust, but its recollected image made for probable cause. Someone with major clout had those juicy rumors traced, and had instigated a genealogical search. This someone was no mere middle-school math teacher, though. The someone could be none other than the Führer who had opined how "It has been indisputably established that, in the case of Jews, if the physical characteristics of the race are sometimes absent for a generation or two, they will inevitably reappear in the next generation." The posthumous pedigree search on this otherwise forgotten cleric traced church records back to 1750, in Lasberg, upper Austria. But alas, the facts on file refused to conform. Schwarz's forebears proved simple Catholic country stock. They were farmers, innkeepers, butchers, weavers. Every last one of them checked out Aryan pure.

To sum up the record on Hitler versus Schwarz:

- At some point—just when is not known—rumormongers alleged Father Franz Schwarz to be of Jewish stock.
- Adolf's encounter with Schwarz came at a time when he too, bearing a surname shared mainly with Jews, had to endure the suspicion of descent from some baptized Jew.
- Schoolboy Hitler's animosity toward Father Schwarz grew deeply *ad hominem,* mutual, and abiding during 1903–04.
- Yet Adolf pursued the feud at that time by challenging Catholic dogma, not at first as a racial cause.
- Schwarz stayed on Hitler's mind. He talked about Schwarz to his roommate August Kubizek, doubtless more than once, between 1906 and 1908. In 1910 he was still railing about Schwarz to Josef Greiner at a men's hostel in Vienna. But neither Kubizek nor Greiner related whether Hitler took Schwarz for a crypto-Jew. He evidently had not, yet.
- The Schwarz lineage mattered to Hitler only later. When it did, though, it mattered enough to launch a quest for a very bygone Jewish scion of a bygone local priest. This genealogical probe on Schwarz took place some time before 1938.
- The full-grown Führer thereupon came to learn there was nothing to tales out of school about a crypto-Jewish priest. The hypothesis of Schwarz as a Jew flopped.
- By then, however, new old facts mattered more. Hitler went on repeating the same anecdotes he had told Greiner thirty-two years earlier in 1910. In the latter retelling, he performed a nose

job, grafting onto the wraith of Father Schwarz the stereotypical feature of a Nazi hate-sheet, cartoonish Jew.

Apart from Father Franz Sales Schwarz, Hitler never blamed woe on any contemporary Jew, proven or presumed, among those he personally came across. The mention of actual Jewish individuals is strangely but significantly sparse in all his rants. But it is explicable, since he had a personal arch-foe already in his mind's eye. Jewry was but a tribal extension of this nemesis. Like the assimilated Saul/Paul and Mordechai/Marx, the villain turns out to be no ghetto Jew. He was a (wrongly supposed, as it turned out) Jew-for-Jesus, and as such the face of *Judeo*-Christianity writ large. Hitler had elevated Schwarz, the object of his personal hate, to an apotheosis.

First, though, appeared his thespian bent. This defining trait of the man made itself manifest by age fifteen, well before he gave much thought to the Jews. He reserved his bile then for Father Schwarz. Steeped in theater, the Hitler boy wrote a script crafted, he said, to annoy his religion teacher. That is: From the account of the Führer himself, he made drama his tool to taunt this padre. Again in the spring of 1908, upon reading Ibsen, Hitler outlined his own play where the pagans slay the priests. Then, though he shelved the script, he had set a pattern. As with many a project vowed in frenzy but postponed, this one could only rankle within.

World War I came and went. Only then did the expelled schoolboy, quirky artist, and would-be architect find his calling to eradicate the Jews. Voicing that call, for Hitler, was a man of the stage who styled himself as an Ibsen creation. Taking Eckart seriously meant taking Ibsen as a seer. Others also vaunted Ibsen as a prophet, one even pointing to him, Adolf Hitler, as prophecy's earthly hand. A revived paganism was foretold. A new Julian would bring it about, this time extirpating Christianity by destroying its root, Jewry. To complete Emperor Julian's task required working a final solution into the prophet's allegorical script.

Thus was the holy pogrom joined to a deferred drama-in-progress, maniacally adapted to the continental stage. Enacting the allegory marked just the start of a long planned struggle against the faith taught by Franz Sales Schwarz, he who expelled young Adolf the Apostate from the garden. The ensuing grudge battle for a "third Reich" was waged in the memory of Emperor Julian. Hitler explicated that much for the record, at last, while preparing for the curtain to the last act.

And so the play became the thing in the German Third Reich.

15

DISCOVERING THE UR-SCRIPT

DR. THOMAS STOCKMANN: Well, now the
town will have something new to talk about! . . .
MRS. STOCKMANN: What is this? . . .
DR. STOCKMANN: A great discovery, Katherine.
MRS. STOCKMANN: A discovery of yours?
DR. STOCKMANN: A discovery of mine. Just
let them come saying, as usual, that it's all
fantasy and a crazy man's imagination! But
they will be careful what they say this time, I
can tell you!
—HENRIK IBSEN, *AN ENEMY OF THE PEOPLE*, ACT I

IF THREE OF Ibsen's plays comprise the essential Ur-script for Hitler's plans, then how could such a stupendous fact go unsuspected for so long? What rabbit hole of discovery finally led to the hidden nightmare Wonderland of the Adolf Hitler Show? And how does this new finding affect what historians believe about World War II and the Holocaust?

MISSED CUES

The short answer to why no one previously linked Ibsen's plays and Hitler's plans is that Ibsen still wears a halo, while Hitler is cast wearing devil's horns. Furthermore, their social circles scarcely overlap. Few scholars of drama are moved to read the Nazi dictator's memoirs and monologues, while few Third Reich specialists enjoy the leisure to study nineteenth-century Scandinavian theater. Even so, certain telling clues went overlooked. The short answer thus falls short.

Among available clues, there is the brief report by August Kubizek to the effect that his roommate read Ibsen's plays sometime in the first six months of 1908. That alone should have raised the question, to what effect? But Kubizek added, in a caveat, that the plays did not seem to make much impression on Adolf, at least none that Kubizek observed. So biographers were deflected when they should have looked further, since another acquaintance reported that Hitler was still reading Ibsen in 1910, a circumstance that nullified Kubizek's caveat. Kubizek also recalled how Hitler tried to write a play about Bavarian pagans resisting Christianity. When considered beside Hitler's own stated enthusiasm for Julian the Apostate, the vectors converge on *Emperor and Galilean.* Then the Otto Wagener account of Hitler's soliloquies (1931) and the subsequent "Table Talk" transcriptions (1941–42) duly yield evidence that the Führer knew the Ibsen epic about a "third Reich."

The failure of biographers to follow these leads may owe something to the distaste for the Julian play felt by many of the academic guardians of Ibsen's legacy. Rarely performed, *Emperor and Galilean* was forgotten once the cultist fuss around the play had passed. Sidelined too were Paul Schulze-Berghof (*Ibsen's Emperor and Galilean as an Allegory of the Times*) and Rolf Engert (*Ibsen as Harbinger of the Third Reich*), with their message of the play as "prophecy." For generations to come, literature professors focused instead on Ibsen's later, more psychological and introspective plays. Critics thus dispelled metahistorical designs in Ibsen just as *Emperor and Galilean* became, it would appear, a metahistorical blueprint for the self-described neopagan who led the German state.

One individual who offered a potential entrée into the labyrinth of Hitler's secret Ibsen world was Dietrich Eckart, had he only been accorded his due. Eckart's *Peer Gynt* became the favored German version and, not surprisingly, the most oft-produced Ibsen play on the Nazi German stage. The troll characters were rendered with the stereotypical features by which anti-Semites depicted Jews. Surely this happenstance showed that the Nazis were up to something regarding the legacy of Ibsen.

Yet Hitler's signed copy of *Peer Gynt* (signed by Eckart, a.k.a. Peer Gynt) shows little sign of being read: no thumbprints, no pencil marks, no pastry flakes wedged between the pages. And Eckart himself was reviled by dramatists once Nazidom fell. As thesis material, he offered a quick ticket to an academic dead end. Eckart's purported dialogue with Hitler (published 1924) was also disdained by historians, thus missing this historical point: The words may not be verbatim Hitler, but he surely read them once in print and they accord with his monologues at table nearly two decades later. So the thoughts are vintage Hitler after all. They were set down by the man who for all intents reinvented corporal Adolf Hitler as "der Führer."

Historians averted their gaze from Eckart because he was a dramatist. He dwelt on alien academic turf and fell between the cracks. Psychohistorians, meaning Freudians, also ignored this tutor to the Führer. He failed to fit their paradigm. Here was a figure esteemed by Hitler as his "fatherly friend"; but fathers, even surrogates, are supposed to be loathed by Oedipal sons. So no one bothered to ask: If Dietrich Eckart took himself for an Ibsen character, and if Hitler adored Eckart, might not Hitler too have donned an Ibsen persona of his very own?

Then there is the issue of Hitler's taste in general. He confirmed his shallowness in *Mein Kampf* by acknowledging that he read not to learn anything new, but to reinforce prejudice. Thus he might cite Schopenhauer on occasion, but always the same few phrases, indicating that he had not really read the philosopher's works. His stated enthusiasm was reserved for lowbrow or middlebrow fare—e.g., popular novels by the German writer Karl May about the American Wild West. Ibsen, the onetime iconoclast, rose to highbrow icon by the end of his career. But preconceptions of a lowbrow Hitler ruled him out as an Ibsen devotee. Another factor to divert attention was the tyrant's much-celebrated yen for Wagner. The opera composer was an overt anti-Semite, whereas Ibsen was never deemed anti-Semitic at all. Pomp and circumstance attended a Nazi Wagnerian cult, including an enhanced annual festival at Bayreuth, showing how theatricals indeed meant a lot to the Führer. Many postwar scholars accordingly emphasized the Wagner hold. But—not for want of trying—no researchers ever spotted any paraphrase from a Wagner opera in any Hitler utterance, much less a steady sequence of restaged plot events. Since Wagner seemed to be publicly the bard that mattered, though, there was no apparent cause to search for others.

MICROBE HUNTER

Mein Kampf concealed another approach to the Ibsen in Hitler. Part of chapter 3 was composed with the text of Ibsen's *An Enemy of the People,* Act IV arguably close at hand. Did no reader ever notice? The trouble is that the Führer's memoir makes for dreary reading. Few even among the ranking Nazis actually pored over it cover to cover. A former Nazi bigwig later recounted a 1927 dinner chat with some half dozen colleagues, minus Hitler, at which the topic of *Mein Kampf* came up. It emerged that no one, not even Goering or Goebbels, had ever finished the book. Some had never started it. Goering let out a laugh. Goebbels looked ashamed, like a schoolboy caught with homework undone. Even then, Goebbels waited another four years before attending to the task.

Hitler himself grew guarded about *Mein Kampf,* encouraging sales but not actual readership: "If in 1924 I had had any inkling that I would become chancellor, I would not have written the book." He forbade an exhibition of the original typescript with all its scribbled corrections. First drafts reveal too much about thought processes. They show that authors are human.

For National Socialist party members to critically dissect *Mein Kampf* would be *lèse majesté.* For non-Nazi critics, subjecting the book to textual analysis would grant it undeserved stature. Exalted or condemned (with nothing in between), *Mein Kampf* went unstudied in any serious sense, by friend and foe alike. For example, the anti-Nazi

German scholar and diarist Victor Klemperer waited til February 1944 to tackle *Mein Kampf,* having long put off the task. Here was a former professor of linguistics and literature, a man of Jewish origins married to a gentile and thus spared deportation while so many other German Jews perished. He, as a man of letters, understood full well that the Nazi holy writ offered insights on the mind of the monster. Yet like many others, he had found it too tedious even to read, let alone plumb in depth as scholars do with Shakespeare or the Bible.

Given such neglect, the Ibsen paraphrase in *Mein Kampf* lay dormant for over three quarters of a century, like some dud bomb left over from a war. Had an alert student detected it, the next step would have been to ask what more from Ibsen might lie buried. But the scholarly bomb squad failed to probe. The anomalous phrase about "leather dealers" went unnoticed. Astonishing as it may seem for all the hundreds of thousands of books and articles devoted to Hitler, during the years after World War II there was never a thorough, critical, line-by-line textual dissection of his famous book, not even by a graduate degree candidate choosing a dissertation topic. More in the way of careful textual commentary has been devoted to the Mother Goose nursery rhymes, *The Wizard of Oz,* and the lyrics to "A Whiter Shade of Pale" than to the memoirs of the man who sparked the world's worst war.

The standard English translation of Hitler's book (by Ralph Manheim) bears this blurb on the back of its paperback edition, by the anti-Nazi German journalist Konrad Heiden:

> For years *Mein Kampf* stood as proof of the blindness and complacency of the world. . . . Once again it was demonstrated that there was no more effective method of concealment than the broadest publicity.

Those words were written in 1943.

As it happened, *An Enemy of the People* was the second-most-often performed Ibsen play in Germany during the Third Reich years, after *Peer Gynt* as-told-to Dietrich Eckart. A feature film version of *Ein Volksfeind* in 1937 starred the prominent actor Heinrich George in the role of Dr. Stockmann. Conceivably someone in the stage or cinema audiences may have felt a sense of *déjà vu* in the scene where the doctor confronts the complacent townsfolk, at the climax of Act IV. If sufficiently curious and motivated, such a spectator might have gone home and compared Stockmann's words to *Mein Kampf,* chapter 3. They would have done so in private. For taking the issue any farther risked a Gestapo summons to a literary seminar at Dachau.

What factor accounts for the active stage history of *Ein Volksfeind* during the Nazi years? It is not unlikely that a theatrical individual at the pinnacle of authority had expressed a wish for this Ibsen play to be produced often, and filmed as well. The drama warned of an unseen enemy, Hitler's very message when he presented himself as a battler against the Jewish "virus." He seems to have been less concerned about any copycatting being brought to light. What endured, until 1942, was the Hitlerian self-image embodied by the adoption of the Dr. Stockmann character.

It is interesting to digress on the character's roots. Stockmann, it appears, goes back a very long way. Ibsen's source may be found in a set of passages in the published diary of the Danish Christian existentialist Soren Kierkegaard (1813–55). Back in 1850 and 1854, a Kierkegaard glorying in his own isolation had carried on about "the crowd":

> Truth always rests with the minority, and the minority is always stronger than the majority, because the minority is generally formed by those who really have an opinion, while the strength of a majority is illusory, formed by the gangs who have no opinion—and who, therefore, in the next instant (when it is evident that the minority is the stronger) assume *its* opinion, which then becomes that of the majority.... [1850]
>
> "The crowd" is essentially what I am aiming my polemical arrow at; it was Socrates who taught me to do so.... I will call the attention of the crowd to their own ruination. And if they don't want to see it willingly, I shall make them see it by fair means or foul.... I will force them to beat me.... He who turns around to combat the "crowd" from which all corruption issues, must seek his own fall. [1854]

Here was the model for Dr. Stockmann confronting the assembled townsfolk in *An Enemy of the People,* Act IV. Kierkegaard's source for Socrates appears to have been a set of lines in the dialogue *Gorgias,* composed by Plato in 380 B.C.E., where Socrates demolishes the idea that majority rule provides its own justification. Expertise—in this case, that of a physician—ought to prevail over the clever arguments of rhetoricians able to win over the foolish majority.

> SOCRATES: You were saying, in fact, that the rhetorician will have greater powers of persuasion than the physician, even in a matter of health?
>
> GORGIAS: Yes, with the multitude—that is. . . .
>
> SOCRATES: . . . you will refute me after the manner which rhetoricians practice in courts of law. For there the one party think that they refute the other when they bring forward a number of witnesses of good repute in proof of their allegations, and their adversary has only a single one or none at all. But this kind of proof is of no value where truth is the aim; a man may often be sworn down by a multitude of false witnesses who have a great air of respectability.

Imbued by Socrates via Plato and Kierkegaard, Ibsen wrote to another Dane, Georg Brandes, on January 3, 1882, taking a poke at his greatest rival in Norwegian letters:

> [Björnstjerne] Björnson says "The majority is always right"; and as a practical politician he is bound, I suppose, to say so. I, on the contrary, must of necessity say "The minority is always right." Naturally I am not thinking of that minority of stagnationists who are left behind by the great middle party, which with us is called Liberal; but I mean that minority that leads the van, and pushes on to points which the majority has not yet reached.

An inspired Ibsen went on to construct Dr. Stockmann, implacable physician in the deadly fight against germs. He dashed off *An Enemy of the People* during the next few months of 1882 and submitted it for stage production by the year's end. Drawing upon several newsworthy incidents of bacterial contamination, it is thought that Ibsen may have incorporated one near Munich into the play. Ibsen himself was, of course, in no way responsible for the later Hitlerian warping of the play's message to equate germs with Jews.

Inadvertently, though, he supplied a role model. He bequeathed it as well to Peter Benchley, the author of *Jaws*. The popular novel (1974) and film (1976) track *An Enemy of the People* closely enough. Again a certain danger lurks, out there. Again the townsfolk (of a beach resort called Amity) are complacent. Alarming publicity would hurt the tourist trade. It takes one determined, selfless scientist to rally a community to save itself despite itself.

Posterity counts Dr. Stockmann, along with Kierkegaard, Socrates, and Benchley's ichthyologist Matt Hooper, all among the good. The Führer too never viewed himself as evil, but instead as an honest voice crying in the wilderness, endowed with the knack to identify a deadly unseen foe, and committed to a mortal fight for the world's salvation. That same world, looking for the source of Hitler's "evil," missed the source as well as the point.

ADOLF THE APOSTATE

By far the most revealing sources on the inner Hitler are the transcribed records of his informal monologues. Authenticity may be gauged in inverse proportion to the time elapsed between speaking and recording—the less editing, the truer to what the speaker said. When he was relaxed, he spoke what he thought; that much must be presumed. The best record is the "Table Talk" for 1941–42, Hitler's *Tischgespräche*. These talks have been mined, albeit selectively, by historians and biographers since their publication in 1951.

And that is the problem. The "Table Talk" record has been quoted countless times to make this or that point. That is, historians approached this most primary of sources after being conditioned by other documents. Hitler's out-loud musings were then used as fill-in. Where he said something anomalous, it was left as just that, an unexplained anomaly. These Hitlerian ramblings were never exhaustively analyzed as an integral text, per se, for their guiding philosophy and particular metaphors. As a source, the Führer's laid-back spoken thoughts are comparable to Richard Nixon's casual Oval Office tapes. Yet far more lawyerly attention has been lavished upon the White House riddle, "what-did-he-know-and-when-did-he-know-it," than historians have devoted to what Hitler thought and what prompted him to think it—according to these authentic stenographic words of the man himself.

On three separate occasions, the man alluded specifically to Emperor Julian the Apostate. Here was a proper anomaly. The proper question should long have been: Why Julian? It was asked just once and answered, incorrectly, in an early German edition of the *Tischgespräche,* where a commentator speculated that the prompt was a German translation of an historian's biography of Julian. But Hitler said, explicitly, that he was moved by a book of Julian's sayings, not a history tome. The question then should have been: What edition of the sayings? And what prior prompt had brought the supreme leader to read and recommend this anomalous ancient work amidst the wintry crises of his own grim, titanic war?

Anomalies were the keys to Sherlock Holmes's success. As Watson looked on in baffled wonderment, while Scotland Yard adduced the obvious and irrelevant, Holmes would delve for that which did not fit. Oddities, he knew, led the way to solutions. He worked back from seeming trifles, the clues trodden over by Inspector Lestrade. From an oddity, Holmes would infer the best explanation. This process differed from either deductive or inductive logic. Deductive reasoning proceeds from a general rule to a specific case. Inductive reasoning tests general rules by experiment and seeks verification from the regularity prevailing in nature. But where a phenomenon is intrinsically aberrant, these forms of reasoning are insufficient. Holmes's logic presumed every anomaly to have an antecedent cause. Proceeding from an effect (i.e., the anomaly) back to a cause, more relevant data should result. A yield of such data constitutes the proof of the process: QED, in almost every (fictional) Holmes case as recorded by Conan Doyle.

Pursuing the anomaly of Julian in the "Table Talk" ought to have done the trick, had Holmes been on the job. As it happened, there were a couple of near misses. At least two contemporaries guessed, correctly, at the role of Julian in the thinking of Hitler. They did so even before Hitler spoke the name of the apostate emperor on the record in 1941–42. Both prescient observers were men of the cloth.

In October 1938, Pope Pius XI made one of his last public appearances. The pontiff was eighty-one years old and weakening. Not long before, he had condemned Nazi racism in an encyclical pointedly titled, in German, *Mit Brennender Sorge* ("With Burning Despair"), but its nuanced phrases had failed to dissuade the Führer from his anti-Semitic program. Now in the autumn of 1938 with war on the horizon, the papal rhetoric gained fervor. Pius XI ventured to compare Hitler to Flavius Claudius Julianus—that is, to Julian the Apostate. Intuitively, perhaps, the leader of Roman Catholicism had verged upon discovering that the Führer's private role model was indeed the apostate emperor. Pius XI noted how the two respective neo-pagan rulers, ancient and modern, had each blamed his Christian victims for the torments they endured while persevering in their faith.

That was all. Nothing explicit followed from the Vatican along these lines. Near the end of his life, Pius XI did order an American priest to draft a position paper denouncing Nazi anti-Semitism. It was filed away, then eventually published long afterward, billed as a "hidden encyclical." Yet it contained no more allusions to Hitler as a second Julian. In February 1939, Pius XI died. Europe soon went to war, but the succeeding pope, Pius XII, said no more about Julian the Apostate or his modern imitator.

Pius XI had raised a point, though. Did no one then draw the vectors tracing from Hitler as a drama fan, and from Hitler as a Julian admirer, to converge on Hitler as the Julian dramatized by Ibsen? Both Ibsen's Julian and Germany's Hitler each aimed for a "third Reich." Did no one ever presume a connection?

It turned out that someone did. Like Pius XI, he too was a clergyman. Under the name "Ernst Fischer," he wrote a pamphlet including the essay "Ibsen und das Dritte Reich" ("Ibsen and the Third Reich"), published in Basel, Switzerland in 1941. The small volume contained three other essays written between 1938 and 1941, although the one about Ibsen is the lead item. In it, Fischer suggested that Hitler's enchantment with the term "Third Reich" owed something to Ibsen's *Emperor and Galilean*. Fischer moreover took the pagan trappings displayed at a November 1933 Berlin rally to hint that Hitler's ultimate purpose, like Julian the Apostate's, was a pagan revival.

So who was "Ernst Fischer"? It is a common name, but the content of this essay does not seem to match the views and interests of any other Ernst Fischer who wrote in the mid-twentieth century. This Ernst Fischer refers to "we Swiss," although that self-identification may be seen as suspect since a German writing anti-Nazi essays published abroad would have every reason to conceal his nationality. An "Ernst Fischer" who was not necessarily a genuine Swiss but instead a German also need not have been a genuine Ernst Fischer. With "Ernst Fischer" presumed to be a pseudonym, a candidate presents himself. This man too, like "Ernst Fischer," had written about the relationship of church and state. This man too, like "Ernst Fischer," published comments on Ibsen. And this man's names too began with the initials E.F.

He was Emil Felden (1874–1959), a Lutheran pastor who had been a classmate and friend of Albert Schweitzer (1875–1965) during their student years in theology at Strasbourg. Felden spent most of his subsequent career at Bremen. A man of left-wing views, he served as a Social-Democratic deputy in the Reichstag during the Weimar Republic. Prior to then, he had written a book on ethical lessons in Ibsen's plays, *Alles oder Nichts!* ("All or Nothing"), published in 1911. He also wrote a novel published in 1921, *Die Sünde wider das Volk* ("The Sin Against the People"), attacking the Nazi dogma that Jesus Christ had not really been a Jew. In Felden's novel, a budding demagogue named "Adolf Finster" (literally "Adolf Darkness" or "Adolf Gloom") appears. He was a parody of Hitler, the target no less obvious than Charlie Chaplin's satirized character in *The Great Dictator*. Adolf Finster spouts lines about how Christ "the Galilean" really must have been an Aryan, since Christ was too creative to have been a Jew, and the Galileans were not racially Jewish. All this was precisely what that other Adolf, Hitler the politician, was saying in speeches during 1920–21.

So the following points are noted: Across the length of Germany, far from Bavaria, Felden was concerned enough about the danger Hitler posed to lampoon him in print as early as 1921. Felden also had a keen interest in Ibsen, and he remarked in print on Christ as "the Galilean," a point in common with both Hitler and the Julian of Ibsen's play. These were all interests in common as well with the "Ernst Fischer" of "Ibsen und das Dritte Reich." Felden's writings came under a Nazi ban during the Third Reich years. To make his opinions known, he had to publish them somewhere outside German control. After France fell to the Germans in 1940, Felden was transferred to German-annexed Alsace, nearer to neutral Switzerland. In 1943, he was interrogated by the Gestapo but freed, and returned after the war to Bremen. Were "Ernst Fischer" and Emil Felden actually the same person? Whether or not they were one and the same, these writings, both by clergymen with the initials "E.F.," appear to have been the closest anyone came to discerning the Ibsen in Hitler during the years Hitler lived.

DOWN THE RABBIT HOLE

Several logical pathways might reasonably have opened into the rabbit hole leading down to Hitler's hidden Ibsen world. The Hitler–Eckart relationship offered one such likely path, given Eckart's insistence that he himself embodied the character Peer Gynt. The paraphrase from *An Enemy of the People* in *Mein Kampf* presented another pathway, as too did Hitler's expressed adulation of Julian in the "Table Talk." Someone like Ernst Fischer who suspected an Ibsen influence on Hitler had enough material on hand after World War II to explore the question, had he been so inclined. By contrast, the Hitler material from *The Master Builder* seems to offer a somehow vaguer route, if a path may be perceived at all.

And yet that material was what illuminated this discovery for me. (The time has come to descend from the aloof scholarly third person.) My step-by-step journey began with research I was doing on Hitler's master builder, Fritz Todt.

As stated, Todt for a long time remained a figure obscured, in the popular view, by his successor, Albert Speer. Apart from brief entries in biographic compendia, there existed only one book-length work about him, published in 1986 by the German author Franz W. Seidler, well known for Third Reich apologetics. Todt remained even less accessible in English. Among the few items available, a master's thesis and a doctoral dissertation (1967 and 1970) submitted by an American graduate student had lauded Todt's role in the building of Hitler's Westwall, but offered no hint of any parallels to the Ibsen play. This thesis and dissertation, neither of which was published in book or article form, would most likely have stayed unnoticed indefinitely. Decades later, however, their author became the subject of a probe triggered by his penchant for Nazi displays and for academic frauds committed while chairman of a history department at a university in the American South. That circumstance placed the long-forgotten thesis and dissertation under renewed scrutiny.

In addition to investigating this miscreant's other suspected frauds and felonies, my attention to his thesis and dissertation incidentally suggested Fritz Todt to be a topic of merit unto itself. Todt, as a major Nazi leader, deserved a more reliable and critical study. I then commenced research on this overlooked Third Reich person of consequence. Todt held the informal title as Hitler's master builder, a term appearing in the subtitle of Seidler's adulatory biography called *Todt: Baumeister des Dritten Reiches*—i.e., "Master Builder of the Third Reich." Apart from that shared word *Baumeister*, though, the Seidler book contained no suggestion that Todt's career might have actually reflected the fictional life of Ibsen's master builder in any way at all. But as I approached the material from scratch, the "master builder" title carried a beguiling hint. It vaguely recalled the Ibsen play, which I had seen long before. So I commenced to read the script, actually in search of some ironic quotation that might be used as an epigraph—i.e., a literary accent for an historical work.

Shortly into the research process, however, the following parallels emerged:

- Todt's career and that of Solness had each taken off in the wake of a mysterious fire of an "ancestral mansion," if the Reichstag be counted as such.
- Todt and Solness each rose to dominate the building profession in their respective realms, displacing or subordinating all rivals. The rise of Todt owed to Hitler's favor, that of Solness to an "unseen power."
- Solness promised to build Hilde Wangel a "castle in the air with a view for miles around," whereas Todt oversaw the project to construct a similar hideaway for Hitler, above Berchtesgaden, Ibsen's favorite alpine resort.
- Neither Todt nor Solness was a qualified architect, but each had talented, architecturally trained understudies waiting in the wings.
- Todt and Solness each perished in a fall from a height, each shortly after speaking to a close acquaintance of ten years. In each case, the acquaintance was the one for whom the "castle in the air" had been promised, or built.
- Todt and Solness each either wore or carried aloft visible wreaths at the moment of their deaths; in Todt's case, Hitler had been musing aloud about wreaths just days before.

These parallels departed from the usual stuff of staid academic history. Finding such curiosities hadn't been planned, and I stayed wary at first. I didn't want to be like Professor Jack Gladney in Don DeLillo's classic novel *White Noise* (1985). Gladney imagines he's on to something when he founds a "Hitler Studies" program at his college. He's clueless and pathetic.

So I set aside the odd parallels as mere anomalies. I shouldn't think about them. Anyway, not too much.

Yet the stage play beckoned to be re-read. Could there be still more parallels, usable for epigraphs, maybe one epigraph to a chapter? The impetus at this stage was still sort of a game for me. I had not yet seriously considered that Hitler had anything substantive to do with guiding Todt's career so as to reenact that of Halvard Solness. That seemed preposterous. Ibsen was highbrow, while Hitler was a boor. Hitler had read Ibsen, but the plays were said to have made no impression; at least his own roommate, August Kubizek, had so written. And as a rule, the leaders of modern industrial states do not take their plans out of plays. But some rulers do break rules. . . .

More serious research continued. It entailed a reading of the Hitler "Table Talk," which happened to mention Todt in a few places. *Tischgespräche* still vied for cluttered desk space with *The Master Builder.* In that way, perhaps a month into the project, came a purely chance find. There seemed to be a paraphrase of sorts, lines from *The Master Builder* reworked among Hitler's words, but still close enough to suspect that play as a source. As seeming paraphrases go, this example could not be deemed conclusive; yet neither would it go away. And this example did fit within the context of those parallels between the lives of Todt and Solness.

It is the nature of rabbit holes that one can fall into them unaware. Research on the life and career of Todt subsequently contended, more and more, with a quest for further evidence of Ibsen in Hitler. The idea was to substantiate the unconfirmed, but still suggestive, possible echo of Hilde Wangel's words among those of the Führer. Additional leads were clearly needed, and so they were actively sought. A keyword search, +Hitler +Ibsen, then turned up references to Dietrich Eckart. That spun off in yet another direction: Hitler's mentor had once adapted an Ibsen play into German verse. And the German items available on Eckart included his strange claim that he embodied the Peer Gynt character, in the flesh. So, if Hitler had similarly entertained such a relationship to Hilde Wangel, it would explain both the paraphrased words and the parallel deeds, with Todt cast as Solness. But that seemed too anomalous, like something one might encounter in Wonderland after stumbling down a rabbit hole.

Matters languished for several months. The research got properly back to Todt, builder of the Autobahn and a worthy historical topic in his own right. An impasse had been reached in finding more about Hitler's fixation on Ibsen, if one there truly was. Or had the appearance of a fixation just been an artifact of coincidence?

Meanwhile, an academic colleague of mine was researching a dissertation about nineteenth-century European spas. A conversation led to Ibsen's play *An Enemy of the People*. The colleague suggested that this script might be worth reading in a search for what the Führer could have borrowed. She turned out to be right; the reading proved well worth the time. Stockmann's speech in Act IV seemed, if anything, Hitlerian. A search for its resonance found first a Hitler speech from 1921, and then, some weeks later, the pentimento passage in *Mein Kampf*, chapter 3. This was the "Eureka!" moment— or, as another, grudging colleague put it *sotto voce*, "Okay, you got him."

When I informed him of the find, Hitler's British biographer, Ian Kershaw, wrote to me with encouraging words: "fascinating," and "an excellent bit of detective work." At that point, Hitler's 1942 paraphrase from *An Enemy of the People* in "Table Talk" had still not been identified, nor had any of the material from *Emperor and Galilean*. But for me, a book about Todt would henceforth have to wait.

The discovery that the Ibsen influence on Hitler went beyond *The Master Builder* prompted my reading all the plays, including *Emperor and Galilean*. In due course, it became evident to me that the epic about Julian counted heavily for Adolf Hitler, if not to the academic guardians of Ibsen's legacy. The dual role of Geli Raubal in two plays was discerned; the timing of her death matched the appearance of Hilde at Solness's door.

Noted too was the series of Hitler paraphrases of lines in *Emperor and Galilean*, the Führer's mentions of Julian in the "Table Talk," and the step-by-step sequence of parallel deeds from what Ibsen wrote to what Hitler did. Most prominent were these instances where historical deed matched literary text:

- Julian and Hitler shared the concept of a neo-pagan "third Reich."
- Julian and Hitler each took a blood relative as consort.
- Their respective consorts each died just prior to the protagonist's bid for power against an ailing chief of state.
- The bodies of the respective consorts were each transported to a place called "Vienna" for a proper Christian burial, despite the pagan sympathies of Julian and Hitler.

- Upon coming to power, Julian and Hitler each staged a ceremonial public burning of objectionable books.
- Julian and Hitler each broke an object from its handle in public, and then made a speech of reassurance to onlookers that this act was actually a positive omen.
- Upon coming to power, Julian and Hitler each pledged to tolerate the Christian churches.
- Julian and Hitler then forthwith proceeded to betray their pledges of religious tolerance.
- Julian and Hitler each rebuilt fortifications paralleling the Rhine river, called by Hitler the *limes* as in the Roman style.
- Jewish temples were obliterated in a signal act, just before Julian and Hitler launched their respective campaigns of eastward expansion.
- Julian and Hitler each signed a peace pact with the neighboring empire to the east.
- Julian and Hitler each shortly betrayed that pact and proceeded to launch an eastward invasion.
- Julian and Hitler each commanded their armies to swerve northward away from the enemy's capital city, postponing its capture til later.
- Julian and Hitler each voiced a plan to "exterminate" a religious minority on the flimsy pretext that it posed an active military threat in the rear.

Next came the "Why," the larger literary-cult context within which Hitler could reenact Ibsen's neo-pagan drama. That search led at length to the works by Rolf Engert and Paul Schulze-Berghof on *Emperor and Galilean* as a "prophecy" of the coming Third Reich. Both men had moved within the locus of Hitler's own personal and political associations, and both had written on drama, a topic of paramount interest to him. Some of Schulze-Berghof's own words seemed to resonate in *Mein Kampf.*

My quest had begun through an inadvertent find from the least likely opening, some curious observed parallels to *The Master Builder.* Substantiation came by and by, with the more solidly demonstrable material relating *An Enemy of the People* and *Emperor and Galilean* to what Hitler said and did. Given the totality of the circumstances and the textual evidence, to consider these three plays as anything other than a consciously interrelated reenactment would seem to be demanding a bit much of mere coincidence. No special insight is claimed for the discovery, only perseverance in research once the outlines were perceived. Sherlock Holmes would doubtless have spotted it all much sooner. He knew enough to act on an anomaly from the outset.

THE FINAL SOLUTION TO THE HITLER PROBLEM?

The evidence that drama scripts guided the Nazi dictator may come as a surprise to many, but here and there a few observers already suspected something of that sort. As the Dutch novelist Harry Mulisch put it in 2001, "Perhaps Hitler, the man of the theater who regarded himself as the greatest commander of all time, had only played theatrically with toy soldiers, albeit of flesh and blood." The late Jewish philosopher Emil Fackenheim had earlier judged that Hitler's histrionics were what decisively counted. This factor trivialized everything, however. Fackenheim lamented: "I don't think he knew the difference between acting and believing. Of course, it's a shocking thing to consider that six million Jews were murdered because of an actor."

Actors follow scripts. Hitler's are at last identified here. Three Ibsen plays gripped him over decades, their omnipresence ascertained by sufficient instances of verbal pentimenti. The words have been adapted but they trace to the same three scripts. Did the actor-dictator speak these lines with their source consciously in mind? The complete parallelism between *An Enemy of the People* Act IV and *Mein Kampf* chapter 3 runs for several pages. It is thus hard to avoid the conclusion that Hitler had at some point either memorized Dr. Stockmann's diatribe, or else had re-read it not long before he dictated the derivative passage of his memoir to his scribe. He may or may not have had the Ibsen text open in front of him at Landsberg fortress prison, but he did not recite, per se. Instead he had deeply internalized the material to make Stockmann's case his own. That leaves moot whether the passages in *Mein Kampf* were deliberately copied from Ibsen, or should be attributed to cryptamnesia. Whether absent minded or not, this example falls well within the bounds of plagiarism. As for the subsequent, shorter pentimenti, all the known instances from all three plays occur in Hitler's ad hoc, informal speech. They are clearly inadvertent, amounting to giveaway manifestations of the dramas' hold on him. But his parallel actions to their plots comprise another matter. Each move required cool calculation. Thus was the play the thing, a consciously restaged parable that interwove three scripts.

Like the visible tip of an iceberg, elements of the scripts appear, each on successive occasions. To ignore the berg's hulking mass below is to sail at risk. It should henceforth be impermissible to judge Hitler without accounting for the Ibsen factor. Just as total immersion in *Taxi Driver* compelled Hinckley the almost-assassin, the Ibsen scripts furnish a master narrative for what Hitler sought, and wrought. Generating the World War II known to all for its blood, suffering, and destruction was a parallel universe now revealed, the scripted war that raged in Hitler's head. The analogy of a film projected onto a screen comes to mind, and the queasy question as to which war was more "real." Let philosophers and ethicists grapple with that one.

Here, however, the discipline is not philosophy or ethics, but history. And, since historians are rational, tireless, and open-minded in their search for truth, they will discuss the empirical evidence purely on the basis of merit, then cheerfully accept the logical conclusion and duly set about revising the textbooks. Right?

Not necessarily, as the town mayor cautioned in Act II of *An Enemy of the People:*

> Believe me, the public has no need of new ideas; it's better off without them. The best way to serve the public is to give it what it's used to.

Built-in constraints will doubtless cause some historians to recoil from even deigning to consider the evidence, let alone accept what it implies. The constraints begin with a guild disdain for biography as, somehow, a lesser form of historical research. Such snobbery is an ongoing, collective reaction to the excesses of nineteenth-century scholarship, when historians writing in the penumbra of Napoleon would reflexively link great events to great men, their virtues and their foibles. The twentieth century knew better.

Biographies continue to be written. But most biographers choose subjects more manageable than The Great Dictator, and portray them as fitting into the trends of their times rather than boldly charting the course of history. Furthermore, within academic biographical writing there is a prejudice against connecting affairs of state too closely with a subject's private life. And should the subject under study show an undisputed mystical side, such as Hitler did, then scholarly biographers nonetheless tend to marginalize the occult factors even when common sense tells us that belief in the occult is what counts most to those enticed by its lure.

All the constraints are present. Hitler is the presumed prime mover, granting Biography dominance. That much alone taints the case. More anathema: State policies are intertwined with Hitler's household affairs, notably the arcane ritual murder of Geli Raubal. No matter how neatly the data fit, to demonstrate such a sweeping solution for Hitler, and from such theatrical material, oversteps hubris, heresy, chutzpah, and impertinence. Worse, it is uncollegial.

Truth be told, within Holocaust studies Hitler has become something like the elephant in the living room. Those who work in the field are so habituated to his presence as to scarcely take heed. They tiptoe around him (and the droppings). If pointed out by an occasional guest, his presence cannot be denied. He is even discussed, albeit in perfunctory manner, should some naïve visitor breach decorum by insisting on it. Yet he is all but omitted from scholarly topics of choice. This may seem counterintuitive to members of the general public. How is it possible to minimize Hitler in a published work of history or a museum exhibit on the Nazi era?

The climate was not always so, and certainly not while Hitler bestrode Europe or in the years soon thereafter. Alan Bullock wrote the first professionally respected biography, published in 1952 as

Hitler: A Study in Tyranny. At the very outset, the author offered a modest disclaimer wherein he diminished the scope of his task, taking care to differentiate the loftier reaches of History from a mere exercise in Biography:

> I have not attempted to write a history of Germany, nor a study of government and society under the Nazi regime. My theme is not dictatorship, but the dictator, the personal power of one man...

Bullock then immediately proceeded to disclaim the disclaimer:

> ...although it must be added that for most of the years between 1933 and 1945 this is identical with the most important part of the history of the Third Reich.

So, as seen by Hitler's first authoritative postwar chronicler some seven years after V-E Day, there have been exceptional times when Biography does amount to History after all. The period of the Third Reich was one such time, to which Bullock himself had been witness.

As of 1952, a prominent Nazi slogan from the Führer's heyday still resonated in the minds of those who had heard it firsthand or in newsreels: *"Hitler ist Deutschland! Deutschland ist Hitler!"* Such a statement of mystical unity cannot be uttered by the official media of a modern state unless the ruler really does possess something close to absolute power. It is, to be sure, absurd to take such phrasing in a fully literal sense. Moreover, nowhere near every German actually believed those words. Here and there, intelligent persons kept a grip on reality amidst a nation gone hysterical. And yet other world leaders, hostile and friendly alike, responded as if the slogan were, in practical terms, true. They dealt with Hitler like an unpredictable, albeit unchallenged, warlord. Thus when it came to negotiations, Hitler was, for all intents, the living embodiment of Germany. One critical biographer writing in the mid-1930s, Konrad Heiden, gave expression to the prevalent regard for the dominance of one man: "*He* [italics in original] shaped the movement; *he* bewitched men's minds; *he* erected the mightiest supremacy over Germany that has ever existed—mightiest because magical."

"*Bewitched* men's minds." "Mightiest because *magical*" [italics added]. From the vantage point of 1936, the Nazi leader's charismatic hold could unabashedly be related to some extraordinary, unworldly appeal. Fully in keeping were Hitler's own assertions to be the tool of Providence. That is, Hitler and his contemporaries took his mastery for granted, along with his professed personal conviction of an otherworldly mandate.

Accepting that mandate, Germany did as its leader bid, to the end. He had acted through the machinery of a party and a state, but no one at the time seriously suggested that these entities could preempt or dissuade the Führer. So Wehrmacht plotters made a vain try at assassination in the summer of 1944, when the war looked lost. There was no other way to switch course. Also during the war, the U.S. Office of Strategic Services proceeded on the premise that Hitler was the supreme lord of the German Reich, de facto and de jure. That is why the OSS commissioned a team of psychologists to produce detailed personality profiles of the man. His lackeys got far less attention, notwithstanding their appearance at the Nuremberg Trials of 1945–46. And at that judicial hearing, the defendants ascribed their criminal acts to orders. Hitler made them do it.

The Nazi henchmen regained their own historical place in the sun only with the passing of a generation after V-E Day. Pursuing justice against smaller-fry murderers like Adolf Eichmann required an examination of how Nazidom operated below the dictator. Professor Raul Hilberg's pioneering, magisterial work on *The Destruction of European Jewry* had already set the tone. It is true that Hitler needed helpers, and their help is what Hilberg documented in fine detail. But more work still remained. An emphasis on bureaucratic processes could keep many historians busy and employed, whereas there was only one Führer to go around. Meanwhile, more trials of lower-ranking perpetrators were held in Germany and the Soviet Union. These stimulated further academic research. By the 1970s, Holocaust studies had begun emerging on elite campuses in the United States as a recognized concentration within History. Publishers offered a widening array of titles. Documentary and feature films revitalized the topic's mass appeal.

Ironically, then, these trials, along with the outpouring of victims' memoirs and local studies, tended to eclipse the role of Hitler. Lesser figures in the dock seemed not ghouls but pathetically ordinary people, aging and shabby. Thus the Holocaust took on more of the character of an impersonal historical force than a berserk program percolating down a chain of command. Some found the trend eerie enough to protest in print. "Hitler has been disappearing behind abstractions. If he is mentioned at all, it is likely to be as a metaphor," wrote the late Milton Himmelfarb in a 1984 article. It was titled straight and to the point: "No Hitler, No Holocaust." Published perceptions had shifted so much in the four decades since the Nazi collapse that Himmelfarb felt obliged to remind readers how . . .

> . . . Hitler willed and ordered the Holocaust, and was obeyed. Traditions, tendencies, ideas, myths—none of these made Hitler murder the Jews. All that history, all those forces and influences, could have been the same and Hitler could as easily, more easily, not have murdered the Jews. . . . Anti-Semitism was a necessary condition for the Holocaust, it was not a sufficient condition. Hitler was needed. Hitler murdered the Jews because he wanted to murder them.

No matter. Even as "Holocaust denial" was discredited, a trend toward what might be called "Hitler denial" continued strong. Those who continued to insist that it had always been Hitler's intent to murder the Jews became a minority, dubbed intentionalists. A rival school of thought, called functionalism, focused instead on the processes lower down. This interpretation saw the massacre of Jews as an ad hoc solution growing out of bureaucratic processes. Functionalists emphasized how the steps that culminated in mass murder seemed to follow a twisted, uncertain path. Instead of one direct Führer order, there had been many variations in local and regional implementation of the Nazi policy toward the Jews. The differences suggested that the supreme leader had been uninvolved or only loosely involved, and that the initiative for killing really sprang from below. Thus, over the years, Hitler himself became a virtual non-topic for many postwar historians of the Third Reich, both in collegial discourse and in the way they presented the story to the general public.

At the Holocaust Museum in Washington, D.C., the downplaying of the tyrant happened by design, not by default. To stress the dictator's rise "is to fall into a revisionist trap," as one museum executive put it. There was a fear of inadvertently glamorizing the Nazi leader by emphasizing the appeal he once had exerted. This approach is ingrained in scholarly work as well, much of it in a functionalist vein. Occupying the fifth floor of the Museum is a superb archive and library belonging to the Center for Advanced Holocaust Studies. It, and Yad Vashem in Jerusalem, are the world's two leading research institutes dedicated to the field. The Center awards coveted fellowships (including one to this author) and provides a collegial working atmosphere. Scholars of renown assemble there for conferences. The Center's library duly acquires biographical materials on the Nazi ruler. But since the start, no fellowship has been awarded for work on Hitler per se. No conference at the Museum has ever focused on the man or his writings. Yad Vashem slights him in a similar way. This diminishing by Holocaust historians of the man Germany once called its Leader may sardonically remind some outside observers of how the name "Moses" is oddly missing from the Passover *Seder* service, or how the Deity goes unmentioned in the Bible's *Book of Esther.* But the state of affairs continues.

In such an environment, a finding that Hitler borrowed the outlines of his program from drama scripts may be taken as a curiosity by many specialized scholars, while others may view it as irrelevant. The basic evidence, after all, consists of mere traces in Hitler's speech of the Ibsen plays, i.e., verbal pentimenti.

But in painting, pentimenti offer a decisive way to distinguish an authentic original from copies made by lesser hands. Once glimpsed, these faint but telling traces cannot be ignored.

So, are the Ibsen pentimenti in Hitler historically significant? The observed, consistent linkage between Ibsen's plays and Hitler's plots comprises a set of empirical facts. These facts too will not go away, nor will their implications. Implicit in the re-enactment of a script is that the ending is foreordained. A Hitler adopting the Stockmann role from *An Enemy of the People* becomes a physician vowed from the outset to exterminate the noxious germs infesting his town. A Hitler self-cast as Julian the Apostate from *Emperor and Galilean* becomes a ruler sworn to extirpate Christianity by its roots. Both scripts, as adapted by Hitler to the world stage, inexorably decreed a war against the Jews to override all else. Even territorial expansion was subordinate. The Greater German Reich turns out to have been but a means to achieve the apocalyptic end. At the very end of his rule in spring 1945 the defeated Führer admitted as much when he condemned the German people as unworthy of him. He had merely used them to pursue his larger, cosmic mission.

If Hitler had amounted to a mere cog or a prisoner of events, then whatever scripted, "prophetic" fantasies played out in his head would have meant little at the time and still less today. In that case, it matters not which particular Ur-texts impelled him. The Ibsen evidence might be consigned to a footnote. However, if Hitler is taken to have been the prime mover as his contemporaries saw him, then the corollary now becomes almost too much to bear: It appears that what set the world aflame was a theatrical production by an unbridled lunatic. In the course of his repertoire he turned everyone else into a bit player, a cameo, an extra, or a prop.

PRINCIPAL SOURCES

LISTED BELOW ARE the most relevant items for substantiating the present discovery of a set of consistent links between the spoken lines and plots of three drama scripts by Henrik Ibsen, and their subsequent echoes in Hitler's words and actions. For a comprehensive political biography of the Nazi Führer, readers should consult the two volume work by Ian Kershaw, *Hitler* (volume 1, *Hubris* and volume 2, *Nemesis*; New York: Norton, 1999–2000).

HITLER'S TRANSCRIBED WORDS

Hitler Reden, Schriften, Anordnungen covering February 1925-January 1933 (Munich: K.G. Saur, 1996)

Hitler: Sämtliche Aufzeichnungen, 1905–1924, edited by Eberhard Jäckel and Axel Kuhn (Stuttgart: Deutsche Verlags-Anstalt, 1980); abbeviated "Jäckel and Kuhn"

Hitlers Tischgespräche im Führerhauptquartier 1941–1942, edited by Henry Picker (Stuttgart: Seewald, 1963); abbreviated *Tischgespräche*. The English translation was first titled *Hitler's Secret Conversations* (New York: Farrar, Strauss, and Young, 1953) and subsequently *Hitler's Table Talk, 1941–44* (London: Weidenfeld and Nicolson, 1973); abbreviated *Table Talk*

Mein Kampf (numerous German editions, cited by chapter); the English translation used here is by Ralph Manheim (Boston: Houghton Mifflin, 1943), abbreviated *MK*

Monologe im Führerhauptquartier, 1941–1944 (Hamburg: Albrecht Knaus, 1980); abbreviated *"Monologe"*

⊕

Eckart, Dietrich, *Der Bolschewismus von Moses bis Lenin: Zwiegespräch zwischen Adolf Hitler und mir* (mimeographed typescript, Munich: Eher, 1924)

Wagener, Otto, *Hitler–Memoirs of a Confidant* (edited by Henry Ashby Turner, Jr.; translation of *Hitler aus nächster Nähe*, New Haven and London: Yale University Press, 1985)

IBSEN

The Correspondence of Henrik Ibsen, ed. Mary Morison, 1905 (republished New York: Haskell, 1970)

GERMAN EDITIONS OF IBSEN'S PLAYS AVAILABLE TO HITLER

Baumeister Solness [*The Master Builder*], translated by Sigurd Ibsen (Leipzig, Reclam, 1892)

Kaiser und Galiläer: welthistorisches Schauspiel [*Emperor and Galilean*], translated by Ernst Brausewetter (Leipzig: Reclam, n.d.)

Kaiser und Galiläer: ein weltgeschichtliches Schauspiel in zwei Teilen, translated by Paul Hermann, in *Henrik Ibsens sämtliche Werke in deutscher Sprache* volume 5 (Berlin: S. Fischer, 1899)

Ein Volksfeind [*An Enemy of the People*], volume 7 of *Henrik Ibsens Sämtliche Werke in deutscher Sprache* (Berlin: S. Fischer, 1899)

Ein Volksfeind, translated by Wilhelm Lange (Leipzig: Reclam, n.d.)

IBSEN IN ENGLISH

Emperor and Galilean in *The Oxford Ibsen*, volume IV, translated by James Walter McFarlane (London: Oxford University Press, 1963) is the edition used here for quoted passages, abbreviated *E&G*. Readers may also wish to consult the more widely available translation prepared for actors, *Emperor and Galilean: a World Historical Drama*, translated by Brian Johnston (Lyme, NH: Smith and Kraus, 1999)

An Enemy of the People (the Michael Meyer translation is used here; it is available in several reprint editions; Hitler's paraphrases in *Mein Kampf* and the Table Talk were from Act IV.)

The Master Builder (Translations by Rolf Fjelde and Michael Meyer are used here, available in several reprint editions; quoted passages are cited by Act.)

IBSEN CRITICISM AND TREATISES ON IBSEN AS "PROPHET"

Eckart, Dietrich, *Abermals vor der Höhle des Grossen Krummen* (Berlin: Herold, 1915)

———, *Ibsen, der grosse Krumme, und ich* (Berlin: Herold, 1914)

Engert, Rolf, *Der Grundgedanke in Ibsens Weltanschauung nach Ibsens eigenen Hinweisen an seinem Wegewonnen und entwickelt* (Leipzig: Voigtländer, 1917)

———, *Ibsen als Verkünder des dritten Reiches* (Leipzig: Voigtländer, 1921)

Felden, Emil, *Alles oder Nichts! Kanzelreden über Henrik Ibsens Schauspiele* (Leipzig: Verlag die Tat, 1911)

Fischer, Ernst (pseudonym ?), "Ibsen und das Dritte Reich," in *Zum Geisteskampf der Gegenwart* (Basel: c.1941)

Hallström, Per, *Der Volksfeind* (Munich: Bruckmann, 1916)

La Chesnais, P.G., "Ibsen traducteur de français" in *Edda*, volume XXVIII, no. 1 (1928)

———, "Les sources historiques de 'Empereur et Galileen'" in *Edda*, volume XXXVII, no. 4 (1937)

———, "L'Historicité de 'Empereur et Galileen" in *Edda*, volume XXXVIII (1938 no. 4)

Mayrhofer, Johannes, *Henrik Ibsen: Ein literarisches Charakterbild* (originally published 1911; 2nd ed. Regensburg: Kösel and Pustet, 1921)

Schmitt, Eugen Heinrich, *Ibsen als Prophet* (Leipzig: Fritz Eckardt Verlag, 1908)

Schulze-Berghof, Paul, "Das ethische Zeitgeist in Ibsens Dichtung" pp. 87–91 in *Die Kulturmission unserer Dichtung* (Leipzig: Fritz Eckhardt Verlag, 1908)

———, *Ibsens Kaiser und Galiläer als Zeitsinnbild* (Rudolstadt: Greifenverlag, 1923)

———, *Wettersteinmächte* (Leipzig: Theodor Weicher, 1924)

———, *Zeitgedanken zu Ibsens 'Peer Gynt'* (Leipzig: Oldenburg, 1918)

MAJOR SECONDARY SOURCES

Eggers, Kurt, ed., *Der Kaiser de Römer gegen den König der Juden, aus den Schriften Julians des "Abtrünnigen"* (Berlin: Nordland, 1941)

———, *Der Scheiterhaufen: Worte grosser Ketzer* (Dortmund: Volksschaft Verlag, 1941)

Hoffman, Heinrich, *Hitler wie ich ihn sah* (Munich: Herbst, 1974)

Jetzinger, Franz, *Hitlers Jugend: Phantasien, Lügen—und die Wahrheit* (Vienna: Europa, 1956); translated by Lawrence Wilson as *Hitler's Youth* (London: Hutchinson, 1958)

Kubizek, August, *Adolf Hitler, mein Jugendfreund* (Graz: Leopold Stocker, 2002, unabridged reprint of the 1953 edition), translated as *The Young Hitler I Knew* (Boston: Houghton Mifflin, 1955): abbreviated "Kubizek"

Rabitsch, Hugo, *Aus Adolf Hitlers Jugendzeit* (Munich: Deutscher Volksverlag, 1938); abbreviated "Rabitsch"

Rauschning, Hermann, *Hitler Speaks: a Series of Political Conversations with Adolf Hitler on his Real Aims* (London: Thornton Butterworth Ltd., 1939)

Speer, Albert, *Inside the Third Reich* (New York: Macmillan, 1970)

ENDNOTES

1. AN ENEMY OF THE PEOPLE

p. 1 Judgment against Mr. Hitler: in Eberhard Jäckel and Axel Kuhn, eds. *Hitler: Sämtliche Aufzeichnungen*, 1905–1924, pp. 1227–1228.

p. 1 He boasted of seeing the same play seventeen times, the same opera forty times: Günter Scholdt, *Autoren über Hitler* (Bonn: Bouvier, 1993), pp. 736–737); and *Hitler's Table Talk, 1941–44*, entry for February 22–23, 1942 (London: Weidenfeld and Nicolson, 1973), p. 333.

p. 1 His real classroom was a darkened theater in Linz: That is how Hitler was recalled in a friendly work on his youth by Hugo Rabitsch, a Linz theater director. Hugo Rabitsch, *Aus Adolf Hitlers Jugendzeit* (Munich: Deutscher Volksverlag, 1938).

p. 2 from theater's grip: Schramm preface to Henry Picker, ed., *Hitlers Tischgespräche im Führerhauptquartier 1941–1942* (Stuttgart: Seewald, 1963), p. 27.

p. 2 "extremely partial to the theater": Record of interrogation of Schaub at Nuremberg, December 7, 1946, in *Staatsarchiv*, Nazi criminal interrogations S-35.

p. 2 "Theater always played a leading role in his life": Quoted in Manfred Koch-Hillebrecht, *Homo Hitler: Psychogramm des deutschen Diktators* (Munich: Siedler, 1999), p. 110.

p. 2 was he the Führer's muse?: Paul Lawrence Rose in *Wagner: Race and Revolution* (New Haven: Yale Univerity Press, 1992); Joachim Köhler, *Wagners Hitler: Der Prophet und sein Vollstrecker* (Munich: Karl Blessing, 1997); Fritz C. Redlich, M.D., "The Impact of Richard Wagner on Adolf Hitler", in Peter Ostwald and Leonard S. Zegans, ed., *The Threat to the Cosmic Order: Psychological, Social, and Health Implications of Richard Wagner's Ring of the Nibelung* (Madison, CT: International Universities Press, 1997); also Christine Ann Colin, *Der Meister and der Führer: A Critical Reappraisal of the Thought of Richard Wagner and Adolf Hitler* (College Park, PA: unpublished doctoral dissertation, 1997; M. Brearley, "Hitler and Wagner: The Leader, the Master, and the Jews," in *Patterns of Prejudice* (vol. XXII, 1988), pp. 3–22; and G.C. Windell, "Hitler, National Socialism, and Richard Wagner", in *Penetrating Wagner's Ring: An Anthology* (Rutherford, NJ: 1978), pp. 219–238.

p. 2 Wyndham Lewis . . . wrote in 1939: Wyndham Lewis, *The Hitler Cult* (London: Dent, 1939), p. 61.

p. 3 in the transcripts of Hitler's dinnertime chats: Published in German as *Tischgespräche*; and *Monologe im Führerhauptquartier, 1941–1944* (Hamburg: Albrecht Knaus, 1980).

p. 6 *An Enemy of the People*, Act IV: The English translation of *An Enemy of the People* by Michael Meyer is used here. There are no differences in fundamentals of meaning from the German translations available to Hitler in 1924.

p. 6 "petty tradesman": edition published by Stackpole, 1939; p. 88.

p. 6 This was Cleon: Aristophanes' *The Knights* had lampooned Cleon under the thinly disguised name Paphlagon for having brought the petty outlook of his trade to politics, hitherto an aristocratic preserve. Joseph Greiner, who was acquainted with Hitler at a Vienna men's hostel in 1910, recalled Aristophanes among the latter's reading.

p. 6 a contribution to the *Illustrierte Beobachter*: "Politik der Woche", reprinted as Document 83 of volume III, part 2, *Hitler Reden, Schriften, Anordnungen* covering February 1925 to January 1933 (Munich: K.G. Saur, 1994) p. 399.

p. 7 at least two German versions: The Reclam universal library series published the plays both as a set and individually in pocket size format. S. Fischer put out a rival complete edition of all the plays in ten paperback volumes.

p. 8 how one translator put it: Eva Le Gallienne, *Six Plays by Henrik Ibsen* (New York: Modern Library, 1951), p. viii.

p. 8 Swedish novelist Per Hallström: *Folkfienden* (Stockholm: Bonniers, 1915).

p. 9 in an authorized Nazi collection: edited by Ernst Boepple, *Adolf Hitlers Reden* (1934), pp. 126–127.

p. 9 bears the date May 4, 1923: Jäckel and Kuhn, item no. 525, p. 923.

p. 9 More notes, in Hitler's handwriting, are dated July 20, 1921: Handwritten facsimile in Werner Maser, ed., *Hitlers Briefe und Notizen* (Düsseldorf and Vienna: 1973), pp. 340–341.

p. 10 the chance of forced deportation: Professor Ian Kershaw noted the repercussions of the dilatory Bavarian moves to deport Hitler; once proceedings were instituted the Austrian authorities refused to take back their wayward son. Personal communication to author, December 2, 1998.

p. 10 a curiously titled article in the Nazi party's daily organ: "Ein Volkfeind und seine Bekämpfung" in *Völkischer Beobachter*, June 6, 1923, p. 6.

p. 11 a 1920 pamphlet by his mentor Dietrich Eckart: It appeared as a special issue of *Auf gut deutsch* and bore the subtitle *Laienpredigt über Juden- und Cristentum* (A Lay Preaching about Jewry and Christendom). The Bruno quote was also featured in a short book by Rudolf John Gorsleben, *Die Überwindung des Judentums* ("Overcoming Jewry"), published in Munich by E. Boepple in 1920 (p. 31).

p. 11 Paul de Lagarde had also brandished a rhetorical test tube: Ian Kershaw, *Hitler volume I, 1889–1936 Hubris* (New York: Norton, 1999), citing Alexander Bein, "Der judische Parasit" Bemerkungen zur Semantik der Judenfrage, *Vierteljahrshefte für Zeitgeschichte* 13 (1965), pp. 121–149.

p. 11 "racial tuberculosis of the nations": letter to Konstantin Hierl in Jäckel and Kuhn, p. 156, also p. 176.

p. 12 he again used the formula on May Day 1923: "Das Judentum bedeutet Rassetuberulose der Völker," in Jäckel and Kuhn, item no. 524, p. 918.

p. 12 during his Landsberg jail time: in Jäckel and Kuhn, item no. 654, p. 1242.

p. 12 on the evening of July 10, 1941 he remarked at headquarters: This and the following quotation appear in Martin Broszat, "The Genesis of the Final Solution", *Yad Vashem Studies*, volume XIII (Jerusalem: 1979), pp. 87–88. The Hitler quotation from February 10, 1941, is according to a note by Werner Koeppens among Irving Collection archival items in the Institut für Zeitgeschichte, Munich. I am indebted to Professor Christopher Browning for calling this source to my attention, and for his judgment on its validity.

p. 13 on February 22, 1942 Hitler expounded: *Table Talk*, p. 332.

p. 13 The Jew's life as a parasite: Manheim translation of *Mein Kampf*, p. 305.

p. 14 chat at midday on February 08, 1942: Author's translation of the German from *Tischgespräche*, p. 105; and from *Ein Volksfeind*, volume 7 of *Henrik Ibsens Sämtliche Werke in deutscher Sprache* (Berlin: S. Fischer, 1899–1909), p. 185.

p. 15 a point perennially at issue among Hitler scholars: This question was the focus of the journalist Ron Rosenbaum's study, *Explaining Hitler* (New York: Random House, 1998).

2. "ADOLF READ IBSEN'S DRAMAS IN VIENNA"

p. 20 architecture as Adolf's "mania": August Kubizek, *Adolf Hitler, mein Jugendfreund* (Graz: Leopold Stocker, 2002, unabridged reprint of the 1953 edition), pp. 97–110 on Hitler's architectural mania; this quotation from p. 99.

p. 20 "He found it very difficult to fit into a school situation": Dr. Eduard Huemer delivered this assessment to the court in Munich which tried Hitler for treason in March 1924.

p. 20 a British term then in fashion, Ibsenize: Prefatory "Note" to *An Enemy of the People* (Dover reprint ed.).

p. 21 It reveals much despite an adulatory intent: Hugo Rabitsch, *Aus Adolf Hitlers Jugendzeit* (Munich: Deutscher Volksverlag, 1938).

p. 21 the priest as a "sick old man": Rabitsch, pp. 66–69.

p. 21 simple parochial school teacher: Monologue of January 8–9, 1942; a microfilm photocopy of the original typescript is at the Library of Congress Manuscripts Division, Captured German Documents collection, container 263, reel 163.

p. 22 twelve installments of three hours each: This incident and other details appear in Joseph Greiner, *Das Ende des Hitler-Mythos* (Zürich: Amalthea Verlag, 1947), pp. 46–50. While the meticulous Hitler biographers Brigitte Hamann and Ian Kershaw have cast doubt on aspects of the Greiner source, it may still be used, albeit cautiously, to verify certain facts. Greiner is mentioned as a fellow lodger of Hitler's by Reinhold Hanisch, whom they both knew at a men's hostel in 1910 ("I Was Hitler's Buddy," in *The New Republic*, April 12, 1939, p. 272). With respect to Franz Sales Schwarz, Greiner mentions Hitler's flaunting the black-red-gold tricolor to provoke the priest. That item does not appear in any printed reminiscence until the publication of Hitler's wartime "Table Talk," which came out after the Greiner book. The fair conclusion is that Greiner heard the story in 1910 from Hitler, who repeated it three decades later for the stenographic record that became the Table Talk.

p. 23 recounting the operas he attended: Jäckel and Kuhn, pp. 44–45.

p. 24 a grownup Hitler revered the moment: Kubizek, p. 118; pp. 99–105 in the English translation.

p. 24 provided with a letter of introduction: Joachim Fest, *Hitler* (New York: Harcourt, Brace, Jovanovich, 1974), p. 29.

p. 25 the leading names from Europe and the Americas: *Bericht über den VIII Internationalen Architekten Kongress Wien 1908* (Vienna: Anton Schroll, 1909).

p. 25 he rented a room at No. 29 Stumpfergasse: The landlady, Frau Zakreys, was incidentally Jewish, a fact noted by Gerald Fleming in *Hitler and the Final Solution* (rev. ed., Berkeley and Los Angeles: University of California Press, 1994, p. 6).

p. 26 "I go to his concerts as others go to church": Frederick Oechsner, et al., *This Is the Enemy* (Boston: Little, Brown, 1942), p. 87.

p. 26 staged the Wedekind play during May and June 1908: Kubizek, p. 218; *Wiener Zeitung*, 15 May 1908, p. 5.

p. 26 two performances in late February 1908: *Wiener Zeitung*, February 21, 1908, p. 20; *Wiener Abendpost*, February 26, 1908, p. 6.

p. 27 The same spirit, or *Geist*: The historical Zenobia reigned 267–272; i.e. she and Odenathus, the model for "Apelles," were both long gone by the time Wilbrandt's fictionalized play ends.

p. 29 He supports the Roman emperor Julian the Apostate: Adolf von Wilbrandt, *Der Meister von Palmyra*, ed. by Theodore Henckels (New York: American Book Company, 1900), p. 67.

p. 29 Maximus hints: *The Oxford Ibsen* volume IV, edited and translated by James Walter McFarlane (London: Oxford University Press, 1963), pp. 401–402; hereafter cited as *E&G*. The German text consulted here is volume 5 in *Henrik Ibsens sämtliche Werke in deutscher Sprache* (Berlin: S. Fischer, 1899–1909), p. 247.

p. 31 The prophesied one shows up periodically: *E&G*, pp. 412–413.

p. 32 a rare one month run: *Berlin Tägliche Rundschau*, February 27, 1908, p. 4 and theater listings through March, for a total of 28 recitals.

p. 32 doting favorably on the Julian play: George Bernard Shaw, *Ein Ibsenbrevier: die Quintessenz des Ibsenismus* (Berlin: Fischer, 1908).

p. 32 "The Ethical Spirit of the Times in Ibsen's Works": "Das ethische Zeitgeist in Ibsens Dichtung" pp. 87–91 in *Die Kulturmission unserer Dichtung* (Leipzig: Fritz Eckhardt Verlag, 1908).

p. 32 Another book published in 1908: by Eugen Heinrich Schmitt (Leipzig: Fritz Eckardt, 1908).

p. 32 consecrated an oath: Kubizek, p. 189.

p. 33 August Kubizek recalled: "Die Dramen Ibsens hat Adolf in Wien erlesen, ohne dass er davon einen besonderen Eindruck empfangen hätte. Ich kann mich jedenfalls nicht daran erinnern." Kubizek, pp. 218–219.

p. 33 would likely have been noted before: The derivation of "third Reich" from the Ibsen drama was suggested, then forgotten. Ernst Fischer published it in "Ibsen und das Dritte Reich," the first of four essays in his *Zum Geisteskampf der Gegenwart* (Basel: 1941). Fischer offered this conjecture before the appearance of Kubizek's published memoir stating Hitler had read Ibsen. No one paid any attention.

p. 33 published three years after: Franz Jetzinger, *Hitlers Jugend: Phantasien, Lügen—und die Wahrheit* (Vienna: Europa, 1956); translated by Lawrence Wilson as *Hitler's Youth* (London: Hutchinson, 1958).

p. 34 he did remember Hitler having relished the light dramas of Otto
Ernst: Otto Ernst was the pseudonym of Otto Ernst Schmidt.

p. 34 Jetzinger . . . held back fair credit: Brigitte Hamann, *Hitlers Wien*
(Munich: Piper, 1996) reviewed both accounts and concluded that,
despite mistakes on fine points the Kubizek account remained a
reliable portrait of the young Hitler. Jetzinger's work too is marred
by some error, as regards the Hitler genealogy.

p. 35 *Gespenster* ("Ghosts") played at the Hofburg: Information on shows
from theater listings in *Wiener Zeitung.*

p. 36 Cheap paperback editions were readily available: The point here,
of course, is to not to convey precisely what Henrik Ibsen wrote
but what Adolf Hitler read, in German.

p. 36 quadruple the number: Wolfgang Pasche, *Skandinavische Dramatik
in Deutschland* (Basel and Stuttgart: Helbing and Lichtenhahn,
1979), p. 206.

p. 37 in a memoir published in 1947: Joseph Greiner, *Das Ende des Hitler-
Mythos* (Zürich: Amalthea Verlag, 1947), p. 83 does not elaborate
on what Ibsen plays Hitler favored.

3. PEER GYNT, A.K.A. DIETRICH ECKART

p. 39 *life as I know it, psychology. operetta cum masquerade*: Ibsen
letter to Ernst Motzfeldt, quoted Michael Meyer in *Ibsen: a Biography* (Garden City, New York: Doubleday, 1971), p. 695; Eckart
in *Abermals vor der Höhle des Grossen Krummen* (Berlin: 1915),
pp. 24–25.

p. 40 "a broad, rather brutal chin": *Memoirs of Alfred Rosenberg*, with
commentaries by Serge Lang and Ernst von Schenck (Chicago: Ziff
Davis, 1949), p. 37.

p. 40 Eckart had made a cause of Ibsen: Uwe Englert, *Magus und Rech-
enmeister, Henrik Ibsens Werk auf den Bühnen des Dritten Reiches*
(Tübingen and Basel: Francke, 2001).

p. 40 Eckart appointed himself to rework *Peer Gynt*: The matters of autho-
rization and of royalties still raised questions in the German theater
world long after Eckart's death and well into the Third Reich. Nazi
officials contended that Eckart had permission for his *Peer Gynt*
from Sigurd Ibsen, the playwright's son (Der General Intendant der
Preussischen Staatstheater, March 14, 1938, on reel 138, container
234 of Captured German Documents in the Manuscripts Division,
Library of Congress).

p. 40 Productions proliferated, Eckart's among them: Statistics on performances are given by Uwe Englert and by Sylvia Rauer in her
doctoral dissertation, *Henrik Ibsens "Peer Gynt" als szenisches
Problem* (Free University of Berlin: 1991), pp. 248–263.

p. 40 "Anyone who wishes to understand me fully must know Norway":

Michael Meyer, *Ibsen: a Biography* (Garden City, New York: Doubleday, 1971), p. 17.

p. 41 "a symbol of earth bound man": *Memoirs of Alfred Rosenberg* (Chicago: Ziff-Davis, 1949), p. 38.

p. 41 It is my own life . . . with frightening clarity: Quoted in Wilhelm Grün, *Dietrich Eckart als Publizist* (Munich: Hohenreichen Verlag, 1941), pp. 50, 56–59; see also Paul Wilhelm Becker, *Der Dramatiker Dietrich Eckart* (Cologne, university doctoral dissertation, 1969), pp. 84–85.

p. 41 Eckart secured release by marrying: Inmates of such institutions would be subject to euthanasia during the Third Reich. Eckart wed Rose Marx on September 15, 1913 as noted by Paul Herrmann Wiedeburg in *Dietrich Eckart* (Hamburg: Hanseatischen Verlagsanstalt, 1939), p. 33.

p. 42 Eckart resorted to attacking . . . Morgenstern: Dietrich Eckart, *Ibsen, der grosse Krumme, und ich* (Berlin: Herold, 1914); and *Abermals vor der Höhle des Grossen Krummen* (Berlin: Herold, 1915).

p. 42 ethnic Jewish origins: Hitler called Morgenstern's work "a Jewish translation" in conversational ramblings recorded on February 19–20, 1942; see *Table Talk*, pp. 260–261.

p. 42 Eckart's very first article: "Die Hypnose im Roman," in Rudolf Heinrich Greinz, ed., *Kultur und Literatur Bilder* (Erfurt and Leipzig: 1892), pp. 49–52.

p. 43 The writer of *Peer Gynt* was already a prophet of his time: Paul Schulze-Berghof, *Zeitgedanken zu Ibsens 'Peer Gynt'* (Leipzig: Oldenburg, 1918), pp. 92 and passim.

p. 43 Nietzsche's *Zarathustra*, the "god-man": Paul Schulze-Berghof (1918), pp. 7, 85.

p. 44 Peer Gynt as . . . a Mammon-workshiping: Paul Schulze-Berghof (1918), p. 94.

p. 44 Eckart promoted a pan-German union: Dietrich Eckart, *Abermals*, p. 15.

p. 46 the rhymed verse play *Lorenzaccio*: Dietrich Eckart, *Lorenzaccio, Tragodie in fünf Aufzügen* (Munich: Hoheneichen, 1920).

p. 46 really took himself to be Peer Gynt: Alfred Rosenberg, *Dietrich Eckart: Ein Vermächtnis* (Munich: Eher, 1938), pp. 14, 24; *Obersalzberg: Wanderungen zwischen Gestern und Heute* (Munich: Eher, 1937), p. 45.

p. 47 "like the polar star": Entry from January 16–17, 1942 in *Table Talk*, p. 217.

p. 47 secretaries confirmed: Christa Shroeder, *Er war mein Chef* (Munich: Langen Müller, 1985), p. 65.

p. 48 leaning toward the mystical: Claus-Ekkehard Bärsch, *Die politische Religion des Nationalsozialismus: die religiöse Dimension der NS-Ideologie in den Schriften von Dietrich Eckart, Joseph Goebbels,*

Alfred Rosenberg, und Adolf Hitler (Munich: W. Fink, 1998), pp. 52–91; 145–148.

p. 49 mimeographed typescript: The Library of Congress preserves a copy of the remarkable first edition, which was distributed by the Eher publishing house in Munich.

p. 50 a trend which went back to Johan Fichte: J.G. Fichte, *Die Grundzüge des gegenwärtigen Zeitalters* (1804–1806; ed. by A Diener, Hamburg: 1956), pp. 102 ff.

p. 50 Eckart argued: Dietrich Eckart, *Der Bolschewismus von Moses bis Lenin: Zwiegespräch zwischen Adolf Hitler und mir* (mimeographed typescript, Munich: Eher, 1924), p. 16.

p. 50 Eckart's further Bible study: Dietrich Eckart, *Das ist der Jude: Laienpredigt über Juden und Christentum* (special issue of *Auf gut deutsch*; Munich: Hoheneichen, 1920), p. 59.

p. 51 precedent in denying Christ's Jewishness.: George L. Mosse, "The Occult Origins of National Socialism" in his *The Fascist Revolution: Toward a General Theory of Fascism* (New York: Fertig, 1999; the essay originally appeared in 1961).

p. 51 ("Was Jesus a Jew?"): published also as a 28-page pamphlet in several editions. Widar Wälsung, *War Jesus ein Jude?* (Nuremberg: 1934).

p. 51 Dollinger's illustrated book: Hitler's copy became property of the Nazi party archives in 1937. An illustration of its front cover is included among odds and ends of Hitleriana, including doodles and transcribed monologues, on reel 163, cont. 263 of the Captured German Documents collection in the Manuscripts Division of the Library of Congress. In his evening soliloquy of January 25–26, 1942 Hitler compared Nordic legends to those of the ancient Near East, as did Döllinger at some length in *Baldur und Bibel*. See *Table Talk*, p. 249.

p. 51 Origen, who had passed on a tale: The story appears in the writings of Epiphanius (320–403 C.E.), citing Origen (185–254 C.E.), who had it from the pagan writer Celsus, who in turn alleged he heard it from a Jew in 178 C.E.

p. 51 The Talmud incidentally refers: e.g., Avodah Zarah 2.40d and Shabbath 14.14d in the Jerusalem Talmud, and Targum Sheni on Esther 7.9 in the Babylonian Talmud.

p. 51 gravestone of a Roman soldier: The stone is exhibited in the Bad Kreuznach museum.

p. 52 "The War on Spiritual Teaching": Artur Dinter, *Der Kampf um die Geistlehre* (Leipzig: Matthes, 1921), p. 38.

p. 52 Hitler had caught on by April 21, 1921: Eberhard Jäckel and Axel Kuhn, eds., *Hitler: Sämtliche Aufzeichnungen, 1905–1924* (Stuttgart: Deutsche Verlags-Anstalt, 1980), item #223, p. 357. Hitler's hobby horse of an Aryan, Galilean, non-Jewish Christ was already noteworthy enough by 1921 for inclusion in a novel appearing that year: *Die Sünde wider das Volk* ("The Sin against the People"; Berlin: Oldenburg, 1921), written by Emil Felden, a Catholic priest. A half-educated character called "Adolf Finster" is lampooned on pp. 146–147, carrying on in this precise vein.

p. 53 "The Jew Graetz": It may be doubted whether Hitler really read Graetz or whether he even uttered these exact words as set down by Eckart. Having been quoted at great length in the *Dialogues*, though, he had to have seen fit to read *that* item at some point.

p. 53 a parable-like quality: Bruce Maylath, "The Trouble with Ibsen's Names" in *Names: A Journal of Onomastics*, volume 33, no. 1 (March 1996), pp. 41–58.

p. 53 "Rolf upholds the oath": Alfred Rosenberg devised it as a cryptonym in messages passed by courier. Ian Kershaw, *Hitler 1889–1936 Hubris* (New York: Norton, 1999), p. 226.

p. 54 "Herr Wolf": *Table Talk*, pp. 212–214.

p. 54 nicknamed Wolfchen: According to Hitler's other secretary Christa Schroeder in her pseudonymous memoirs. See Albert Zoller, *Hitler Privat: Erlebnisbericht einer Geheimsekretärin* (Düsseldorf: Drosste, 1949), pp. 142–143.

p. 54 Eckart's exit: Ernst Hanfstaengl, *Unheard Witness* (Philadelphia: J.B. Lippincott, 1957), p. 86; Alfred Rosenberg, *Memoirs* (Chicago: Ziff-Davis, 1949), p. 70; Ian Kershaw, *Hitler 1889–1936 Hubris* (New York: Norton, 1999), p. 155 and notes, p. 651.

p. 54 Eckart . . . reputedly told associates: "The Secret Doctrine" was incidentally the title of a theosophical tract assembled by Madame Helena Blavatsky from prior occult writings. The quotation from Eckart appeared without attribution in *Le Matin des Magiciens* (Paris: Gallimard, 1960; translated as *The Morning of the Magicians*, New York: Stein and Day, 1963, p. 193). This book rightly stressed the importance of magical thinking in Hitler, but is unreliable in many particulars.

p. 55 Hitler attended . . . Peer Gynt: The Hitler reminiscence came on the night of February 20–21, 1942 and is recorded in *Table Talk*, pp. 260–261.

p. 55 its pages pristine: It is included among the books comprising what remains of Hitler's personal library, in the Third Reich Collection at the Library of Congress.

p. 55 *Peer Gynt* held but a low priority: Hitler saw the play in Berlin in March 1920. Years later he said this was his first theater visit after the war, and complained that the "Jewish" translation by Morgenstern still played at Munich (*Table Talk* entry for February 19–20, 1942, pp. 260–261).

4. THE IMITATION OF CHRIST, ET AL.

p. 57 Adolf Hitler in a speech, August 31, 1920: Jäckel and Kuhn, p. 220–221; *E&G*pp. 446; 95. "Two souls live in my breast": From *Faust* Part One, Scene I, "Outside the City Gate".

p. 58 Stensgaard, from *The League of Youth: The Oxford Ibsen*, volume IV, translated by James Walter McFarlane (London: Oxford University Press, 1963), p. 30.

p. 58 Ibsen's first play to be written in Germany: Halvdan Koht, *Life of Ibsen* (New York: Benjamin Blom, 1971), p. 251.

p. 60 Hitler rang out: Jäckel and Kuhn, p. 1211.

p. 61 Hanns Johst, *Der König* (Munich: Albert Langen, 1920). He had seen *König* seventeen times: "Er habe den 'König' siebzehnmal gesehen, er sei by ihm das liebste Stück, mehr: So wolle er, Hitler, einmal untergehen": Günter Scholdt, *Autoren über Hitler: Deutschsprachige Schriftsteller 1919–1945 und ihr Bild vom "Führer"* (Bonn: Bouvier Verlag, 1993), pp. 736–737. John Lukacs called cursory attention to this astonishing statement in *The Hitler of History* (New York: Knopf, 1997), p. 85. A theater schedule in *Völkischer Beobachter* for Thursday, January 13, 1921, p. 5, provides the Kammerspiele venue. The play enjoyed enough readership to warrant a reprinting in 1921, when five thousand copies were in circulation. The story of Johst's scripted monarch bears more than a little resemblance to the reign of Henri Christophe, self-proclaimed ruler of Haiti (r. 1806–1820), including Christophe's suicide.

p. 64 He [Hitler] never ceases from watching himself and playing a conscious part . . . : Otto Strasser, *Hitler and I* (Boston: Houghton Mifflin, 1940), pp. 66–67.

p. 65 Something has gone completely wrong with Adolf: Hitler's German-American press aide Ernst Hanfstaengl recalled the Eckart remarks from 1922 or 1923 in *Hitler: the Missing Years* (New York: Arcade reprint, 1994), p. 83.

p. 65 When I came to Berlin a few weeks ago: Included among Hanfstaengl statements in the wartime Office of Strategic Services *Source Book on Hitler*. The quoted portion was read online at: www.ess.uwe. ac.uk/documents/osssection1.htm.

p. 65 a whip . . . made of rhinoceros hide: One contemporary account gives it as hippopotamus hide. Rudolf Olden, *Hitler* (New York: Covici-Friede, 1936), p. 187.

p. 65 as a costume accessory: E.g., Kurt Ludecke notes the whip in a photograph in *I Knew Hitler*, facing p. 408.

p. 66 I am Marius: Joachim Fest, *Hitler* (New York: Harcourt, Brace, Jovanovich, 1973), p. 196.

p. 66 Hitler could even liken himself . . . to Sulla: Henry A. Murray, M.D., *Analysis of the Personality of Adolph Hitler* (unpublished typescript done for the Office of Strategic Services; Cambridge, MA: Harvard Psychological Clinic, October 1943), p. 20.

p. 69 Hitler ... regarded the Autobahn as his Parthenon: Speer included this item in a memorandum to Joachim C. Fest who then included it in *Hitler* (New York: Harcourt, Brace, Jovanovich, 1973), p. 382.

p. 69 In a published interview Speer confirmed: James P. O'Donnell, "Conversations with Speer," in *Encounter* volume 47, no. 4 (October 1976), pp. 6–16.

p. 69 A likely source appears in *Vers une architecture:* Hitler's middle school French should have been sufficient for him to muddle through Le Corbusier's uncomplicated text in a work consisting mainly of photographs. *Vers une architecture* (reprint; Paris: Arthaud, 1977) was published in English as *Towards a New Architecture* (New York: Payson and Clarke, 1927), see pp. 140–145.

p. 70 Of Goethe's *Faust* he [Hitler] once remarked: Kubizek, p. 218; or pp. 182–183 in English translation.

p. 71 performed again in Vienna on April 25, 1908: *Wiener Zeitung,* April 25, 1908, p. 16.

p. 72 You know the story of the Hound of the Baskervilles: *Table Talk* p. 283 and *Monologe* pp. 258–259.

p. 72 *Der Hund von Baskerville* was current in 1907: The German script was by Ferdinand Bonn (Leipzig: P. Reclam, 1907).

p. 72 A German sound film version: Carl Lamac of the Ondra-Lamac studio adapted Conan Doyle's story as a German screenplay; it starred Peter Voss and Friedrich Kayssler. The novel was translated by Heinrich Darnoc (Stuttgart: Franckh'sche Verlags-Handlung, 1937).

p. 73 There are plenty of Jews with blue eyes and blond hair: *Tischgespräche,* pp. 333–334; *Table Talk,* p. 384.

p. 74 "I am fighting for the work of the Lord": Concluding lines of *MK,* chapter 2.

5. CONNECTING THE DOTS: FROM THE IBSEN CULT TO HITLER

p. 75 "Ibsenites" and their "Ibscene" style: Oxford English Dictionary entry for "Ibsen".

p. 76 Alfred Schuler scrawled in notes: Paul Bishop, "'Mein eigenstens, wärmstes Herzblut will ich preisgeben': Alfred Schuler's Reception of Henrik Ibsen and its Context," in *Oxford German Studies* (volume 28, Oxford: 1999), pp. 153–193.

p. 78 Ibsen owed much to William Archer: Thomas Postlewait, *Prophet of the New Drama: William Archer and the Ibsen Campaign* (Westport, CT: Greenwood Press, 1986); also Kenneth Edward Jansen, *The Ibsen Movement in England: Ibsen Misunderstood* (Athens, OH: University of Ohio Ph.D. dissertation, 1969).

p. 78 Huneker ... elevated Ibsen: James Gibbons Huneker, *Iconoclasts* (New York: Scribner, 1905); and *Egoists* (New York: Scribner, 1909).

p. 78 GBS's 1891 book: George Bernard Shaw, *Ein Ibsenbrevier: die Quintessenz des Ibsenismus* (Berlin: Fischer, 1908).

p. 78 despite the waning of Ibsen productions: Wolfgang Pasche, *Skandinavische Dramatik in Deutschland* (Basel and Stuttgart: Helbing and Lichtenhahn, 1979), pp. 200–201 notes the "Ibsen-Dämmerung," or twilight.

p. 79 Felled by a stroke in 1900: Rüdiger Bernhardt's *Henrik Ibsen und die Deutschen* focused on the life of the playwright in Germany and his influence there up to the time of his death, without discussing the cultist activity which followed thereafter (Berlin: Henschelverlag, 1989).

p. 79 his "political legacy": Mathilde Lucca Prager, *Henrik Ibsens politisches Vermächtnis* (Vienna: Wiener Verlag, 1906). Prager wrote under the pseudonym "Erich Holm."

p. 79 *Ibsen als Erzieher* ("Ibsen as Teacher"): Leipzig: Xenien Verlag, 1908.

p. 79 *Ibsen als Prophet* by Eugen Heinrich Schmitt: Leipzig: Fritz Eckardt Verlag, 1908.

p. 80 "the great magus of the north": Johannes Mayrhofer, *Henrik Ibsen: Ein literarisches Charakterbild* (originally published 1911; 2nd ed. Regensburg: Kösel and Pustet, 1921), p. 1; While admiring Ibsen on the whole Mayrhofer rued (p. 95): "What's the use to us, ultimately, of the prophet of the misty 'third Reich'?" Mayrhofer wrote from a Catholic standpoint and criticized the solar-worshipping apostate Julian in *Der Kaiser des Sonnengottes* (Regensburg: Manz, 1918).

p. 80 about two dozen major books on Ibsen: e.g., the 610 pages of Josef Collins' *Henrik Ibsen: Sein Werk, seine Weltanschauung, sein Leben* (Heidelberg: C. Winter, 1910).

p. 80 Dietrich Ekart's pamphlet war: Dietrich Eckart, *Ibsen, der grosse Krumme, und ich* (Berlin: Herold, 1914); *Abermals vor der Höhle des Grossen Krummen* (Berlin: Herold, 1915); and the prefatory material to Eckart's rendition of *Henrik Ibsens Peer Gynt* (Munich: Hoheneichen, 1917).

p. 81 *Alles oder Nichts!* ("All or Nothing"): Leipzig: Verlag Die Tat, 1911.

p. 81 *Die Weltanschauung Henrik Ibsens:* Leipzig: Xenien Verlag, 1913.

p. 81 Engert's dissertation on Ibsen: Rolf Engert, *Der Grundgedanke in Ibsens Weltanschauung nach Ibsens eigenen Hinweisen an seinem Wegewonnen und entwickelt* (Leipzig: Voigtländer, 1917); see back flyleaf for notice of the book's projected postwar version under the *"Herald"* title.

p. 82 Ibsenism was polarizing: Johannes Mayrhofer stated that as a convinced Catholic he had to reject the cult of the "prophet," in a preface written in late 1920 for a second edition of his *Henrik Ibsen: Ein literarisches Charakterbild* (Regensburg: Kösel and Pustet, 1921).

p. 82 cited favorably by John Maynard Keynes: Keynes put it, "I believe that the future will learn more from the spirit of Gesell than it will from that of Marx." See chapter 23 of Keynes' *General Theory of Employment, Interest, and Money* (London: 1936).

p. 82 No particular group of usurers: The 1917 edition of Engert's book reproduced a a poem by Ibsen in German from 1870, musing about the character and motivations of Judas Iscariot (p. 22), the disciple said to have betrayed Jesus for money. For Jew-baiters, Judas long symbolized all of Jewry. By 1921 when anti-Semitism had emerged from the shadows, Engert took care to delete the poem from his completed book on Ibsen.

p. 82 the title of Bavarian finance minister: Gesell was named finance minister of the so-called Soviet regime. Rolf Engert described the debacle in *Silvio Gesell in München, 1919: Erinnerungen und Dokumente aus der Zeit vor, während, und nach der ersten bayerischen Räterepublik* (Hannover: Fachverlag für Sozialökonomie, 1986).

p. 83 the visionary Joachim of Fiore: Marjorie Reeves, *Joachim of Fiore and the Prophetic Future* (London: SPCK, 1976).

p. 83 *Ibsen als Verkünder des dritten Reiches* ("Ibsen as Herald of the Third Reich"): Leipzig: R. Voigtländer Verlag, 1921.

p. 83 His booklet appeared in 1923: Paul Schulze-Berghof (a.k.a. Paul Schulze) *Ibsens Kaiser und Galiläer als Zeitsinnbild* (Rudolstadt: Greifensverlag, 1923).

p. 84 "a parable . . . of the German cultural soul": Paul Schulze-Berghof (1923), p. 12.

p. 86 "Who really is this Herr Hitler?": Eduard Gugenberger, *Hitlers Visionäre: Die okkulten Wegbereiter des Dritten Reichs* (Vienna: Ueberreuter, 2001), p. 29.

p. 86 Schuler . . . feared Hitler might be insincere: Karl-Heinz Schuler, "Alfred Schuler under der Nationalsozialismus", in *Jahrbuch der deutschen Schillergesellschaft* (volume 41, Stuttgart: 1997), pp. 397–398.

p. 87 Hitler knew enough about Gesell: In a speech given April 21, 1922, in Jäckel and Kuhn, item no. 380, p. 630.

p. 89 on occasion with "kosher": speech in Munich May 24, 1921, Jäckel and Kuhn, item no. 248, p. 411.

p. 90 "Mosaic-Christian tyranny of Sinai": Paul Schulze-Berghof (1923), p. 111.

p. 90 The Roman Caesar with the soul of Christ as leader (*Führer*): Paul Schulze-Berghof, *Wettersteinmächte* (Leipzig: Theodor Weicher, 1924), p. 380.

p. 91 "Heil!—Heil!—Heil!": Paul Schulze-Berghof (1924), p. 571.

6. FROM BERCHTESGADEN, A WORLD DRAMA

p. 93 *I call the book "A World-Drama."*: *The Correspondence of Henrik Ibsen*, ed. Mary Morison, 1905 (republished New York: Haskell, 1970), p. 255.

p. 94 Julian . . . reigned less than two years: Robert Browning, *The Emperor Julian* (Berkeley and Los Angeles: University of California Press, 1976), pp. 228–232.

p. 94 Schiller's published letter: The text of this letter was quoted in Ernst Fischer, *Zum Geisteskampf der Gegenwart* (Basel: 1941), p. 11.

p. 94 "the romantic on the throne": David Friedrich Strauss, *Der Romantiker auf dem Throne der Cäsaren* (republished Bonn: Emil Strauss, 1896); an interpretation of this essay as a covert critique of the Prussian monarch appeared in the July 1848 issue of *Edinburgh Review*.

p. 94 "Neander focused on Julian": *Ueber Kayser Julianus und sein Zeitalter*. Neander also gave coverage to Julian in his general church history *Allgemeine Geschichte der Christlichen Religion und Kirche*.

p. 94 Auer had . . . written a major tome: J.E. Auer, *Kaiser Julian der Abtrünnige im Kampfe mit dem Kirchenvätern seiner Zeit* (Vienna: 1855).

p. 94 Kettenburg's *Julianus Apostata*: Kuno von der Kettenburg, *Julianus Apostata: Tragödie* (Berlin: Salfeld, 1812).

p. 94 by . . . Ingersoll: Charles Jared Ingersoll, *Julian: A Tragedy in Five Acts* (Philadelphia: Carey & Lea, 1831).

p. 95 Ibsen . . . refused to read: Halvdan Koht, *Life of Ibsen* (New York: Benjamin Blom, 1971), p. 277.

p. 95 Riotte released: Hermann Riotte, *Julian der Abtrünnige, Trauerspiel in fünf Akten* (Leipzig: Ferber & Seydel, 1870).

p. 95 verses rhymed by . . . Seeberg: P. Seeberg, *Kaiser Julian, der Abtrünnige: Trauerspiel in fünf Akten* (Berlin: L. Rauh, 1874).

p. 96 Julian as . . . superstitious: R.C. Blockley noted the criticism of the historian Ammianus Marcellinus toward Julian in this regard, in *Ammianus Marcellinus* (Brussels: Latomus, 1975), p. 77.

p. 96 another ancient source states: P.G. la Chesnais, "Les sources historiques de 'Empereur et Galileen'" in *Edda*, volume XXXVII, no. 4 (1937), p. 334.

p. 99 the *Kulturkampf*: Alan Palmer, *Bismarck* (New York: Scribner, 1976), p. 167.

p. 99 writing with . . . Brandes, as an imagined reader: Ibsen letter to Frederick Hegel, July 12, 1871, in *The Correspondence of Henrik Ibsen*, pp. 215–216; also Georg Brandes, "Aus meinen Lebenserinnerungen," in *Die Neue Rundschau*, September 1923, p. 818.

p. 99 A refreshing lift . . . at Berchtesgaden: Letter of August 8, 1872, in *The Correspondence of Henrik Ibsen*, p. 243.

p. 100 a letter to . . . Daae: Item no. 100 in *The Correspondence of Henrik Ibsen*, p. 249.

p. 100 Ibsen . . . told his publisher: Item no. 101 in *The Correspondence of Henrik Ibsen*, p. 250.

p. 101 a chagrined letter to Daae: Item no. 103 in *The Correspondence of Henrik Ibsen*, pp. 254–255.

p. 101 "the most strictly historical": William Archer, *The Collected Works of Henrik Ibsen* (New York: Scribner's, 1910–1913), volume V, p. xvii.

p. 102 only minimal direct resort to other ancient texts: P.G. la Chesnais, "Les sources historiques de 'Empereur et Galileen'," in *Edda*, volume XXXVII, no. 4 (1937), pp. 543–545.

p. 102 Lines from an essay by Julian: These lines consist of the paired biblical allusions from Deuteronomy and the Gospel of St. John which Hitler too would later paraphrase in tandem; see chapter 8 here.

p. 102 Ibsen . . . via a secondary source . . . Albert de Broglie: P.G. la Chesnais, "Les sources historiques de 'Empereur et Galileen'," in *Edda*, volume XXXVII, no. 4 (1937), pp. 547–548.

p. 102 "I . . . made extracts from . . . ecclesiastical history": Letter to Roman Wierner of July 07, 1899, item no. 235 in *The Correspondence of Henrik Ibsen*, p. 453.

p. 102 "translation from French": P.G. la Chesnais, "Ibsen traducteur de français" in *Edda*, volume XXVIII, no. 1 (1928), pp. 97–116 ; also P.G. la Chesnais, "Les sources historiques de 'Empereur et Galileen'" in *Edda*, volume XXXVII, no. 4 (1937), p. 552; P.G. La Chesnais, "L'Historicité de 'Empereur et Galileen" in *Edda*, volume XXXVIII (1938 no. 4), pp. 549 ff.; and Paulus Svendsen in "Om Ibsens kilder til "Kejser og Galilaer," *Edda*, XXXIII.2, 1933, pp. 230, 251, and P.G. La Chesnais, "L'Historicité de 'Empereur et Galileen" in *Edda*, volume XXXVIII (1938 no. 4), p. 564.

p. 109 Gregory complained: Gregory Nazinanzen (Gregory of Nazinanzus) "First Invective against the Emperor" paragraphs 58 and 61, translated by Charles William King, in *Julian the Emperor* (London: Bell and Sons, 1888), pp. 33–25.

p. 110 first German translation: George B. Bryan, *An Ibsen Companion* (Westport, Connecticut: Greenwood Press, 1984), p. 86.

p. 111 Fastenau . . . and 1905: Johann B. Fastenau, *Julian der Abtrünnige: Roman aus dem 4 christlichen Jahrhundert* (Passau: Waldbauer, 1888); Marie Tyrol, *Kaiser Julian der Abtrünnige: Historischer Roman* (Leipzig: W. Friedrich, 1889); Felix Dahn, *Julian der Abtrünnige* (Leipzig: Breitkopf & Härtel, 1893 and 1898); Nikolaus Heim, *Christus Victor: Kampf und Sieg der Kirche Jesu unter Kaiser Julian dem Apostatem* (Kempten: Koesel, 1902); Wilhelm Vollert, *Kaiser Julians religiose und philosophische Ueberzeugung* (Gütersloh: Bertelsmann,

1899); G. Dittmar, *Julian Apostata: Tragödie* (Elberfeld: 1876); von Malsen, *Kaiser Julian: Ein Trauerspiel in fünf Akten* (Stuttgart: 1881); Adam Trabert, *Kaiser Julian der Abtrünige: dramatisches Gedicht* (Vienna: 1894); Marie von Najmájer, *Kaiser Julian: Trauerspiel in fünf Akten*; and Hermann Lüdke, *Kaiser Julian: Dramatische Dichtung in 5 Aufzügen* (Leipzig: Wigand, 1905).

p. 111 August Strindberg paid tribute: In the German theatrical review *Die neue Rundschau*, vol. 17 (July 1906), pp. 858–873, and republished in Munich and Leipzig in 1918 by G. Müller in the series *Historische Miniaturen*.

p. 111 Carl Jung was drawn . . . to Julian: Richard Noll, *Aryan Christ* (New York: Random House, 1997), pp. xv, 67, 98, 109, 134, 309; and Noll, *The Jung Cult: Origins of a Charismatic Movement* (Princeton: Princeton University Press, 1994).

p. 111 Stories by . . . Merezhkovsky: Adam Josef Cüppers, *Die Töchter des Schatzmeisters: Erzählung aus der Zeit Julians des Abtrünnigen*; Gerhard Hennes, *Der Sieger: Erzählung aus dem 4. Jahrhundert*; Therese Kellner, *Der Sieg des Kreuzes: Erzählung aus der Zeit des Kaisers Julian des Abtrünnigen*. All were published in Cologne by Bachem in 1910; Johannes Geffcken, *Kaiser Julianus* (Leipzig: Dieterich'sche Verlagsbuchhandlung—Theodor Weicher, 1914); Johannes Mayrhofer, *Der Kaiser des Sonnengottes* (Regensburg: Manz, 1918); Friedrich Doldinger, *Kaiser Julian, der Sonnenbekenner* (Stuttgart: Christengemeinschaft, 1926); *Julian Apostata: Der letzte Hellene auf dem Throne der Cäsaren* (Leipzig: Schulze, 1918; translated by Carl von Gütschow).

p. 111 Savitri Devi: Savitri Devi, *A Warning to the Hindus* (Calcutta: Brachmachari Bijoy Krishna Hindu Mission, 1939). A subsequent, post–World War II book by her (*The Lightning and the Sun*) extolled Hitler as a supra-historical reincarnation of the Egyptian pharoah Akhnaton and of Genghis Khan; Philip Käte, *Julianus Apostata in der deutschen Literatur* (Berlin and Leipzig: Walter de Gruyter, 1929).

p. 112 I really hadn't known how clearly a man like Julian: *Table Talk*, p. 317.

7. AN ALLEGORY OF THE TIMES

p. 115 *I have seen the characters: The Correspondence of Henrik Ibsen.*

p. 115 Degrelle . . . observed: Degrelle's piece "The Enigma of Hitler" appeared in *The Journal of Historical Review* (May/June 1994, p. 24), an outlet generally apologetic towards the Nazis, but there are no reasons to doubt the Degrelle recollection.

p. 118 Nabokov's novel *Lolita* . . . followed a very similar story: Michael Marr, *The Two Lolitas* (London: Verso, 2005).

p. 118 Camus' . . . Diderot: René Stolbach, a graduate student in French Literature at Johns Hopkins University, made this discovery about Camus and Diderot which he revealed in a seminar paper in 1967.

p. 124 Julian scolds the man: *E&G*, p. 206.

p. 124 I'm as much in the dark as ever: *E&G*, pp. 219, 225.

p. 125 I was blind then: *E&G*, p. 254.

p. 125 exposure to searing gas: The official chronology of Hitler's war record is included as item no. 56 in Jäckel and Kuhn, pp. 84–86. In *Mein Kampf* Hitler identified the chemical as captured stocks of German yellow cross gas, used by the British against their adversaries. This was stated at his trial, on February 26, 1924.

p. 126 begun an autobiography during 1922: Robert Payne, *The Life and Death of Adolf Hitler* (New York and Washington: Praeger, 1973), p. 176. Payne cites no source for the abortive autobiographical attempt.

p. 126 a journalist's report in early 1923: Ludwell Denny, "France and the German Counterrevolution," in *The Nation* (volume CXVI, 1923), pp. 295–297.

p. 126 statement to a Bavarian court on February 26, 1924: Jäckel and Kuhn, item #605, p. 1064.

p. 127 In *Mein Kampf* the tale was further reworked: *MK*, Manheim translation, p. 203.

p. 127 *The Eyewitness (Der Augenzeuge)*: reprinted Berlin: Aufbau-Verlag, 1973

p. 131 The wreath is seen . . . in photographs showing Hitler: Hans Kallenbach, *Mit Adolf Hitler auf Festung Landsberg* (Munich: Parcus, 1933), photographs facing p. 161; Otto Lurker, *Hitler hinter Festungsmauern* (Berlin: Mittler, 1933), plate 13.

p. 131 Hoffmann also recalled . . . a wreath: Heinrich Hoffmann, *Hitler wie ich ihn sah* (Munich: Herbig, 1974), p. 40.

p. 132 The emperor is thinking of making you his successor: *E&G*, pp. 223–224.

p. 133 He called himself but a "drummer": Ian Kershaw, *Hitler 1889–1936: Hubris* (New York: Norton, 1999), pp. 183–185. Hitler as self-proclaimed "drummer" was treated fully by Albrecht Tyrell in *Vom Trommler zum Führer* (Munich: Fink, 1975).

p. 133 Part One, Act III of *Emperor and Galilean*: *E&G*, pp. 256–260.

p. 134 *Das dritte Reich,* written by Arthur Moeller van den Bruck: Mary Agnes Hamilton, Introduction to "Germany's Third Empire" (a 1934 translation by E.O. Lorimer of *Das dritte Reich*). See also Fritz Stern, *The Politics of Cultural Despair; a Study in the Rise of the Germanic Ideology* (Berkeley, CA: University of California Press, 1961).

p. 135 "Third Reich" as an exclusively Nazi patent.: e.g., in the title of a 1927 Goebbels tract, *Wege ins Dritte Reich: Briefe und Aufsatze für Zeitgenossen* (Munich: Eher, 1927).

8. DEATH IMITATES ART: THE SACRIFICE OF GELI RAUBAL

p. 137 mid-morning on September 19, 1931: In April 1992 a masterful piece of sleuthing by Ron Rosenbaum appeared in *Vanity Fair*, spotlighting Raubal's death which also made the fulcrum event in Rosenbaum's *Explaining Hitler* (1998). Anna Maria Sigmund in *Des Führers bester Freund: Adolf Hitler, seine Nicht Geli Raubal, und der "Ehrenarier" Emil Maurice—eine Dreiecksbeziehung* (Munich: Heyne, 2003) offered useful background material and a review of the forensics surrounding the death. Here is added the finding of *Kaiser und Galiläer*, Part One, Act V as paradigm for the Hitler relationship to Raubal and part of his formula for her murder.

p. 137 locked from the inside: It made for the very stuff of popular crime fiction—detective stories by John Dickson Carr had featured corpses found alone in bolted rooms, after which Agatha Christie adopted the device for *The Mysterious Affair at Styles* (1921).

p. 138 "The special quality of Hitler's affection": Kurt Lüdecke, *I Knew Hitler* (New York: Scribner's, 1937), p. 178.

p. 138 An aide brings word to Julian: *E&G*, p. 268.

p. 139 "an empty headed little slut": Ernst Hanfstaengl, *Hitler: The Missing Years* (London: 1967; New York: Arcade reprint, 1994), p. 162.

p. 140 Geli remaining as commanded at the Munich apartment: Anna Maria Sigmund, *Des Führers bester Freund: Adolf Hitler, seine Nicht Geli Raubal, und der "Ehrenarier" Emil Maurice—eine Dreiecksbeziehung* (Munich: Heyne, 2003), p. 167.

p. 140 According to the Führer's valet, Heinz Linge: Linge as quoted in Erich Kuby, *Die Russen in Berlin, 1945* (Munich: Scherz, 1965), p. 204.

p. 140 According to Heinrich Hoffmann: *Hitler wie ich ihn sah* (Munich: Herbig, 1974), pp. 127–133.

p. 140 the Deutscher Hof hotel: Ron Hansen, author of the novel *Hitler's Niece* (New York: Harper Collins, 1999), has rightly suggested this stay at the Deutscher Hof as one of the more suspicious aspects of the episode (e-mail post to this author, September 2, 1999). However, Hansen's fictional treatment commits the error of having Hitler personally shoot Geli.

p. 141 interviewed by an officer Sauer,: Ron Rosenbaum, "Hitler's Doomed Angel", *Vanity Fair*, vol. 55, no. 4 (April 1992), pp. 178ff, 238 ff.; Heinrich Hoffman, *Hitler wie ich ihn sah* (Munich: Herbst, 1974), p. 129; Konrad Heiden, *Der Fuehrer: Hitler's Rise to Power* (New York: Knopf, 1936; republished London, H. Pordes, 1967), p. 307; Felix Gross, *Hitler's Girls, Guns, and Gangsters* (London: Hurst & Blackett, 1941), pp. 24 ff.

p. 142 the locked door story: Ronald Hayman wrote in his scrupulous study of the case, "Perhaps the truth behind the confusion is that the door was not locked at the time of the shooting. It may have been locked by the Nazis just in time for them to break it down before the police arrived." *Hitler and Geli* (London: Bloomsbury, 1997), p. 184.

p. 143 autopsy . . . was waived: Otto Wagener wrote in error after World War II that an autopsy had been conducted, and with Hitler in attendance. But having a family member present, and a non-medical practitioner at that, would violate elementary forensic procedure. Wagener was in personal touch with Hitler a week after Geli's death although apparently neither on the day of the event nor during the days immediately following. It may be that Hitler had misinformed Wagener about an autopsy. Otto Wagener, *Hitler—Memoirs of a Confidant* (translation of *Hitler aus nächster Nähe*), edited by Henry Ashby Turner, Jr. (New Haven and London: Yale University Press, 1985), p. 226.

p. 143 Hitler responded to a hostile story: Full text of the Hitler letter is in *Hitler Reden, Schriften, Anordnungen* covering February 1925-January 1933 (Munich: K.G. Saur, 1996), volume IV, part 2, pp. 109–111.

p. 143 withdrew . . . for three days: Anna Maria Sigmund, *Des Führers bester Freund: Adolf Hitler, seine Nichte Geli Raubal, und der "Ehrenarier" Emil Maurice—eine Dreiecksbeziehung* (Munich: Heyne, 2003), pp. 182–183; Albert Zoller (pseudonym for Christa Schroeder), *Hitler Privat: Erlebnisbericht einer Gehimsekretärin* (Düsseldorf: Drosste, 1949), pp. 89, 92.

p. 144 dialogue . . . between Julian and an aide, Sallust: *E&G*, pp. 252–253.

p. 148 memoirs of Heinrich Hoffman: *Hitler wie ich ihn sah* (Munich: Herbig, 1974, p. 130). "Dr. Kurt Krueger," the pseudonym of a purported psychoanalyst of Hitler, also had his "patient" ascribing to Angelika Raubal the decision for the Vienna burial. "My sister made all the arrangements, and I did not have the heart to interfere" (*Inside Hitler*, New York: Avalon, 1941).

p. 150 his letter to the *Münchener Post*: *Hitler Reden, Schriften, Anordnungen* covering February 1925-January 1933 (Munich: K.G. Saur, 1996), volume IV, part 2, pp. 110–111.

p. 151 "That is why she had to go": *E&G*, p. 279.

p. 151 Constantius . . . appoints Julian: *E&G*, p. 304.

p. 152 Wagener recalled enough: That is, in the late 1940s Wagener was remembering what he had already written down, which is always easier than remembering someone's exact words over a decade later. This is the view of Henry Ashby Turner, Jr., in his preface to *Hitler—Memoirs of a Confidant* (the translation of *Hitler aus nächster Nähe*, New Haven and London: Yale University Press, 1985).

p. 152 Wagener reconstructed direct quotations: The economic historian Ralf Banken has examined the policy aspects of Otto Wagener's memoir and found its information consistent with other contemporary sources, thereby buttressing the overall reliability of Wagener as an observer; in "An der Spitze aller Künste steht d. Staatskunst" (Das Protokoll der NSDAP-Wirtschaftsbesprechungen Februar/ März 1931; unpublished draft article kindly supplied by Ralf Banken to this author, August 2005).

p. 152 *Emperor and Galilean*, Part Two, Act III: *E&*, p. 402; Otto Wagener, *Hitler—Memoirs of a Confidant*, p. 222.

p. 153 "Against the Galileans": "Against the Galileans" translated by Wilmer Cave Wright in *The Works of the Emperor Julian* (Loeb Classics, London: William Heinemann, 1913), pp. 396–399.

p. 154 I really hadn't known how clearly: *Table Talk*, p. 76.

p. 155 The Führer . . . quibbled about . . . *logos*: Otto Wagener, *Hitler— Memoirs of a Confidant*, pp. 295; 314–316. A broad meaning has attached to *logos* ever since the pre-Socratic thinker Heraclitus. But Hitler was no Greek scholar. What matters most in present context, however, is not the widespread discussion of what *logos* meant but instead the source for the curious Hitlerian juxtaposition of the St. John *logos* phrase and the First Commandment.

p. 155 a mystical tract on rebirth . . . in Hitler's . . . library: Hans Görges, *Der zerfallene Mensch: drei Bücher von Tod und Wiedergebürt* (Rudolstadt: Greifenverlag, 1926), p. 79. The same small publisher had also released Paul Schulze-Berghof's book hailing *Emperor and Galilean* as prophecy. Hitler's copy of the Görges book, inscribed by the author on the title page, is kept in the Third Reich Collection at the Library of Congress.

Hitler could on occasion draw selectively on other gospels as well. Like Jesus he once reminded a disciple that "I have come to Germany not to bring peace but a sword—" words taken from Matthew 10:34, as quoted by Robert G.L. Waite in *The Psychopathic God*, p. 32.

p. 156 "So, now begins the battle": Anna Maria Sigmund, *Des Führers bester Freund: Adolf Hitler, seine Nicht Geli Raubal, und der "Ehrenarier" Emil Maurice—eine Dreiecksbeziehung* (Munich: Heyne, 2003), p. 191.

p. 156 She had to sacrifice herself for this: Otto Wagener, *Hitler—Memoirs of a Confidant*, pp. 222–223.

p. 156 five English-language fiction and non-fiction works: Ronald Hayman, *Hitler and Geli* (London: Bloomsbury, 1997); Kristine Rusch, *Hitler's Angel* (New York: St. Martin's, 1998); Ron Rosenbaum, *Explaining Hitler* (New York: Random House, 1998); Ron Hansen, *Hitler's Niece* (New York: Harper, 1999); Andrew Nagorski, *Last Stop Vienna* (New York: Simon & Schuster, 2003), pp. 248–256.

9. FÜHRER AND GALILEAN

p. 159 *Emperor and Galilean,* Part One, Act V: *E&G,* p. 355.

p. 162 he took it as an omen: Heinrich Hoffmann, *Hitler Was My Friend* (translation of *Hitler wie ich ihn sah*; London: Burke, 1955), pp. 135–137.

p. 162 "Hitler Breaks Hammer. Germans See Evil Omen": *New York Times,* October 16, 1933, p. 1.

p. 162 German press, . . . was more upbeat: News articles were "Kein Wiederaufstieg ohne Wiedererweckung deutcher Kultur und Kunst"; "Der Hammerschlag des Führers"; Die Grundsteinlegung zum ‚Haus der Deutschen Kunst' and "Tag der Deutschen Kunst" in *Völkischer Beobachter,* October 17, 1933.

p. 163 commissioned an artist to sketch the scene: An album of these sketches in chalk is among the surviving items of Hitler's personal library which are housed in the collections of the Library of Congress.

p. 164 "With victory in your heart . . . you must surmount the Galilean": *E&G,* p. 311.

p. 164 I will in no way tolerate malicious attacks on the churches of the Christians: *E&G,* pp. 324–325.

p. 165 of our national morality: Adolf Hitler, *Speeches and Proclamations, 1932–1945,* edited by Max Domarus (Wauconda, Illinois: Bolchazy-Carducci, 1990–1997), volume I, p. 250.

p. 165 a concordat with the Holy See: John Cornwell, *Hitler's Pope* (New York: Viking, 1999), chapters 4–8.

p. 166 told his aide Kurt Lüdecke: Kurt Lüdecke, *I Knew Hitler* (New York: Scribner's, 1937), pp. 520–521.

p. 166 We are not out against the hundred and one different kinds: quoted in *The Nazi War Against the Catholic Church* (Washington: U.S. National Catholic Welfare Conference, 1943), p. 27.

p. 166 Catholic sources for 1936: Miles, pseud. *Hitler gegen Christus* (Paris: 1936), pp. 166–191; see also John Cornwell, *Hitler's Pope* (New York: Viking, 1999), pp. 157–166 on Pacelli's reaction to Hitler's betrayal of the concordat.

p. 167 *Emperor and Galilean* Part Two, Act III: *E&G,* pp. 384, 385, 388.

p. 168 Part One, Act IV of *Emperor and Galilean: E&G,* pp. 283, 285.

p. 168 the *limes* project: Dieter Bettinger and Martin Büren, comp., *Der Westwall: Die Geschichte der deutschen Westbefestingingen im Dritten Reich* volume 1 (Osnabrück: Biblio Verlag, 1990), pp. 99 ff.

p. 169 Try, powerless as you are: *E&G,* p. 372.

p. 169 Julian sends his general Jovian: *The Oxford Ibsen,* volume IV, translated by James Walter McFarlane (London: Oxford University Press, 1963), pp. 389–391.

p. 170 Hitler's analogous action: Saul Friedländer, *Nazi Germany and the Jews: Volume I, The Years of Persecution 1933–1939* (New York: Harper Collins, 1997), pp. 269–278). False flag provocations were Nazi stock in trade. A duped assassin need not even know for whom he was working when induced to commit his deed.

p. 170 "sole instigator": Otto Dietrich, *Hitler* (Chicago: Regnery, 1955), p. 41.

p. 171 The king of Persia has offered me tenders of peace: *E&G*, p. 402.

p. 172 Hitler . . . confided to a military adjutant: The adjutant was Colonel Rudolf Schmundt. Hitler's remark was recalled at the Nuremberg war crimes trials. *Trial of the Major War Criminals* (Nuremberg: 1947–1949) volume 7, pp. 158–160.

p. 173 Wehrmacht general Günther Blumentritt: Günther Blumentritt in Seymour Freidin, et al., ed. *The Fatal Decisions* (New York: William Sloan, 1956), pp. 39–40.

p. 173 stocks of grain and oil in Ctesiphon?: *E&G*, p. 427.

p. 174 We are going to modify slightly our line of advance: *E&G*, p. 437.

p. 175 Directive No.21 issued on December 18, 1940: The order is officially catalogued by the German *Bundesarchiv* as OKW/WFSt./Abt.L (I) Nr. 33408/40; text given in Werner Haupt, *Sturm auf Moskau, 1941* (Friedberg: Podzun-Pallas Verlag, 1986).

p. 175 he stated an intention to destroy the city along with its wharves: A memorandum of September 29, 1941 by the *Kriegsmarine* (navy) chief of staff records the naval command's failed attempts to reason with Hitler about sparing at least the Leningrad harbor and wharf facilities. The translated text is given in Robert Payne, *The Life and Death of Adolf Hitler* (New York: Praeger, 1973), p. 437.

p. 176 Franz Halder recorded his dismay in a war diary: Franz Halder, *The Halder War Diary* (Novato, California: Presidio, 1988) is the edition of Halder's *Kriegstagebuch* consulted here. Since other editions exist, the portions cited in text are given by date rather than page number.

p. 177 "But for one . . . decision, Germany could have won . . . in . . . 1941": jacket blurb to R.H.S. Stolfi, *Hitler's Panzers East: World War II Reinterpreted* (Norman, OK: University of Oklahoma Press, 1991).

p. 177 John Lukacs confessed: John Lukacs, *The Last European War: September 1939-December 1941* (Garden City, Long Island: Doubleday, 1976), p. 146; Klaus Reinhardt, *Die Wende vor Moskau: Das Scheitern der Strategie Hitlers in Winter 1941/42* (Stuttgart: Deutsche Verlags-Anstalt, 1972); also Alan F. Wilt, "Hitler's Late Summer Pause in 1941" in *Military Affairs* vol. 48 (December 1981), pp. 187–191. John Erikson, Albert Seaton, and Alan Clark in their histories of the Russo-German war were also at a loss to explain Hitler's move in rational military terms.

p. 177 much discussed southward move of Guderian's tanks: The turn south toward Kiev of panzers under general Heinz Guderian has been exhaustively studied by Bryan I. Fugate in *Operation Barbarossa* (Novato, California: Presidio, 1984).

p. 178 Peace feelers from a shaken Stalin: The peace feeler was revealed to the world by Dmitri Volkogonov in *Stalin: Triumph and Tragedy* (London: Weidenfeld and Nicolson, 1991), pp. 412–413. Additional material culled by Volkogonov from the Soviet archives is reviewed in Laurence Rees, *War of the Century: When Hitler Fought Stalin* (New York: The New Press, 1999), pp. 52–55. The Soviet approach was made through the Bulgarian ambassador to Moscow, Ivan Stamenov, who handled German interests. He met with Pavel Sudoplatov, an envoy of Stalin's secret policeman Lavrenti Beria. Stamenov on his own initiative urged the Soviets to stand firm against Germany.

p. 178 from *Emperor and Galilean*, Part Two, Act V: *E&G*, pp. 454–455.

p. 178 in February 1945, Hitler looked back and lamented 1941: *The Testament of Adolf Hitler: The Hitler-Bormann Documents, February–April 1945* (London: Cassell, 1961) p. 74. Looking back, Hitler judged he could have won had he started Barbarossa on May 15. He blamed the delay, without cause, on Mussolini. The later start made the more reason for keeping to plan and avoiding the diversions of July and August 1941.

p. 179 Part Two, Act II of Ibsen's play: *E&G*, pp. 358–360.

p. 180 The Galileans in Caesaria shall pay with their blood: *E&G*, p. 381.

p. 181 the Führer rehashed: *Monologe*, p. 263.

10. FINALLY, A SOLUTION TO THE "FINAL SOLUTION"

p. 183 "The Roman's spear from Golgotha!": A Hitler quotation showing interest in the spear as early as 1912 is not attributed to any source in Trevor Ravenscroft, *The Spear of Destiny* (New York: Putnam, 1973), p. 7. The online Wikipedia entry "Spear of Destiny" relates Hitler's removal of the relic from Vienna to Nuremberg, although again without source attribution.

p. 184 Julian . . . mentions these treatises: *E&G*, pp. 374–375.

p. 184 The Führer's fare: He ascribed his fare by a reference to ancient practice: "There's an interesting document from the time of the Caesars showing how the armies of that time were nourished without meat" (entry for 05 November 1941, *Monologe*, p. 127. The "interesting document" was no doubt Tacitus, *Annals*, XIV, 24.1.

p. 184 Martin Bormann did some limited editing: Richard C. Carrier, "Hitler's Table Talk: Troubling Finds" in *German Studies Review*, volume 26, no. 3 (2003), pp. 561–576.

p. 185 Hitler . . . put the name of Julian on record: *Hitler's Table Talk, 1941–44* (London: Weidenfeld and Nicolson, 1973), p. 76.

p. 185 Genghis Khan: Richard Breitman discovered Himmler's fascination with Genghis Khan, revealed in *The Architect of Genocide: Himmler and the Final Solution* (New York: Knopf, 1991) pp. 39–43.

p. 185 gentile makeup of Jesus' homeland: Since his tutelage under Eckart in the early 1920s more reinforcing literature to that effect had come into the Hitler library. One such item was Max Erich Winkel's *Der Sohn* ("The Son"; Berlin: Kampmann, 1938; especially pp. 26–32 and 382–387 on Jesus as a Galilean and hence supposedly a non-Jew). The author had incidentally written a previous book (1928) touting a scientific basis for astrology. Winkel presented Hitler an inscribed copy for Christmas 1939, now housed in the Third Reich Collection at the Library of Congress. Hitler need not have read it deeply; the book's point is summed up in a subtitle: *Die evangelischen Quellen und die Verkündigung Jesu von Nazareth in ihrer ursprünglichen Gestalt und ihre Vermischung mit jüdischem Geist.*

p. 186 "spirit of Judas" . . . in Paul Schulze-Berghof's treatise: Paul Schulze-Berghof (1923), p. 65.

p. 187 The book with the sayings of emperor Julian: *Table Talk*, p. 87.

p. 187 What Christianity wrote against Julian: Was das Christentum gegen Julian geschrieben hat, ist dasselbe Wortgeblödel, welches die jüdische Schriftum über uns ergossen hat, während die Schriften des Julian reine Wahrheiten sind. In *Hitlers Tischgespräche im Führerhauptquartier* (Stuttgart: Seewald, 1976), p. 96.

p. 188 postwar German editor . . . guessed: *Hitlers Tischgespräche im Führerhauptquartier*, ed. by Henry Picker (Stuttgart: Seewald Verlag, 1963), p. 168. Bidez's book was originally published in Paris by Les Belles Lettres.

p. 188 over seven hundred pages of text in Greek: *The Works of the Emperor Julian*, with an English translation by Wilmer Cave Wright, in three volumes, Loeb Classics series (London and New York: Heinemann, 1913).

p. 189 *Der Scheiterhaufen* . . . a thin, large-print volume: Kurt Eggers, ed., *Der Scheiterhaufen: Worte grosser Ketzer* (Dortmund: Volksschaft Verlag, 1941). Eggers's own attempts at writing for the stage had failed to meet critical acclaim, most notably a play based on the biblical story of Job. It bombed in 1934. After Eggers's combat death in 1943 the propaganda and psychological warfare component of the Waffen-SS was named for him, *Kriegsberichter Regiment Kurt Eggers.*

p. 190 Eggers . . . had visited a library: The available German version was *Kaiser Julians Bücher gegen die Christen*, as translated by Karl Johannes Neumann (Leipzig: Teubner, 1880). Eggers failed to grant credit to this source. Also available was *Die Religionsphilosophie Kaiser Julians in seinen Reden auf König Helios und die Göttermutter*, with German translation by Georg Mau (Leipzig: Teubner,

1907). The scholar Johan Rudolf Asmus had moreover prepared *Kaiser Julians philosophische Werke* for a wide German readership (Leipzig: Dürr, 1908).

p. 193 *Kaiser Julian und das Judentum*: Leipzig: J.C. Hinrichs, p. 40.

p. 195 the German text of his remarks: Richard C. Carrier, "Hitler's Table Talk: Troubling Finds" in *German Studies Review*, volume 26, no. 3 (2003), pp. 569–570.

p. 198 Hitler's subsequent remarks: These quotations give the author's own translation of the German text as in *Monologe* pp. 302–303; the English translation given in *Table Talk* introduced wording not present in the German text. The English version of Ibsen given here is translated from the German text of *Kaiser und Galiläer*, volume 5 in *Henrik Ibsens Sämtliche Werke in deutscher Sprache* (Berlin: S Fischer, 1899–1909), p. 293.

p. 201 Himmler's notation: A photograph of the handwritten note is given as the frontispiece to Peter Witte, Michael Wildt, Martina Voigt, Dieter Pohl, Peter Klein, Christian Gerlach, Christoph Dieckmann, Andrej Angrick. *Der Dienstkalender Heinrich Himmlers 1941/42. Im Auftrag der Forschungsstelle für Zeitgeschichte in Hamburg bearbeitet.* Hamburg: Hans Christians Verlag, 1999. The *Dienstkalender* source is also sometimes referred to as the *Terminkalender*.

p. 203 Julian's words via Ibsen: *E&G*, p. 422

11. THE MASTER BUILDER

(In Chapters 11 and 12, textual citations to *The Master Builder* follow the division of acts and scenes in Sigurd Ibsen's German rendering of the play, *Baumeister Solness*.)

p. 207 Today is the 19th of September!: Ibsen had the date inscribed in a ring he presented to the Norwegian concert pianist Hildur Andersen, one of the two women upon whom the composite character Hilde Wangel is believed based. He also gave Hildur a manuscript copy of the play. An amorous relationship is suspected but not confirmed.

p. 208 Todt was . . . a "white raven": Schwerig von Krosigk, *Es Geschah in Deutschland* (Tübingen, Hermann Leins, 1952), pp. 296–300.

p. 212 Geli had died . . . during the night: The detective fiction of the time is informative regarding forensic inexactitude in fixing an hour of decease. In chapter 4 of *Trent's Last Case* (1913), the sleuth Trent opines, "That Dr. Stock will make an ass of himself at the inquest is almost as certain as that tomorrow's sun will rise. I've seen him. He will say the body must have been dead about so long, because of the degree of coldness and rigor mortis. I can see him nosing it all out in some textbook that was out of date when he was a student. Listen, [Inspector] Murch, and I will tell you some facts which will be a great hindrance to you in your professional career. There are many things that may hasten or retard the cooling of the body . . . As for rigidity, if Manderson died in a struggle, or labouring under sudden emotion, his corpse might stiffen practically instanteously." And thus convey a superficial, wrong impression of death earlier than it actually occurred. Techniques had not improved when Dorothy L. Sayers wrote *Whose Body?* (1923). Chapter 2 has Lord Peter Wimsey going over the dubious medical references: "Wimsey walked over to the bookshelf and took down a volume of *Medical Jurisprudence*. 'Rigor mortis—can only be stated in a very general way—many factors determine the result.' Cautious brute. 'On the average, however, stiffening will have begun—neck and jaw—5 to 6 hours after death'—m'm—'in all likelihood have passed off in the bulk of cases by the end of 36 hours. Under certain circumstances, however, it may appear unusually early, or be regarded unusually long!' . . . 'modifying factors—age—muscular state—or febrile diseases—or where temperature of environment is high'—and so on and so on—any bloomin' thing."

p. 213   twenty-three years had passed since . . . Adolf read: Besides Ibsen there is Wedekind. According to Kubizek, he and Hitler saw the Frank Wedekind drama *Frülingserwachen* together. Vienna newspapers show it was performed during three weeks in late May and early June 1908. The climax of the play is the suicide of a young woman. Geli Raubal was born on June 4, 1908. When Geli died 23 years later the hit film in German movie theaters was Fritz Lang's *M*. In it a depraved character played by Peter Lorre stalks young girls, entices them with candy, and kills them. *M* had been released in May 1931 and played all summer. Either or both *Frülingserwachen* and *M* may be suspected of some ancillary stimulus but as will be seen, Ibsen's *The Master Builder* makes the closest fit for Hitler's repertoire.

p. 215   What does 'heart' mean?: Matthias Schmidt, *Albert Speer: The End of a Myth* (New York: St. Martin's, 1984), p. 36.

p. 216   not necessarily . . . homosexual: Lothar Machtan, *The Hidden Hitler* (New York: Basic Books, 2001) dwells on the homosexuality of persons in Hitler's entourage but falls short of making a provable, let alone probable case for the Führer himself as a practicing homosexual. Despite the suggestive title, *Homo Hitler* by Manfred Koch-Hillebrecht (Munich: Siedler, 1999) also failed to prove him a practicing homosexual.

p. 216   "He is not a homosexual": Wyndham Lewis, *The Hitler Cult* (London: Dent, 1939), p. 78.

p. 216   Hitler did admire Joan: On July 2, 1942, at dinner, Hitler pronounced

George Bernard Shaw's *St. Joan* a more faithful portrayal of the Maid of Orleans than Friedrich Schiller's *Die Jungfrau von Orleans* (*Table Talk*, p. 549). A Hitler identification with Joan cannot be ruled out but no literary basis for it has yet been shown.

p. 216 Adolf maintained a crush on: Her surname has variously been given as Jantsen and Rabatsch. Later in life she stated unawareness that Hitler had followed her around. He did write her one anonymous love letter, which she recalled.

p. 217 Hitler kept in touch . . . via postcards: A photograph of the postcard is included as a plate in August Kubizek *Adolf Hitler, Mein Jugendfreund* (Graz: Stocker, 1953), facing p. 224). See also Jacques Brosse, *Hitler avant Hitler: Essai d'interpretation psychoanalytique* (Paris: Fayard, 1972), p. 282.

p. 217 In America he is being burlesqued: Kurt Kreuger (pseudonym), *Inside Hitler* (New York: Avalon, 1941), p. 323.

p. 218 A certain departure from heterosexual masculine norms: Robert G.L. Waite in *The Psychopathic God* (New York: Da Capo press reprint, 1977), p. 234.

p. 218 the blend of inborn feminine and masculine: *OSS Hitler Source Book*, quoted at http://www1.ca/nizkor.org/hweb/people/h/hitler-adolf/oss-papers/text/oss-sb-deuss-01.html.

p. 218 "his feminine side": These articles were clipped and entered in the Nazi party archives among the biographical material on Hitler. Quoted by Ian Kershaw in *The 'Hitler Myth': Image and Reality in the Third Reich* (Oxford: Clarendon, 1987), p. 33.

p. 218 Hitler as . . . a shapely nude: Reproduced in Claudia Koonz, *The Nazi Conscience* (Cambridge, MA: Harvard University Press, 2003), p. 95.

p. 218 his feminine characteristics—: Walter C. Langer, *The Mind of Adolf Hitler: The Secret Wartime Report* (New York: Basic Books, 1972), pp. 172–173.

p. 219 the large gynic (feminine) component: W.H.D. Vernon, "Hitler the Man—Notes for a Case History", in Henry A. Murray, M.D., ed., *Analysis of the Personality of Adolph Hitler* (unpublished; Cambridge, MA: Harvard Psychological Clinic, October 1943), pp. 86–87, 200. Typescript copy on file at Cornell University Law School Library, Ithaca, NY.

p. 220 an observed effeminacy: Anton Joachimsthaler, *Korrektur einer Biographie* (Munich: Herbig, 1989) p. 162.

p. 220 inclinations as based on his effeminacy: Jacques Brosse, *Hitler avant Hitler: Essai d'interpretation psychoanalytique* (Paris: Fayard, 1972), pp. 334–335.

p. 220 the decorator pierces tranquility: frontispiece quotation in Karl Lärmer, *Autobahnbau in Deutschland 1933 bis 1945* (East Berlin: Akademie Verlag, 1975).

p. 220 Wyndham Lewis ventured: Wyndham Lewis, *The Hitler Cult* (London: Dent, 1939), pp. 47, 77, 78, 103, 122, 123.

pp. 221–222 "his walk! . . . It was very ladylike": William L. Shirer, *Berlin Diary* (New York: Knopf, 1941), pp. 136–137.

p. 222 "The intuition which mastered him instead of pure logic": Halder correspondence of 1971, cited by John Toland in *Adolf Hitler* (New York: Doubleday, 1976), p. 720 and endnote.

p. 222 most profoundly feminine man: Harold Nicolson, entry for October 03, 1939 in *Diaries and Letters*, edited by his son Nigel Nicolson, volume 2, *The War Years, 1939–1945* (New York: Atheneum, 1967), p. 39. Although married, Nicolson was himself homosexual. The dinner was hosted at the Carlton Grill in London by Diana Cooper, wife of Duff Cooper who was urging the formation of a war cabinet under Winston Churchill.

p. 222 Burckhardt had gotten to know the subject: Burckhardt went on to become a noted historian with a superb biography of cardinal Richelieu. Lamentably, he never undertook a biography of Hitler, whom he knew so well, close up.

p. 223 In the eyes of a woman: *Table Talk*, p. 285.

p. 224 two persons . . . to whom I was really, inwardly attached: Elsa Bruckmann related her words to Hitler when speaking shortly afterwards with Ilse Hess who included the conversation in *England—Nürnberg—Spandau: Ein Schicksal in Briefen* (Leoni am Starnberger See: Druffel, 1952), p. 26.

p. 224 "the sexual impulse" . . ."without making any fuss": Hermann Rauschning, *Men of Chaos* (New York: Putnam, 1942), p. 233.

p. 225 her encounter with her first man: *Monologe*, p. 71; English from Hitler's *Table Talk*. He elaborated on the newsreel views of the war, "I am extremely happy to have witnessed such scenes." And, a moment later, the normal cliché for the task of empire building would be "Herculean," not "Cyclopean." The latter term in architecture denotes structures of large, uncut stones.

p. 226 Why shouldn't I go hunting, too?: *Henrik Ibsens sämtliche Werke in deutscher Sprache* (Berlin: S. Fischer, 1899–1909), volume 8, p. 405. The phrase echoes in Norwegian literature, e.g., in Jostein Gaarder's *Sophie's World* as part of a dialogue between Sophie and Alberto: "'What do you see,' asked Alberto. 'I see that you're a strange kind of bird.'" (New York: Farrar, Straus, & Giroux, 1996), p. 376. The words come within two pages of a specific Gaarder allusion to Ibsen.

12. "DER BAUMEISTER IS TOT!"

p. 230 "my most persistent opponent": *Table Talk*, entry for May 21, 1942, p. 500.

p. 231 burning of the Glass Palace: Only some 250 of the art works destroyed were covered by insurance, according to *The Times of London*, June 10, 1931, p. 16.

p. 232 a cubist monstrosity: Adolf Hitler, *Reden, Schriften, Anordnungen 1925–1933* (Munich: K.G. Saur, 1996) Volume IV, part 2, p. 62, n. 12.

p. 232 the Nazis' daily press organ: "Glaspalast" in *Völkischer Beobachter*, June 5, 1923, p. 2. The fire followed exactly eight years and one day later. The Nazi newspaper article was printed on the fifteenth birthday of Geli Raubal, plus one day. In this context of near-exact anniversary observances, it may be stated as well that the Glass Palace burnt down on the five hundredth anniversary, plus one week, of the day when Joan of Arc was burnt at the stake. Hitler's interest in Joan is a matter of record, from *Table Talk*. Given all the other Hitlerian quirks, some contrived connection cannot be ruled out.

p. 233 Writing in Spandau prison: Albert Speer, *Inside the Third Reich* (New York: Macmillan, 1970), p. 49; and *Spandau, the Secret Diaries* (New York: Macmillan, 1976).

p. 235 to purchase it outright: Otto Dietrich, *12 Jahre mit Hitler* (Munich: Isar, 1955) p. 210.

p. 235 renamed it the Berghof.: Hitler's risible excuse on the record for choosing this property over others is worth quoting: "My choice lay between the Berghof and a property at Steingaden. Fortunately, I chose the Berghof. If I had taken the Steingaden place, I should have been compelled to become a producer of the famous Steingaden cheese, in order to keep the place up. Suppose, then that for some reason or other the price of cheese rose. Everybody would immediately say, 'Of course! The Führer is himself personally interested in the price of cheese'" in *Table Talk*, entry for July 26, 1942, p. 595.

p. 235 mad King Ludwig: Greg King, *The Mad King: A Biography of Ludwig II of Bavaria* (Secaucus, N.J.: Birch Lane Press, 1996). Hitler sympathized with Ludwig and rambled on about him at some length in the *Table Talk* monologues for 1942.

p. 235 "Führer Tagebuch": Along with other items of biographical interest this document is included on Reel 163, Container 263 in the Captured German Documents collection, part of the Manuscripts Division of the Library of Congress.

p. 236 A photograph shows Todt... undertaking a reconnaissance: Eduard Schönleben, *Fritz Todt: Der Mensch, der Ingenieur, der Nationalsozialist* (Oldenburg: Gerhard Stalling, 1943), p. 23; also *The Bormann Letters*, edited with an introduction by H.R. Trevor-Roper (London: Weidenfeld and Nicolson, 1954), pp. 14–15.

p. 236 Bormann was assigned the blame after World War II: Albert Speer, Inside the Third Reich (New York: Macmillan, 1970), p. 193.

p. 236 ready at last on September 16, 1938: Frederick Oechsner, *This is the Enemy* (Boston: Little, Brown, 1942), pp. 75–76

p. 236 the eyrie seemed . . . dreamed up by an abnormal mind: Hitler was well aware of François-Poncet's remarks, as is shown by the *Monologe* entry for midday, February 02, 1942.

p. 237 miserable accommodations ... the norm: As Todt put it, the camps were run "in the fashion that had been established in past centuries "wherein everybody was used to deficiencies for years". Fritz Todt, "Adolf Hitler and His Roads," in *Adolf Hitler: Pictures from the Life of the Führer, 1931–1935* (translation of *Bilder aus Leben des Führers*, Indianapolis: Peebles Press, 1978), p. 95.

p. 238 if anything should happen to Todt: Albert Speer, *Inside the Third Reich*, p. 194.

p. 239 an odd tasking for the architect: Speer, *Erinnerungen*, p. 197 and Dietrich Eichholtz, *Geschichte der deutschen Kriegswirtschaft* (East Berlin: Akademie-Verlag, 1969) vol. II, pp. 57–59, citing Bundesarchiv Koblenz R 43 II/607.

p. 239 to ensure Speer would eventually step into Todt's position: Albert Speer, *Inside the Third Reich*, pp. 194, 535.

p. 239 Speer ... and his staff ... a unit of Organisation Todt: Albert Speer, *Inside the Third Reich*, p. 185.

p. 239 Solness confides his forebodings in Act I: Michael Meyer translation.

p. 240 The Führer mused ... about medals: *Table Talk*, pp. 64–65.

p. 241 Todt's usual plane ... was being overhauled: Nicolaus von Below, *Als Hitlers Adjutant 1937–1945* (Mainz: Von Hase & Koehler, 1980), pp. 305–306.

p. 242 The aircraft ... radioed back the message that all was in order: Report of field marshall Erhard Milch, quoted in Franz W. Seidler, *Fritz Todt* (Munich: Herbig, 1986), p. 369.

p. 244 sabotage ... was "possible": Milch testimony quoted verbatim in Franz W. Seidler, *Fritz Todt* (Munich: Herbig, 1986), p. 369.

p. 244 Hans Baur ... wrote: Hans Baur, *Hitler at My Side* (translation of *Mit Mächtigen zwischen Himmel und Erde*; Houston: Eichler, 1986), pp. 144–146.

p. 246 no such explosive device abroad: Franz W. Seidler, "Der Flugzeugabsturz des Reichsministers Dr. Todt 1942: Attentat oder Unfall?" in *Geschichte und Gegenwart* volume IV, no. 3 (1985), pp. 224–225, citing the sworn testimony of Elspeth Todt in a postwar hearing.

p. 247 parcels ... in the central on rearward sections: Heinz Nowarra, *Heinkel He 111: A Documentary History* (London: Jane's, 1980), especially pp. 37, 171.

p. 247 Todt and Bäuerle ... more physical trauma: Franz W. Seidler, *Fritz Todt*, p. 370, quoting verbatim the postmortem data appended to the Luftwaffe crash report of Luftgau I, March 08, 1943 (sic); original in Institut für Zeitgeschichte, Fd 44. The data describe only five bodies as opposed to the six persons mentioned in Baur's account.

p. 248 Gestapo then ordered Haasemann to desist: Franz W. Seidler, "Der Flugzeugabsturz des Reichsministers Dr. Todt 1942: Attentat oder Unfall?" p. 225, citing hearing testimony from 1947.

p. 248 "For a pretty remarkable fall!": Entered into the Introduction p. 35E, volume I of the German high command war diary (*Kriegstagebuch des Oberkommando der Wermacht*; Frankfurt am Main: Bernard & Graefe, 1961–1965) for March 4, 1942, compiled by Grenier who included his private comment.

p. 250 he climbs to the top of his building to crown it with a wreath: Hermann Rauschning, *Hitler Speaks: a Series of Political Conversations with Adolf Hitler on his Real Aims* (London: Thornton Butterworth Ltd., 1939), p. 264. Rauschning was president of the senate of the Free City of Danzig in 1933–1934 before being eclipsed by rival Danzig Nazis. He fled Germany in 1936. The English language edition of this book preceded its German version, *Gespräche mit Hitler* (New York: 1940).

p. 250 Rauschning . . . likened Solness: The Solness passage follows immediately after an image of Hitler pacing up and down like the Ibsen character John Gabriel Borkmann from the play of that name. Again, it had to be either Hitler or Rauschning who was the Ibsen fan.

p. 250 wreaths . . ."I've preserved one ever since": *Monologe*, p. 260.

13. FROM SCRIPT TO SCRIPTURE—A MIMETIC SYNDROME

p. 257 "For doing what Brutus was honored for": *"Right or Wrong, God Judge Me"—The Writings of John Wilkes Booth*, ed. by John Rhodehamel and Louise Taper (Urbana and Chicago: University of Illinois Press, 1997), pp. 149–150; see also Michael W. Kauffman, *American Brutus: John Wilkes Booth and the Lincoln Conspiracies* (New York: Random House, 2004).

p. 257 Booth's sister expressed the opinion: quoted in Albert Furtwangler, *Assassin on Stage: Brutus, Hamlet, and the Death of Lincoln* (Urbana and Chicago: University of Illinois Press, 1991), pp. 50, 99; also John F. Andrews, "Was the Bard Behind It?", *Atlantic*, vol. 266 no. 4 (October 1990), pp. 26–32.

p. 260 Hercule Poirot . . . profiled the hypothetical suspect: *The A.B.C. Murders* (New York: Berkeley, 1991), pp. 37, 78. In the final (inevitable) Christie suspension, Mr. A.B.C. turns out to be a patsy who was set up by the real killer. What counts here, though, is the canny profile of a murderer by-the-book which serves to rivet readers' suspicions on A.B.C. almost to the very end.

p. 262 "I really felt I could kill someone": Quoted by the federal penal psychiatrist Dr. Sally C. Johnson in her "Forensic Evaluation for Theodore John Kaczynski," U.S. District Court for the Eastern District of California, docket number CR 5–96–259 GEB.

p. 262 A reputedly half-Jewish chauffeur: Emil Maurice.

p. 264 unaware of his patient's fixation on the film: Lincoln Caplan, *The Insanity Defense and the Trial of John W. Hinckley, Jr.* (Boston: David R. Godine, 1984), pp. 65–66.

p. 268 Dissociative Identity Disorder: It is described in DSM-IV, the Diagnostic and Statistical Manual of Mental Disorders, 4th ed., revised (Washington, D.C.: American Psychiatric Association, 2000).

p. 269 "Osiris Complex": Colin A. Ross, M.D., *The Osiris Complex: Case Studies in Multiple Personality Disorder* (Toronto: University of Toronto Press), p. 10. Isis and Osiris were a mythological sister and brother who mated.

p. 270 the basis for *Der Augenzeuge*: Ernst Weiss, *Der Augenzeuge* ("The Eyewitness"). Rudolph Binion earlier described the circumstances in a forward to *The Eyewitness* (New York: Houghton Mifflin, 1977), pp. v-viii and in *Hitler among the Germans* (New York: Elsevier, 1976), pp. 10–13.

p. 270 "the man who invented Hitler": David Lewis, *The Man Who Invented Hitler* (London: Headline, 2003); also Berhhard Horstmann, *Hitler in Pasewalk* (Munich: Droste, 2004).

p. 270 spell under hypnosis reasonably suspect: The link of "hidden selves" to experiences with hypnosis was discussed by E.R. Hilgard in "Divided Consciousness in Hypnosis" in Erika Fromm and Ronald E. Shor, ed., *Hypnosis: Developments in Research and New Perspectives* (New York: Aldine, 1979) and by Nicholas P. Spanos in "Past-Life Hypnotic Regression: A Critical View" in *Skeptical Inquirer* (Winter 1987–1988), pp. 174–180.

p. 270 "a somnambulist certainty": Harold Nicolson, entry for October 03, 1939 in *Diaries and Letters*, edited by his son Nigel Nicolson, volume 2, *The War Years, 1939–1945* (New York: Atheneum, 1967), p. 39.

p. 271 "some kind of trance": NSDAP Hauptarchiv, Hoover Institution microfilm, Reel II, Folder 35.

p. 271 "I have to hypnotize Quisling": Quoted by Robert G.L. Waite in *The Psychopathic God: Adolf Hitler* (New York: Da Capo Press reprint, 1993), p. 375.

14. JUDENFRAGE: HITLER'S "JEWISH QUESTION"

p. 273 "is an energy of hatred": Quoted in Harold Nicolson, entry for October 03, 1939 in *Diaries and Letters*, edited by his son Nigel Nicolson, volume 2, *The War Years, 1939–1945* (New York: Atheneum, 1967), p. 39.

p. 274 "a gap between explanation and event": Bullock Foreward to Franz Jetzinger, *Hitler's Youth* (London: Hutchinson, 1958), p. 10.

p. 274 "No work has yet been produced": Lucy S. Dawidowicz, *The Holocaust and the Historians* (Harvard University Press, 1981), p. 34.

p. 274 Eberhard Jäckel, the scholarly compiler: *Hitler's Weltanschaung: Entwurf einer Herrschaft* (Stuttgart: Deutsche Verlags-Anstalt, 1981), p. 158; and *Hitler in History* (Hanover, N.H.: Brandeis University Press, 1984), p. 1.

p. 274 Arnold Beichman carped: "The Holocaust Mystique Myth", *The Washington Times* op-ed page A-21, September 20, 1999.

p. 274 Christopher Browning . . . the cave denizens in Plato's *Republic*: "The Decision Concerning the Final Solution," unpublished lecture in Paris as reported by Eberhard Jäckel in *Hitler in History* (Hanover, N.H.: Brandeis University Press, 1984), p. 45.

p. 274 "enigma" a "black hole": Kershaw volume I pp. xxv–xxvii.

p. 274 "an 'X'": As quoted in Robert G.L. Waite in "Afterword" to Walter Langer, *The Mind of Adolf Hitler* (New York: Basic Books, 1972), pp. 221–222.

p. 275 "We do not know and will never know": John Lukacs, *The Duel: May 10—July 31, 1940, the Eighty Day Struggle between Churchill and Hitler* (New York: Ticknor and Fields, 1991), p. 224.

p. 275 "Once Hitler's obsession is understood": George Victor, *Hitler, the Pathology of Evil* (Washington: Brasseys, 1998), chapter 1, "The Enigma".

p. 275 a tract or a pamphlet: On inconclusive evidence, Wilfried Daim arbitrarily asserted the strongest formative influence to be that of Lanz Liebenfels, in *Der Mann, der Hitler die Ideen gab* (Munich: Isar, 1958). But Hitler doubtless read other screed as well. For studies of what was available, see George L. Mosse, *The Crisis of German Ideology* (New York: Grosset and Dunlap, 1964), p. 138; and Fritz Stern, *The Politics of Cultural Despair* (Berkeley and Los Angeles, University of California Press, 1961), pp. 38 ff.

p. 276 an apparition in a black caftan and black hair locks: Adolf Hitler, *Mein Kampf*, translated by Ralph Manheim (London: Hutchinson, 1969), volume I, chapter 2, pp. 52–55.

p. 276 Adolf . . . was likely projecting.: Thomas Weyr records this intriguing anecdote in *The Setting of the Pearl: Vienna Under Hitler* (Oxford University Press, 2005), p. 115: "Around 1910 my father took the entrance exam to the Vienna Academy of Fine Arts. Next to him sat a man who clearly had neither bathed nor shaved recently and who wore the caftan-like cloak popular among eastern Jews. My father assumed he was one of them. But he was not. His name was Adolf Hitler. My father passed. Hitler flunked." While the account is of interest, there is always the likelihood that the memory of Weyr's father had been colored by the *Mein Kampf* account.

p. 276 in the trenches: John F. Williams, *Corporal Hitler and the Great War 1914–1918: The List Regiment* (London: Cass, 2005), pp. 13–14, 23, 131, 159, 207–208.

p. 278 at least not before 1876: The spelling "Hitler" is said by one source to have been the maiden name of Alois' mother-in-law; see W.H.D. Vernon, "Hitler the Man—Notes for a Case History," part of Henry A. Murray, M.D., ed., *Analysis of the Personality of Adolph Hitler* (O.S.S. confidential report, Cambridge, MA: Harvard Psychological Clinic, October 1943), p. 55.

p. 278 "The name Hitler is a common Jewish one": W.H.D. Vernon, "Hitler the Man," p. 75.

p. 281 actually derived from "Hüttler": Walter Rohland, *Erlebnisse in der Familie, im Freundeskreis und in der weiten Welt* (Ratingen: 1977)

p. 282 a Nuremberg death row memoir: Hans Frank, *Im Angesicht des Galgens* (Munich: Beck, 1953)

p. 283 Kimberly Cornish: Kimberley Cornish, *The Jew of Linz: Wittgenstein, Hitler, and Their Secret Battle for the Mind* (London: Century, 1998). This work is mostly a vehicle for Cornish's views on Wittgenstein's philosophy, but the Hitler gimmick no doubt boosted sales.

p. 283 Wittgenstein was two grades ahead: Djavid Salehi, "Ludwig Wittgenstein als Schüler in Linz", in *Wittgenstein Studies*, no. 1, 1997, and at http://www.phil.uni-passau.de/dlwg/ws07/15-1-97.txt.

p. 283 Binion . . . surmised: Rudolf Binion, *Hitler among the Germans* (New York: Elsevier, 1976), pp. 10–17, 130–143.

p. 283 personal consideration for . . . Bloch: Bloch's reminiscences, originally appearing in *Collier's* magazine, were reprinted by the (pro-Nazi) *Journal of Historical Review* in its May/June 1994 issue.

p. 284 sold . . . Hitler's paintings: Brigitte Hamann, *Hitler's Vienna: A Dictator's Apprenticeship* (Oxford: Oxford University Press, 1999), pp. 164–168; 356–359.

p. 284 "Dr.Kurt Krueger": Kurt Krueger, *Inside Hitler* (New York: Avalon, 1941), pp. 40–41, 75–78, 233–235. This book later gained an endorsement from Upton Sinclair. It bore an introductory essay by the Nazi renegade Otto Strasser who had ample grounds for casting slurs on Hitler. He may be suspected as the actual "Kurt Krueger" or perhaps a source, since the book, while peddling disinformation in many places, still displays some inside knowledge.

p. 284 Guttmann . . . recommended corporal Hitler for the Iron Cross: John F. Williams, *Corporal Hitler and the Great War 1914–1918: the List Regiment* (London: Cass, 2005), pp. 131–135, 191.

p. 286 popes of alleged Jewish ancestry: *Bolschewismus von Moses bis Lenin*, p. 28. Hitler did not identify which particular popes he had in mind.

p. 286 On the night of September 27–28, 1941: *Monologe*, p. 26.

p. 287 six SS divisions, entirely free of religion: *Tischgespräche*, p. 80.

p. 287 on the night of January 08–09, 1942: *Monologe*, p. 187. The school class roster with the correct name is given by Rabitsch, , p. 94.

p. 288 on February 08, 1942: *Table Talk*, p. 304.

p. 288 on August 30, 1942: *Monologe*, p. 377.

p. 289 with his long nose: "Ich habe mir oft vorgenommen, dass ich mich zurückhalte, aber es hat sich immer wieder gegeben. Was ich gehasst habe, war die Verlogenheit. Ich sah' ihn heute noch mit seiner langen Nase, und das hat mich so gereizt, dass ich dann immer wieder losgegangen bin und etwas angestellt habe." Monologue of January 08–09, 1942, at the Library of Congress Manuscripts Division, Captured German Documents collection, container 263, reel 163.

p. 289 the mathematics and science teacher: The rumor monger was Theodor Gissinger, according to Rabitsch, p. 66.

15. DISCOVERING THE UR-SCRIPT

p. 296 Few...ranking Nazis: Otto Strasser, *Hitler and I* (Boston: Houghton Mifflin, 1940), pp. 57–58.

p. 296 Goebbels waited another four years: Goebbels diary entry for 10 June 1931, *Die Tagebücher von Joseph Goebbels: Sämtliche Fragmente*, Teil 1, Band 2 (Munich: K.G. Saur, 1987), p. 62.

p. 296 "I would not have written the book": Hans Frank, *Im Angesicht des Galgens* (Munich: Beck, 1953), pp. 45ff.

p. 297 Klemperer waited til February 1944: Victor Klemperer, *I Will Bear Witness: A Diary of the Nazi Years*, volume II, 1942–1945, entry for February 10, 1944 (London: Weidenfeld and Nicolson, 1999), p. 295.

p. 297 never...textual dissection: Early studies of *Mein Kampf* all failed to deliver as textual dissection. E.g., Hans Staudinger, *The Inner Nazi: A Critical Analysis of Mein Kampf* (Baton Rouge: Louisiana State University Press, 1981) offers little in the way of textual analysis. An article by Michael McGuire, "Mythic Rhetoric in *Mein Kampf*: A Structuralist Critique" in The *Quarterly Journal of Speech*, volume 63, no. 1 (February 1977) remained too preoccupied with theory to trace the sources of the mythic rhetoric. Another such venture in promoting theory at the expense of empirical investigation was Michael Foldy, "The Emotional Logic of Mein Kampf: Kohutian and Bakhtinian Perspectives on Hitler's Internment in Landsberg Prison" in *The Psychohistory Review*, volume 26, number 2 (winter 1998).

p. 298 Soren Kierkegaard: *The Diary of Soren Kierkegaard*, translated from the Danish by Gerda M. Andersen; edited by Peter P. Rohde (New York: Philosophical Library, 1960), pp. 104–107. The Norwegian writer Jostein Gaarder ironically characterized Kierkegaard as an "enemy of the people" type in *Sophie's World* (New York: Farrar, Straus, & Giroux), p. 378.

p. 299 Ibsen wrote...Georg Brandes: *The Correspondence of Henrik Ibsen*, p. 350.

p. 300 best record is the "Table Talk": Useful in calling attention to some incidental discrepancies in various translated editions is an article by Richard C. Carrier, "Hitler's Table Talk: Troubling Finds," in *German Studies Review*, volume 26, no. 3 (2003).

p. 302 Pius XI ventured to compare Hitler to Flavius Claudius Julianus: *L'Osservatore Romano*, October 21, 1938.

p. 302 "hidden encyclical": Georges Passelecq and Bernard Suchecky, *The Hidden Encyclical of Pius XI* (translated from the French; New York: Harcourt Brace, 1997).

p. 302 "Ibsen und das Dritte Reich": It appears as the first item in *Zum Geisteskampf der Gegenwart*, a collection of four essays bearing no publication date other than 1938–1941.

p. 303 he had written a book on ethical lessons in Ibsen's plays: Emil Felden, *Alles oder Nichts! Kanzelreden über Henrik Ibsens Schauspiele* (Leipzig: Verlag die Tat, 1911); *Die Sünde wider das Volk* (Berlin: Oldenburg, 1921), especially pp. 146–149

p. 304 returned after the war to Bremen: Albert Schweitzer eulogized Felden upon the latter's death in 1959. See Horst Kalthoff, biographical entry for Emil Felden in "Biographisch-Bibliographisch Kirchenlexikon" (version as edited September 26,1999; posted in Bd. XVII for Year 2000 at website http://www.bautz.de/bbkl/f/ felden_e.shtml; monitored May 07, 2001.

p. 310 murdered because of an actor: Quoted by Ron Rosenbaum in "Explaining Hitler," *The New Yorker*, May 01, 1995, p. 58.

p. 313 I have not attempted to write a history of Germany: Alan Bullock, *Hitler, a Study in Tyranny* (New York: Harper, 1952), p. 7

p. 314 bewitched men's minds: Konrad Heiden, *Hitler, a Biography* (New York: Knopf, 1936), p. 303

p. 315 "No Hitler, No Holocaust," *Commentary*, March 1984, p. 37

p. 316 "a revisionist trap," Alvin Rosenfeld, quoted in Edward T. Linenthal, *Preserving Memory: The Struggle to Create America's Holocaust Museum* (New York: Viking, 1995)

INDEX